PRODUCING MASS ENTERTAINMENT

STUDIES IN COMICS AND CARTOONS
Jared Gardner and Charles Hatfield, Series Editors

PRODUCING MASS ENTERTAINMENT

The Serial Life of the Yellow Kid

Christina Meyer

THE OHIO STATE UNIVERSITY PRESS | COLUMBUS

Copyright © 2019 by The Ohio State University.
All rights reserved.

The various characters, logos, and other trademarks appearing in this book are the property of their respective owners and are presented here strictly for scholarly analysis. No infringement is intended or should be implied.

Library of Congress Cataloging-in-Publication Data is available online at catalog.loc.gov.

Cover design by Laurence J. Nozik
Text design by Juliet Williams
Type set in Palatino Linotype

CONTENTS

List of Illustrations		vii
Abbreviations		xiii
Acknowledgments		xix
INTRODUCTION		1
CHAPTER 1	Diffusions, or, How Did the Yellow Kid Go Serial?	19
CHAPTER 2	Serial Aesthetics and Consumption Practices of the Yellow Kid Comic-Tableaux	71
CHAPTER 3	Branching Areas of Interest in the Comic-Tableaux	117
CHAPTER 4	Spawning Continuation? Dynamics of Repetition and Variation, Once More	149
CONCLUSION	Serial Returns, or the Afterlife of the Yellow Kid?	185
Bibliography		199
Index		229

ILLUSTRATIONS

FIGURE 1.1 William B. Howell, "'Yellow Kid' Copyright," *Synopsis of Decisions of the Treasury Department*, p. 363.   28

FIGURE 1.2 E. Rosenfeld & Co., "For the Rest of the Country," *Clothier and Furnisher*, vol. 26, no. 2, Sept. 1896, p. 32.   31

FIGURE 1.3 Rudolph Dirks, "First, the Anti-Cartoon Bill. Then, Perhaps This!" *New York Journal and Advertiser*, 20 Feb. 1898, American Humorist, p. 5. San Francisco Academy of Comic Art Collection, The Ohio State University, Billy Ireland Cartoon Library & Museum.   40

FIGURE 1.4 J. B. Lowitz, "The Intercollegiate Boat Race in the Jungle," *The World*, 18 Oct. 1896, Comic Weekly, p. 8 (detail). San Francisco Academy of Comic Art Collection, The Ohio State University, Billy Ireland Cartoon Library & Museum.   40

FIGURE 1.5 *The Yellow Kid*, vol. 1, no. 2, March 1897 (detail). Library of Congress, Prints and Photographs Division.   45

FIGURE 1.6 *The Yellow Kid*, vol. 1, no. 4, May 1897 (detail). Library of Congress, Prints and Photographs Division.   45

FIGURE 1.7 "The Corps of Guides, Whose Services Were Donated to the Fair," *The Home Magazine*, vol. 8, no. 1, Jan. 1897, p. 6.   57

FIGURE 1.8	Marks Arnheim Tailoring Est., "The Brilliant Results of Truth and Perseverance," *The World*, 13 Dec. 1896, Comic Weekly, p. 8 (detail). San Francisco Academy of Comic Art Collection, The Ohio State University, Billy Ireland Cartoon Library & Museum.	64
FIGURE 1.9	EDGE, and Robert H. Ingersoll & Bro., "The Ingersoll Yankee Dollar Watch," *The World*, 20 Dec. 1896, Comic Weekly, p. 4 (detail). San Francisco Academy of Comic Art Collection, The Ohio State University, Billy Ireland Cartoon Library & Museum.	65
FIGURE 2.1	George Benjamin Luks, "The Open-Air School in Hogan's Alley," *The World*, 18 Oct. 1896, Comic Weekly, p. 3 (Alex and George, detail). San Francisco Academy of Comic Art Collection, The Ohio State University, Billy Ireland Cartoon Library & Museum.	88
FIGURE 2.2	George Benjamin Luks, "The Great Prize Fight in Hogan's Alley," *The World*, 6 Dec. 1896, Comic Weekly, p. 4 (Alex and George, detail). San Francisco Academy of Comic Art Collection, The Ohio State University, Billy Ireland Cartoon Library & Museum.	88
FIGURE 2.3	George Benjamin Luks, "Thanksgiving Day in Hogan's Alley," *The World*, 22 Nov. 1896, Comic Weekly, p. 4 (Alex and George, detail). San Francisco Academy of Comic Art Collection, The Ohio State University, Billy Ireland Cartoon Library & Museum.	89
FIGURE 2.4	George Benjamin Luks, "President-Elect M'Kinley Visits Hogan's Alley," *The World*, 29 Nov. 1896, Comic Weekly, p. 5 (Alex and George, detail). San Francisco Academy of Comic Art Collection, The Ohio State University, Billy Ireland Cartoon Library & Museum.	89
FIGURE 2.5	Jimmy Swinnerton, "Is It Possible That Messrs. George and Alexander—Put Up a Job on the Journal Tigers?" *New York Journal and Advertiser*, 27 Feb. 1898, American Humorist, p. 5 (detail). San Francisco Academy of Comic Art Collection, The Ohio State University, Billy Ireland Cartoon Library & Museum.	92

ILLUSTRATIONS • ix

FIGURE 2.6   George Benjamin Luks, "Thanksgiving Day in Hogan's Alley," *The World*, 22 Nov. 1896, Comic Weekly, p. 4 (Alfy, detail). San Francisco Academy of Comic Art Collection, The Ohio State University, Billy Ireland Cartoon Library & Museum.   96

FIGURE 2.7   George Benjamin Luks, "President-Elect M'Kinley Visits Hogan's Alley," *The World*, 29 Nov. 1896, Comic Weekly, p. 5 (Alfy, detail). San Francisco Academy of Comic Art Collection, The Ohio State University, Billy Ireland Cartoon Library & Museum.   96

FIGURE 2.8   George Benjamin Luks, "The Great Baby Show in Hogan's Alley," *The World*, 25 Oct. 1896, Comic Weekly, n. pag. (Flying Machine Boy, detail). San Francisco Academy of Comic Art Collection, The Ohio State University, Billy Ireland Cartoon Library & Museum.   97

FIGURE 2.9   George Benjamin Luks, "President-Elect M'Kinley Visits Hogan's Alley," *The World*, 29 Nov. 1896, Comic Weekly, p. 5 (Flying Machine Boy, detail). San Francisco Academy of Comic Art Collection, The Ohio State University, Billy Ireland Cartoon Library & Museum.   97

FIGURE 2.10 George Benjamin Luks, "New Year's Celebration in Hogan's Alley," *The World*, 27 Dec. 1896, Comic Weekly, p. 4 (Flying Machine Boy, detail). San Francisco Academy of Comic Art Collection, The Ohio State University, Billy Ireland Cartoon Library & Museum.   97

FIGURE 2.11 George Benjamin Luks, "A Genuine Horse Show in Hogan's Alley," *The World*, 8 Nov. 1896, Comic Weekly, p. 5 (Journalist, detail). San Francisco Academy of Comic Art Collection, The Ohio State University, Billy Ireland Cartoon Library & Museum.   98

FIGURE 2.12 George Benjamin Luks, "President-Elect M'Kinley Visits Hogan's Alley," *The World*, 29 Nov. 1896, Comic Weekly, p. 5 (Journalist, detail). San Francisco Academy of Comic Art Collection, The Ohio State University, Billy Ireland Cartoon Library & Museum.   98

FIGURE 2.13 George Benjamin Luks, "A Snowball Battle in Hogan's Alley," *The World,* 20 Dec. 1896, Comic Weekly, p. 4 (Journalist, detail). San Francisco Academy of Comic Art Collection, The Ohio State University, Billy Ireland Cartoon Library & Museum. 98

FIGURE 3.1 Richard Felton Outcault and Edward Waterman Townsend, "McFadden's Row of Flats—The Studio Party in McFadden's Flats," *New York Journal,* 3 Jan. 1897, American Humorist, p. 4 (detail). Library of Congress, Serial and Government Publications Division. 122

FIGURE 3.2 Richard Felton Outcault and Edward Waterman Townsend, "McFadden's Row of Flats—The Studio Party in McFadden's Flats," *New York Journal,* 3 Jan. 1897, American Humorist, p. 4 (detail). Library of Congress, Serial and Government Publications Division. 122

FIGURE 3.3 George Benjamin Luks, "A Genuine Horse Show in Hogan's Alley," *The World,* 8 Nov. 1896, Comic Weekly, p. 5. San Francisco Academy of Comic Art Collection, The Ohio State University, Billy Ireland Cartoon Library & Museum. 135

FIGURE 3.4 Richard Felton Outcault and Edward Waterman Townsend, "The Season Opens with the Horse Show in McFadden's Row of Flats," *New York Journal,* 8 Nov. 1896, American Humorist, n. pag. Library of Congress, Serial and Government Publications Division. 135

FIGURE 4.1 Richard Felton Outcault and Rudolph Edgar Block, "Around the World with the Yellow Kid. Off for Europe—Where They Won't Do a Thing to the Effete Monarchies," *New York Journal,* 17 Jan. 1897, American Humorist, p. 4 (detail). San Francisco Academy of Comic Art Collection, The Ohio State University, Billy Ireland Cartoon Library & Museum. 167

FIGURE 4.2 Richard Felton Outcault and Rudolph Edgar Block, "Around the World with the Yellow Kid—Mickey and His Friends Hobnob with Royalty," *New York Journal,* 31 Jan. 1897, American Humorist, p. 4 (Goat, detail). San Francisco Academy of Comic Art Collection, The Ohio State University, Billy Ireland Cartoon Library & Museum. 178

FIGURE 4.3 Richard Felton Outcault and Rudolph Edgar Block, "Around the World with the Yellow Kid. High Life in Paris—The Yellow Kid (L'enfant Jaune) Takes an Airing," *New York Journal,* 21 Feb. 1897, American Humorist, p. 4 (Goat, detail). San Francisco Academy of Comic Art Collection, The Ohio State University, Billy Ireland Cartoon Library & Museum. 178

FIGURE 4.4 Richard Felton Outcault and Rudolph Edgar Block, "Around the World with the Yellow Kid. A Bull Fight in Honor of the Yellow Kid," *New York Journal,* 21 Mar. 1897, American Humorist, p. 4 (Goat, detail). San Francisco Academy of Comic Art Collection, The Ohio State University, Billy Ireland Cartoon Library & Museum. 179

FIGURE 4.5 Richard Felton Outcault and Rudolph Edgar Block, "Around the World with the Yellow Kid. Fortune Smiles Upon the Yellow Kid in Monte Carlo," *New York Journal,* 7 Mar. 1897, American Humorist, p. 4 (Goat, detail). San Francisco Academy of Comic Art Collection, The Ohio State University, Billy Ireland Cartoon Library & Museum. 179

FIGURE 4.6 Richard Felton Outcault and Rudolph Edgar Block, "Around the World with the Yellow Kid. In the Louvre—The Yellow Kid Takes in the Masterpieces of Art," *New York Journal,* 28 Feb. 1897, American Humorist, p. 4 (Molly, detail). San Francisco Academy of Comic Art Collection, The Ohio State University, Billy Ireland Cartoon Library & Museum. 180

FIGURE 4.7 Richard Felton Outcault and Rudolph Edgar Block, "Around the World with the Yellow Kid. Mickey and His Friends Climb the Alps," *New York Journal,* 28 Mar. 1897, American Humorist, p. 4 (Molly, detail). San Francisco Academy of Comic Art Collection, The Ohio State University, Billy Ireland Cartoon Library & Museum. 180

FIGURE 4.8 Richard Felton Outcault and Rudolph Edgar Block, "Around the World with the Yellow Kid. The Yellow Kid in Cairo," *New York Journal and Advertiser,* 9 May 1897, American Humorist, p. 4 (Molly, detail). San Francisco Academy of Comic Art Collection, The Ohio State University, Billy Ireland Cartoon Library & Museum. 180

FIGURE 5.1 Richard Felton Outcault, "A Few Things the Versatile Yellow Kid Might do for a Living," *New York Journal*, 22 Nov. 1896, American Humorist, p. 8. San Francisco Academy of Comic Art Collection, The Ohio State University, Billy Ireland Cartoon Library & Museum.   197

ABBREVIATIONS

McFadden's E1   Richard Felton Outcault and Edward Waterman Townsend, "McFadden's Row of Flats," *New York Journal,* 18 Oct. 1896, American Humorist, p. 5.

McFadden's E2   Richard Felton Outcault and Edward Waterman Townsend, "McFadden's Row of Flats," *New York Journal,* 25 Oct. 1896, American Humorist, n. pag.

McFadden's E3   Richard Felton Outcault and Edward Waterman Townsend, "McFadden's Row of Flats— Receiving the Returns in McFadden's Row on Election Night," *New York Journal,* 1 Nov. 1896, American Humorist, p. 4.

McFadden's E4   Richard Felton Outcault and Edward Waterman Townsend, "McFadden's Row of Flats— The Season Opens with the Horse Show in McFadden's Row of Flats," *New York Journal,* 8 Nov. 1896, American Humorist, n. pag.

McFadden's E5   Richard Felton Outcault and Edward Waterman Townsend, "McFadden's Row of Flats—Inauguration of the Football Season in McFadden's Row," *New York Journal,* 15 Nov. 1896, American Humorist, p. 5.

McFadden's E6   Richard Felton Outcault and Edward Waterman Townsend, "McFadden's Row of Flats—A Turkey Raffle in Which the Yellow Kid Exhibits Skills with the Dice," *New York Journal,* 22 Nov. 1896, American Humorist, p. 4.

McFadden's E7   Richard Felton Outcault and Edward Waterman Townsend, "McFadden's Row of Flats—The Yellow Kid Introduces A. Monk, Who Enlivens the Pool Tournament in McFadden's Flats," *New York Journal,* 29 Nov. 1896, American Humorist, p. 4.

McFadden's E8   Richard Felton Outcault and Edward Waterman Townsend, "McFadden's Row of Flats—McFadden's Flatters' Skating and Tobogganing Expedition," *New York Journal,* 6 Dec. 1896, American Humorist, p. 4.

McFadden's E9   Richard Felton Outcault and Edward Waterman Townsend, "McFadden's Row of Flats—A Merry Christmas in McFadden's Flats," *New York Journal,* 13 Dec. 1896, American Humorist, p. 4.

McFadden's E10   Richard Felton Outcault and Edward Waterman Townsend, "McFadden's Row of Flats—The Opening Night in Kelly's Bowling Alley," *New York Journal,* 20 Dec. 1896, American Humorist, p. 4.

McFadden's E11   Richard Felton Outcault and Edward Waterman Townsend, "McFadden's Row of Flats—The New Year's Fancy Dress Ball in McFadden's Flats," *New York Journal,* 27 Dec. 1896, American Humorist, p. 4.

McFadden's E12   Richard Felton Outcault and Edward Waterman Townsend, "McFadden's Row of Flats—The Studio Party in McFadden's Flats," *New York Journal,* 3 Jan. 1897, American Humorist, p. 4.

McFadden's E13   Richard Felton Outcault and Edward Waterman Townsend, "McFadden's Row of Flats," *New York Journal,* 10 Jan. 1897, American Humorist, p. 4.

AW E1	Richard Felton Outcault and Rudolph Edgar Block, "Around the World with the Yellow Kid. Off for Europe—Where They Won't Do a Thing to the Effete Monarchies," *New York Journal*, 17 Jan. 1897, American Humorist, p. 4.
AW E2	Richard Felton Outcault and Rudolph Edgar Block, "Around the World with the Yellow Kid," *New York Journal*, 24 Jan. 1897, American Humorist, p. 4.
AW E3	Richard Felton Outcault and Rudolph Edgar Block, "Around the World with the Yellow Kid—Mickey and His Friends Hobnob with Royalty," *New York Journal*, 31 Jan. 1897, American Humorist, p. 4.
AW E4	Richard Felton Outcault and Rudolph Edgar Block, "Around the World with the Yellow Kid. At Balmoral Castle—A Lawn Party in the Yellow Kid's Honor," *New York Journal*, 7 Feb. 1897, American Humorist, p. 4.
AW E5	Richard Felton Outcault and Rudolph Edgar Block, "Around the World with the Yellow Kid," *New York Journal*, 14 Feb. 1897, American Humorist, p. 4.
AW E6	Richard Felton Outcault and Rudolph Edgar Block, "Around the World with the Yellow Kid. High Life in Paris—The Yellow Kid (L'enfant Jaune) Takes an Airing," *New York Journal*, 21 Feb. 1897, American Humorist, p. 4.
AW E7	Richard Felton Outcault and Rudolph Edgar Block, "Around the World with the Yellow Kid. In the Louvre—The Yellow Kid Takes in the Masterpieces of Art," *New York Journal*, 28 Feb. 1897, American Humorist, p. 4.
AW E8	Richard Felton Outcault and Rudolph Edgar Block, "Around the World with the Yellow Kid. Fortune Smiles Upon the Yellow Kid in Monte Carlo," *New York Journal*, 7 Mar. 1897, American Humorist, p. 4.

AW E9 Richard Felton Outcault and Rudolph Edgar Block, "Around the World with the Yellow Kid. The Yellow Kid Shakes His Trotters in Old Madrid," *New York Journal*, 14 Mar. 1897, American Humorist, p. 4.

AW E10 Richard Felton Outcault and Rudolph Edgar Block, "Around the World with the Yellow Kid. A Bull Fight in Honor of the Yellow Kid," *New York Journal*, 21 Mar. 1897, American Humorist, p. 4.

AW E11 Richard Felton Outcault and Rudolph Edgar Block, "Around the World with the Yellow Kid. Mickey and His Friends Climb the Alps," *New York Journal*, 28 Mar. 1897, American Humorist, p. 4.

AW E12 Richard Felton Outcault and Rudolph Edgar Block, "Around the World with the Yellow Kid. The Yellow Kid Invades Germany," *New York Journal and Advertiser*, 4 Apr. 1897, American Humorist, p. 4.

AW E13 Richard Felton Outcault and Rudolph Edgar Block, "Around the World with the Yellow Kid. The Yellow Kid Afloat on the Grand Canal," *New York Journal and Advertiser*, 18 Apr. 1897, American Humorist, p. 4.

AW E15 Richard Felton Outcault and Rudolph Edgar Block, "Around the World with the Yellow Kid. The Yellow Kid in Cairo," *New York Journal and Advertiser*, 9 May 1897, American Humorist, p. 4.

AW E16 Richard Felton Outcault and Rudolph Edgar Block, "Around the World with the Yellow Kid. An Eruption in Honor of the Yellow Kid," *New York Journal and Advertiser*, 16 May 1897, American Humorist, p. 4.

AW E17 Richard Felton Outcault and Rudolph Edgar Block, "Around the World with the Yellow Kid. The Yellow Kid Returns," *New York Journal and Advertiser*, 30 May 1897, American Humorist, p. 4.

AW Leaflet 5	Richard Felton Outcault, "The Yellow Kid in Gay Paree," *New York Journal*, 20 Feb. 1897, p. 6.
AW Leaflet 6	Richard Felton Outcault, "A Leaflet from the Yellow Kid's Diary," *New York Journal*, 28 Feb. 1897, p. 6.
AW Leaflet 7	Rudolph Edgar Block and Richard Felton Outcault, "A Leaflet from the Yellow Kid's Diary—Monte Carlo," *New York Journal*, 6 Mar. 1897, p. 6.
AW Leaflet 8	Rudolph Edgar Block and Richard Felton Outcault, "A Leaflet from the Yellow Kid's Diary," *New York Journal*, 13 Mar. 1897, p. 6.
AW Leaflet 9	Richard Felton Outcault, "The Yellow Kid at the Seat of War. A Leaflet from the Yellow Kid's Diary," *New York Journal*, 23 Mar. 1897, p. 6.
AW Leaflet 12	Richard Felton Outcault, "The Yellow Kid in Russia," *New York Journal and Advertiser*, 19 Apr. 1897, p. 6.
AW Leaflet 13	Richard Felton Outcault, "The Yellow Kid at the Seat of War," *New York Journal and Advertiser*, 7 May 1897, p. 6.

ACKNOWLEDGMENTS

I DON'T WANT TO BLAME Art Spiegelman for what follows. But it was the Comic Supplement in the concluding pages of his *In the Shadow of No Towers* that sparked my interest in the late nineteenth-century newspaper comics, and in particular in the serialized comics with a recurring character named Mickey Dugan, also known as the Yellow Kid. Due to other obligations, I had to put my ideas and questions into my (virtual) files for quite some time. But my curiosity to learn more about the newspaper comics and the cultural work that they performed for readers in the 1890s and the desire to inquire into the "life" of one of the first popular comic figures, the Yellow Kid, remained. Finally I was able to begin my research and writing adventure, which has led to this book.

The past years have been a journey full of unpredictable discoveries, of hours rolling reel after reel through the microfilm machines; of days and nights sitting in front of the computer screen, typing, procrastinating, and searching through online resources and databases; of weeks looking through magnifying glasses; and of opportunities to present the material discussed here. This book is the result of all these activities. It is time to express my gratitude to those who have helped me conduct my research, formulate and revise my ideas into a coherent text, and finish my book.

First of all, I would like to thank the German Research Foundation (DFG) for the research grant awarded for my project. This book would not have been possible without their generous financial support.

I am grateful to all of those with whom I have had the pleasure to discuss my project: first and foremost, the members, associate members, and fellows of the research unit "Popular Seriality—Aesthetics and Practices" (PSRU, 2010–2016, funded by the German Research Foundation), without whose knowledge, critical comments, questions, and encouragement this book would not exist. I owe thanks to Frank Kelleter, director of the research unit, who invited me to be part of the seriality Think Tank in Siggen in February 2015. Of the entire Siggen group, I would especially like to thank Bettina Soller, Kathleen Loock, Ilka Brasch, Andreas Sudmann, Regina Bendix, Maria Sulimma, and Britta Lesniak for the extended discussions and valuable suggestions, for the long strolls through Siggen and its surroundings, and for the after-work quizzes and talks.

Two special (popular seriality) friends, colleagues, and mentors must be mentioned individually: I cannot express enough thanks to Ruth Mayer, without whose guidance, genuine affection and encouragement, and constant feedback the completion of my project would have been far more difficult to accomplish. Thank you, Ruth! I would also like to say a very big thank you to Daniel Stein for his invaluable advice, for his generous input, and for being so supportive of my work throughout the years.

This book has also benefited from comments and suggestions made by the members of the American Studies research colloquium at the Leibniz University of Hannover, Germany. Thanks are due to Florian Groß, Shane Denson, Kirsten Twelbeck, Felix Brinker, Svenja Fehlhaber, Stefan Hautke, Jana Wachsmuth, Stefanie John, Sandra Dinter, and Anna-Lena Oldehus, who read chapters of my manuscript and who helped me shape my final draft. I am indebted to them for their friendship, inspiration, and insightful discussions.

Among the amazing community of scholars in the field of comics studies that I have met and worked with over the past years and to whom I owe thanks for their questions, comments, and advice, I would like to single out Christian Bachmann, whose knowledge about "old" comics and ephemeral material of the nineteenth century has greatly impacted my work, and Lukas Wilde, with whom I have had the most thought-provoking and inspiring discussions about characters and figures/*kyara*.

I would like to offer my sincere thanks and appreciation to all the staff members at the Library of Congress in Washington, DC, the New York Public Library in New York City, and the Billy Ireland Cartoon Library and

Museum in Columbus, Ohio. I met the warmest welcome at all of these libraries. To the librarians I have had the pleasure to meet and talk to I wish to express my gratitude for their expert advice, help, and patience. My special thanks go to Georgia Higley, head of the newspaper section at the Library of Congress, and Sara W. Duke, curator of popular and applied graphic art in the Prints and Photographs Division of the Library of Congress, for drawing my attention to artifacts I would probably have overlooked, and for providing expertise and support along the way. Special thanks are also due to the curators and librarians working at the Billy Ireland Cartoon Library and Museum, in particular Lucy Shelton Caswell, Jenny Robb, Caitlin McGurk, and Susan Liberator, for their support and for providing an atmosphere of enthusiastic scholarship. The Billy Ireland Cartoon Library and Museum is a marvelous place to visit and I consider myself very lucky to have had the opportunity to conduct my research there.

My gratitude goes out to Lindsay Martin, Kristen Elias Rowley, and Ana Jimenez-Moreno at The Ohio State University Press for giving valuable support, encouragement, and advice during various stages of the project's development and for responding to my questions so promptly. I would also like to extend my warm thanks to the series editors of Studies in Comics and Cartoons, Jared Gardner and Charles Hatfield, and the staff members of the editorial board at The Ohio State University Press. My appreciation goes to the reviewers who provided valuable feedback and suggested cuts and amendments; to my copyeditor, John Miller Jones, for his assistance in the production process of the final draft; and to Ann-Sophie Toldema for editing my bibliography. Their attention to detail has turned the manuscript into a book.

I owe a debt of gratitude to all my dear friends (and colleagues) who have listened over and over again to what I had to say about the Yellow Kid and late nineteenth-century newspaper comics. They have helped me to stay sane. My special thanks to Sylvia, Vanessa, Marita, Julia, Robert, Maike, Esther, and Sabine for providing support, laughter, and good food along the way. Je vous embrasse tous bien fort.

Finally, I wish to thank my dad, who has always been there for me, who has encouraged me to continue, and who has pushed me to finish this book; and my brother, Thomas, who served me a glass of sparkling wine when most needed, and who has taught me how to keep calm and be patient (and he continues to do so). Words cannot express how thankful I am to have them.

Christina Meyer

INTRODUCTION

> The auricle . . . stood out from the head after the fashion suggested by the comic pictures of the "Yellow Kid."
> —John O. McReynolds 268

> For some unaccountable reason the weekly doings of the "yellow kid" became immensely popular with the readers of the New York *World,* and throughout the week these highly coloured prints of the infant monster were distributed and broadcast all over the city of New York and the country. Bushel-baskets of them were daily carried to the towering dome of the World Buildings, and from there thrown to the four winds of heaven, which carried them away into distant regions.
> —"'Yellow' Journalism"

> The most modern creation . . . is without question the effervescent "Yellow Kid" . . . . [P]eople throughout the country have followed Mickey Dugan, the saffron colored globe trotter.
> —"The Yellow Kid" 3

THE YELLOW KID mentioned in the three epigraphic quotations is a comic figure that originated in the Sunday colored supplements of the New York mass press in the 1890s. The figure has a bald round head, jug ears, and two buck teeth. His official name was Mickey Dugan, but he was and still is remembered as the Yellow Kid. The Yellow Kid is an orphaned child (age unknown), who walks barefoot, dressed in a long, yellow shirt onto which words are printed in vernacular language. He appeared as the leading character in a number of unrelated cartoons and comic strips and became a recurring, immediately recognizable protagonist in different, serialized comics in the Sunday supplements. The Yellow Kid comics series were popular, and they were consumed not only by New York residents but also by readers living outside of the city, not only by the person who bought the paper but also by other family members, friends, and neighbors. The Yellow Kid was one of the first nationally syndicated newspaper comic figures in the US in the final decade of the nineteenth century, but his fame reached beyond the American borders, too. The Canadian magazine illustrator and cartoonist John Wilson Bengough, known for his sketches in *Grip* magazine, drew editorial cartoons for the Toronto *Globe*, some of which showed the Yellow Kid (see Bengough). Moreover, the Yellow Kid "traveled" to Europe and left traces there. There are copies of the comic figure in newspapers and magazines in Britain and Italy (and possibly in other countries). Pictures of the Yellow Kid were printed in British newspapers during the Spanish-American War in 1898, for example ("The War Scare"). And even before that, the Yellow Kid appeared "in bootlegged form as *The Pink Kid*" in the *Comic Home Journal* in Britain in 1897, with "local flavor added," and copies of the Yellow Kid, drawn by other artists, also appeared in such papers as the *Big Budget* (Connerty 539; see also Nicholson). In Italy, Yellow Kid comics were reproduced in periodicals targeted for children. For instance, a 1901 issue of *Novellino: foglio illustrato e colori per bambini* printed the 1896 comic strip "The Yellow Kid and His New Phonograph," which was shortened and translated into "Il fonografo di bébé" (see Castelli 3).[1]

Why were the Yellow Kid newspaper comics so popular? What distinguishes them from other comics and from other cultural products and practices of the same time? What are the structuring narrative and aesthetic principles in the Yellow Kid comics? What cultural work did the comic series the Yellow Kid appeared in perform? What are the reasons for the Yellow Kid's success? At what moment and why did the comic figure become famous and under which sociohistorical and economic circumstances? Who or what made "it" famous? How and why did the Yellow Kid appeal to a large audience? What pleasures were afforded by the Yellow Kid? At what point did the Yellow Kid's popularity end? *Did* it end, and if yes, why? These questions frame this study, which contributes to the growing body of scholarship dealing with mass-cultural phenomena, and the *serial* practices and aesthetics of the late nineteenth century. It will place the Yellow Kid's emergence and mass appeal within the larger framework of seriality studies.[2] Scholars working in this field of research investigate, among other things, serializations in and across different media, past and present; examine the "close entanglement of production and reception of

---

1. My thanks to Eddie Campbell for drawing my attention to this.
2. The following is a selection of scholarly publications dealing with the forms, aesthetics, practices, and media of serial storytelling in an Anglo-American context that have inspired my study: Hagedorn, "Technology" and "Doubtless"; Robin Myers; Brake; Mark W. Turner, "Periodical" and "Unruliness"; Jess-Cooke and Verevis; Goris; Eco; Wiltse; Jared Gardner; Denson and Mayer; Budra and Schellenberg; Allen and van der Berg. I heavily draw on Ruth Mayer's study *Serial Fu Manchu* and Frank Kelleter's edited volume *Populäre Serialität*, which brings together a collection of essays approaching the aesthetic principles and practices of popular seriality.

serial storytelling" (Kelleter, "Five Ways" 13); and outline or delineate the interrelations between popularity and seriality and the historical circumstances that support serial structures. We are surrounded by all kinds of serial forms and practices today and have been for at least two centuries. In my study, I will foreground one of the first mass-produced and mass-consumed commercial cultural artifacts, the Yellow Kid; will identify the medial, technological, and economic environments in which the comic figure was enmeshed; and will investigate the wide, fast, and seemingly uncontrollable dispersal of the comic figure in the last decade of the nineteenth century. I take the Yellow Kid as a case study to gain insights into the processes of serialization at a specific historical moment in which communicative practices and consuming activities began to change and in which mass-medial forms underwent particular (serial) dynamizations (see Kelleter, "Five Ways" 20; see also Kelleter, "From Recursive" 99). With this study, I wish to offer a more complete understanding of the reciprocity of the medial, institutional, economic, and formal facets of the comic figure's "serial career" (Mayer, *Serial* 161) as well as the mass appeal of such figures as the Yellow Kid. In what follows, I will give answers to the questions posed above and by so doing also explain the structure of this study, its argumentations, and its objectives. In the next pages, I will first outline the print context of the Yellow Kid's emergence because this backstory plays a crucial role for my argument about what I describe as the *serial life* of the Yellow Kid.

In the 1890s, city papers in the US began to print extras for their Sunday editions—in color. Newspapers had experimented with color plates in the 1870s, and offered special "colored wrappers" ("The Graphic Christmas Number") on holidays, but only in the 1890s did this become a common practice. In June 1892, the Chicagoan *Inter Ocean* launched an Illustrated Supplement in color. It presented multicolor drawings (first and foremost of the forthcoming world exhibition), short articles, feature stories, and comics (see West 11). Shortly afterward, other city newspapers started printing supplements in color regularly as well, including colored cutout features that were meant to be preserved and (re)used for do-it-yourself games or paper dolls.[3] Local papers—as, for instance, the *Newburgh Daily*

---

3. Readers were first introduced to a model figure/scenery (e.g., a theater stage, a fairground, a circus, a doll) that they were supposed to cut out, paste on cardboard, and preserve, and with each new issue of a newspaper's Sunday supplement they would get additional elements (e.g., a new costume plate for the paper doll), again to be cut out and preserved. Once completed, the newspaper reader was able to play with the do-it-yourself game or doll. These were enticement strategies to create loyal consumers.

Register in New York, or the Utica *Journal*—printed extra sections in color, too, but these usually appeared on special occasions and on holidays only. A year after the *Inter Ocean* presented its Illustrated Supplement, Joseph Pulitzer's New York *World* introduced a Colored Supplement (on May 21, 1893), which was soon to become the weekly sensation of the paper; it was a four-page section filled with diverse illustrations, short human-interest stories and prose miscellanea, and a number of comics. Three years after the inception of the Colored Supplement, Pulitzer's Sunday *World* had three different sections: the Sunday Magazine, the Women's Pages (renamed as Woman's World in 1897), and the Comic Weekly, which carried different captions throughout the years (see Baker and Brentano 31). Further Sunday extras would follow later, as for instance the Art Portfolio, which was launched in 1898.[4] One reason why Pulitzer compartmentalized his Sunday *World* was to make the newspaper more readable for consumers; they would know what to find in each supplement immediately. From 1895 onward, most of the mass-circulation papers along the East Coast in such cities as Boston, New York, and Philadelphia offered different sections in their Sunday editions, in color.

The Sunday Comic Weekly became the eye-catching wrapper for Pulitzer's *World,* in which the other parts of the newspaper were embedded. It first contained four pages, and starting in autumn of 1896, the supplement was eight pages long. The Comic Weekly was huge—it measured approximately eighteen by twenty-two inches (forty-six by fifty-five centimeters)—and it was spectacularly bright. The comic extra section offered a variety of one-panel cartoons, multipanel strips, and half- or full-page comics, but it also contained song sheets, short gags, "Children's Corner" columns, and many more "funny" things. It is in this Comic Weekly that the Yellow Kid originally emerged. The comic figure was drawn by Richard Felton Outcault (1863–1928; see Feinstein), and it started as an occasionally appearing Sunday feature in the supplement. In the first three months of 1896, the comic figure evolved into a regular, weekly, continual Sunday feature in Pulitzer's *World* in a series titled *Hogan's Alley*. An article printed in the *San Francisco Call* suggests that Outcault got his idea for the *Hogan's Alley*

---

4. Pulitzer ran an Art Supplement in 1892 but it did not appear regularly and the contents were not printed in color. This extra showed political figures, especially the leaders of the Tammany Hall. A new Art Supplement was launched in 1897 but dropped again. Pulitzer's 1898 Art Portfolio seems to be an attempt to imitate and compete with the Art Supplement of the *New York Herald*, which the paper had started printing—irregularly—in December 1893 (with reproductions of a selection of paintings) and an attempt to compete with the art prints in diverse (high-priced) periodicals of that time period.

setting from a song he listened to while watching the performances in "an Ed Harrigan play" ("The Evolution"). Together with an entourage of animals—a goat, a dog, a green parrot, and a black cat—and other children, the Yellow Kid lives in the middle of an imagined tenement-house district in the metropolis of New York. These other children include "Kitty Dugan and her theatre hat; 'Liz,' whose beauty has captivated the Dugan kid; little Molly Brogan, whose face always wears an expression of astonishment," and more (Outcault, "The Sunday World's Hogan's Alley Folk"). Because of the simple outer appearances of these "funny little people," the reader of the Yellow Kid comics was able to find each of them in every episode "at a glance" (27).

Before the Yellow Kid and his entourage became a steady feature in the Sunday *Hogan's Alley* series in 1896, the color of his nightshirt varied: The color changed from gray (Outcault, "At the Circus") to green (Outcault, "The Day After") to red polka-dotted (Outcault, "Merry Xmas Morning") to yellow. This gave way to a fiction that has for a long time been accepted, namely, that newspaper and magazine printers in the 1890s had great difficulties in producing the color yellow and that the Yellow Kid is the "result" of a successful production of the color (see Olson; Sheridan; Becker; Couperie and Horn). In recent years, scholars have shown that this long-standing myth about the color yellow is false (see Blackbeard 32; see also 30–31 and 60). In fact, American weeklies, humor magazines such as *Puck,* and the newspapers began printing in color before the implementation of the Yellow Kid in the Sunday Comic Weekly and brought to the public their first colored pages (see McCardell; see also De Vinne, esp. 44–45 and 291–96; McDonald, esp. 53–55). The Sunday supplement staff of Pulitzer's *World* experimented with the color of the robe, and then, as James Lee recounts, settled on yellow because it would stick out, and would make the *Hogan's Alley* inhabitant an easily identifiable figure (James Melvin Lee 382). Later it was suggested that the engraving room foreman, Gus Thom, was responsible for inking the kid's shirt in yellow ("R. F. Outcault"; see also Outcault, "How the Yellow Kid Was Born"), after consultation with Charles W. Saalburg, who had started as the head of the art department of the *World* in 1895 (see Feinstein 4). When Outcault began to produce Yellow Kid comics regularly, these carried such varying titles as "Shantytown" or "Reilly's Pond," but they soon disappeared from the Sunday supplement when the Yellow Kid and his entourage moved into the urban setting. From then on, the corner of Hogan's Alley became the recurrent geographic space in which the Yellow Kid is situated. There are a few exceptions; these are episodes in which the Yellow Kid leaves Hogan's Alley to go to Coney Island, for example. Predominantly, the events take place on and in the streets of New York City.

A few months after the first episodes of the *Hogan's Alley* series had been printed in Pulitzer's comics extra section, William Randolph Hearst, who had previously lived and worked in San Francisco, hired Outcault to do the popular Yellow Kid comics for a Sunday supplement titled *American Humorist*, which Hearst introduced to his newspaper *New York Journal* in October 1896.[5] In an essay printed in the trade journal *Inland Printer* in 1899, the anonymous author summarized that Hearst pursued the policy of "[drawing] away from his rival . . . any man who proved valuable to the latter paper. So he sent for Outcault . . . and offered him $150 a week, twice what he was being paid at the *World*, to join the *Journal* staff and bring the 'Yellow Kid' with him" ("The Salary"). As a reaction, Pulitzer's staff members offered Outcault "the same salary to remain on the *World*. [Outcault] returned to Hearst and told him he thought he would stay on the *World*, but Hearst added $1,000 spot cash to his previous offer" ("The Salary"). How much of this is actually true I am not able to tell, but what it suggests is that profit-making policies were the driving force behind employment and payment agreements. Hearst believed that Outcault (and other artists still working for Pulitzer at that time) would contribute to making the *Journal* the best-selling newspaper, and this was all that he cared about. What tends to be forgotten in the scholarship on Outcault is that though he stopped creating *Hogan's Alley* episodes, he still continued to draw comics for Pulitzer's *World*—thus his name did not vanish from this paper. Time and again, Outcault self-reflexively commented on this double burden, working for both Hearst's *Journal* and Pulitzer's *World*; he was assigned to do different things for each of the papers (see Outcault, "R. F. Outcault"). And, though Outcault was no longer in charge of the *Hogan's Alley* series, the title of this series did not vanish from the *World*. Pulitzer reassigned the *Hogan's Alley* series to another artist: From October 11, 1896, onward, George Benjamin Luks, who is today remembered primarily as an Ashcan artist (see Kasanof; Gambone), created episodes for the popular Sunday comics series. Luks had been a staff member of the newspaper ever since

---

5. When Hearst came to New York in 1895, he bought the *Morning Journal*, previously owned by Joseph Pulitzer's brother Albert, and renamed it the *New York Journal*. In April 1897, the title was changed to the *New York Journal and Advertiser*, the reason being that Pulitzer vetoed Hearst's paper from becoming a member in the Associated Press syndicate; as a result, Hearst bought another paper (the New York *Advertiser*), which had an Associated Press subscription, and merged it with the *Journal* (Nasaw 110).

he had left the *Philadelphia Evening Bulletin* in early 1896. Before he was in charge of drawing the Yellow Kid series, Luks had regularly contributed illustrations, caricatures, and half-page comics for Pulitzer's *World,* and he had already penned a *Hogan's Alley* episode for the paper's Sunday supplement in May 1896 (Luks, "Hogan's Alley Attacked"). In October 1896, his signature replaced Outcault's.

Starting in October 1896, two competing Yellow Kid series were printed in two rival New York newspapers. Outcault composed Yellow Kid pages for Hearst's *Journal,* and Luks penned Yellow Kid comics for the *World.*[6] While Pulitzer's Sunday paper suffixed each Yellow Kid adventure with *Hogan's Alley,* the respective episodes of Outcault's Yellow Kid series in Hearst's Sunday American Humorist carried the recurrent caption *McFadden's Row of Flats.* This series was the result of collaborative work between Outcault and Edward Waterman Townsend, who was the author of the very popular *Chimmie Fadden* (1895) stories—these were first serialized in Charles A. Dana's New York newspaper *Sun* and later collected in book format (see Kibler; see also Blackbeard 64–65, 68). In the *McFadden's Row* series, Townsend wrote short narratives and Outcault contributed the illustrations. These two also worked together to write and draw a Yellow Kid *Diary Leaflets* series, which was printed weekdays and on Saturdays in the editorial page of Hearst's *Journal* between October 1896 and January 1897 and which content-wise interconnected with the *McFadden's Row* series, and referred to extra-textual, topical issues and (sporting) events printed in the main section of the newspaper (see Guarneri 134).

In both the *McFadden's Row* and the *Hogan's Alley* series, the alleys and rows function as the topographical venue for critical, parodistic, satirical, and/or affirmative messages concerning the conditions of city life at the end of the nineteenth century. The weekly Yellow Kid comics are comedic, entertaining, colorful, and spectacular versions of New York City; they reflect the spatial transformations of the rapidly sprawling metropolis in the verticality of the page format. In the background of each episode, printed in the vertical format, there are multistoried tenement buildings and the tall poles with connecting clothing lines, or fire escapes with hung bedding and clothes, and a crowd of people (tenants) scattered in all corners and levels of the page; in Outcault's and Townsend's *McFadden's Row* series, the high-size text columns further add to the vertical format of the respective installment. Both of the Yellow Kid series focus on the fissures

---

6. Questions concerning Outcault's copyright registration request will be tackled in chapter 1.

and transformations in American society at the end of the nineteenth century, the social and economic inequities in the new urban space, the question of mobility within urban space, and the concomitant question of who is included in and who is excluded from the expansionist city demography, from social practices, events, and leisure activities—and in what ways and to what extent. In each episode, the artists implicitly or explicitly, visibly and less palpably, inquire into the possibilities and restrictions of access to, and forms of participation in, urban modernity. Yet they do this, I shall point out immediately, without offering answers to the question of how these social inequalities might be eliminated. Both artists take the tenements as recurrent settings to visually and verbally negotiate how social relations evolve, how human interaction takes places in the big city, and they focus in particular on how working-class tenants, immigrants, and poor inhabitants are integrated in, or excluded from, modern city life, along the lines of (financial) power and social status, and along the lines of literacy, gender, race, ethnicity, and age.

With the beginning of the new year, Outcault created another series, which shows the Yellow Kid and his friends in a number of adventures abroad in a graphic narrative titled *Around the World with the Yellow Kid*; together, the kids embark on a ship and leave New York in the first episode printed on January 17, 1897, travel through Europe, and return to New York in May of the same year. *Around the World* was collaboratively produced by Richard Outcault and Rudolph Edgar Block, the editor of the Sunday American Humorist at that time. Block wrote the narrative columns and Outcault contributed the drawings. A year later, Outcault illustrated *The Huckleberry Volunteers*, a weekday Yellow Kid series in black and white that appeared in the *New York Evening Journal* from April 8, 1898, through April 22, 1898. Text passages (written by Paul West) were affixed below Outcault's illustrations (reprints are in Blackbeard 118–25). In line with Hearst's editorial policies, or rather his explicit support of a military intervention in Cuba, *The Huckleberry Volunteers* series clearly helped perpetuate a pro-war statement via the popular comic figure.[7]

---

7. In the second half of the serialized *The Huckleberry Volunteers*, the Yellow Kid becomes the "Commander in Chief" (Outcault and West, "The Huckleberry Volunteers—An Old Acquaintance") of a brigade of volunteer fighters about to set for Cuba. A couple of episodes later, the Yellow Kid leads the horse-riding and sword-swinging brigade to victory (see Outcault and West, "The Huckleberry Volunteers—They Make"). An in-depth analysis of the ways in which the serialized graphic narrative instrumentalizes the Yellow Kid for political reasons, and the ways in which it builds on and perpetuates ethnic and racial stereotypes, is long overdue. In this study, however, the series is excluded from my analysis.

Shortly before the Yellow Kid disappeared from Hearst's comic supplement in 1898, Outcault created a variety of one-panel and multipanel Yellow Kid comics titled "The Yellow Kid . . ." (followed by an activity such as hunting, golfing, or inspecting the streets of New York). And, he drew a short-running Yellow Kid series that carries the alternating titles *Ryan's Alley* and *Ryan's Arcade*, which appeared between September 1897 and January 1898—not in a weekly rhythm, though. On May 1, 1898, Outcault ended the Yellow Kid installments. In Pulitzer's *World*, readers were able to find weekly *Hogan's Alley* episodes until September 1897; afterward they appeared irregularly (until the end of the year) until the moment when Luks began to work on new comics series. These included the *Kalsomine Family* (1897), or the *Great Trained Chicken*, which transformed into the *Mose's Incubator* series in 1898 (see Gambone). What we have, then, is a comic figure that originated in Pulitzer's Comic Weekly, which then appeared in competing series—and in different comics formats—in two rival newspapers.

The weekly installments in both *Hogan's Alley* and *McFadden's Row* are composed in the form of half-page or full-page, unpaneled *comic-tableaux* (see Blackbeard 36; Meinrenken, "Ver-rückte" and "Künstlermythen"). Similar to the living pictures performed on the theater stage—forms of entertainment that had their heyday in the nineteenth century (see Lewis, "Tableaux"; Assael)—the episodes in the Yellow Kid series capture a dynamic moment in time. The comic-tableaux present the occurrences in the life of the Yellow Kid in the form of what Frank Kelleter and Daniel Stein describe as overflowing abundance[8] (95; see also Duval 98 on the "pullulement de l'image"). The only frames or material constraints that these comic-tableaux have are the borders of the newspaper page. The large format and the seemingly chaotic compositions of the Yellow Kid comic-tableaux are quite like the American humor magazines' colored center-spreads that started to be printed in the late 1880s (see Kunzle, "Precursors" 159; Gordon, *Comic Strips* 15–20). But there is one big difference: Apart from the fact that the weekly humor magazines were fairly expensive (*Judge* and *Puck* cost ten cents per issue, whereas the Sunday editions of Pulitzer's and Hearst's newspapers cost five cents only), and the fact that the magazines were geared toward a middle-class audience and were only accessible to a limited readership via subscription (at least some of them), the center-spreads in such a magazine as *Judge* were not organized serially. By contrast, the Yellow Kid pages were a new, serialized form of commer-

---

8. "überquellende[s] Simultangeschehen"; my translation.

cial mass entertainment, and a new form of affordable *and* widely available and accessible reading material that appealed to, as I will be arguing in this study, a diffuse audience.

What made the Yellow Kid comics series so successful? How did they reach large, mass audiences? What pleasures did they offer? Here, I would first like to heed Joshua Brown's insightful study, which reflects on the transforming urban space in the nineteenth century and argues that "city life might be composed of a series of shocks and collisions, but there were signs and procedures with which one might comprehend" these impressions, and the "pictorial press played a crucial role in making the city seem decipherable." The illustrated press, Brown further maintains, "mapped the city by gathering separate representations of distinct and contrasting social [and ethnic] types" (81; see also Lehuu). Although he focuses on a different time period (mid-1860s to the 1880s) than I intend to cover and puts emphasis on the engravings of street scenes and the turbulent urban life in *Frank Leslie's Illustrated Newspaper,* with a predominantly middle-class target audience, Brown's assumptions about the illustrated press providing models and interpretative schemes for its readers are useful with respect to the weekly Sunday Yellow Kid comics. These offered reading patterns and, to refer to Ian Gordon, they "project[ed] new understandings" (*Comic Strips* 6) of the urban space for a diffuse audience (see also Soper, "From Rowdy" 143). This book will adopt Brown's and Gordon's ideas, bring them to an analysis of the Yellow Kid comic-tableaux, and examine the interpretive schemes these comics pages presented to their readers each week. To be clear, the investigations to follow do not attempt to trace *actual* reading experiences and interpretations of the comic-tableaux. As Charles Johanningsmeier rightly states, historical readers are "elusive beings who rarely recorded how they reacted to written material" (*Fiction* 184). Rather, the analyses to follow attempt to trace the reading options that are inscribed in and the potential uses generated by the Yellow Kid comics (in and through the pictorial parts, including color and typography, as well as in and through the words in speech balloons, captions, and narrative columns). I am talking about the frictions that the Yellow Kid pages are built upon to fulfill the different reader needs; in other words, I am talking about strategic versus nearly playful inscriptions, affirmative versus or next to critical messages, and so on, in the words and pictures and between the different modes of representation, which allow for diverse—and continued—engagements with them. Thus, I am interested in the ways in which the Yellow Kid newspaper comic-tableaux encourage specific activities. I maintain with Jared Gardner that the newspaper comics are "*crowded* field[s] where meaning is both *collaborative* and *competitive*" (xi; see also Hatfield 132). This also means that they are composed of multiple addressees, and that meaning "proliferates" in the pages (see Frahm 43; Yaszek 30; Blackbeard 72). With reference to Jared Gardner, who has argued that the turn-of-the-century newspaper comics were "the most important of the new vernacular modernisms . . . [that] diagram the serial complexities of modern life and fix the fragments of modernity on the page . . . [to be] repeatedly viewed and analyzed" (7, 19), I argue that the Yellow Kid comics afforded reading possibilities and enabled consumption practices that the products of other cultural fields of modernity such as, for instance, documentary photography, literature, or art, did not provide (see Meyer, "Serial Entertainment"). Each episode in itself offered multiple readings and could be enjoyed without knowledge of a previous or future installment. The pages were accessible to "a wide spectrum of readers" (Blackbeard 72; see also Yaszek 30). Literacy was high, but not everybody was concerned with reading the words and dealt with the pages in the same way. This has to do with the tableaux' heterogeneous composition—that is, their combination of competing modal elements (such as, for instance, words, pictures, or lines to indicate spatial relationships) as well as their diverse and at times conflicting messages, which offered different forms of interaction. This copresence of manifold reading options is crucial for meaning-making processes of *Hogan's Alley* and *McFadden's Row*. Thus, I aim to illustrate that and how the Yellow Kid series, to use Blackbeard's wording, "operate on multiple levels" (72).

Identifying the different manifestations of serial storytelling in and of the Yellow Kid comics and the audience engagements mobilized by them also includes an examination of the highly standardized, formulaic elements that the Yellow Kid series relied on, and which readers would reencounter every week, with only slight variations (Kelleter and Stein 103–4; on the "promise of perpetual renewal," see Kelleter, "Five Ways" 8). In this context, Jared Gardner speaks of the "repeated interaction of fixed and predictable 'types' within the new urban environment, bounded by a crowded visual plane and within a limited narrative time" (7; see also Eco 192–93 on the "fixed repertoire of topoi"). The Yellow Kid pages are built on a principle of seriality that is reminiscent of the "'serial killer'—the compulsive, violent, and fragmented return to the scene of the crime. It is an economy . . . that simultaneously epitomizes and travesties the logic of consumer capitalism—an economy that celebrates its own sterility" (Jared Gardner 26; see also Eco, esp. 199). Recyclability and simplification of form and content are, however, not the only structuring, formulaic patterns of the weekly comic-tableaux. The Yellow Kid pages also operate with dynamisms of branching out and multiplication—the twin figures named Alex and George in Luks's *Hogan's Alley* series (see chapter 2 of this study) and other *serial props,* as I call them, make evident that the aesthetic principle of varied repetitions is also informed with operations of expansion, which enable multiple reading practices.

Repetitions such as the Yellow Kid comics series are, of course, intricately tied to the production culture of nineteenth-century newspapers. The periodicity of the mass papers—the serial mode of publication—allowed for newspaper comics in general and the Yellow Kid pages in particular to be consumed regularly, in rhythmic ways. The rapid and extensive dissemination of the Yellow Kid comics outside New York was made possible by an elaborate distribution system such as the syndication network and the street sales, which was dependent on modern transportation infrastructure—such as the transcontinental railroad and extended postal service (see Johanningsmeier, *Fiction;* Nalbach)—and through cheaper delivery costs (Joshua Brown 22–24; Emery and Emery 200–205; Ferre 8–9; Henkin, esp. the introduction and the second chapter; on services to rural areas, see Fuller). New technologies that allowed low-cost duplications had a huge influence on the newspaper industry, as Ted Smythe points out (see also Savory and Marks; Harris, esp. chs. 14 and 16), yet it was in particular the presses that "enabled papers to expand production, extend deadlines, and in a few cases, improve printing quality. In any case larger editions were run off at faster speeds, which enabled editors to meet earlier deadlines" (Smythe 123). Production costs would in addition be impressively cut down through the "manufacture of white paper or newsprint from wood pulp produced through mechanical and chemical techniques" (Smythe 124). Of course, the Sunday colored comic supplements would not have been possible without the prior invention of, for example, moveable type, ready-prints, galley-proof forms and plates, linotype machines, the aforementioned color presses, and new techniques of image (re)production such as lithography and photozincography—all of which lowered production and labor costs (see Johanningsmeier, *Fiction* 34–63). Although this study acknowledges the importance of new mechanical as well as chemical processes for the print market and the impacts they had, and while it endorses the assumption that "[new technologies spur[] new audiences" (Strychacz 13; see also Dryer 547–50; Emery and Emery 107–278; Gossel 96–102; Alfred McClung Lee 97–106; Joshua Brown esp. 235–43), it puts stronger emphasis on the question about the cultural circumstances and medial and economic environments in which the comic figure emerged and thrived and reflects on the consumption practices elicited by the Yellow Kid comics pages.

This study is not exclusively about the medium of comics, however. Instead, the chapters to follow will unfurl the Yellow Kid's development from a recurrent, readily identifiable comic figure in the Sunday newspaper pages to a seemingly uncontrollable "force" outside of the supplements and will trace the circumstances of its proliferation. It will look into the conditions and processes of how one of the first serial comic figures in American cultural history kept a diffuse, promiscuous audience engaged, across media. My usage of the term *serial figure* is based on Ruth Mayer's definition. She writes: "For a figure to be 'serial,' my defining criteria are that it is flat, immediately recognizable, iconic, and fated to execute a stock repertoire of actions and attitudes in ever changing settings and contexts, against a backdrop of increasingly complex scenarios and devices" ("Image Power" 398). She has furthermore stressed that, "more than a narrative character, the serial figure extends outside the diegesis into various forms of public discourse and circulation" ("Image Power" 398; see Denson and Mayer; Mayer, *Serial* 7–12). These are claims Mayer has formulated in regard to the popular and iconic Fu Manchu figure of the twentieth century; while the ideological work of this Fu Manchu figure is sharply demarcated from the cultural work and logic of the Yellow Kid, the criteria Mayer describes grasp some of the fundamental principles of the comic figure: He is flat—meaning, there is no lengthy character development of the Yellow Kid. Furthermore, he is a transformable, portable, versatile figure, whose iconic, emblematic shape lends itself to multiple appropriations in other medial forms. The Yellow Kid comic figure was implemented as a kind of "module" in the newspaper supplements, which was repeated each week with only slight variations (see Denson and Mayer 199 on the modular quality of serial figures); but then the comic figure "left" the original context and began to spread. Throughout his "life," the Yellow Kid had been invested with all kinds of meanings and functions, and he quickly permeated consumer culture and infiltrated the public space. Audience interactions with the Yellow Kid were quite diverse, as I will illustrate in this study. The comic figure moved between and migrated across different media but remained easily identifiable. To refer to Mayer again, "if they were not conceived as serial figures in the very first place, they jumped from medium to medium, adapted, shapeshifted, mutated, and yet stayed always recognizably the same" ("Machinic" 192). In the semibiographical account titled "How the Yellow Kid Was Born," which was published in 1898, Outcault stated: The Yellow Kid "never grows up, or, if he does, he immediately reincarnates himself in his old form and goes through the same programme again" (7; see also Outcault, "The Bud"). A longer passage from the same essay bespeaks the iconicity of the Yellow Kid and furthermore explains the comic figure's versatility:

> He was on earth before the flood and boarded in the ark for forty days and nights. He was one of the first to leave when the waters subsided, and ever since then has been a denizen of this sphere—and always will be. Who was it, away back in Bible times, that threw stones at an elderly gentleman and remarked: "Go up, thou bald head?" Why, the Yellow Kid, of course, in one of his many incarnations. Who followed the Pied Piper out of Hamelin? The Yellow Kid, for a certainty. (7)

Interestingly enough, the Yellow Kid himself also comments on his status as a recurrent and identifiable comic figure. In the fictional autobiography *The Yellow Kid in McFadden's Flats* (1897), the Yellow Kid, in the first-person narrative mode, explains to his readers: "If I didn't [remove all the dirt from the yellow dresses so often,] you wouldn't know they were yellow, and if you didn't know that I'd have to be introduced to you every time I met you, dear reader, unless you might remember me by my sweet and innocent smile" (Townsend and Outcault 16). This self-awareness about his own status as a commercial, recurring figure is marked also in the comics series, as I intend to show in this study, together with a reflection on the implications of such "moments" of self-referentiality.

The Yellow Kid's serial reproductions are, however, not limited to the two leading New York newspapers. The Yellow Kid, which populated Pulitzer's *World* and Hearst's *Journal*, had begun to wander, and quickly percolated from the Sunday supplement pages of these papers into other newspapers and magazines. For example, in 1897, the New York–based Ainslee & Co. Publishers brought to the market a magazine titled *The Yellow Kid*. It cost five cents per copy, and it contained a potpourri of short essays, poems, and short stories, as well as sketches, cartoons, prize contests, advertisements, and photographic engravings. Outcault contributed several Yellow Kid drawings for the cover pages of the first couple of issues, which were produced by the H. A. Thomas & Wylie Lithographic Company in New York. In the same year, the New York G. W. Dillingham Company published an illustrated, fictional autobiography titled *The Yellow Kid in McFadden's Flat*, which cost fifty cents. And, variants of the Yellow Kid appeared in theater, music, retail, and advertising. As I will illustrate in this study, the comic figure began to set off in various directions outside of its original setting in the supplement comics series in March 1896. Outcault took notice of the seemingly self-propelling replications of the Yellow Kid in different media: Reflecting on the Yellow Kid's life from "Bud to Blossom" (Outcault, "The Bud"), he said that the comic figure "loomed up in spite of me" (Outcault, "How the Yellow Kid"). Outcault had no control over the "product." *When, how,* and *why* the Yellow Kid gained momentum are questions I will answer in this study. It will develop the argument that the Yellow Kid's success and mass appeal were contingent on the comic figure's serial unfolding. By this I mean two things: First, the Yellow Kid's serialization in the newspapers, and second, the term *serial* describes the comic figure's proliferations outside of the carrier medium, and in forms other than the two-dimensional drawings. As I have pointed out elsewhere, the comic figure not only had its place in the newspapers but also circulated outside the original medium, taking the forms of consumer wares (such as, for instance, toys), advertisements, and billboard signs and acting as a name-giver for and protagonist in dramatic and musical compositions and songs (see Meyer, "Serial Entertainment"). My contention is that because the Yellow Kid spilled into different areas of public life—as, for instance, into theaters and music halls and into the streets (in the form of parading Yellow Kids and in the form of posters)—and into private lives and households, embodied by purchasable and collectible articles such as dolls, card games, or other Yellow Kid artifacts, we need to take into account a whole range of cultural practices, new means of production and distribution, and innovative revenue strategies in order to understand the comic figure's success.

The Yellow Kid is a frequent reference point in comics scholarship and in research projects about yellow journalism, the mass papers of the nineteenth century, or leisure activities, urban life, and city language, yet few publications take seriously, and thoroughly discuss, the prolific logic of the Yellow Kid and the serial dynamics of the newspaper comic-tableaux he originated in. This study works to remedy this gap in scholarship and brings into focus the undertheorized sprawl of this comic figure. I hope to shed light on the *energy* of the Yellow Kid *within* and *outside* the Sunday supplement pages. Against the backdrop of Kerry Soper's contention—namely, that comic figures such as the Yellow Kid "are useful vehicles for exploring the cultural, institutional, and economical mechanisms which shape nascent, mass art forms" ("From Rowdy" 143)—the chapters to follow will unfold the serial "life" of the Yellow Kid. It is argued that this life is informed with both the processes of replication and multiplication and the dynamics of sprawl and proliferation, and that these accrete mechanisms of the popular, iconic Yellow Kid comic figure were embedded in and spawned by the economic structures, technologies, and medial environments of capitalist culture (see Mayer, *Serial* 17, 133). This study will situate the emergence of the comic figure within the larger research area of the media-historical developments of popular seriality in the final decades of the nineteenth century, unravel the cultural work that the Sunday comics pages performed, and explore the expansive spread of the Yellow Kid.

The chapter following this introduction will focus on the "becoming" of the Yellow Kid. It will unfurl the comic figure's implementation and regularization in the newspaper supplements as well as its proliferation in areas other than the Sunday sections and in enactments other than the two-dimensional drawings. With recourse to Mayer's claim about serial figures—namely, that they "extend outside the diegesis into various forms of public discourse and circulation" ("Image Power" 398)—chapter 2 will examine the various channels of dissemination and the diverse forms and formats the Yellow Kid figure was appropriated in and with what implications. The existence of multiple versions of the Yellow Kid in print format and in other medial forms prompts questions about authorship that I will tackle in this chapter. Outcault may have initially had the idea for the Yellow Kid, but he is certainly not the sole author who instigated and was responsible for the career of the Yellow Kid. There were other social agents involved in this career, as I will illustrate. In this context, chapter 1 will furthermore look at the ways the Yellow Kid, using the wording by Kelleter, "[stimulated] creative activities on the part of [its] recipients, who ... operate as *agents of narrative continuation* (Kelleter, "Five Ways" 13). Reactions included not only drawings by the newspaper readers who were fans of the Yellow Kid, for example, but also such things as letters to newspaper and magazine editors (see "The Bookman's Letter-Box," *Bookman* and Letter).

Chapters 3, 4, and 5 serve to gain insights into the different processes and modes of serialization in regard to the Yellow Kid newspaper comics. In chapter 3, I first examine the specificity of the Sunday comics and the ways in which they distinguish themselves from the practices and modes of consumption from other cultural fields of the same time, for instance, vaudeville acts. Phenomena such as the Yellow Kid and the tremendous success of this comic figure offer insights into cultural practices at a specific historical moment; this is why it is also relevant to reconstruct the aesthetic principles of the newspaper comics series that the Yellow Kid appeared in. I will demonstrate that the structuring patterns of the weekly comic-tableaux are not just defined by the rhythmic (and infinite) repetitions of the same, predictable, easily recognizable "stuff" with variations. The Yellow Kid pages also operate with the serial dynamisms of duplication and imitation, as well as growth, thrust, and expansion.

Following this, chapter 4 will offer close readings of Yellow Kid comic-tableaux from the *Hogan's Alley* and *McFadden's Row* series. The abundance of available primary material proves to be quite a challenge. To offer historically situated close readings of each and every Yellow Kid full-page or half-page comic-tableau is simply impossible. In chapter 4, I will concentrate on a selection of installments in the *Hogan's Alley* and *McFadden's Row* series, which appeared from October to December 1896 only—for these were the months of the most heated competition between Pulitzer and Hearst and when different and competing Yellow Kid series started to appear in the rival newspapers. How these two comics series enter into and negotiate a relation of competition, and what reading possibilities are incited in one episode, between episodes in one series, and between the episodes of the different series are the key questions I will seek to answer in this chapter. I aim to show that the Yellow Kid comics could (and can) be enjoyed as single, one-time installments (read one, then toss it away) or as episodes in a continuous yet nonlinear series. Pleasure can emerge not only through the reading options within one episode of either *Hogan's Alley* or *McFadden's Row*; pleasure can emanate between the installments in *one series* and also *between* the episodes of the competing comics series.

While chapter 4 will put center stage episodes from the two rivaling series set in New York, chapter 5 will foreground the uncharted *Around the World with the Yellow Kid* narrative by Outcault and Block, with the aim of analyzing how this serialized travelogue probes the dynamisms of repetition and variation as outlined above. The graphic narrative raises interesting questions concerning the economic, medial, and aesthetic principles of seriality. *Around the World* is a different form of serial storytelling. While it offers repeated variations of the same cast of characters in similar ways as Outcault's and Townsend's *McFadden's Row* series, it is graphic narrative that also operates with a progressing, continuous story arc—the journey from New York to Europe and back. It expands the geographic space of action and adventure, moving the Yellow Kid's actions beyond the city borders, and it reinvents the Yellow Kid comic figure and the entourage of animals and other characters in another context. At the same time, however, the narrative hinges on mechanisms of recursivity, folding back as it were, and securing what had been established previously. In the end, *Around the World with the Yellow Kid* is only a gesture of expansion; it testifies to Outcault's repeated efforts to bring under control the rampant product called the Yellow Kid.

Before I move to the first chapter, I would like to add that the different parts in this study do not have to be read consecutively. Each of the chapters in my study can be read without the knowledge of the preceding or the following one. The structure of this study, however, was chosen quite purposefully; it reflects the various dimensions, excrescences, and repercussions of the serial life of the Yellow Kid, and the angles from which one may approach this serial life.

CHAPTER 1

DIFFUSIONS, OR, HOW DID THE YELLOW KID GO SERIAL?

IN THE SCHOLARSHIP on the history of comics, the Yellow Kid is commonly placed in the context of the circulation wars between the two newspaper barons Joseph Pulitzer and William Randolph Hearst. Their fight was a story of continuous outbidding, which took place in all sections of the respective newspapers (see Smythe, esp. 140–43; Campbell) and certainly included the Yellow Kid. For instance, when Pulitzer printed Yellow Kid headline ears on the front page of his newspaper, Hearst would do the same in one of the next editions of his *Journal*. When Hearst printed Yellow Kids in the classified and wanted ads sections, Pulitzer would do so, too. And, both Pulitzer and Hearst exploited the Yellow Kid in the form of posters or recruiting cards in order to serve as an advertising tool to promote their newspapers (see Nasaw 108). Of course, the circulation war impinged on the Yellow Kid's career, but it does not suffice, I argue, to look at the battles between the two newspaper owners in order to understand the comic figure's fame. First of all, the Yellow Kid had begun to go astray months before Pulitzer and Hearst fought over the Sunday supplement feature— the comic figure appeared in the form of diverse manufactured goods (as early as April 1896), went theatrical (to appear in a variety of dramatic compositions), and infiltrated the trade press. Second, rivalries were not confined to Pulitzer's *World* and Hearst's *Journal* but included competitions between retailers, different manufacturing companies, music composers, and producers of theater plays. Last but not least, the comic figure inspired consumer wares, especially toys, and was used in numerous advertising campaigns and populated billboard signs. While it is certainly helpful to differentiate between the two- and three-dimensional iterations and the serialized newspaper comic-tableaux of the Yellow Kid, we should not see these multiple channels and diverse media formats in isolation but consider them as constitutive and coexisting parts of the serial life of the Yellow Kid (see Meyer "Medial Transgressions"). My line of argumentation thus moves beyond Mark Winchester's contention about the Yellow Kid's mass appeal and success—he has convincingly argued that the multiple theater adaptations of the comics series "have not been seriously addressed as an extension of promotional strategy nor as a possible factor in a feature's success," but they contribute to our understanding of "the *Yellow Kid* mania" (*Cartoon Theatricals* 62 and fn. 3). I endorse his claim, but I think it is still too narrowly formulated.

This chapter looks more closely at the requirements and conditions of the Yellow Kid's dispersal. I intend to show when and how the Yellow Kid gained momentum. It will unpack the medial, economic, and technological contexts in which the Yellow Kid spread and trace the forms, channels, and practices of the comic figure's proliferation. The comic figure initially operated as a recurrent feature in the Sunday newspaper pages, but then the original plan "somehow" went out of control, and I am interested in how and to what extent this happened.

My answers to the questions of how the Yellow Kid started to spread, from where and in which directions, will unfold in six parts: I begin by discussing the implementation of the Yellow Kid in the newspapers and examine the distribution infrastructure of the late nineteenth-century newspaper industry, that is, the various modes that "moved" the Yellow Kid to areas outside of New York City, including transmission technologies and the network of wire services. Examining how the city newspapers distributed the Yellow Kid allows for a better understanding of the conditions under which the comic figure first emerged, before it exited the original carrier medium and spilled into other media formats. Next, I deal with the multiple copies of the Yellow Kid and juridical questions regarding the ownership over the comic figure. I explore the various efforts to assert control over this popular creation, which had begun to go astray before the two competing series were printed in the two rival newspapers. The existence of multiple, competing versions of the Yellow Kid prompts questions not only about ownership but also about authorship. Outcault may have initially had the idea for and penned the comic figure, but he is certainly not the sole author who was responsible for the career of the Yellow Kid. There were other individuals and institutions involved in this career. These observations on how the comic figure defied authorial and legal control serve as a backdrop in the ensuing sections, in which I will explore the print derivatives of the Yellow Kid in newspapers and in a number of humor magazines, on the one hand, and other two- and three-dimensional proliferations of the comic figure, on the other. I examine the ways in which the Yellow Kid permeated consumer culture in advertising campaigns, some of which were serialized, and in the form of commercial products. The aim in the concluding pages is to bring to light another aesthetic dimension or another form of the serial excrescences of the Yellow Kid's career, namely, the comic figure's *self-observational narrative* (see Kelleter, "Five Ways" 18–19) about his evolution, effects, and enactments outside of the original core text and medium. By this I mean two things: First, there are text passages in the comic-tableaux and on the comic figure's yellow shirt that serve to reflect on the medial status of the Yellow Kid. Second, the Yellow Kid comments on his existence outside of the Sunday comics pages in the form of mass-produced consumer items and as an advertising device.

This chapter, then, develops the idea that the career of the Yellow Kid comic figure is a career of "serial agency," which is, referring to Kelleter, "dispersed in a network of people, roles, organizations, machineries, and forms" ("Five Ways" 26), including the practices of self-description about his own possibilities. It argues that the Yellow Kid's career hinged on multiple, interconnected "forces, [that is,] acting persons [and] institutions [as well as] action-conducting forms, [objects] and technologies" (Kelleter, "Five Ways" 24, 26). To explore these is the overall goal in this chapter.

ACTION-CONDUCTING TECHNOLOGIES

If we believe a story that was printed in William Hearst's *Journal* in autumn 1896, the Yellow Kid comic figure was the first pictorial Sunday feature to be propagated electrically through the wires: An illustrated article in the American Sunday Magazine supplement depicted the successful transmission of the first pictures "by wire." These "dotted" pictures that were presented to the newspaper readers on that day included "the portraits of Bryan and Sewall, of Edison," and a picture of the "Journal's famous

Yellow Kid"—in other words, figures of political, scientific, and commercial significance ("Here Are"). Note that the newspaper is trying to retain proprietary rights over the comic figure by promoting it as "the Journal's" feature; I shall return to this issue shortly. The idea of electrically cabled images was a recurrent topic in many magazine essays and newspaper reports published at that time; they tell of a new experience of intimacy and simultaneity.[1] In the *Journal*'s account, the Yellow Kid is imagined making contact to recipients outside of New York via the wires. The veracity of the report aside, what it suggests is that the emblematic form of the Yellow Kid comic figure—that is, both his shape and the words he speaks—can be easily encoded and decoded through electric transmission devices. What it furthermore suggests is that copies of the Yellow Kid can be reproduced quickly and distributed widely. The story proposes and points to the possibilities of wire technology to connect vaster areas of society and expand audiences that know about a cultural artifact such as the Yellow Kid. In the context of the serial unfolding of the Yellow Kid, what the story of the cabled images of the Sunday feature allegorizes is the velocity with which the Yellow Kid "traveled" and the geographic distance he was able to traverse. And in fact, the comic figure did reach demographically dispersed audiences. One way this happened, and the most important means of fast and wide dissemination, was through syndication.

Syndicate networks that emerged and branched in the nineteenth century had an enduring impact on the press. Syndicate companies of the nineteenth century such as the American Press Association, the United Press, the Ansel Nash Kellogg Company, or the International Literary and News Syndicate, to name but a few, played an important role in the print industry, because they both supplied all kinds of material (e.g., stories, snippets, illustrations) to a growing number of dailies, weeklies, and periodicals and exposed a greater number of people to the same reading material (see

---

1. Silhouettes were successfully transmitted in the latter half of the nineteenth century by means of a photo-telegraph, a device invented in the 1880s. In the 1890s, pictures could be transmitted via telegraph lines. Edwin J. Houston and A. E. Kennelly explain the technical operations and principles of information transmission (see esp. 293–94; see also Baxter 24–25; Coppersmith, esp. 9–36). The first so-called telediagraph, an early fax-like machine, which was invented in 1895, was installed in the office of the *New York Herald* in 1898, and shortly afterward in Chicago, Boston, Philadelphia, and St. Louis. In January 1898, the *New York Herald* announced that the first pictures were successfully transmitted from New York to Chicago with the help of a telediagraph (see Cook 345–47).

Johanningsmeier, *Fiction* 1–2; see also Watson, esp. 31–32, 70²). Syndicates helped cultivate regular readerships and contributed to condition their consumption habits (see Kaestle 531–38; Galow 314). Through syndication, print material could be multiplied without multiplying the costs; the transmission of news items and other features was speeding up, and, important too, the reach of printed matter expanded considerably. While in 1896, readers in Denver would have to wait a couple of days to see the episodes of a comics series, two years later, the newspaper readers in New York and St. Louis would be able to see the same feature on the same day. To allow for simultaneous publication, printing plates were shipped to St. Louis in advance via railroad.[3] As a system of nationwide distribution, syndication, then, contributed to the greater visibility and greater availability of Yellow Kid images. They functioned as engines of multiplication of Yellow Kid material.

It is often assumed that comics were marketed nationwide only after the turn of the century, but feature syndication began earlier, and included the Sunday supplement comics.[4] The Sunday newspaper comics were usually distributed to other newspapers with the help of printing plates. Already in the antebellum years, wood-engraved illustrations of art were shipped via railroad in the form of electrotype plates.[5] This afforded the other newspaper or magazine or book publisher to print them easily and to add and rework texts (Joshua Brown; Kielbowicz, "Regulating"; McNair). Printing plates were syndicated to other newspapers regularly from the 1920s onward, but already in the 1890s Sunday features such as the *Hogan's Alley* and *McFadden's Row* series circulated this way.

---

2. Elmo Scott Watson differentiates between syndicate agencies (delivering *features* to other publishers) and press associations (gathering and distributing national as well as international *news dispatches* to other papers). The Associated Press, however, quickly held monopoly and functioned as both news and feature "vendor" (see Johanningsmeier, "Newspaper"; Kielbowicz, "Postal Subsidies" and "Regulating," esp. 24–26).

3. Outcault's first episode of the *McFadden's Row of Flat* series, which was printed on October 18, 1896, arrived in Denver a few days later, and was printed in the Friday edition of the *Denver Evening Post*, with minor changes (Outcault and Townsend, "McFadden's Row," 23 Oct. 1896). Episodes of Outcault's 1898 comics series *Kelly's Kindergarten*, which he sketched for Pulitzer's *World*, appeared in the *St. Louis Post-Dispatch* on the same day (see Outcault, "An Illustrated," *The World* and "An Illustrated," *St. Louis Post Dispatch*).

4. Rudolph Dirks's serialized *The Katzenjammer Kids*, which was introduced in Hearst's newspaper in December 1897, were also syndicated to Canadian newspapers (see Gabriele and Moore).

5. Early uses can be traced back to the 1840s (see von Lintel).

Thus, it was in the 1890s that comics developed into "a shared national cultural artifact," as Ian Gordon points out ("Mass Market" 55–56; see also Bergengren 271). Pulitzer's *World* and Hearst's *Journal* had subscribers all over the continent, and the comics were not just read by the person who bought the paper but also, as letters, (auto)biographies, and telegrams of that time prove, by other family members, and they were often shared with friends or neighbors. Representative in this regard is the autobiography by Joseph "Yellow Kid" Weil, in which the following dialogue is recounted: "One evening [I glanced] at a newspaper. . . . A comic sheet had caught my eye. It was called 'Hogan's Alley and the Yellow Kid' . . . said Coughlin. 'I like that comic sheet,' I told him. 'Then I'll save it for you every day,' said Coughlin. He did. And I read the comic regularly" (17). What this suggests is not only that the number of readers that bought and then shared the Sunday supplements is difficult if not impossible to determine (see Johanningsmeier, *Fiction* 17).[6] It also suggests that through technologies such as syndication, consumption practices were synchronized, just as it suggests that the Yellow Kid newspaper comics were able to build (actual and imagined) communities of readers.[7]

In addition to this, the rapid and extensive dissemination of the Yellow Kid was dependent on modern transportation infrastructure. Through the improved and expanded transportation system (e.g., the Eastern Erie Railroad routes that connected New York and Chicago), the transit time from New York to Chicago and other cities and towns could be shortened, which helped the physical circulation of material, including the newspaper comics series and other Yellow Kid forms. In an 1898 report about a transcontinental train ride, one of the passengers noted: "The rear car . . . was christened 'Hogan's Alley' in the early stages of our trip, because of the spirit of fun and frolic that at times ran rampant there," another reason being that one of the guests "procured a number of large cards with 'Hogan's Alley' printed upon them, and hung them up through the car" (Shaw 210). This passage attests to the popularity and relatability of the Yellow Kid, on the

---

6. In the nineteenth century, catalogs such as N. W. Ayer & Son's *Ayer & Son's American Newspaper Annual* (1896) provided circulation figures. Statistical reports such as Robert Chapin's *The Standard of Living among Workingmen's Families in New York* (1909) give insights into how money was spent on newspapers (see Chapin, esp. 211–18).

7. On the notion of imagined communities, see Benedict Anderson's theory of modern nation(ness) and nationalism. According to Anderson, the nation "is an imagined political community"; it is imagined to the extent that "the members of even the smallest nation will never know most of their fellow-members, meet them or even hear of them, yet in the minds of each lives the image of their communion" (6).

one hand—the title of the comics series serves as a metonymic reference in order to describe specific (inter)actions of the passengers on a train. On the other hand, it points to consumption practices of collecting and possibly exchanging. Activities such as hanging up the cards and thus exhibiting the Yellow Kid to the train passengers contributed to the coast-to-coast reach of the comic figure.

The technologies of distribution (i.e., syndication, steamships, and the railroads, and presumably the wires) and reproduction (i.e., the presses) sped up, synchronized, and expanded the availability of the Yellow Kid artifacts; they are engines of the Yellow Kid's success and helped to generate an awareness of popular culture. Other forms of exhibiting and disseminating the Yellow Kid, which impacted the public prominence of the comic figure, were drawing lectures. I am mentioning these here in the section about technologies because the events were recounted in the newspapers and communicated to the readers. By means of illustrated reports about Yellow Kid drawing lectures and chalk talks performed on stage in diverse theaters or in other contexts, the newspaper readers would be informed about how to make one's own version of the Yellow Kid (see "Outcault at Olympia"; see also Pinkowski 170–71; Wikoff, esp. 24–27; Bartholomew). I would like to point out one such performance briefly: In February 1897, Outcault together with other comics artists was invited to the New York Sing Sing prison to give a lecture on drawing. Hearst's journalists covered this event, and in the next Sunday edition a full-page report was printed on the cover page of the American Sunday Magazine. The prisoners "knew all about the 'Yellow Kid,'" the report suggests, and "they knew all about Outcault, they knew all about McFadden's Flats" ("Our State Art Studio"). During the session, Outcault showed the prisoners how to draw the comic figure, and the participants were then invited to resketch the Yellow Kid. A number of the drawing results were then reproduced in Hearst's *Journal*. Apart from the fact that the article serves to promote the *Journal* as the favored newspaper that everybody (including the prisoners) reads, it also showcases the reproducibility of the Yellow Kid; talented or not, to copy the Yellow Kid is easy (see also "Newspaper"). What this article furthermore indicates is that the comic figure inspires creative consumption—you can add the utterances you would like the Yellow Kid to communicate via his long shirt.

That Outcault himself contributed to the dispersal of the comic figure in the form of drawing courses, and thus had an active part in the implementation of the Yellow Kid in the public imagination, does not mean, however, that he was able to control the channels of the Yellow Kid's quick and wide spreading, and neither were the two newspapers that printed the comics series, as the next part will illustrate. Other engines of the Yellow Kid's dispersal included institutions such as music sheet companies and theater show producers and their competitions over copyright.

ACTION-CONDUCTING COMPETITIONS

Three weeks before the first *McFadden's Row* installment appeared in William Randolph Hearst's *New York Journal*, trade journals, advertising periodicals, and other magazines and newspapers started to debate copyright questions with regard to the Yellow Kid. One of the earliest accounts that discussed intellectual property rights and the legal status of the comic figure was printed in the *Fourth Estate* on October 1, 1896, whose editor, Ernest Birmingham, stated:

> An interesting question is raised by the employment by the New York *Journal* of one of the *World*'s artists who ran a distinctive Sunday feature. . . . The question is, has the artist the right to take to a rival a great feature of the *World*, or has that paper any ownership in his work other than that it paid for in the past? The universe will not be disturbed by this quarrel over a man, and yet he and the two papers have a most interesting question to settle in the courts. ("Note and Comment," Oct. 1896, 6)

This idea about a lawsuit reoccurred a number of times in the press in 1896: In another brief comment of the same year, an anonymous author noted that Outcault, allegedly, "has purchased the copyright [for the Yellow Kid] from *Truth* and future yellow kids in the *World* may cost $1 each" ("Troublesome Yellow Kid"). A few months later, *Fourth Estate* would explain to its readers: "In the fight between the New York *World* and *Journal*, the 'yellow kid' has played a prominent part. . . . Outcault sought an injunction prohibiting the *World* from using his idea. This has not yet been decided by the courts, and the *World* still prints its 'yellow kid'" ("Yellow Kid Trouble"). Despite the suggestion of a lawsuit and a court case, there never was a hearing; there never was a court case. Browsing through the *Reports of Cases Heard and Determined in the Appellate Division of the Supreme Court of the State of New York* (from volume 1 in 1896 to volume 27 in 1898), through the *Supreme Court Reporter*, Arthur Hamlin's *Copyright Cases* (1904), and a number of online resources shows that no record exists about any lawsuits or cases with respect to Outcault and the Yellow Kid (see also Winchester, "Litigation" 20). Though Outcault—or the *New York Journal*—may have attempted to enjoin the *World* from printing comics with the Yellow Kid, there are no records of legal actions undertaken, either by Outcault or by the newspapers.

It is true that Outcault tried to obtain legal protection for the Yellow Kid in September 1896 in a letter he sent to the Copyright Office of the Library of Congress, in which he requested protection for "this little character" (Outcault, "The Yellow Dugan Kid"; see also Blackbeard 49). Outcault's attempt to get copyright protection had much more to do with the proliferating copies of the comic figure and his wish to guard his own commercial interest rather than with the impending move to Hearst's newspaper in October of the same year (see also Gordon, "Mass Market" 54). Outcault took notice of the diverse imitations of the Yellow Kid in print and especially in other media. In his letter, Outcault highlighted that the comic figure "is not intended for an article of manufacture" ("The Yellow Dugan Kid"). Outcault, however, never "completed" his copyright application (see Ginsburg 66–68). This is documented in the decisions through the Treasury Department. In figure 1.1, I show the statement of the assistant secretary in the Treasury Department, William Howell, from April 15, 1897.

The title Howell is referring to in this statement is the fictional autobiography *The Yellow Kid in McFadden's Flats*, which was published by Dillingham in March 1897, and which was copyrighted in 1897 (and Outcault's name is given in the *Catalogue of Title Entries*); the specific "design" of the Yellow Kid comic figure, however, has no copyright entry in the copyright catalogues of 1896–1897, and neither Outcault nor the newspaper held copyright over the Yellow Kid (see Treasury Dept., *Catalogue* Nos. 248, 286, 287, 291, 294, 297, 298, 302, 314, 315, 336, 339). In contrast to this, Yellow Kid dramatic and musical compositions have title entries, and so do Yellow Kid games, such as William A. DeGroot's *Hogan's Alley Puzzle* (see Treasury Dept., *Catalogue* No. 287, 23, 28–30; see also Treasury Dept., *Catalogue* No. 286, 15), as well as a number of Yellow Kid lithographs (Treasury Dept., *Catalogue* No. 315, 22).[8]

Musical and dramatic compositions that were based on the *Hogan's Alley* newspaper series originated between March and July 1896, and a number of show producers and composers began to send out applications for copyright registrations (see Library of Congress, *Dramatic Compositions*,

---

8. Yellow Kid lithograph posters were abundant. The Library of Congress and the New York Public Library websites provide digitized copies of a selection of Yellow Kid posters promoting the *World* and the *Journal*.

(17990.)

"Yellow Kid" copyright.

TREASURY DEPARTMET, *April 15, 1897.*

SIR: The Department is in receipt of your letter of the 5th instant, in which you state that Mr. R. F. Outcault holds the copyright of the design commonly known as the "Yellow Kid;" and you ask that the importation of articles infringing on such copyright be prohibited.

In reply, I have to inform you that the Department is advised by the Librarian of Congress, under date of the 10th instant, that the record of copyrights printed weekly in the "Catalogue of Title Entries" is, by law, confined to such publications as have had the copyright perfected by deposit of two copies in his office; that the copyright of Mr. Outcault was not perfected, as the copies of the design were not forwarded to him, but that copyright entry by printed title was duly made. He also states that many other entries under title of the "Yellow Kid" have been made by various claimants, of books, dramatic compositions, etc.

Copies of the Catalogue of Title Entries are furnished by this Department to the officers of the customs at all ports for their guidance, and on completion of the copyright of the design it will be included in said publication.

It is understood by the Department that the title only and not the design itself has been copyrighted.

Two circulars inclosed in the letter of the Librarian of Congress are herewith transmitted for your further information.

Respectfully, yours,

(5707 h.)

Mr. W. Y. CONNOR,
"*New York Journal,*" New York, N. Y.

W. B. HOWELL,
Assistant Secretary.

FIGURE 1.1. William B. Howell, "'Yellow Kid' Copyright," *Synopsis of Decisions of the Treasury Department*, p. 363.

vol. 1, 984).[9] Furthermore, the Sunday comic-tableaux with the Yellow Kid were utilized for other consumption purposes than reading: Outcault's uncle, the singer and comedian Will S. Rising, announced in June 1896 that he "would use the cartoons as the basis for a series of 'illustrated songs'"

---

9. Announcements for a *Hogan's Alley* production began in April 1896 (see "Hogan's Alley"; "Gossip of the Town," *New York Daily Mirror*; "Gossip of the Town," *New York Dramatic Mirror*). The copyright for this piece was completed later that year (Treasury Dept., *Catalogue* No. 294, 25; see also Winchester, *Cartoon Theatricals*, 70–71, 77–79). Harry S. Miller's musical composition *Down in Hogan's Alley* was copyrighted in March 1896 (Treasury Dept., *Catalogue* No. 248, 22).

(qtd. in Winchester, *Cartoon Theatricals* 64; see also "Plays and Players").[10] In the July issue of the *New York Dramatic Mirror,* it is mentioned that Rising drew a large audience when he was "doing his illustrated songs, including 'Hogan's Alley'" at Herald Square Theatre ("Reflections," July 1896; see also "Reflections," June 1896). In August 1896, the *Philadelphia Inquirer* announced that the vaudeville houses at Union Square would show "New York World 'Yellow Kid" skits ("Footlight Flashes"). These and other musical arrangements and dramatizations had an impact on the growing publicity of the comic figure during the summer months of 1896, and helped increase the number of people who would know about the Yellow Kid and the comics series he appeared in.

In addition to this, Yellow Kid consumer items had started to proliferate in the summer months of 1896. *Fourth Estate* editor Ernest Birmingham noted in July 1896: "A manufacturer of campaign buttons is using this [Yellow Kid] figure.... They have caught the popular fancy" ("Note and Comment," July 1896, 7). From April 1896 onward, tobacco companies sent out free pin-back buttons, for example—I come back to this later. Attendees of various theatrical compositions with the Yellow Kid were able to acquire souvenir buttons. And, Yellow Kid political pin-back buttons circulated in 1896, endorsing the presidential candidate William McKinley. Thus, the diverse manufacturers played a role in turning the comic figure into a fashion item and a cheap, mass-produced good for both advertising and political promotion to be worn or shown in public spaces.

Imitations of the Yellow Kid in advertising campaigns had likewise begun to propagate before Hearst entered the competitions. In one of the editorial comments in the trade journal *Printers' Ink,* Oscar Herzberg states that "for several months past [the] 'Yellow Kid' has been going the advertising rounds" (36). Herzberg explains: "There has been an eruption of him all over the country. He has been used to advertise shoes, and clothes, and jewelry, and tooth powder, and consumption cures, and porous plasters, and about everything that is advertised" (36; see also "The 'Yellow Kid' of the New York *World*"). In August 1896, the E. Rosenfeld & Company, which manufactured nightwear garments, and which sold their products in stores

---

10. To perform illustrated songs was a popular form of live entertainment (and a tool for marketing new sheet music). Illustrated songs usually "involved a vocalist and pianist [who would perform] a popular song, backed by a projected set of twelve to sixteen colored glass slides that, in a sequence, 'illustrated' the lyrics" (Abel 127). Audiences were encouraged to participate in these live performances. On the emergence of an audio-visual culture in the second half of the nineteenth century, see Abel, esp. 127–38.

in Baltimore and New York, hired different artists to create advertisings and posters in the form of Yellow Kid comic-tableaux, which were then reproduced in the trade press between September 1896 and January 1897 (see Rosenfeld, "For the Rest," Sept. 1896, "For the Rest," Oct. 1896, "Xmas," Dec. 1896, and "Xmas," Jan. 1897; see figure 1.2; see also Meyer, "Medial Transgressions"). They are full-page advertisements, in which the Yellow Kid is utilized to promote the trademark "Faultless" night-robes. The ads do not just make use of the Yellow Kid comic figure but imitate the Sunday comics full-page-spread layout as well. The crowded page, and the artistic strategies of space-filling words and using sign carriers' banners and the clothes as promotional space, are transferred to the full-page advertisement tableaux; the techniques of dialect speech presentation and language puns, which are used in the *Hogan's Alley* series, are likewise imitated in these ads. In these advertising campaigns, the consumption of leisure material (the comics) and consumer goods (the pajamas) is intertwined. Moreover, the recognition value of the Yellow Kid is transposed to the tableau advertisement, which functions as celebrity endorsement here.

Around the same time (the months between April and September), the Yellow Kid was appropriated by the theater stage and the plays were performed outside of New York in such cities as Philadelphia and Baltimore (see Winchester, *Cartoon Theatricals*), and the publication of music sheets that referenced the Yellow Kid or celebrated the Hogan's Alley setting increased. In a comic titled "A Crying Need of the Day Is a Few More Popular Songs," printed on April 5, 1896, Outcault offers his ironic take on the role the Yellow Kid played in observing and participating in this entertainment business. In "A Crying Need," the city of New York is supplied a steady stream of sheets of paper carrying the newest pieces of music, which are performed on stage and which are also imitated by its residents (and animals), who are singing, whistling, warbling, and screaming from music, and by so doing creating a soundscape of popular tunes on the streets. At the center of Outcault's comic, the Yellow Kid, his mouth wide open, takes part in this ear-deafening noise by promoting a piece called "Hogan's Alley" via a speech balloon (Outcault, "A Crying Need"; see Keightley, "Hogan's," esp. 45–46).

In October 1896, things got a lot more complicated; then, theater producers dueled for audiences by staging different *Hogan's Alley* and *McFadden's Row* shows, and publishers of sheet music in various cities brought to the market diverse song sheets that celebrated the Yellow Kid (see also Meyer, "Medial Transgressions"). Both theatrical competitors and music producers had a part in the construction of the Yellow Kid's career, and the

FIGURE 1.2. E. Rosenfeld & Co., "For the Rest of the Country," *Clothier and Furnisher*, vol. 26, no. 2, Sept. 1896, p. 32.[11]

strategy in media competitions—that is, protection by copyright—was also played out in the fights between Hogan's Yellow Kid and McFadden's Yellow Kid dramatic and musical compositions.

On October 12, 1896, Albert Herman Woods asked for copyright protection for *The Yellow Kid of Hogan's Alley*; three days later, Daniel A. Kelly's *The Yellow Kid in McFadden's Row of Flats* was copyrighted. One week after this, Lemuel North Woolcott requested copyright protection for his three-act farce comedy titled *A Yellow Kid*. In November 1896, George I. Pitt's Yellow Kid comedy, W. B. Watson's *McFadden's Yellow Kid* as well as his *That Yellow Kid*, and Jason C. Fulton's play were registered (see Library of Congress, *Dramatic Compositions*, vol. 2, 1672, 2303, 2634; see also Winchester, *Cartoon Theatricals*, esp. ch. 2; see Thomas Allston Brown). Sometimes, a

---

11. Originally, the ads were printed in vertical format in the journal, taking in a full page; for convenience I realigned the sample image horizontally.

theater producer created more than one Yellow Kid show, as for instance, Henry Edwin O'Grady, who produced a show titled *Yellow Kid of Hogan's Alley* as well as a show named *Yellow Kid of McFadden's Flats* (see Library of Congress, *Dramatic Compositions*, vol. 2, 2634); both were three-act farce comedies, both were copyrighted on March 19, 1897, and both premiered in Philadelphia.[12]

The diverse theatrical adaptations of the Yellow Kid comics series and Yellow Kid skits—in the form of musical comedy, farce, or burlesque—had a national reach across age, class, and gender (see Winchester, *Cartoon Theatricals*, esp. 72–75). Matinees and evening performances were attended by diverse audiences. The Yellow Kid plays are "full of fun," it was often said, suited to delight everybody, "so bring your wife, your children and sweetheart and enjoy and [sic] evening of hilarity with Mickey Dugan, the 'Yellow Kid'" ("A news snippet "). The copyright catalogues give evidence of the many different musical and dramatic productions, but only a few scripts have survived, which makes it difficult to make any claims about the plays' respective contents and structures (see Winchester, *Cartoon Theatricals* 80 and fn. 37; see also Meyer, "Medial Transgressions"). One script that did survive is Frank Dumont's *The Yellow Kid Who Lives in Hogan's Alley, a Burlesque*. The Yellow Kid serves as name-giver for, and protagonist in, this play. In the stage directions, it reads: "Enter Yellow Kid, seated in a toy express wagon, and drawn by a real goat. The Kid wears large ears, yellow gown, feet with toes to look large; in fact, to make up like the Yellow Kid *as seen in pictures*" (Dumont 5; my emphasis). The Yellow Kid "as seen in pictures" shaped the way the farce is presented to the theater audience; papier-mâché masks that covered the head completely, yellow-dress costumes, and face masks were used to impersonate the Yellow Kid.

The various theater show producers competed for time and money that people would allocate for diversion. The two most famous plays in the season of 1896–97 were Gilmore & Leonard's *Hogan's Alley* and the *McFadden's Row of Flats* by Gus Hill. The popular Gilmore & Leonard company—the name of which derives from the two leading performers/producers, Bar-

---

12. Oftentimes, rival *Hogan's Alley* and *McFadden's Row* plays opened in theaters in different cities at the same time: They could be seen in New York (at Proctor's, the Olympia, and Weber and Fields, for example), in Brooklyn (at the Bijou), in Philadelphia (at the National), in Lockport (at the Hodge Opera House), or in Syracuse (at the Grand as well as the Bastable). And then, traveling comedian groups took both *Hogan's Alley* and *McFadden's Row* shows to the stages in cities and towns in the West. The "Drama" or "Theater" sections as well as the play advertisements in the various newspapers, and especially in the theatrical press, give insights into where and how often Yellow Kid acts were performed throughout the country.

ney Gilmore and John F. Leonard—staged a comedy titled *Hogan's Alley*, which ran successfully at least until the season of 1905–6 (see Chapman and Sherwood).[13] Repeatedly the shows' producers claimed that theirs was the only one with the "original" Yellow Kid, often impersonated by the famous actor Richard (Dick) Gardner. Gilmore and Leonard promoted their show thus: "The attraction that has caused more laughs, more talk, more originality, and draws more money than any Farce-Comedy in existence, this or last season. It is the recognized home of the Original 'Yellow Kid'" ("Gilmore and Leonard"; see also "At the Lyceum Theater"; "At the Theatres"). Pulitzer's *World* reviewed the show time and again, usually claiming that it was based on the Sunday comics series that appeared in his newspaper. In one of the reviews, the anonymous author states that

> "Hogan's Alley" is one of the brightest and liveliest of farce-comedies produced in many years. It faithfully presents many of the peculiar phases of New York life which have been recorded in the Sunday World from week to week in a most original and laughable manner. All of the characters which have become household words were there, even the parrot.... But the "Yellow Kid" made the great, unmistakable hit of the evening. ("'Hogan's Alley' A Big Hit")

This show soon competed with another Yellow Kid show: Edward Waterman Townsend wrote and directed a musical comedy titled *McFadden's Row of Flats*, which was copyrighted by Gus Hill.[14] It debuted before an audience in New York, and then was seen in theaters in cities and small towns across the country (see Townsend, *McFadden's*). In addition to these,

---

13. There exists also a record of a film titled *Trouble in Hogan's Alley*, produced by the American Mutoscope and Biograph Company, in cooperation with Richard Outcault. The film was first released in July 1900 and then re-released and copyrighted in August 1903. Unfortunately, I was unable to get a hold of this film, but I do have catalogue entries that give evidence of its existence (see Walls 63; see also Niver 101). The plot summary provided in Niver suggests that it is loosely based on the *World*'s comics series; the film seems to focus on fighting scenes between the Hogan's Alley tenants. Moreover, there is a record of a film titled *Yellow Kid* that circulated in 1897 (see Maguire & Baucus Ltd. 14), but I haven't been able to find a copy. In the 1920s, the titles of both newspaper comics series were adopted to film productions, as Winchester notes, but the Yellow Kid has no appearances in the films (see *Cartoon Theatricals* 111–14).

14. Gus Hill was involved in a number of stage productions of theatrical cartoons (see Winchester, *Cartoon Theatricals* 115). Hill produced and copyrighted another musical farce comedy that was written by Edward Townsend: *Yellow Kid's Trip around the World* was performed first in 1897 (see Library of Congress, *Dramatic Compositions*, vol. 2, 2375).

the Woolcott & Jackson's company regularly performed a piece titled *A Yellow Kid*. This show traces "a humorous dramatic history of Mickey Dugan, the famous yellow kid" ("Local News and Notes"). And, the newspapers widely announced a play titled *Town Talk in McFadden's Flats,* in which the well-known songwriter William Jerome, together with the Herald Square Comedians, performed Yellow Kid acts (see, for instance, "An Entertainment"). The producer of *Town Talk in McFadden's Flats* touted that he had the "original Yellow Kid" ("Glens Falls"); in the advertisements for this show, it is also mentioned that this original Yellow Kid "has just moved from Hogan's Alley to McFadden's Flats," and that the farcical conceit had been officially authorized by the *New York Journal* ("Glens Falls"; see "Amusements," *Auburn Bulletin*; see also Meyer, "Medial Transgression"). Thus, the story of the rival comics series is (re)told and repeated in the theater adaptations of *Hogan's Alley* and *McFadden's Row,* as well as in the diverse newspaper ads promoting them. These competitions become manifest in the lithograph posters, too, which were produced for the plays. Lithograph companies such as H. C. Miner or Russell and Morgan in New York often printed posters for both *Hogan's Alley* and *McFadden's* shows (*Gilmore & Leonard* n. pag.; "The Old Reliable McFadden's Flats—Le'Ggo the Anchor"; "The Old Reliable McFadden's Flats—An Awful Bump"), which were then also reproduced in diverse newspapers (see, for example, "New McFadden's Row of Flats" 5).

Similar to the continuous competitions between the diverse Yellow Kid theatrical performances, music sheet publishers competed for customers and likewise contributed to the spawning of serial variants of the Yellow Kid. Sheet music (classical, popular songs, or folk) was distributed in different ways in the nineteenth century: by means of periodicals with a thematic focus on music, and through newspapers and mass magazines such as *Ladies Home Journal*; in these two media, sheet music usually appeared in the form of cutout extras (supposed to be preserved) or in the form of foldouts attached to the papers. Apart from that, music pieces also circulated via mail-order, and they were sold in stores (see Chanan; Charosh; Furia; Levy; on the history of music marketing, see Odgen et al.; on the history of music periodicals, see Krummel).

The Yellow Kid adorned the covers of many music folios. The Tin Pan Alley firm Howley & Haviland, run by Patrick Howley and Frederick Benjamin Haviland (see Keightley, "Tin Pan"), issued different Yellow Kid sheet music in 1896. They published both a piece titled *The Belle of Hogan's Alley* (composed by James Blake and Michael Bernard, and the content of which is only loosely related to the newspaper comics series) and a piece titled *McFadden's Row of Flats*. Moreover, the Yellow Kid comic figure was celebrated in a number of songs, waltzes, piano music of marches and two-steps, and more.[15] Musical compositions that celebrated the Yellow Kid include, among other things, such pieces as Tony Stanford's *The Yellow Kid of Hogan's Alley* (1896; see Treasury Dept., *Catalogue* No. 287, 28), compositions with the same title such as Thomas J. Armstrong's *The Yellow Kid's Patrol* (1897; see Treasury Dept., *Catalogue* No. 314, 16) and M. G. Wittman's *The Yellow Kid's Patrol* (1897; see Treasury Dept., *Catalogue* No. 336, 57), or Cora Vandersloot's *Yellow Kids on Parade* (1897; see Treasury Dept., *Catalogue* No. 286, 15). Copies of Vandersloot's music sheet—which was published by the Pennsylvania company Fisk & Achenbach—were first given to friends, but the *Yellow Kids on Parade* was then also publicly performed by, among others, the famous John Philip Sousa band, and was included in Gilmore & Leonard's *Hogan's Alley* play.

Next to Howley and Haviland, which distributed Yellow Kid music folios, the Russell Hunting company produced songs and was one of the first to make Yellow Kid records for the "talking machines" ("New Records"). The title of their 1897 Yellow Kid record is *The Yellow Kid of Hogan's Alley* ("New Records"; see also Laing). People who possessed either a phonograph ($40 to $200) or one of the newly invented (and much cheaper) echophones ($8) could thus listen to the Yellow Kid record and also sing along.

Other composers and sheet music publishers from other states in the country realized the recognition value of the Yellow Kid and also attempted to capitalize on the popular comic figure. They used not only the name of the Yellow Kid and printed it on the cover but also included illustrations of the comic figure to promote their sheets; these were often drawn by anonymous artists. Though the—distorted—copies of the Yellow Kid all look slightly different from Outcault's or Luks's drawings, the comic figure remains identifiable in all of the sheet covers (see Shardlow; Gene Myers; Elliot; Meyer and Schlott; Baker). There was a relentless process of distribution—and commodification—of the Yellow Kid.

---

15. The comic figure also inspired dance choreographies. The Yellow Kid dance was quite popular at that time. The dance consisted mainly of high steps and kicks and is reminiscent of the cakewalk that Luks had also visualized in several *Hogan's Alley* episodes (see Luks, "A Seeley" and "A Cake Walk"). The dance was performed, among other things, by the Leander Sisters at the Sutro Baths in San Francisco in August 1897. In their performance, the smaller sister wears a Yellow Kid mask with flap ears and a long (presumably yellow) coat to imitate the comic figure's appearance. The dance was captured on film and is viewable online at the Library of Congress (see "Leander Sisters").

In September 1896, the Homer Tourjée Music Company entered the competitions by producing two different Yellow Kid songbooks. The opening line in *The Dugan Kid Who Lives in Hogan's Alley*, composed and written by William H. Friday Jr. and Homer Tourjée, reads: "Who does-n't know the Du-gan Kid, . . . He wears a dan-dy yel-low dress" (n. pag.). The piece represented a pleasurable and entertaining feature and made possible another engagement with the Yellow Kid, in both words and images. For those unfamiliar with the "Dugan Kid" mentioned in the title and in the lyrics of *The Dugan Kid Who Lives in Hogan's Alley*, this songbook served as an invitation to buy Pulitzer's *World* and to search for the "yellow dress" of the street urchin in the pages of his newspaper: "You'll find his pic-ture in the World, most ev-e-ry Sun-day morn" (n. pag.). Just a few of months after *The Dugan Kid Who Lives in Hogan's Alley* had appeared in Pulitzer's *World*, the company presented another Yellow Kid theme song, but instead of celebrating the *World* and the Dugan Kid's place within this paper, Friday and Tourjée's new song situated the famous comic figure in the context of Hearst's *Journal*. Before it was printed in the American Humorist, readers of the newspaper were informed that the music folio would not only be framed by Yellow Kid "illustrations in five colors" ("Just in Time"), created by Outcault, but that it was arranged in such a way that they could cut out the pages and "Bind [them] in a Book" ("Just in Time"; see also "The Best Song Yet") and perform the song at home. While Tourjée and Friday's sheet music *The Dugan Kid Who Lives in Hogan's Alley* situates the life of the Yellow Kid in the *World*, "The Yellow Kid" songbook printed in the *Journal*'s Sunday supplement tells another story. Here, the Yellow Kid's outer appearance, his characteristics, his doings, his vernacular language, and his place of origin are linked to the *Journal* (Friday and Tourjée, "Yellow Kid" 7–8). The music folio is an advertisement jingle for both the Yellow Kid and the newspaper he appears in. It advises its readers that if you don't want to miss the "latest," "greatest," "up-do-datest," go buy yourself the next issue of the *New York Journal* (7–8).

What both of Friday and Tourjée's Yellow Kid music folios convey is that the comic figure has an impact on New York residents: In the songbook for the *World* and in the music folio for the *Journal*, it is suggested that the vernacular language of the Yellow Kid has impacted everyday communication in such a way that some of his recurring expressions of the comics series can now be heard "if you listen on the street" (Friday and Tourjée, "Yellow Kid," 7; see also "Children Sing"). In addition to that, both of the Yellow Kid songbooks made by the Homer Tourjée Music Company tell the origin story of the Yellow Kid comic figure again—an origin story that changes according to, or is adapted to, the respective newspapers. Thus, the circulation war between the rival papers of Pulitzer and Hearst has repercussions in other media, and questions of originality and authenticity infused the competitions between theatrical compositions and music sheet producers, too.

Music publishers across the country (such as, for instance, W. J. Dyer & Bro. in Saint Paul; M. D. Swisher in Philadelphia; August Meyer in Anaconda, Montana; G. M. White in Detroit; Louis Francis Haaren in Richmond, Virginia; Uedemann in Jacksonville; or Judson W. Elliott in Minneapolis) took notice of the developments in New York and soon entered these competitions. The Mark Ament Music Company, located in Peoria, Illinois, is an interesting case in point in this regard: In 1896, the company distributed a music folio titled *The Little Yellow Kid* (copyrighted in January 1897). It was written by Annie G. Callender and composed by William H. Penn (who held the copyright). On the cover of *The Little Yellow Kid*, the Yellow Kid, drawn by an anonymous artist, greets the audience: "Hully Gee! But I'm Hot Stuff" (Penn and Callender n. pag.). The lyrics of this musical piece are written in first person and in the vernacular style that is known from the dress of the Yellow Kid in the Sunday comics pages. The music folio addresses not only the Yellow Kid's popularity but also the comic figure's various enactments outside of the newspapers. The first couple of lines of the lyrics read: "Oh! Talk a-bout yure reel hot stuff, just cast yure I on me, De lit-tle yel-low kid is all de rage . . . . Me talk is in de papers, and me pic-ture's in de stores, An' now dey tries to ring me on the stage" (Penn and Callender 2). That the various reconfigurations of the Yellow Kid were also negotiated in other medial forms at that time attests to an awareness of the competing media that attended the Yellow Kid's rise to fame; notions of the comic figure's iterability and the Yellow Kid's proliferations were self-consciously addressed in such music sheets as Penn and Callender, and thus became part of the Yellow Kid's narrative of serial unfolding.

That theater producers and music publishers attempted to capitalize on the Yellow Kid's fame seems evident. However, these competitions point to something else, too: For one thing, the comic figure's career was activated and conditioned by the different dramatic and musical compositions that foster intermedial relationships (see also Keightley, "Hogan's"). The context in which readers consumed the comics series was also shaped by the practice of the Yellow Kid's adaptation for theater and musical compositions. For another thing, the Yellow Kid lent himself to appropriations in other medial forms, but it seems that the "power" of these (and other) imitations and variations would emanate from the comic figure itself. The iconicity of the Yellow Kid was stabilized through repetitions and the various replications; but then again, the iconization of the comic figure "evolved," to use the wording from Mayer, "very much on its own" (*Serial* 59). Following this paradigm, the next section sets out to demonstrate that even in his "medium of origin" (Mayer, *Serial* 38) the Yellow Kid did not stay in his allocated "space"—the comics in Sunday supplement pages. The comic figure meandered through the newspaper pages of both Pulitzer's *World* and Hearst's *Journal*.

ACTION-CONDUCTING PRINT FORMS

The Yellow Kid exited the settings of his original Sunday comics series and branched out: He was adopted in other comics, he moved to other sections of the newspapers, and he appeared in other formats. Not only Outcault and Luks penned the Yellow Kid. Other newspaper illustrators of both Pulitzer's *World* and Hearst's *Journal* appropriated the Yellow Kid in diverse ways and with different effects in the Comic Weekly and the American Humorist, respectively, as well as in political cartoons that appeared outside of the supplement pages. The Yellow Kid was invested with new meanings and served different functions (see, for instance, Cory, "Four Days" and Political cartoon; Shultz; Kemble). The artists attested to the popularity of, while at the same time they contributed to, the comic figure's expansive dynamics; the Yellow Kid extended to other comics-worlds. But there is something else that one can learn: The comics pages give insight into the Yellow Kid's status as a flat and recyclable figure. With recourse to Ruth Mayer's claim about the versatility of serial figures, I argue that the Yellow Kid is a modifiable, adaptable figure that could be bent and put into various contexts and used and reused for any purpose.

In Rudolph Dirks's ironic commentary on the Anti-Cartoon Bill (1897), titled "First, the Anti-Cartoon Bill. Then, Perhaps This!" (see figure 1.3), the Yellow Kid has a cameo appearance. Here, he is situated in the foreground and turns his back to the readers, holding a red brick in his right hand behind his back. Other famous characters from Hearst's Sunday newspaper comic supplement rush forward to the tree in which a "poor artist" (Dirks) is seeking shelter—among them are James (Jimmy) Swinnerton's famous Tigers (one of them is placed in the top right-hand corner, sitting on a hippo), Edward Kemble's so-called Coons (next to the Yellow Kid, to the right), and animals from Dirks's serialized animal cartoons (1897–98) as well as his characters Hans and Fritz from the *Katzenjammer Kids* series, who hold a rifle, a knife, a sword, and a miniature cannon tube (bottom left corner of the page). There are some unhappy faces, and some of the animals and characters in the "First . . . Then" comic-tableau have their mouths open as if ready to say something, or inquire, or complain about something. Through his gesture with his finger, the Yellow Kid orders the baffled artist to come down from the tree. In Dirks's humorous "First . . . Then" half-page comic-tableau, the Yellow Kid and the other characters and animals surrounding the tree serve to allegorize unrequited love between a comics artist and his creations. Instead of affection and thankfulness, the comics characters who had been given life through the pen of an artist chase this "chap" (Dirks) into a tree and beleaguer him. The Anti-Cartoon Bill targeted the drawings of political figures and other personalities and was meant to outlaw the publication of caricatures, political as well as editorial cartoons, and illustrated portraits of social and political people in the newspapers; in this comic-tableau, however, the newspaper comic characters themselves threaten the creator. So, "first," newspaper comics artists and illustrators had to fight against press censorship, and now they face the attacks from their own creations. In Dirks's comic-tableau, the Sunday supplement characters and animals seem to come after the artist because they are exposed to the public without prior permission. That the Yellow Kid is part of this revolt adds another facet to the humor of the comic-tableau because he was one of the most often copied comic figures in that time period, and now the Yellow Kid seems to want to throw the red brick for having been imitated (exploited), yet again.

In J. B. (John Buckingham) Lowitz's comics series *In the Jungle* (renamed *Gazoozaland* in February 1897), which was printed in Pulitzer's *World* and which consisted of half-page comic-tableaux and was collaboratively created with Albert Bigelow Paine (who contributed text columns in verse), something else happens; the recurrent protagonist of this series, an ape, is endowed with a number of the characteristic features of the Yellow Kid comic figure (see figure 1.4): The animal wears a long yellow dress, "wid ruffles" (Lowitz, "Valentine's"), onto which, in the tried and tested way, the words this ape wants to communicate are printed—of course, in vernacular form (see Barker 28). Moreover, in each of the episodes of the series, the readers of *Gazoozaland* encounter the same cast of characters in different settings. Lowitz drew on the already established, recognizable elements of the Yellow Kid and the comic series, and rewrote the formulaic elements into another context, superimposing the typical features of the Yellow Kid onto a new character in a new setting.

FIGURE 1.3. Rudolph Dirks, "First, the Anti-Cartoon Bill. Then, Perhaps This!" *New York Journal and Advertiser*, 20 Feb. 1898, American Humorist, p. 5. San Francisco Academy of Comic Art Collection, The Ohio State University, Billy Ireland Cartoon Library & Museum.

FIGURE 1.4. J. B. Lowitz, "The Intercollegiate Boat Race in the Jungle," *The World*, 18 Oct. 1896, Comic Weekly, p. 8 (detail). San Francisco Academy of Comic Art Collection, The Ohio State University, Billy Ireland Cartoon Library & Museum.

The comic figure was altered, distorted, and adapted in all kinds of ways. The malleability hinged on its flatness. In addition to these guest appearances and appropriations of emblematic features of the Yellow Kid in other newspaper comics, the comic figure was used as a foil for caricature. There were numerous parodistic rewritings of the Yellow Kid, both in the newspapers and in other print media, such as humor magazines. In Walt McDougall's cover page comic titled "New York's Great Reform Freak Show," he represents the famous Republican congressman and senator Thomas Collier Platt (in office from March 1897 to March 1909) as an elderly, white-bearded "Yellow Kid of Parkhurst Alley" and endows him with the typical—and distinct—features of the Yellow Kid: the big round head, the large ears that stick out, the bare feet, a boyish physique, and a yellow dress (with sleeves that are slightly too long), which conveys a message. The characteristic traits of the Yellow Kid are reconceptualized as a means for social satire; the elements of the Yellow Kid's appearance are transplanted onto a real-life person and serve to poke fun at the (wrong) doings and bossing around of the political figure T. C. Platt. In similar ways, the artists Grant Hamilton and Bernhard Gillam, who worked for the humor magazine *Judge*, used the Yellow Kid and other famous characters such as, for instance, Palmer Cox's so-called Brownies to mock different political figures (see Hamilton and Gillam; Hamilton, "The Yellowest" and "Political 'Kids'"). In their illustrations for *Judge*, the Yellow Kid is mainly used to poke fun at the Democrat governor of New York, and later US senator, David Bennett Hill—Hamilton's Yellow Kid wears muttonchops and a moustache and has quite a high forehead in order to "represent" Hill. That *Judge* magazine printed these and other political cartoons satirizing the members of Tammany Hall is not very surprising given the fact that *Judge*'s editor, William J. Arkell, supported the Republican Party. Pulitzer's *World* and Hearst's *Journal*, on the other hand, had a Democratic leaning and strove for readers supporting the Democratic Party.

The Yellow Kid was nomadic; he meandered through his medium of origin and permeated other print formats. In the college journal titled the *Makio*, which was published by the Fraternities and Literary Societies of the Ohio State University, the journal's contributors reproduced the Yellow Kid multiple times in various sections to perform both entertaining and advertising functions (see Sullivan, A Yellow Kid illustration, "Miscellaneous," and "A Chapter" 303, 305; Kiler's Pharmacy Co.). The distinctive shape and memorable looks of the Yellow Kid, the comic-tableau layout design, and the vernacular language seem to have drawn audiences and stimulated imitations. Such rewritings of the Yellow Kid's iconic features bespeak that readers outside New York consumed the Sunday supplement comics and also other appearances of the comic figure in the newspapers. The diffuse audiences had a part in the construction of the Yellow Kid's career by multiplying and propagating the comic figure in formats other than the Sunday comics series.

Other print media formats in which the Yellow Kid was appropriated include a literary magazine bearing his name (*The Yellow Kid*) and the fictional autobiography titled *The Yellow Kid in McFadden's Flats*. This was published by Dillingham in 1897 (the first print counted 30,000 copies) and was extensively promoted in Hearst's *Journal*. In this book, Edward Townsend and Richard Outcault recycled installments from the *McFadden's Row* series; details from the illustrations of the Sunday series were reproduced in black and white, and Outcault added a few new drawings. The book tells the "sweet young life" of "Master Mickey Dugan, better known as the Yellow Kid" (15, 11). This life really only began, the text suggests, "the day I went to the Flats to live" (19). The fictional autobiography is intertextually related to the *McFadden's Row* series as well as to the *Around the World* narrative in Hearst's *Journal*. The diegetic setting of the Sunday *McFadden's Row* series is integrated into the autobiography—both in words and in images. This is also made quite explicit in the acknowledgments of the book: "Many of the illustrations in this book were originally published in the New York *Journal*. They are reproduced here by permission of W. R. Hearst, editor and proprietor of the *Journal*" (5). The publication of *The Yellow Kid in McFadden's Flats* was certainly a means to exploit the success of the Yellow Kid, and to enable yet another way of extended reader engagement with the comic figure. But I think that the distribution of the fictional autobiography can also be viewed in the context of the many efforts by the artists and the newspapers to claim ownership and regain control over the Yellow Kid. By relating the Yellow Kid's life to the comics series in the *Journal*, the authors Townsend and Outcault set out to determine the "real" place of belonging of this vagabond figure—namely, *McFadden's Row of Flats* in Hearst's newspaper.

The Yellow Kid is the narrating agency of the events in *The Yellow Kid in McFadden's Flats* (though there are some shifts in focalization and levels of narration, I should mention). In the introduction of the book, an unnamed fictional editor traces how the book came into being and gives details about who was involved in its production: The Yellow Kid wrote the draft, we are told, which was then handed over to the "artisan" (Townsend and Outcault 11) friend named Terence McSwatt. The editor continues that McSwatt "had taken advantage of his opportunity . . . to garnish [it] with certain literary dressing of the high and excellent style . . . and also to insert [aspects] which had been overlooked in the Kid's original draft. As McSwatt left the manuscript, the present Editor herewith leaves it of the reader" (12). For those familiar with the newspaper comics series in Hearst's *Journal,* this mentioning of "high and excellent style" is a tongue-and-cheek reference to the (un)skills of Terence McSwatt, who was implemented as a recurrent character and poet laureate in *McFadden's Row*—in the comics series, he usually plagiarizes other poets, performs poorly composed verses, or laments his life.

What makes this autobiography an important case in point for this study is that next to the implicit and explicit relations to the newspaper comics series, which invite extended consumption practices of and between two media, the text is informed with self-reflexive moments about the Yellow Kid's iconicity, about his serial status, and about his impact. The Yellow Kid narrator comments on his own material status as a two-dimensional drawing in the newspapers—"gentle reader, . . . I am a picture myself" and you "will find my way of spelling printed on my dress" (42, 149)—and on the artist Richard Outcault, who "made" him and who seems to have had "no time to draw any hair on my dear young head" (42), and thus interrogates the relationship of himself to the carrier medium. Furthermore, the Yellow Kid reflects on his life as a national celebrity: On the one hand, "it must be terrible to have your picture printed where all may gaze" (45), which is a self-ironic remark on his own omnipresence; on the other hand, "I am glad I am so popular" (143) and "beloved" (44). Pondering on his mass appeal, he self-mockingly states that "it is not my beauty, so much as my modesty, that makes me so" (143). Last, the Yellow Kid deliberates on his own serial existence: He tells the readers that he removes all the dirt from the yellow dresses each week because otherwise "you wouldn't know they were yellow, and if you didn't know that I'd have to be introduced to you every time I met you, dear reader" (16). These self-descriptions about his renewings and his remarks about his material and medial "being" are certainly designed to generate humor. But there is something else to them. They are meta-comments that trigger an awareness of the Yellow Kid's permeability and versatility, and that invite us to engage with the evolution and reception of the Yellow Kid.

At around the same time that the fictional autobiography hit the market, the forty-eight-page *Yellow Kid* magazine (see *Yellow Kid: A Semi-Monthly Magazine*) began its publication with the help of the face and name of the comic figure. The *Yellow Kid* is a magazine that contained an assembly of short essays, poems, and short stories, as well as sketches, cartoons, prize contests, advertisements, and photographic engravings. Outcault contributed several Yellow Kid drawings for the cover pages of the first couple of issues of the magazine. The publishing company seemed to consider the Yellow Kid a guarantor for success, and he became the representative of this magazine. The first issue was launched on March 20, 1897, and was sold for five cents per copy, or one dollar per yearly subscription. The *Yellow Kid*'s first editor was Joe Kerr—a pseudonym of William Melville Kerr. Under the editorship of Kerr, the *Yellow Kid* magazine also printed advertisements promoting the next New York Sunday *Journal*. While the *Journal* sponsored the *Yellow Kid* magazine through advertising, the magazine provided another means for Hearst to promote his *Journal*. In the ensuing pages, I wish to draw attention to a selection of illustrations from the cover pages of the magazine (see figures 1.5 and 1.6). The settings in which the Yellow Kid is shown in these illustrations are middle-class locations such as a nicely furnished room, a restaurant, or a ship, to mention but a few. The magazine advertised the cover images as follows: "Watch for it! On April 17, the Easter edition of *The Yellow Kid* magazine will appear. A new illuminated cover by R. F. Outcalt [sic] will show *the jolly little degenerate* in still more genteel guise" (Yellow Kid advertisement; my emphasis). Obviously, these cover-page illustrations are further multiplications of the Yellow Kid, but this is not what interests me here (or only partially). What I am interested in is how the advertisements printed on the cover or back of this magazine function in relation to and exchange with other Yellow Kid texts.

In figure 1.5, we see a Yellow Kid with a cigar in his hand. In front of the Yellow Kid lies a pack of Yellow Kid cigarettes. In figure 1.6, a framed Yellow Kid poster hangs on the wall of a restaurant, and the Yellow Kid, who is sitting at a table and toasting (and spilling) some alcoholic beverage, wears a Yellow Kid pin-back button on his yellow dress—which is a reproduction of number 32 in the series of the Yellow Kid buttons manufactured by the Neuberger Company. What these images on the *Yellow Kid* magazine do, then, is to visualize the role the comic figure played as a brand "ambassador" for, among other things, tobacco companies such as those producing High Admiral cigarettes and cigars.

Tobacco companies—and their distributors and cigar dealers—touted their tobacco wares with the help of the Yellow Kid (see Waples-Platter Grocer Co., A Yellow Kid cigar advertisement 17, 23, and 24 Feb. 1897). The Yellow Kid promoted cigarettes and cigars via trade cards, print advertisements, posters, and the illustrations on the covers as well as the sides and back covers of cigarette packs. Furthermore, the manufacturers distributed Yellow Kid giveaways such as message-bearing pin-back buttons, some

FIGURE 1.5. *The Yellow Kid,* vol. 1, no. 2, March 1897 (detail). Library of Congress, Prints and Photographs Division.

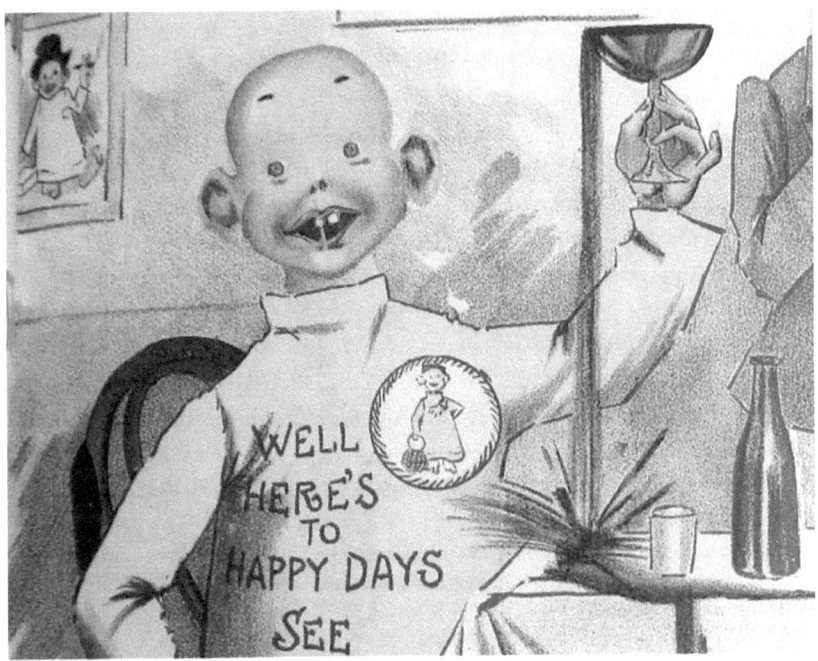

FIGURE 1.6. *The Yellow Kid,* vol. 1, no. 4, May 1897 (detail). Library of Congress, Prints and Photographs Division.

of which show the Yellow Kid in situations or positions that the reader of the Sunday comics series or the fictional autobiography would recognize immediately. "With each package of these the smoker gets one of Outcault's valuable series of *original* comic Yellow Kid buttons," an ad would inform its readers (National Cigarette & Tobacco Co., "The Cigarettes"— my emphasis; see also Marschall and Bernard, esp. 26–35 and 70–75). The give-away pin-back buttons with images of the sloganeering Yellow Kid were only attainable through the purchase of a cigarette pack. "Advertising buttons appear to be as popular as ever," noted a *Printers' Ink* contributor in 1896, and added: "The difficulty with which the manufacturers now have to contend is to keep up the supply of slangy phrases. The National Cigarette and Tobacco Co. has obviated this by using a new series representing Outcault's Yellow Kid in various postures" ("The 'Yellow Kid' of the New York *World*").[16]

Coming back to *The Yellow Kid* magazine: The diverse images of the Yellow Kid on the cover pages refer to the Sunday newspaper comics series and to other Yellow Kid comic formats such as the buttons, while also addressing the comic figure's role in the advertising industry. It is clear, then, that the Yellow Kid operated in a network of different media, which observed and were in dialogue with each other. The Yellow Kid functioned *in, between,* and *across* different media—as a kind of intermediator as well as self-promoter. He was embedded and participated in what Matthew Freeman would call the "cross-promotional consumer culture" ("Branding" 637). These mechanisms become obvious also in High Admiral cigarette advertising campaigns launched in print and other media at that time. Poster advertisements (see National Cigarette & Tobacco Co., "High Admiral") and the print advertisements (see National Cigarette & Tobacco Co., "The Cigarettes") tie into the cross-referencing of *The Yellow Kid* magazine cover images and the competing series of free advertising buttons. For instance, in one of the poster ads, the Yellow Kid says in self-reflexive manner: "SAY I'VE TRADED ME FACE TER DE HiGH ADMiRAL FOLKS AN SAY DE CIGARETTES IS A DREAM P. S. SO iS ME FACE" (National Cigarette & Tobacco Co., "High Admiral"). The message in one of the company's print ads reads like a warning. The Yellow Kid declares: "SAY!

---

16. There were two rival manufacturers involved in the production and dissemination of Yellow Kid pin-back buttons: B. Neuberger, located in New York, and Riley-Klotz, located in Newark, New Jersey. In order to distinguish the series, the tobacco companies printed numbers at the bottom of the buttons, placed either to the right (Neuberger) or to the left (Riley-Klotz). The buttons hit the market in April 1896.

YE WANT TE BE DEAD CAREFUL ABOUT USIN ME FACE CAUSE ITS RENTED SEE!" (National Cigarette & Tobacco Co., "The Cigarettes"). On the back cover of the company's Yellow Kid cigarette pack consumers are cautioned, "Beware of Imitations," and informed that "All Yellow Kid Cigarettes are manufactured by us" (National Cigarette & Tobacco Co., "Outcaults Yellow Kid Cigarettes"). The advertisements not only promote the tobacco wares but also talk about the marketing of the Yellow Kid's face and allude to the fact that the comic figure was widely copied. What those cross-references thus show is that the operations of replication and branching out, which define the Yellow Kid's career, are also informed with intermedial and self-reflexive dynamics. I will further elaborate on this in the concluding three sections of this chapter, in which I historicize the emergence and spread of the comic figure in the interacting fields of modern advertising, retailing, and toy manufacturing. I will trace how and in what ways the diverse agents energized the career of the Yellow Kid and reflect on how the processes of the comic figure's commercial unfolding had repercussions in the comic-tableaux themselves.

YELLOW KID OBJECTS AS INTERACTING AGENTS

That people consumed the Yellow Kid becomes manifest in the form of copycat illustrations or sketches sent in for prize contests (see J. R. Williams), letters to the editors of the newspapers, or short biographical accounts. In her 1905 study *Family Monographs,* social worker Elsa Herzfeld observed that younger family members were busy "drawing 'Buster Brown' and the 'Yaller Kid'" (Herzfeld 16; see also Ethellyn Gardner n. pag.). A reader of the *Omaha World-Herald* wrote a letter sent to the newspaper on December 22, 1898, voicing the following request: "Dear Santa Claus: Bring me some houses, a little table and dishes and a yellow kid" (Dillon 8). I cannot say with certainty how many people engaged with the Yellow Kid and where, and in which medial form(s), but with the help of the records and visual documents I have collected during my research—especially in the trade press—I can say something about the Yellow Kid consumer items, to whom they were targeted, and the affordances they offered. In the following, I discuss the Yellow Kid's multiple incarnations in the worlds of toy manufacturing and advertising (in the form of window cardboards, lithograph posters, etc.), and examine what Steven Connor calls *"fidgetables,* things that hold out the possibility of being fiddled with" (4)—Yellow Kid paraphernalia such as papier-mâché masks, costumes, or souvenir items—and situate these against the background of the rise of mass marketing of fictional characters in the second half of the nineteenth century.

Recurring newspaper comic characters had existed before the Yellow Kid became famous in 1896. In April 1894, Charles W. Saalburg had created one of the first colored comics series titled the *Ting-Lings*—showing a crowd of Asian stereotypes with bloated heads—which was printed in the Sunday supplement of the Chicagoan newspaper *Inter Ocean*.[17] Likewise, the licensing and mass marketing of fictional characters had begun a decade before such comics series as the *Ting-Lings* or *Hogan's Alley* (and others) started to appear in the newspapers. Prominent examples are Palmer Cox's Brownies, mentioned above, or—in Britain—Ally Sloper (see Banville; Bailey; Sabin; Kunzle, "The First Ally Sloper"). These had preceded the Yellow Kid's career.

Ally Sloper became England's first plurimedial "superstar" and "an everyday icon" from the 1880s onward, as Roger Sabin has pointed out (177). The success of Ally Sloper was made possible "through a combination of what we would now call synergistic marketing techniques involving a range of advertising campaigns and reader-response devices such as competitions"—through these and other practices, "the profile of the character was consolidated to become an everyday icon" (Sabin 177; see also 180, 182). Moreover, merchandise articles were sold and free giveaways were distributed in order to "engage the loyalties and participation of its [the comic figure's] readership, gain publicity and boost its circulation" (Bailey

---

17. Despite the repeated efforts to acquaint the newspaper readers with the Ting-Lings (see "Ting-Ling"; see also Saalburg, "The Ting-Lings" and "Ting-Ling Types"), Saalburg's characters did not become iconic characters, and they did not have a nationwide reach. One reason for this was that Saalburg left the *Inter Ocean* (to work for Pulitzer's *World*), and the newspaper did not hire another artist to continue the *Ting-Lings* series (see Adcock). Another reason was that the Chicago newspaper had a fairly small circulation number (approximately 95,000; Pulitzer had approximately 500,000). Moreover, whereas Pulitzer's *World* subscribed to the Associated Press syndicate, the *Inter Ocean* was a McClure's Literary Associate Press subscriber, which really only began distributing Sunday section features, such as comics, in 1898. This changed after the turn of the century, when the role of the McClure syndicate, especially with regard to the marketing and dissemination of comics, grew exponentially (see Johanningsmeier, *Fiction*, esp. 65). And, even though these characters were also appropriated in other medial formats (in the form of paper dolls, for example, and the London-based children's book publisher Dean & Son Ltd. issued a *Ting Lings* toy book in 1898), the Ting-Ling characters never gained widespread popularity. In comparison with other fictional characters of the nineteenth century that were marketed widely and in different media and appealed to large audiences, the Ting-Ling characters and the series they appeared in did not have mass appeal.

10; see also 12). This "circuit of mutually promoting manifestations" that we can trace explains how "the 'contract' between Sloper and his readers is being *extended into areas of everyday consumerism*" (Sabin 179; my emphasis). Sloper was a character that readers from different social classes could relate to (see Sabin 177, 185).[18]

The Brownies have a different backstory. The Canadian-born illustrator and author Palmer Cox (see Cummins 42–66) penned the goblins and wrote limericks that accompanied the drawings. The illustrated narratives were first serialized in the *St. Nicholas* magazine, and then they were reused in a series of prose books. The beginnings can be traced to *Wide Awake*, which printed the first Brownie characters in 1879. The Brownies are a band of characters with the same physical features—bloated belly, large eyes, skinny legs. The initially unspecified sprites gradually turned into recognizable types. Cox developed a cast of over thirty Brownies, each of which was endowed with a specific attire, and each of which was given a name in order to indicate either a profession, an ethnic background, a national identity, or a distinct personality or character trait. The Brownies became popular in the late 1880s, and their popularity lasted well into the twentieth century. Next to the illustrated, serialized stories in the juvenile magazine and in a series of books, the Brownies showed up in the form of, among other things, toy items (see McLoughlin, *McLoughlin Bros' Catalogue 1895*, 89, 93, 108; see also McLoughlin, *McLoughlin Bros' Catalogue 1897*). They "inspired," according to Angela Sorby, "a major consumer craze" (66–67). The Brownies "grew into distinct contemporary social stereotypes. [They] were antecedents of modern character sets" (Cross 88). The Brownies were designed to cater primarily to a consumer market of white middle-class children. "They symbolized," writes Gary Cross, "American urban society in the 1890s in a mythically harmonious way" (89). Moreover, the Brownies were licensed to major advertisers such as Ivory Soap and for the manufacture of a broad range of products (see Olivier 6–7; see also Blackbeard 25–26; Morgan 22–23; Morgan and Ingram; Hake 28–29). Gradually, more and more tie-in products flooded the market. "The effect was," Nelson and Chasar conclude, to "thoroughly blur the line between original and collateral Brownie artefacts, between the impulse to buy a book of Cox's poems and the impulse to buy a patent medicine, a doll, or a box of soap" (144).

---

18. In this context see also Theodore Dreiser, who in his *Newspaper Days* recounts a visit to a friend's house and describes how baffled he was when he discovered that this friend owned what he considered "a gruesome-shaped head of papier-mâché representing some half-demented creature, commonly known in England as Ally Sloper" (Dreiser 167; see also 337).

What is similar about the Brownies and the Yellow Kid is that both the children's magazine characters and the newspaper comic figure were used as promotional tools in advertising and as "spokescreatures" (Olivier 6) of various commercial products, and that they were adapted into three-dimensional toys and other consumer wares. Yet, when one compares the career of the Brownies and the career of the Yellow Kid, what seems different are, however, at least two aspects: Apart from the fact that the Brownies are a crowd of mute fairies (the only voice is the first-person narrator in the text columns), they are characters that invite identificatory engagements—each representing either an ethnic stereotype, a nationality, or a profession. The Yellow Kid, on the other hand, is flat and versatile and is marked by medial and narrative liminality. The liminal quality of the Yellow Kid has to do with his unstable position within his medium of origin as well as outside; a contemporary of Outcault called him a "versatile individual" who shifts and moves between different medial formats ("Baltimore" 1896). Furthermore, as I showed in the previous section, the Yellow Kid cross-referenced the different media in which he operated. The inter- and self-reflexive quality of the comic figure is another aspect that differentiates, I would say, the career of the Brownies and that of the Yellow Kid.

The Yellow Kid catered to a diffuse audience both in regard to the comic-tableaux (the focus in the next chapters) and in regard to his multiple incarnations outside of the newspaper comics series. These included miniature flip books such as H. W. Willcox's *A Story without Words: The Yellow Kid* (1897; see Treasury Dept., No. 302, 8); "yellow kid sofa cushions, . . . yellow kid kites, yellow kid masques, yellow kid cigarettes, and the yellow kid magazine" (Urquhart 524–25); and such items as a "mechanical 'Yellow Kid' [which] takes off its hat, hammers on a bell, wags its head, etc." ("Trade Items," May 1897, 802). It sold for twenty-five cents (at Macy's for thirty-three cents) and was meant "to amuse the Children" (Denholm & McKay Co.). A few months earlier, the book and tablet manufacturer Boorum & Pease had proudly announced: "We have obtained the exclusive right to use 'Yellow Kid designs.'" Outcault designed some of the book-cover illustrations for the company ("Trade Items," Feb. 1897, 256). In the Boorum & Pease ad, a little further down, it is stated that the "'Yellow Kid' is immensely popular, and various things bearing his physiognomy have had enormous sales" (227). By selling stationery items that were endowed with reproductions of the Yellow Kid, the manufacturing company participated in the dissemination of the comic figure at that time; through their diverse products such as Yellow Kid scrapbooks, the Boorum & Pease company offered activities such as cutting, pasting, and saving material of personal value and also contributed to the preservation and memorization of the Yellow Kid (Boorum & Pease Company; see also Walker). The sheer quantity of Yellow Kid items is overwhelming, and the outlets through which manufactured goods were distributed are quite diverse.[19] In addition, the toy industry was fast in adapting the Yellow Kid to diverse toy items such as puzzles, dolls, ten pin blocks, and more (see McLoughlin, *McLoughlin Bros' Catalogue* 1897, 115, 119, 122).

In the 1890s, the expanding toy industry "introduced pressed steel and offset lithography to replace tinplate and hand-painted toys" (Cross 29), which were fairly expensive and time-consuming to produce. "Increased mechanization, new materials, and innovative methods brought lower consumer prices and more toys to the American family. Many of these changes also reduced the time required for getting toys and games to retail shelves, allowing manufacturers to respond effectively to fads and current events" (Cross 29). Toy manufacturers employed fictional as well as real-life celebrities to sell a new item. When the supplement comics began to spread across the country in the 1890s, some protagonists from popular series would also be turned into board games, dolls, pin blocks, card games, and more. One of the leading toy manufacturers that were involved in producing and distributing Yellow Kid toys was the McLoughlin Brothers company (see Whitehill). Through such items as those by the McLoughlin Brothers, the Yellow Kid branched out to other groups of consumers (in particular children) and invited further, different consumption practices of the Yellow Kid comic figure. One of McLoughlin Brother's puzzles—the *Yellow Kid Puzzle*, published in 1896 (it cost sixty cents)—shall serve as a case in point here.

On the cover of McLoughlin's puzzle box, the Yellow Kid, smiling at the potential player in a long yellow dress and pointing to the name *Yellow Kid Puzzle* with his left hand, promises via the words on his yellow dress that it is going to be fun to play the game. When put together, the pieces of McLoughlin's *Yellow Kid Puzzle* show the scene of Outcault and Townsend's episode titled "McFadden's Row of Flats—Inauguration of the Football Season in McFadden's Row."[20] The visual elements and the layout design of the newspaper comic-tableau are transferred to another medium; the text columns that frame the *McFadden's Row* episode are not reprinted on the game pieces. Instead one finds two additional buildings and clothing lines

---

19. The website *Greetings from Mouse Heaven* (http://melbirnkrant.com/collection/page7.html) holds the most extensive merchandise collection of the Yellow Kid figure (see Birnkrant). My thanks to Corey Creekmur for drawing my attention to Birnkrant's website. In addition, see Hake, esp. 166–69; Marschall and Bernard 27.

20. An image of the *Yellow Kid Puzzle*, including an image of the box, can be viewed online (see Birnkrant). Outcault and Townsend's football episode is available in the digital album at Ohio State University Library.

in the background of the puzzle. The speech balloons and captions that are printed in Outcault and Townsend's comic-tableau are, however, also visible to the puzzle game player. These narrative affordances of the comic are transferred to another medium.

Regular readers of the Yellow Kid comics series in Hearst's *Journal* who interacted the puzzle were invited to reactivate their reading experience of the newspaper episode. This is also suggested by the text on the cover of the puzzle box, which states that the scene of the puzzle pieces is taken "From the N. Y. Journal's Famous Series Drawn by R. F. Outcault" (see McLoughlin, *Yellow Kid Puzzle*; this short note is printed on the puzzle pieces as well, just as the—false—information that Outcault copyrighted the Yellow Kid in 1896 is shown both on the cover of the box and on the puzzle pieces). The puzzle affords repetition (with variation); it can be viewed and used as another means to engage with the Yellow Kid and the comics-world he and his entourage appear in. Both the puzzle and the newspaper comic-tableau are separate, different aesthetic (and social) materials that allow for different yet also overlapping aesthetic experiences. Readers familiar with Outcault and Townsend's "Inauguration of the Football Season in McFadden's Row" were able to use the puzzle to review—and revisit—a scene from the Sunday supplement series. Just like the 1897 fictional autobiography mentioned above, in which the reader would find pictorial details of this particular *McFadden's Row* comic-tableau in black and white and in which a first-person narrative account of the event that annotates and expands the narrative in the columns of the newspaper comic-tableau affords repeated interaction with the Yellow Kid, the game enables a repeated, continued, extended engagement with the comics-worlds and the Yellow Kid, which goes beyond the (material and aesthetic) boundaries of the newspaper supplement.

For the reader who was (yet) unfamiliar with the *McFadden's Row* comics series or the fictional autobiography, for that matter, or who followed the *Hogan's Alley* series in the *World*, the *Yellow Kid Puzzle*—in particular the text on the cover of the puzzle box—serves as an invitation to acquaint themselves with the adventures of the Yellow Kid in the *Journal,* and to buy the newspaper regularly in order to become part of the reading community of the "Journal's Famous Series Drawn by R. F. Outcault" (see McLoughlin, *Yellow Kid Puzzle*). In both of these forms, the Yellow Kid functions as the protagonist who directs his audiences to the consumption (i.e., the purchase and interaction) of other commodities. To use the wording of Freeman, the Yellow Kid invites his audiences to engage with "additional iterations" of himself (see "Advertising" 2372).

Putting the puzzle out on the market at nearly the same time of the publication of the *McFadden's Row* comic-tableau did more than simply generate mutual advertising. It generated closer association of two medial forms of the Yellow Kid. McLoughlin's *Yellow Kid Puzzle* and the newspaper comic-tableau can operate in isolation, but the two forms also overlap and afford cross-linking. I consider this important because this gives insights into how consumers (of newspapers and of other commodities) were being habituated to expanded consumption practices—practices that shifted, to use the wording of Matthew Freeman, "across the borders of media like a decorated shop window that steers its onlookers toward products" ("Advertising" 2371; see also Meyer, "Medial Transgressions"). Freeman furthermore states that the turn of the century is a moment in the history of mass-consumer culture when the "practice of recurring fictional characters and serial narratives that unfold across different platforms to better promote the products of an intellectual property was ingrained into the economic fabric of modern advertising" (2372; see also Freeman, "Branding"). After the turn of the century, cross-promotional advertising and merchandising became a common practice (see Freeman, "Advertising" 2363, 2367–72; Freeman, "Branding" 637; on the expansionist impulse in merchandising in the nineteenth century, see Leach 18–19). The Yellow Kid comic figure can thus be regarded as a precursor of the rise of transmedia franchise in the twentieth century.[21]

Shortly after the McLoughlin company had published the *Yellow Kid Puzzle*, other toy companies started to produce their versions of Yellow Kid puzzles—maybe this was even before McLoughlin sold its *Yellow Kid Puzzle* (the only dates I have available are those listed in the copyright catalogues). For instance, in 1896, William A. DeGroot brought to the market a *Hogan's Alley Puzzle* (copyrighted in 1897; see my discussion above), which competed with the *Yellow Kid Puzzle*. Unfortunately, I was unable to take a look at DeGroot's puzzle, but I am certain that similar to McLoughlin's game, the *Hogan's Alley Puzzle* offers a reprint of an episode from Luks's *Hogan's Alley* series published in Pulitzer's newspaper. Each of these puzzles competes for audiences, offering pleasures for a different community of readers, while also helping to create loyal consumers of either *Hogan's Alley* or *McFadden's Row* (or both).

---

21. The scholarship on media practices is extensive. Discussions of the concepts of inter- and transmediality and media convergence are provided by Thon (who approaches transmedial franchises through the lens of narratology), Hills (who investigates transmedia tie-ins), and Jenkins et al. (who elaborate on the concept of memetic sprawl in contemporary culture), for example.

Before I explain the advertising functions of the Yellow Kid and how they fold back to and are articulated in the comic-tableaux themselves, I conclude this section by inquiring into the "unnecessary" paraphernalia such as Yellow Kid papier-mâché masks and costumes, free samples and Yellow Kid souvenirs, and the purposes these fulfilled. I have already spoken about the Yellow Kid message-bearing pin-back buttons that were given away for free by the tobacco companies upon the purchase of a cigarette pack. Yellow Kid giveaways—such as metal pins—were also sent out to wholesalers, retailers, and merchants via mail when they had ordered a particular catalogue (Lynn & Co.; Robert Ingersoll & BRO.). Such marketing strategies—to send out free advertising novelties to diverse agents—were quite common at that time. Another common practice to advertise a particular brand was to supply goods (such as champagne or cigars) to celebrities; these would in turn recommend the product they received to others (see "Giving Away Goods").

In addition to this, I found another channel of distribution of the Yellow Kid to consumers: store receipts. The wholesalers Brucker & Boghien, located in Philadelphia, who specialized in selling tobacco, cigars, and pipes (including the three-cent Yellow Kid cigar), stamped the store receipts with images of the Yellow Kid; with each purchase at Brucker & Boghien, the Yellow Kid would thus be passed on to the consumer—though many of these were disposed at one point, a number of sheets of the store's receipt books have survived and are part of the huge variety of today's Yellow Kid memorabilia that is available for purchase at online auctioneers.

Similar to the tobacco industry's giveaways mentioned above, the chewing gum companies had diverse marketing strategies to lure potential consumers to buy their products: The Adams company distributed Yellow Kid pocket-sized trading cards with the purchase of Adams's chewing gum.[22] Such packaging strategies served to encourage customers to buy the specific product regularly, and thus stimulated "serial repetitions in time"

---

22. Other chewing gum companies, as for instance the Grove Company in Salem, Ohio, registered their chewing gum as trademark with a Yellow Kid slogan on the tinfoil wrappings ("Registered Trademarks"). The Yellow Kid Lucky gum existed in the form of sticks and was consumable also via Yellow Kid chewing gum machines (woodcase and painted-tin gum vending machines). The Pulver gum company started to use such one-cent vending machines in 1899—the year Walton W. Wright's machine was patented. Inside the gum vending machine, a Yellow Kid would hand to you the chewing gum when you inserted the money (see Feinstein 6). The Pulver manufacturing company, based in Rochester (New York), advertised the Yellow Kid gum in the trade press—images of the Yellow Kid continued to appear as the logo on their company letters in the 1930s, and so did the chewing gum wrappers.

(Connor 53). Trade cards, as Richard Ohmann points out, were distributed to customers "after a purchase or included in the manufacturer's package as a kind of bonus," and were often "collected as curiosities in albums or posted as art on people's walls" (201; see also Strasser 9; on the history of trade cards, see Connor, esp. ch. 4). The Yellow Kid trade cards appeared in 1897. A complete set consisted of twenty-five cards, each card with a number; the numbers made it easier for consumers to figure out which of the cards was still missing to complete the series. These cards were meant to stimulate trade between the manufacturer/distributor of the cards and the customer and to turn them into dependable consumers; they also encouraged the exchange of cards between the various consumers.

In similar ways, theater show producers attempted to lure people to attend their programs. They, too, took advantage of and contributed to the Yellow Kid's popularity by disseminating promotional buttons, on the one hand, and Yellow Kid souvenir items, on the other. Months before the previously mentioned Gilmore and Leonard *Hogan's Alley* comedy-farce premiered in September 1896, the company distributed promotional Yellow Kid buttons; these were designed by anonymous artists and served to publicize the show in advance. At the same time, manufacturers started to produce Yellow Kid souvenir items that attendees of a theater show were able to acquire at the end of a performance. In one of the theater reviews for the *Philadelphia Inquirer,* the anonymous reporter discussed the popularity of the Yellow Kid figure and noted that after one of the *Hogan's Alley* shows, Yellow Kid "souvenirs [were] eagerly sought after" ("Programs of the Week"). Through the trade cards, souvenir buttons, and other items, the Yellow Kid was turned into a collectible commodity. They were designed to create desire for ownership.

Yellow Kid souvenirs in gift bags were furthermore distributed at social events such as the annual banquet of the Brotherhood of Commercial Travellers, which took place in New York in December 1896. It is reported that at this annual banquet "the souvenirs of the occasion" that the guests received included "a brass-gilt figure of the idiotic 'Yellow Kid,' designed as a paper-weight, bearing the inscription, 'Say, ain't I heavy?'" ("Brotherhood" 7). This was placed next to the guests' plates (see B. C. T.). I am unable to verify how many of the attendees actually took home these giveaways, but I do know that a few of these Yellow Kid ephemera still exist today—as online auctioneers make obvious.

Apart from these and other promotional products and Yellow Kid consumer wares, the comic figure "existed" in life-size and operated as a funfair attraction—tintypes of the turn of the century give evidence of that:

Amateur actors would wear Yellow Kid papier-mâché masks and long shirts and show up at different occasions (see "False Faces"; American Mask Manufacturing Company; "At the Masque Balls"). At the Commercial Travelers Fair in New York, the Yellow Kid was an exhibit, much to "the screaming delight of little men and women and the children of larger growth, who enjoyed having a laugh" (Allen S. Williams 10–11). Furthermore, Hearst installed a booth in which a large-size Yellow Kid advertisement and Yellow Kid posteramas lured readers and passersby to stop and take a photographic picture in front of the Yellow Kid image ("Brotherhood" 7; see figure 1.7). In addition to that, the *Journal* organized an auction during which Yellow Kid posters were sold, and the actress Yvette Guilbert as well as the vocalist and dancer (and later silent film actress) Louise Beaudet helped promote the newspaper's posters (see Rohrhand; see also Hayden Jones).

It is reported, too, that at various dress balls and theme parties the attendees wore Yellow Kid costumes (see "A 'Yellow Kid' Party"). Moreover, mascot-performers dressed up as Yellow Kids in street parades, at Mardi Gras, and for Halloween (see "The Missouri Travelers"). Oftentimes, the actors of the touring Yellow Kid theater shows dressed in costumes and paraded the streets in the cities in which a show was to be staged. When William H. Macart's *Hogan's Alley* came to small-town Lockwood to perform at the Hodge Opera House, many were attending the arrival of the troupe: "The jolly actors and stylishly dressed actresses . . . came to town on the Central's eastern train this afternoon at 3 o'clock" ("Amusements," *Lockport Daily Journal*). The newspaper report continues: "A great crowd of youngsters were at the station this afternoon when the Hogan's Alley Company arrived. When Mickey Dugan alighted from the train, the children clapped their hand and swung their caps. The popular actor gracefully tipped his hat [and] smiled pleasantly at the crowd" (1). Likewise, in one of the short "Notes" in *Printers' Ink*, it is stated that the "famous 'Yellow Kid' is being used by Geo W. Monroe to advertise his play of Hogan's Alley. A dozen or more men in long yellow mackintoshes and masks with abnormal ears have been patrolling New York streets" ("Notes").

This idea of amateurs in Yellow Kid costumes was taken to the retail business, too. People wearing long yellow dresses and facial masks paraded the sidewalks and streets to announce a specific product or novelty (see "The Shoe Men's Outing"). "An enterprising firm recently put upon the street two live 'Yellow Kids,'" wrote the *Coal Trade Journal* in December 1896, and they were "dressed in the highest of Hogan's Alley fashion, with yellow fez and gloves" ("With the Retailers," *Coal Trade Journal*; see also

THE CORPS OF GUIDES, WHOSE SERVICES WERE DONATED TO THE FAIR.

FIGURE 1.7. "The Corps of Guides, Whose Services Were Donated to the Fair," *Home Magazine*, vol. 8, no. 1, Jan. 1897, p. 6.

"With the Retailers," *Boot and Shoe Recorder*). The words printed on the yellow dresses conveyed "the fact that the firm were the greatest coal dealers in the city" ("With the Retailers," *Coal Trade Journal*).

Observers of the retail business regularly corresponded with the trade press; trade journals such as *Printers' Ink*, the *Inland Printer*, or the *American Stationer*, or, in hardware, *Iron Age* or the *Hardware Reporter*, and diverse journals in medical fields, in clothing, and more provided up-to-date strategies of advertising and marketing. Correspondents wrote about new developments and commented on spectacular window displays and such appearances as those of the parading Yellow Kids: A *Printers' Ink* contributor reported that in Chicago, one could spot "a dwarf dressed in imitation of the Yellow Kid [who] ambles along the streets in the interest of an advertiser" (Severn). In another brief commentary printed in the *Boot and*

Shoe Recorder, it is mentioned that "[one] of the sensations of the day at the ground was the arrival of Val Duttenhofer & Sons' force behind a band dressed as yellow kids with a real yellow kid in the centre of the parade" ("The Shoe Men's Outing" 80–81). The Yellow Kid was used as a site for spectacle. Parades of people wearing the iconic features of the Yellow Kid on the streets were a means of publicity and can be considered another driving force of the comic figure's career.

Apart from such parading Yellow Kid salesmen, retailers hung up posters in their store windows as well as inside, and they placed advertisements on the storefront's sidewalk in order to lure prospective buyers into their stores. One of the correspondents of the *American Stationer* reported in January 1897 that the "Kistler Company has a large [Yellow Kid poster] in its window. . . . The 'yellow kid' seems to be the popular advertising medium at the present time," the author concluded ("Denver"; the Yellow Kid continued to be used in shop windows in the early twentieth century: see Mason 63). In Providence, a shop window of a hatter was spotted who "has in his window several jack-o'-lanterns made of pumpkins, and at night they are lighted with electric lamps, one of them being dressed to imitate the famous Yellow Kid, with the inscription: 'I never was born, but, like Topsy, I just growed'" (FAX). *Printers' Ink*, from which this last comment is taken, regularly printed snippets sent in from other cities and rural areas telling about noteworthy events. L. S. Roby, reader and contributor to *Printers' Ink*, sent in a summary of things discovered in Topeka, Kansas, in September 1897, which were then published a month later in the trade journal. One of the things Roby saw was a show window by a druggist who filled his window with "a large 'yellow kid' with a sign: 'I am a back number, but the things inside are all up to date'" (Roby). Yellow Kid items were on display, and the Yellow Kid promoted goods. A few shop owners would even rename their stores into "The Yellow Kid Store" (Paul) and advertise the stock through the vernacular speech of the comic figure in the hope of attracting the passersby: "We ain't mutch on potry, but we has a way ov knockin 'em when it comes to sellin' de best goods for the least money, and dat's no lie, See?" (Paul). Other strategies of enticement to attract potential consumers into a store and to inspect the goods sold there were advertising formats such as Yellow Kid cardboard cutouts and cards that were used for window dressing, and sometimes window decorators, such as T. R. Marshall (South Carolina's Kinard's window decorator), designed a complete scenery "representing 'Hogan's Alley of newspaper fame. . . . The flats were all there and 'De Yellow Kid,' too. He wore his usual angelic smile . . . . The goat and all the famous ragamuffins were there. People stopped to look and laugh and look again" ("Seen in Windows" 8). The trade press counseled retailers how to develop spectacular window displays and thereby increase their sales. The trade and advertising journal *Printers' Ink*, though annoyed by the "idiotic smile" of the "very prevalent" comic figure, also carried articles about the benefit of placing a Yellow Kid in the window (Herzberg 36; see also Advertising; "Advertising Novelties"). Trade publications encouraged advertisers and retailers to utilize the comic figure, and merchants and shop owners were given instructions on how to promote their wares with the help of self-made Yellow Kid cutouts. The editor of the *American Druggist and Pharmaceutical Record*, Ulysses G. Manning, noted:

> Anyone can draw a recognizable kid that will answer for a window poster. After drawing the outline, color the dress a brilliant yellow and then rack your brain for some Hogan Alley philosophy. A kid can be used for advertising soda, cigars or sundries. . . . Change your signs often and if people do not show symptoms of the hoped for delirium within a few days, take in your kid and burn him. (Manning, "The Yellow Kid")

Time and again, Manning reflected on "the yellow boy and his Hogan Alley Dialect" (Editorial comment), and with a slightly ironic undertone, he warned the readers of his journal that the Yellow Kid "should not be employed by the bilious brand of druggist, but may give the exuberant class a chance to work off some spare humor" ("The Yellow Kid"). Though Manning was unable to explain the "popular craze" that evolved around this comic figure of "R. F. Outcalt [sic]," the editor saw the great advantages of using the kid as an advertising tool for shop window displays, which at times "show a dreary monotony of arrangement" (Editorial comment; see also "A Glimpse" and "Baltimore" 1896). In short, the "flappy ears" of the Yellow Kid "have illumined store windows all over the United States" ("The 'Yellow Kid'" 32). The Yellow Kid occupied the visual window space of the stores.

Merchants reacted and sent in letters that summarized the success of using Yellow Kid posters, cards, cardboard cutouts, and more in windows and inside their stores. In one of the issues of *American Druggist and Pharmaceutical Record*, which was distributed in New York and Chicago, a letter from a reader of this journal (signed with H. W. Reusswig) attests to this usage of the Sunday supplement character as a promotional device. In this letter, Reusswig explains that when he changed his window display and installed a Yellow Kid figure to advertise and promote the chamois skins, this display "has attracted so much attention" and has helped in "decreasing my stock" (Reusswig; see also "Seen in Windows" and "New England Notes"). Similarly, in an article on Christmas season window displays, a *New Haven Register* contributor noted: "Some of the borough merchants are making special efforts this year in the way of holiday displays. One of the most unique is a representation of the yellow kid of Hogan's Alley fame, which is being exhibited to lure the holiday purchaser into leaving his money in town" ("Wallingford"). Finally, in the weekly Boston-based journal *Boot and Shoe Recorder,* one finds short notes about retailers at Ellicott square in Buffalo (New York), who profited from the neighboring "Edison Kinetoscope people"; "they have an imitation 'Yellow Kid' in their window all hours of the day. . . . The 'Kid' succeeds in attracting a great many," and the retailers "come[] in for a share of patronage at [their] expense" ("With the Retailers," *Boot and Shoe Recorder*; see also "Baltimore" 1897). To what extent these and other Yellow Kid formats in the merchants' store windows actually helped sell products and motivated consumers to buy specific items cannot be proven by empirical data. Such letters, notes, and brief editorial comments as quoted above allow only limited views on marketing and sales techniques.

To measure the commercial effectiveness is difficult (see Sassatelli 131). Though contemporaries of Outcault and Luks suggested that if you placed a Yellow Kid in your window, "much amusement and good advertising will result" ("Baltimore" 1896), it is debatable whether Yellow Kid copies in shop windows actually motivated men and women to buy the items that were promoted. I am not entirely convinced that the ads and displays really helped persuade the customer and helped sell the products. In her study *Satisfaction Guaranteed,* Susan Strasser emphasizes that there were a number of turn-of-the-century advertisings that served as "clever promotion that won public attention without increasing sales" (118; see also James D. Norris). A related point is made by Pamela Laird, who says that "determining whether a product or service sold or not because of its advertisements has never been easy"; she warns us not to "[correlate] promotional practices with sales figures" and to easily and quickly "[assume] causal links" (275). With respect to the Yellow Kid, I think it is very likely that he attracted window-gazers but at the same time distracted many prospective consumers—he may have been an eye-catcher who entertained but not necessarily a purchase-stimulating promoter. The Yellow Kid window items, posters, cards, and cutouts may have created more spectators than actual buyers. They may have, in other words, merely pointed to the Yellow Kid himself and functioned as forms of self-promotion rather than a method of selling a specific product.

As a continuation of these reflections, the next section sets out to explore how advertising agents contributed to the proliferations of the Yellow Kid, on the one hand, and to investigate the functions the Yellow Kid performed as an advertising figure, on the other. Advertising was a propelling condition of the Yellow Kid's career, which is, as I will demonstrate in the concluding pages of this chapter, reflected also in the Sunday comic-tableaux of the rival series.

THE YELLOW KID AS ADVERTISING FIGURE

The Yellow Kid had a part in the contested field of advertising. For one thing, the Yellow Kid circulated in advertisements that promoted the Sunday editions of the two competing New York newspapers. Hearst's *Journal* used outdoor advertising to lure new audiences/consumers to buy the newspaper, and he, as well as Pulitzer, distributed small art posters (approximately fourteen by nineteen inches) to merchants in New York and store owners in other cities, and to sellers at kiosks and newsstands (see Outcault and Gunn). Sample posters and cards and a host of other items were sent out to the merchants via the mail (see Laird 84; see also Ewen and Ewen, esp. 127–28). For another thing, the Yellow Kid served as a commercial "agent" outside of the newspapers. The list of venues in which the Yellow Kid appeared is long—too long, in fact, to be covered here in its entirety—but a few examples shall be discussed in the following.

Advertising artists, merchants, and manufacturers as well as a number of different publishing and trading companies—such as, for instance, Maguire & Baucus Ltd. (named after the Kinetoscope marketing and film selling and shipping agents Frank Z. Maguire and Joseph D. Baucus[23])—projected their commercial messages onto the surface space of the Yellow Kid's dress and put his specific features, that is, his grin, his long dress, and his vernacular language (and often his gesturing hand), in the service of hardware, candy, clothing, and more (see J. B. Lewis Co.). They appreciated the marketing value of the Yellow Kid and made use of the comic figure in their ads in different ways. Advertisements that adopted the Yellow Kid filled

---

23. On the cover page of Maguire and Baucus's 1897 catalogue listing Lumière and Edison films, as well as international films, the Yellow Kid welcomes the customers—meaning anyone owning a projecting machine, including, among others, theater house owners and "Lecturers and Church exhibitors" (Maguire & Baucaus Ltd. n. pag.). Via his shirt, the Yellow Kid tells them that he can help sell "GOODS WHILE YER ASLEEP" (Maguire & Baucus Ltd. n. pag.). My thanks to Katrin Horn.

the pages of the press from East to West Coast from 1896 to at least the 1920s (see Filbert Grinding Co.). Anonymous artists created—often poorly sketched—copies of the Yellow Kid in the ads (Castelberg's National Jewelry Co.; Johnson Bros.; Raphael's Inc.; Winchester, "Hully Gee" 31). His face and hand welcomed the readers, and the words on his dress were meant to support the respective product or the wholesaler who sold specific items—jewelry, clothing, hardware, and so on. In most cases, there was no relation between the Yellow Kid and the items or services the comic figure promoted. As Laird has observed, many retailers "could rarely afford to have a special image designed and printed for themselves" (149). For merchants, retailers, and small manufacturing companies, to copy the popular comic figure was easy, and a quick and cheap solution. The Regent Manufacturing Co. worked with advertising repetitions: For their multiple "Whistle" knife ads, they reused Yellow Kid sketches (see Regent Manufacturing Co.; very similar ads by the Regent Manufacturing Company appear in various issues of *The Iron Age* between January 21, 1897, and February 18, 1897). Advertisements that incorporated imitations of the Yellow Kid, such as those quoted above, certainly functioned to draw the readers' attention to the page. On a page filled with stock advertisements or text columns, an ad with a copy of the Yellow Kid and his vernacular language certainly stood out.

The recognizability of the Yellow Kid served the advertisers' purposes—he was, to use the wording from Laird, a "memory hook . . . for advertising appeal" (185). The W. W. Morgan Clothing Co. used the comic figure because the Yellow Kid is, as their text makes explicit, "one of the most important personages in society everywhere he goes"; next to the text passage a copy of the Yellow Kid is dressed "in stile"—with a hat on, an overcoat, and a walking cane (3; see also N. R. Jetic & Co.). Here and on other occasions, the Yellow Kid comic figure is functionalized as a kind of iconic "celebrity" eye-catcher (albeit fictional) in the ads to address consumers—this is a strategy that is widely applied nowadays in advertising (with real-life actors and actresses, in particular) to create an immediate and intimate relation between the recognizable "person" in the ad and the reader of the ad. Whether this strategy of using an image of the Yellow Kid was an effective means to maximize the flow of goods is, however, contestable; there are no statistics available of when, where, and how often the goods that were promoted through the Yellow Kid were actually bought and by whom, and it is very likely that, as indicated earlier, the ads entertained but distracted from consumption. The Yellow Kid operated as a kind of interface figure reaching out and drawing attention to the various consumer goods and to himself as a product and harbinger of a mass-consumer culture.

One of the first colored advertisements printed in the *World*'s Sunday Comic Weekly that made use of the Yellow Kid was Marks Arnheim's tailoring advertisement titled "The Brilliant Results of Truth and Perseverance" (see figure 1.8). In the bottom left corner of the Arnheim ad, a Yellow Kid points to the upper right-hand side of the advertisement to a group of men who are dressed in short and long overcoats, and who wear different kinds of hats. The text that separates the Yellow Kid from the coat-wearing men holds information on the tailoring business—"tailor-made goods for the least money"—and the company's achievements of the past years, as well as architectural details about the Arnheim building. Whereas the text puts stronger emphasis on the history and success of the "colossal" Arnheim Tailoring Company and highlights it as a "wonder of the age," the Yellow Kid points to the variety of garments and announces: "DATS DE WAY ARNHEIM DREʐʐEʐ EM ʐEEį" (Marks Arnheim Tailoring Est.). The Yellow Kid is an additional message-hawking device here to grasp the reader's attention. The ad is built on the recognition value of the Yellow Kid and familiarity perceptions.

Whereas the Arnheim Yellow Kid ad was printed on the final page of the Sunday comic supplement and thus isolated from the contents of this extra section, a week later, Pulitzer's Comic Weekly placed a Yellow Kid advertisement in close connection to the comics and short humorous stories in the inside pages of the supplement (see figure 1.9). Right below an episode of the *Gazoozaland* series by John Lowitz (mentioned earlier in this chapter), one can find a Yellow Kid who advocates the new "Yankee" dollar watch by the Ingersoll Company (founded by Robert Hawley Ingersoll and his brother Charles Henry in 1880). The text in the ad emphasizes not only the "marvel in mechanics" but also the "marvel of cheapness and utility" (EDGE and Robert H. Ingersoll & Bro.). The Yellow Kid, the ad suggests, was among the first to recognize the "reliable time-keeper": "THE KID KNOWS A GOOD THING WHEN HE SEES IT." At the lower part of this ad, a Yellow Kid (wearing a miniature top hat) smiles at the potential consumer and declares in typical dialect speech: "DATʐ ME NEW WATCH—AiNT ʐHE A BOID FUR ONE DOLLAR WELL SAY." Apart from the fact that the ad functions as a reminder that Christmas is coming up soon and that the one-dollar Ingersoll watch would make a nice gift, the ad is turned into an amusing feature that is integral to the Comic Weekly leisure entertainment. The pleasures of reading the comics are transferred to the advertisement, and vice versa—entertainment content and advertising content intertwine (see Freeman, "Advertising" 2368; see also Gordon, *Comic Strips* 105).

FIGURE 1.8. Marks Arnheim Tailoring Est., "The Brilliant Results of Truth and Perseverance," *The World*, 13 Dec. 1896, Comic Weekly, p. 8 (detail). San Francisco Academy of Comic Art Collection, The Ohio State University, Billy Ireland Cartoon Library & Museum.

Advertising and the serialized Yellow Kid comics had a close relationship from the start. This is conveyed not only through the explicit juxtaposition of a Yellow Kid advertisement and a Yellow Kid comic tableau in the same Sunday supplement. The link manifests itself also in the ways in which the comics pages (humorously) promote all kinds of (fictive) products. As Jens Balzer has put it, advertising is ubiquitous; "even the clouds over the city project themselves as a space for advertisements" ("Hully Gee" 24–25). In Outcault's "The Residents of Hogan's Alley Visit Coney Island," a hot-air balloon in the upper half of the page holds a number of advertisements: "DRINK Nothing but BEER FOR THE THIRST" is printed on the balloon's top, followed a bit farther down by the slogan, "USE ONLY SOAP FOR WASHING—WITH A LITTLE WATER ON THE SIDE—(OUTSIDE)."[24] A month later, the whole background of another *Hogan's Alley* episode is filled with advertising messages; the bills posted on a fence warn the passerby to "AVOID AXIDENCE," but as long as you are "INSURE IN DE AXIDENT INSURACNE CO.... YEZ KIN NEVER GIT HURTED" (Outcault, "The Bicycle Meet"). They furthermore advise everybody to "READ DE CRANK" because the magazine "KONTAINS [. . .THE] MOST INTERESTING WHEEL ADVERTISMENTS," promote "MARRIAGE MADE EASY CHEW PEPSIN SOAP," and tell

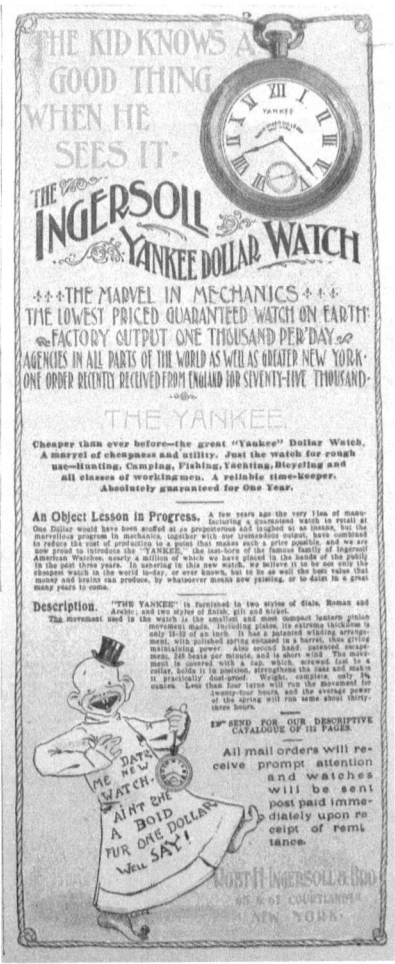

FIGURE 1.9. EDGE, and Robert H. Ingersoll & Bro., "The Ingersoll Yankee Dollar Watch," *The World*, 20 Dec. 1896, Comic Weekly, p. 4 (detail). San Francisco Academy of Comic Art Collection, The Ohio State University, Billy Ireland Cartoon Library & Museum.

everybody to "BUY [THE] NEW BICYCLE BELL-E" (Outcault, "The Bicycle Meet"). Of course, Outcault (and Luks as well) jokingly responded to the myriad promotional campaigns in the form of newspaper ads and bill-

---

24. The Yellow Kid was also a piece of soap himself: The New York–based David S. Brown & Co. sold figural Yellow Kid soaps, for example.

board signs on the streets, which aimed at selling all kinds of products to the potential consumer. At the same time, however, these parodistic advertisements in the comic-tableaux that are printed on a hot-air balloon, fences, walls, and elsewhere (in brief: advertising spaces) bespeak the cross-infiltrations of commerce and art.

"The Bicycle Meet" episode just mentioned became part of an advertising campaign by the headlight company manufacturing the "20th Century" bicycle headlight. A week after Outcault's installment had appeared in Pulitzer's *World*, the *New York Daily Tribune* dedicated a full page to the bicycle parade that took place in New York; in one of the advertisements framing the report, it is mentioned that "The Bicyclists of Hogan's Alley—As Illustrated by the New York Sunday World—last week took the advantage of the Great Leader certain big stores of New York made when they sold at below cost The 20th Century Bicycle Head-Light" ("Bicycles"). A few months later, the Yellow Kid would function as a promoter of bicycle lamps in colored advertisements printed in Hearst's *Journal* (Betts Patent Headlight Company; see also "Sporting Goods"). In "The Bicycle Meet" installment, Outcault furthermore makes use of a kite to promote another product: "NOW IS THE TIME TO TAKE A TONIC OR ANYTHING ELSE RENOVATE YOUR SYSTEM WITH DR. OILTANK'S BENZINE FRITTERS." Again, while this is meant ironically to elicit laughter, these and other ads make clear that the Yellow Kid newspaper comics pages are cultural artifacts that, while they certainly entertained and offered to their readers weekly leisure activities, testify to a growing consumer society (see also Luks, "The Hogan's Alley Inauguration" and "A Ghost Séance").

Readers of the Yellow Kid Sunday comic-tableaux were furthermore encouraged to pay attention to the advertisements in the newspaper, not only because of respective advertising contents but also because of the entertaining delight enabled through them. In one of the installments in *Around the World with the Yellow Kid*, printed in 1897, one of the signs advised readers: "READ OUR ADS THEY ARE THE FUNNiEST THiNG IN THE WHOLE PAPER" (AW E2). The Yellow Kid comic-tableaux do not just comment on the role and impact of advertising in society; the Yellow Kid was entangled in these developments. The episodes of *Hogan's Alley* and *McFadden's Row*, as well as the advertisements promoting the next Sunday edition of the *World* or the *Journal*, also—and repeatedly—draw attention to the comic figure's manifold proliferations outside of the comics series. These instances are part of a self-observational narrative, which is another aesthetic dimension or another form of the serial excrescences of the Yellow Kid.

PRACTICES OF SELF-DESCRIPTION

On June 20, 1896, an unsigned copy of the Yellow Kid appeared in the center of a half-page advertisement announcing the next Sunday edition of the *World*. In the background of this advertisement, we see the outline of a big city, with tall buildings and smoking chimneys. In the foreground the jug-eared Yellow Kid in his long shirt grins directly at the reader; next to him sits a chained and muzzled dog. The two are placed in front of a billboard sign. With his hand, the Yellow Kid points toward this sign, which announces: "THERE'S A FINE PICTURE OF **ME** IN THE EIGHT PAGE COMIC COL SUPP. OF TOMORROWS GREAT SUNDAY WORLD" ("To-Morrow's Great Sunday World"). In this advertisement for the next Sunday *World*, it is not the surface of the dress through which the Yellow Kid speaks to his audiences (as he usually does); in this advertisement, it is the billboard that speaks for and to him and to the readers of the newspaper. Intentionally or unintentionally, humor is elicited by means of deictic incongruence of the pronoun *me* here: Because the pronoun is printed on the billboard, it suggests that the announcement refers to the billboard sign itself and that there is going to be a "fine picture" of the billboard sign in the next comic supplement of the *World*. Another reading is that the comment of the Yellow Kid is extracted from his dress to the surface of the billboard sign. In that sense, the Yellow Kid serves here not only to praise the eight-page colored comic supplement but also to promote himself as part of this supplement, and by so doing marks his own medial status.

This self-referential technique is repeated in other advertisements (see EDGE, "Thanksgiving" and "The Great Sunday"). Three months before the "To-Morrow's Great Sunday World" advertisement appeared, the comic figure showed up in a half-page advertisement announcing the next edition of the Sunday *World* (Saalburg, "The Great Sunday"; see also Saalburg, "Inimitable" and "The Colossus"). In that ad, the comic figure is only a tiny detail, easily overlooked; a few months later, the Yellow Kid would become the central element in the advertisements for Pulitzer's newspaper. As I have argued earlier in this chapter, in March 1896 the Yellow Kid began to exit the *Hogan's Alley* series and started to gain momentum. This development from an unidentifiable feature to an iconic figure is manifest also in the advertisements for the *World*.

In many episodes in both the *Hogan's Alley* and *McFadden's Row* series, the Yellow Kid himself or the surrounding background elements furthermore serve to articulate the comic figure's serial proliferations. Both Richard Outcault and George Luks were aware of these developments and inserted parodistic allusions or explicit references to the Yellow Kid's embodiments in other medial formats. George Luks's "Bargain Day" episode is an interesting example in this context (Luks, "Bargain Day"; see Meyer, "Medial Transgressions" and Gambone 132–33). In the foreground of this episode, the recurring Hogan Alleyites do the (mischievous) things they always do. In the background, one can see a shop whose owner has put up numerous Yellow Kid posters as well as small pictures of the comic figure in his window; a crowd of window-shoppers has gathered to look at the bargains offered in the store. Among other things, what these people see in the window is a picture of an odd-toed artist (a caricature of Outcault, depicted wearing a yellow dress with an oversized red bow tie) who draws a poster with the Yellow Kid waving to his onlookers and saying the words "THE IDEA'S RHINE-OSEROS"; this poster cost "$00,16" and is attributed with "COPYRIGHTED (NIT)" (Luks, "Bargain Day"). Quite obviously, these elements parody Outcault's request for copyright of the Yellow Kid and poke fun at Outcault as the artist giving shape to a specific (same-old) idea. Furthermore, the window-shoppers can look at diverse advertisements promoting all kinds of Yellow Kid consumer wares, such as an "8 CENTS" Yellow Kid doll. Another bargain is "A COLLAR BUTTON" that you get "WITH EVERY YELLOW KID" (Luks, "Bargain Day"). Luks parodies the marketing strategies of manufacturers such as the tobacco companies that distributed free Yellow Kid giveaways to lure consumers to buy further products such as the Yellow Kid cigar and cigarette (see my discussions above). Here and on other occasions, Luks reflects on the comic figure as part of a burgeoning mass-consumer culture. Outcault likewise negotiated the comic figure's status as a commercial commodity. In one episode of the *McFadden's Row* series, it is announced that "EVERY TiNG DESE DAYS iS YALLER KID BUY DE YELLOW KID GLOVE YELLOW KID CIGAR YELLOW FELLER WHEEL &c &c &c &c &c &c SAY!" (*McFadden's* E2).[25] The Yellow Kid has been turned into numerous, ubiquitously available, commercial items. This is echoed in another box on the same page,

---

25. The "yellow kid" gloves are not named after the Yellow Kid. The gloves were a popular fashion item in the nineteenth century, and the delineation "yellow kid" refers to the specific shade of the color yellow. In one of the Yellow Kid diary leaflets, the first-person narrator, who is the Yellow Kid, jokes about the fact that he and the fashion item have similar names (AW Leaflet 6).

which reads: "WE'RE DE HOTTEST TING WOT EVER HAPPENED—SEE! WE HAS KNOCKED DE COUNTRY CRAZY" (*McFadden's* E2). These and other text segments placed on banners, on walls, on posters, or in boxes in the Yellow Kid comic-tableaux epitomize the proliferations of the Yellow Kid outside his medium of origin (see Meyer, "Medial Transgressions").

Before he started working for Hearst, Outcault had already pointed to these processes, and had made the variants of the comic figure—as, for instance, the Yellow Kid campaign buttons—a recurrent visual topic in his comic-tableaux; in "A Wild Political Fight," one of the surrounding characters wears a Yellow Kid campaign button. Moreover, the inhabitants of Hogan's Alley perform a variety of (fictive) Hogan's Alley songs, and background billpostings announce that another upcoming music piece will be available soon, which celebrates the Yellow Kid (see Outcault, "Hogan's Alley Children," "Hogan's Alley Folk Sailing," and "The Bicycle Meet"). In several of Outcault's comic-tableaux, the music folio *The Belle of Hogan's Alley* by Blake and Bernard, which was promoted with the help of the Yellow Kid, is (re)inscribed into the diegesis of the *Hogan's Alley* comics series (see Keightley, "Hogan's" 42–43). In one of the episodes, the song is performed by the "Hogan's Alley Quartette" (Outcault, "Li Hung Chang"). I am putting the *re-* in parentheses because I am not certain which was there first—the illustration of the song in Outcault's comic or the *Belle* sheet of Blake and Bernard. The cover page of their piece reads that the composers "respectfully dedicated" the music sheet to "Mr. R F. Outcault." In the inside pages, however, it is mentioned that this song was first performed on stage by Gilmore and Leonard and is now a seven-page folio for sale at "all" music stores in New York (Blake and Bernard 6; see also "Descriptive Songs"). To speak with Keir Keightley, what we see here is an "intermedial nexus of newspaper, songsheet, and vaudeville stage" ("Hogan's" 30), and this nexus was made into a self-reflexive, recurrent topic in the Yellow Kid comics series.

That the Yellow Kid operated as an advertising figure outside of the newspaper pages is likewise alluded to in the Sunday supplement comics as well as in other cartoons (see "The Art of Advertising"). The Christmas episode in the *McFadden's Row* series is an interesting case in point: In the comic-tableau the Yellow Kid holds up a suit, which he received as a Christmas present. The gift tag attached to the suit reads: "FROM A SNIDE CLOTHIER WHO IS USING YER FACE FER AN ADVERTIZMENT" (*McFadden's* E9). I do not know how many readers were actually familiar with the ads by the Rosenfeld garment manufacturing company, which I have quoted earlier in this chapter. The joke is, however, only fully understandable to readers who knew about the Yellow Kid pajama advertisements that were printed in the trade press. These are instances of reciprocation that infuse the Yellow Kid's career.

The varieties of the Yellow Kid as outlined throughout this chapter—adaptations for theatrical and musical compositions, appropriations in advertising, reconfigurations in the form of merchandise wares, and more—refold to the Sunday comic-tableaux of both *Hogan's Alley* and *McFadden's Row*; that the rival series also observed each other is a topic I engage with in chapter 3. This said, I want to turn the attention to the Yellow Kid comics pages in both Pulitzer's *World* and Hearst's *Journal*. In the next three chapters, I will inquire into the serial dynamics of and between the episodes in the competing Yellow Kid series in order to show that the prolific logic of the Yellow Kid already manifests itself in the Sunday newspaper comics.

CHAPTER 2

SERIAL AESTHETICS AND CONSUMPTION PRACTICES OF THE YELLOW KID COMIC-TABLEAUX

WHILE THE PAST CHAPTER looked at the forces behind the Yellow Kid's plurimedial expansion, this chapter sets out to investigate the seriality of the newspaper comics series in which the Yellow Kid appeared. The basic premise of this chapter is that the mechanisms of repetition, branching out, and multiplication not only define the Yellow Kid comic figure but are fundamental processes that are at work also in the comics themselves. To use the wording of Ruth Mayer, the "semantics of spread" (*Serial* 5) manifest themselves on the plot level in the episodes of both *Hogan's Alley* and *McFadden's Row* as well as in *Around the World,* and are displayed also through aesthetic operations of duplication and spinning out.

In this chapter, I approach the seriality of the comics pages as follows: In the first two sections, I examine the Yellow Kid comic-tableaux in the context of other products and practices of modernity, such as, for instance, theater, especially vaudeville, documentary photography, or realist and naturalist fiction; this includes a discussion of how the vernacular language functions in the Yellow Kid comic-tableaux. This chapter argues that among the various literary, painterly, theatrical, photographic, and journalist "observers," who put center stage, in very different ways, the conditions of modern urbanity in late nineteenth-century American society, the Yellow Kid newspaper comics of the 1890s had a particularly important role as commercial, vernacular, mass-produced, mass-distributed, and mass-consumed reading material and serial forms of pleasure (see Meyer, "Serial Entertainment"). In the second half of this chapter, I will carve out how different modes of consumption are generated through the Yellow Kid newspaper comics series. I will explore the consumption practices that are triggered through the series' protagonist, on the one hand, and through the *serial props* of the competing series, on the other. As well, I will analyze the under-researched columns in the *McFadden's Row* series in order to demonstrate how different reader engagements are activated through oscillating narrating voices and shifts in focalizations. My contention is that the Yellow Kid comics can be enjoyed as single, one-time installments or as episodes in a continuous yet nonlinear series, and that pleasure can emerge by means of the reading options inscribed *within one episode* as well as intraserially *within one series* and also interserially, that is, *between* the episodes of the competing series.

The overall goal of this chapter is to get a better understanding of the specific historical contexts in which the Yellow Kid newspaper comics emerged, the cultural work the comics performed, and the aesthetic principles that enabled this work.

THE YELLOW KID COMICS AND OTHER PRODUCTS AND PRACTICES OF THE 1890s

The world of publishing in the 1890s was "fiercely competitive" (Campbell 8; see also Juergens 48). In the fight over consumers, the newspapers and magazines competed not only against each other but also with other media options of that time and with products and practices from other cultural fields. So, the newspapers had to offer something new if they wanted to make a profit and to distinguish themselves from other artifacts. An important development in this regard—maybe even *the* most important and innovative strategy—was when city papers such as Joseph Pulitzer's *World* added colored extras to their Sunday editions. Each week, his and other newspapers catered to the "widely divergent interest" of their readers ("The Sunday World"; see also French 52). In 1905, Arthur Benington, former member of the *World*'s staff, reflected on the weekend editions of the newspapers and said that the Sunday editor has to give a variety of matter to please all sorts of tastes, for the Sunday paper is read in the farmhouses up the state, and in the drawing rooms on Fifth avenue; in the East Side tenements and the millionaires' clubs; in the suburbs of Flatbush and New Rochelle, and in the dormitories of colleges and universities; by women and children in all walks of life, as well as by the men who form the great mass of readers of the daily papers. (38)

By means of the Sunday supplements, the newspapers reached a broad, diversified, mass readership. Though it was common "to speak lightly" of the Sunday supplements, as John Philip Young (journalist, economist, and former managing editor of the *San Francisco Chronicle*) pointed out, "because [they were] not wholly made up of contributions which a fastidious literary taste could approve" (154), the conservative press, readers, and critics noticed the success of the weekend editions of such papers as Pulitzer's *World*. In particular the comics supplements were popular and eagerly sought after.

Most newspaper pages, including the Sunday supplements and their comics, were at some point tossed away or used for other purposes, as for instance, to wrap up food (see Irvin Lewis Allen 108). They were disposable artifacts, and this included the Yellow Kid comics, too. Yet, as I will show in the following, for the moment of consumption, these offered to the readers "something" and in new ways that made them particularly special and attractive and that distinguished them from other forms of Sunday leisure activity, other forms of reading material, and other cultural products and practices.

In their introduction to *Metropolitan Lives*, the authors Rebecca Zurier and Robert Snyder write that the Ashcan artists—George Bellows, William Glackens, Robert Henri, George Luks, Everett Shinn, and John Sloan (see Mecklenburg; Gambone)—three of whom produced drawings for Pulitzer's *World* (Glackens, Luks, and Shinn) and William Randolph Hearst's *Journal* (Glackens), "forged a contemporary form of realism that conveyed partial but real truths about New York City, its mosaic of communities, and the complexities of life and art in a diverse city where most people were strangers to one another" (13). Furthermore, their respective artworks

> mapped out new territory for American art by identifying moments of interaction between the people of the city and its massive culture of commerce. . . . The dynamics of urban change were essential to the force and complexity of their art, which was largely a response to the challenge of representing a tumultuous era in the city's history. (Zurier and Snyder 13)

Just as the Ashcan artists offered black-and-white as well as colored interpretations of the "dynamics of urban change" (Snyder and Zurier 85) in an unprecedented way, so did the newspaper comics artist create and "give visible form to the dynamic social forces that were shaping and reshaping New York City" (85). In this regard, Albert Boime has declared: "Not fortuitously, the crystallization of the comics concides [sic] with the formation of America's first modern movement in painting, the Ash Can School. Its pioneers, associates and heirs . . . contributed directly to the development of the comic strip" (22). As he furthermore emphasizes: "The relationship of graphic journalism to both the development of the comic strip and the Ash Can School is essentially based on their abiding concern with the actual quality of American life" (22). Of course, there are fundamental differences between the paintings drawn by the "Eight" and the comics penned by the newspaper artists. Whereas both the newspaper and the fine art artists belong to the professional middle class—they are middle-class spectators as well as interpreters and creators of the vibrant urban modernity (see Brand 6)—and while the serialized Yellow Kid comic-tableaux of *Hogan's Alley* and *McFadden's Row* as well as the Ashcan paintings revolve around the topic of city streets and city life and represent "street vernacular of both image and word" (Irvin Lewis Allen 16), their form and modes of representing city life (as well as the products' materiality) and the social usage of the comic-drawings in the mass newspapers and the publicly exhibited paintings differ.

The social reality of the densely populated tenement districts in Lower Manhattan, and the street life—especially of the children—in Gotham city and other growing cities in the country had already been an issue of public interest as well as curiosity and anxiety in the antebellum newspapers, both in the form of articles and in the form of engraved illustrations published in either magazine format or book form affordable only to the middle and upper classes (see Gandal, esp. 27–38). Since the advent of urban life documentary photography in the late 1880s—which was one of the new forms of communication and vehicles to transmit tenement living conditions as a new aspect of increased urbanization in modern America—overcrowded houses and the hardships of the lower classes had become a pictorial reality implemented in the minds of those who encountered the visual representations. The most well-remembered pieces are presumably Stephen Crane's serialized "Tenderloin" sketches, which he began on October 25, 1896, and which were published in Hearst's *New York Journal*, on the one hand, and Jacob Riis's reports about the Mulberry Bend in the area of Five Points in New York City, on the other (see Leary; Strychacz 16–20; Trachtenberg;

Hales, esp. chs. 4 and 5). Ever since illustrations of street life and the tenement housings were running through the presses of, and printed in, the widely distributed city dailies and periodicals, the *street arab* "entered" the home of the readers (Riis, "How the Other Half Lives" and *How the Other Half Lives* 196–209; see also Gilfoyle). Outcault started "drawing 'kid' pictures [and] groups of street gamins of all sorts" for *Truth* magazine in the early 1890s before he moved his work to Pulitzer's *World* (Outcault, "How the Yellow Kid").

That the Yellow Kid Sunday comic-tableaux are related to, or should be read against the backdrop of, documentary photography of big city slum life, in particular the visual capturings of tenement life in New York City by Jacob Riis, is an argument that Bill Blackbeard has made in his *R. F. Outcault's The Yellow Kid: A Centennial Celebration of the Kid Who Started the Comics*. The Sunday Yellow Kid comics may be conceived as humoristic responses to the bleakness and somberness of the black-and-white engravings printed in the main sections of the newspapers, as well as in periodicals such as *Harper's Weekly*, for example (see Graham; Woolf; Woods et al.; see also Snyder, "City"; Gordon, "Mass Market" 50). In this regard, Roger Fischer has claimed that Outcault—as well as numerous other comics artists of that era—placed and depicted their respective comic figures "in a cultural context familiar to [readers]" (Fischer, "Nast" 30; see also Fischer, *Them Damned*). In a similar vein, Irvin Lewis Allen asserts that those who worked in the entertainment business (artists, writers, performers) were "in touch with urban worlds" and familiar with street speech and street life, and "naturally incorporated this social knowledge into their products of mass culture" (Irvin Lewis Allen 17). Outcault and Luks were familiar with the photographs, engravings, and descriptions of the tenement districts in New York, and they both attempted to give expression to their own observations of the "urban world" in the 1890s.

The Sunday *Hogan's Alley* and the *McFadden's Row* comics series offered to their readers serialized experiences of modern urban life; they are visual-verbal attempts to figure out who the working classes and who the ethnically diverse groups of immigrants were in relation to the elite (white) classes. Art historian Günter Metken writes about the newspaper comic pages of Richard Outcault that these are forms of "funny miserabilism," and "studies of the milieu, stuffed to confusion" (25; my translations). Referring to Metken's claim about the visual forms of "Zolaian naturalism" (25; my translation), Dietrich Grünewald contends that the scenes depicted in the comic-tableaux draw on the experiences of newspaper readers, on their everyday problems, their worries and wishes; the comics may not be able to eliminate these, yet by laughing at them the comics present (or give back) a bit of self-assurance, a way of diversion and possibly a little strength (Grünewald 11; see also McLean). Their argument is sound up to a point, but what both are missing are thoughts about the ways in which the comic-tableaux in the mass newspapers are enmeshed in their contexts of production and how their popularity relied on the means of distribution (see Meyer, "Noch besser"), as well as reflections on the pages' intrinsic dynamics, which invite different reader engagements. Moreover, readers did not necessarily observe themselves when consuming these comics. As I argue, it is the multiple, even competing, voices and perspectives inscribed in the Yellow Kid comic-tableaux and their principle of repetition and variation that made the Sunday supplement pages so alluring for a heterogeneous readership. For the moment of consumption, the Yellow Kid comics offered reading options and modes of engagement that distinguished them from other forms of Sunday leisure activity and other forms of reading material.

With respect to *ritualized consumption practices,* such as those offered through the entertainment form of vaudeville performances, which served as background for and a recurrent point of reference in many Yellow Kid comic-tableaux, the Sunday newspaper comics played a particular role. According to Robert Snyder, "vaudeville was essentially a variety show organized around the premise of *providing something for everyone*" (*The Voice* 53; my emphasis)—and with the increasing number of matinee (and evening) shows, the former of which predominantly catered to middle-class families (mothers with their children), the audiences grew more heterogeneous (see Block). In this regard, Irvin Lewis Allen points out that "vaudeville . . . was the chief medium of live, oral entertainment and was part of the web of social life" (18). Furthermore, the "popular forms of stage entertainment reflected more and more the concerns, the interests, the social worlds, and so the speech of their urban audiences. . . . Vaudeville drew a diverse urban audience and through its comedy and songs gave city people an image of their own diversity" (18). As others have stated before me, the Sunday comics in the newspapers of Pulitzer and Hearst offered to their readers printed versions of vaudeville scenes, which made the complexities of modernity and life in a sprawling—and economically polarized—city readable and consumable (see Wood n. pag.; Lewis, *From Traveling,* esp. 68).

The interconnection of, or reciprocal relationship between, the Yellow Kid comic-tableaux and vaudeville performances becomes obvious in two ways: First, as I have demonstrated in the previous chapter, comedy plays adapted the Yellow Kid "as seen in pictures" (Dumont 5) and turned the Yellow Kid into the protagonist of theater stage productions. Second, a number of Yellow Kid episodes are set in a theater and show vaudeville acts on the newspaper page (see *McFadden's* E13). Topical allusions to famous vaudeville actors and acrobats, or opera singers, served as triggers for those readers who were familiar with the theatrical entertainment, and generated satisfaction because of the recognition value inscribed in the pages. Moreover, the "variety package" of vaudeville (Lewis, *From Traveling* 8, 95; Jeanne Thomas Allen 5; DesRochers)—in other words, the repetitive and predictable structure of gags, slapstick, humor based on ethnic stereotyping and national and cultural clichés, songs, dialogues, ill-fitting uniforms, and more—found its way also into the comic-tableaux in the form of visual and verbal quotations, references, or paraphrases.

Similar as these two mass-entertainment forms may be in terms of ritualized, repeated pleasure, there is one key difference concerning the respective consumption habits: What the Yellow Kid pages do and what the vaudeville shows cannot or do not do is to capture an otherwise fleeting moment in time on paper to be looked at several times, and in private or in public with friends, relatives, or other people surrounding. In order to be able to consume the vaudeville acts, you needed to be at a specific place at a clearly defined time (the moment a show would begin), and usually the duration of the show program was defined by a set, or nearly set, time (see Robert C. Allen). In describing the difference between the consumption practices of vaudeville and comics, Alexander Braun emphasizes that the medium (the comics) belonged to readers once they bought it; the reader was not a paying guest during a scheduled and time-limited amusement but the *owner* of the amusement (5). Furthermore, the media environment of the newspaper comics differed from that of the vaudeville entertainment form in regard to the production and the channels of dissemination, as well as with respect to the scale of audience expansion—meaning, although vaudeville theaters attracted large audiences, and though standardized performances would tour across the country, these were not mass-produced, in the sense of rapid reproduction of a specific piece in the same form. In comparison, a newspaper comic page was able to quickly reach larger, demographically diverse audiences.

Publication in installments was a common practice in Victorian England as well as in America, and it included more than fictional works such as novels and poems in periodicals (Hayward 21–83; Hughes and Lund, *The Victorian* 13–21, as well as 51f; Balzer, "Hemd" 144; Cotkin 101f; Johnston, esp. 1–12 and 19–21). As Hughes and Lund show, scholarly texts such as Matthew Arnold's *Culture and Anarchy* were published in serialized form, too (see "Studying" 237; see also 241 on the practice of "serial reviewing").

I have argued elsewhere that in the context of serial forms of storytelling that were established throughout the nineteenth century, the serialized Yellow Kid comics played a particular role: Apart from the fact that they were colorful and funny to look at, the pages were widely available (through syndication) and easily accessible, and they enticed diverse readers with different social, ethnic, and economic backgrounds (see Meyer, "Serial Entertainment" and "Topographien"). Readers without, or with very basic, knowledge of the English language, or readers without interest in reading the words were still able to enjoy the Yellow Kid comics (through the pictorial parts, the colorfulness, and the spectacle presented on the newspaper page). Even without reading the words (in the speech balloons and boxes, or in the narrative columns in the *McFadden's Row* series), the sights offered by Luks and Outcault elicit pleasure. The "anarchic" layout compositions invite visual scanning and searching (for the protagonist, for example, or for other recurrent characters and animals, as I will explicate in this chapter) without necessarily forcing the reader to delve into the details and the words printed in the pages. In short, readers could use the weekly Yellow Kid comics according to their preferences and needs.

Against this backdrop, I show how the comics pages were able to attract a broad audience through different modes of representation, starting with an analysis of the dialect speech presentation and slang idiomatic that serve to convey the imagined tenement talk of the Flatters and the Alleyites. I intend to demonstrate how the Yellow Kid comics relate to and distance themselves from other media of the same time period, media that use dialect as a technique or subject matter.

THE LOCAL COLOR OF NEW YORK? LANGUAGE IN THE YELLOW KID COMICS

Every inhabitant, all the animals in the Yellow Kid comics series, and even nonliving things such as bottles, glasses, pebbles, and coins, converse in nonstandard English. The speech in the comics consists of nonstandard grammatical features, alternative spellings, a mixing of lower- and uppercase letters—even within one word—and more. The Yellow Kid comic-tableaux are filled with what is supposed to be the Bowery dialect. Even the billboard signs and all kinds of written announcements in the background of the respective episodes in *Hogan's Alley* and *McFadden's Row* are printed in nonstandard English. Dialect "echoes" from the walls and the sound fills the streets, metaphorically speaking; it is spreading over the city.

The most common strategy to reproduce the sound of an imagined Irish brogue in the written form are the substitutions of *th* (as, for example, *de* instead of *the* and *dere* instead of *there, dis* instead of *this, ting* instead of *thing, wit* or *wid* instead of *with,* or *close* instead of *clothes*), which are used in order to imitate the tongue in consonant pronunciation of the Hogan's Alley / McFadden's Row inhabitants—that is, the retractions of the tongue in the pronunciation of interdentals. Another technique is the substitution of vowels such as *o* (as in *te* instead of *to* or *fur* instead of *for*) and, third, the omission or replacement of vowels and consonants (e.g., *oney* instead of *only, again* instead of *against*, or *t'* instead of *to*). In his 1896 essay "English of the Lower Classes in New York City and Vicinity," E. H. Babbitt stated,

> The quality of the first vowel varies a good deal. In the pronunciation of the better classes it is a real high-mixed vowel, higher than the usual unaccented *ə*. It runs the gamut down . . . until it reaches the point which leads the comic papers to print "goil," "woild," etc., in attempting to give the "Bowery dialect." (463)

In the 1890s, there was quite a hype for writings in nonstandard English—as a way to apprehend and put into words perceptions of social experiences.[1] With respect to dialect writing in realist and naturalist fiction at the turn of the century, Gavin Jones states: "As both a representational technique and a cultural theme, dialect was absorbing the creative energies of literary minds" (3; see also North 17; Kersten, "Using" 3). As Jones further claims, the popular entertainment forms such as vaudeville "revealed similar sociolinguistic concerns, as it satisfied the needs of its urban and increasingly ethnic audience" (161). In his biography of Stephen Crane, Thomas Beer says: "Comedians aped [the Bowery's] dress on the stage at Koster and Bial's improper vaudeville, and speakers at banquets recited Bowery jokes. There was no other slum in America so settled of speech and habit" (83). The area in Lower Manhattan provided, as Beer would say, a "reservoir of unchaste diction" (84). Because representations of dialect in a variety of

---

1. Dialect writings can be traced further into the history of American culture, yet the first time they gained wide popularity was the time the penny press emerged in the 1830s (see Gavin Jones; Kersten, "The Creative Potential"). Interestingly enough, while there exists quite a pile of scholarly publications on dialect literature of the turn of the century, the newspaper comics pages have been excluded from these works. Gavin Jones points to the "dialect gags and caricatures [that] formed a central part of mass entertainment forms," but the popular Sunday supplement comics do not play any role in his otherwise fruitful and insightful study (6; see also 161 on the ways in which dialect entered the mass market).

texts and media formats developed so quickly and broadly (in literature, in entertainment forms such as vaudeville, in illustrations, and in caricatures and cartoons), many political and cultural forces feared that, as Gavin Jones has observed, "a virulent epidemic was contaminating the nation" and thus loudly and unanimously cried for "linguistic standardization" and regularized usage (1; see also 62; see North 12). The concerns about the English language, formulated in and disseminated through such magazines as *Harper's* or *Scribner's*, and the question about how vernacular variants (including local and regional slang idioms) develop, transform, and presumably threaten "American English" were, as Jones and other scholars in this field of research have pointed out, intricately tied with questions about the "meaning of national identity" (10; see also North 14–15). The "conviction that language was in peril" (North 13; see also Kersten, "The Creative" 93–94), and the fear about a possible contagion of the nation through "impure" language was also expressed in the anti-mass-paper campaigns of the 1890s (see Campbell; Cohen[2]); these included the Yellow Kid not only because the figure itself spread so excessively and uncontrollably but also because the idiomatic expressions printed on Mickey Dugan's shirt and the "improper," nonstandard English language he and his friends and animals speak had, according to the argument, a devastating impact on the "unsuspecting and long-suffering" reading public (Bannister).

With the Sunday newspaper comics series of Outcault and Luks (and, of course, of many other comics artists of that time period, too), dialect speech presentations entered a new mass medium and entertainment form, and the vernacular expressions of the Yellow Kid and his entourage became a standardized mode of storytelling that lasted well into the early years of the twentieth century (see Kersten, "Using"). In the comics, the speech presentations in nonstandard English serve humorous purposes. Partly adopted from dialect literature (such as Stephen Crane's tenement tale *Maggie*), partly copied from stage performances, and partly taken from personal experiences of living in New York City and listening to the diversity of speech in the streets, Luks's and Outcault's (and Townsend's) representations make visible for the reader an imagined tenement street talk in Hogan's Alley and McFadden's Row—or, as E. S. Sheldon would say,

---

2. Here see also the National Purity Congress that took place in 1895; in the papers presented there, the various speakers agreed on the containing of all "seeds of impurity." In her "Address to the National Purity Congress," Pauline W. Holme pronounces herself for the exclusion of the mass papers in private homes, for example (see 189–90). For a broader perspective on postbellum social purity crusades, see Pivar, esp. ch. 5.

the "representation for the eye of the language as spoken" (288). Whereas in vaudeville performances one was able to hear the sound, in the printed comics you would be able to see and read the sound of the people in the streets of Lower Manhattan. The voice of the city was put on paper, to be enjoyed repeatedly, and possibly read aloud and imitated.

The comics medium in the nineteenth century and literary texts that use dialect as technique and subject matter have one thing in common (in terms of reader reception): "In the act of reading vernacular literature," writes Siglinde Lemke in her study *The Vernacular Matters*, "one is caught between simultaneous desires to both decode the nonstandard language and be absorbed by its sound.... This sonic dimension prolongs the act of reading and facilitates a mode of reception in which the reader approaches the text with caution—and inevitably becomes a listener" (128). A related point is made by Holger Kersten, who asserts that "these unconventional linguistic forms ... provided their audiences with a different kind of aesthetic experience and created opportunities for new and surprising insights and sensations" ("The Creative" 117). In the serialized *Around the World* narrative, analyzed in chapter 4 of this study, Outcault and Rudolph Block also intersperse "Frentch langwidge" (AW E6), or German words, or others, depending on the country the Yellow Kid is in; these are written imitations of spoken language in the ways the protagonist hears and reproduces them. In one of the episodes, the Yellow Kid says, for example: "Joiminny ... I guess I'll stay heer an' be d' gelber knabe witch is wot dey caul mi in joimin I speek joimin elligint" (AW E12). In another episode, when the crowd visits Paris, the Yellow Kid recounts:

> mong share billy polly voo frongsay? wot? say de way I c'n tauk Frentch is de envy uv d' hole town. Ware did'je loin t' speek so good sed me frend sara Boinhart. Sady I sez, I hav alwuz spoke Frentch toozhure, ma share Sady. esker vooz 8 ung garsong frongsay? sez Sady. We, I sez, je swee ung peach. An' t' jolly 'er along I sed vooz 8 ung peach o.c. (AW E6)

In the Yellow Kid comics, the sonic dimension is furthermore sustained with the help of typography. The doggerel that is represented in *Hogan's Alley, McFadden's Row,* and *Around the World*—in the boxes, in banners, on the walls, and in the speech balloons—is hardly regular, which becomes graphically visible also through the mixing of lower and uppercase letters within one word and the backward writing of letters. The "anarchic" lettering in the Yellow Kid comic-tableaux and the orthographic misspellings are entertaining in themselves. Furthermore, the comics mesh together various typefaces and font sizes, and sometimes forms of handwriting are included, too. In the Yellow Kid comics, typography represents an additional device to convey the—class-inflected—vernacular language of the Hogan Alleyites and McFadden Flatters.[3]

As a subject matter, dialect in the Yellow Kid comic-tableaux carries varying undercurrents and has quite diverse implications for the meaning-making processes. In one episode, dialect is related to the social issues of language acquisition in immigrant communities and literacy among the inhabitants, and the "wrong" spellings in the comic-tableau draw explicit attention to language itself, as a medium of communication and as a criterion for citizenship (see Meyer, "Urban America"). In another episode, it is announced that "NO ENGLiSH KIN BE USED" in McFadden's Row because "WE ARE iRiSH AN NOT ANGLOMANIACS" (*McFadden's* E7). Here, Outcault writes himself into the page as a kind of linguistic critic who formulates tongue-in-cheek his reactionary ideas to the authority of standard (British, that is) English. Dialect speech in cases like these becomes political. On other occasions, the Yellow Kid comics self-reflexively draw attention to the fact that most of the time, the tenants in Hogan's as well as McFadden's tenement flats are faking dialect. Because of these many ways in which the Bowery dialect is functionalized and made graphically visible in the Yellow Kid episodes, readers' investment in the reading of the pages can be manifold.

The following pages tie into these observations by showing that multiple reading options in the respective episodes are generated not only by means of the various visual-verbal modes of speech presentation but also through the Yellow Kid himself. The Yellow Kid comic figure's proneness to medial proliferations, as discussed in the previous chapter, resonates in the volatility of the Yellow Kid figure in the comics and the openness to projection.

WHO IS THE YELLOW KID?

When Robert Harvey describes the Yellow Kid's "vaguely Oriental visage" (37), and when Lisa Yaszek says about the Sunday supplement child that "the Yellow Kid appears to be a Chinese, Irish or Slavic (depending on how you look at him)" (35), they point to one of the ambiguities in the com-

---

3. On typography as a mode of representation in comics, and its impact on reading experiences, see Holbo; Kaindl; Kress and Leeuwen.

ics series, namely, the Yellow Kid's protean quality. Whether Outcault was aware of this "floating signifier," I am not able to tell, but already in June 1896, the artist attempted to establish an ethnic background for the Yellow Kid: He christened the unnamed, vagabond, bald-headed figure and gave him the name Mickey Dugan (see Outcault, "The Bicycle Meet") and gave him a sister named Kitty Dugan.[4] I am not able to verify whether Outcault was explicitly requested to establish the Yellow Kid as an Irish leader of the Alleyites in the comic-tableaux, which wouldn't be surprising given the fact that the Irish were common subjects in caricatures, political cartoons, and vaudeville at that time (see Appel; Conolly-Smith; Kibler; Knobel; Murphy; Soper, "From Swarthy"; Stivers). In any case, from then on the name Mickey Dugan, which was only known to those who were familiar with the *Hogan's Alley* episode in which the kid was christened, or to those who later during that year read the narrative columns in the *McFadden's Row* episodes (and thus considered the two competing series as belonging or referring to one another), was meant to serve as an ethnic marker to identify the comic figure as an Irish immigrant child living in New York City.

In episodes of *Around the World*, the reader is furthermore informed about the Yellow Kid's ancestors; in the first installment, the first-person narrator Mickey Dugan says that he is a fourth-generation, Irish American child (his "grate-grand'fadder faut in d'revvolooschun"; AW E1). In another episode, the Yellow Kid visits Ireland, and the words on his shirt say, "DE LAND OF ME 4 FADDERS" (AW E6). Yet, the attempt to categorize the Yellow Kid, to endow him with a name, and to gain control over him through the creation of a backstory, seemed to show little success. Mickey Dugan was (and still is) not remembered as Mickey Dugan but as the Yellow Kid, or the other way around: The Yellow Kid was and is not remembered as Mickey Dugan but as the Yellow Kid.

Even with the knowledge about the "real" name and the place of origin of his ancestors in mind, and even with the words printed on his long yellow shirt, the series' protagonist in both Luks's *Hogan's Alley* and Outcault and Townsend's *McFadden's Row* episodes invites different readings and allows for projections. One way this becomes obvious is by looking at the debates that evolved around the Yellow Kid, in the form of articles, in the form of brief theater announcements, or in the form of other comics. A car-

---

4. In the *McFadden's Row* series, the name of Kitty Dugan was changed to Kitty Hogan. In Townsend's accompanying narrative columns her name is spelled differently (Kittie Hogan). Quite obviously, the child's name is not relevant; far more important to the recognition of Kitty Dugan/Hogan in the individual episodes is her wardrobe, especially the large hat.

toon penned by George B. Luks, accompanying an article about one of the theater adaptations of *Hogan's Alley*, proves insightful here. In the cartoon, the Yellow Kid grins at the reader of the newspaper and explains: "I'M YELLOW BUT I'M IRISH SEE!" (Luks, "A Sunday World Cartoonist's"; see also Townsend and Outcault 144). What I would say is that this comment, or plea, on the shirt suggests that the yellow color of the kid's attire, and his outer appearance (i.e., the reduced facial and bodily features), invited readers and theatergoers to interpret the kid in different ways than intended, or rather to ascribe an ethnic identity to the comic figure that differed from the Irish American background that Outcault had (intentionally or not) envisioned for him.

Contemporaries of Outcault would categorize the Yellow Kid as, among other things, a "Chinese-Irishman" ("Baltimore" 1897; see also Dale and Gunn[5]). One reason why newspaper readers and theatergoers would ascribe a non-Irish ethnic identity to the Yellow Kid might have to do with the ubiquitous anti-yellow-press publications, in which people fought against such mass papers as the *World* or the *New York Journal*—in articles, editorial comments, and short essays, in the form of illustrations, in newspapers and magazines—and in the course of which the color yellow was implemented in the readers' minds as a symbolic power to connote anything and anyone (allegedly) threatening, epidemic, or contagious (see Boutelle; Duer; Gallienne; Wardman, "Yellow" and "On"; Warner; see also Constable; Winwar). This included also fears about anarchism, or anti-immigrant sentiments, which would, in the closing decades of the nineteenth century, in particular be directed toward Chinese and Japanese immigrants. Another possible explanation for why readers and theatergoers would ascribe a non-Irish ethnic identity to the Yellow Kid might have to do with the fact that in the early episodes we find versions of the bald-headed child with facial features that would replicate stereotyped images of Asians: In "At the Circus in Hogan's Alley" (May 1895), the soon-to-be-popular Yellow Kid comic figure—not yet in his typical yellow nightgown—is endowed with high eyebrows and slanted eyes. In Outcault's "The War Scare in Hogan's Alley" (March 1896), we see the Yellow Kid prominently located in the foreground of the page, and next to him two children hold up their fists; one of them is bald-headed and dressed in a long yellow shirt, while the other is dressed in a long blue shirt, has black pigtailed hair and carved eyebrows, and has a fierce expression on his face. The kid in the yellow gown punches

---

5. For further information on representations of Chinese and Irish in nineteenth-century visual art (in particular caricatures) see, for example, Tchen, esp. 214–24. My thanks to Ian Gordon.

his counterpart, as if Outcault wanted to suggest that this kid punches his own mirror image from the early versions. In the episode "Li Hung Chang Visits Hogan's Alley," the Yellow Kid, on the quiet, explains to the readers: "ME & LI HAS MADE A BIG HIT WIT EACH OTER! SAY HE TINKS I'M A CHINAMAN—DON'T SAY A WOID" (6). The point is not that the Yellow Kid figure contributed to the popularization and proliferation of yellow peril ideology. Rather, the point is that the Yellow Kid is a flat and "content-free" figure that allows for multifarious projections. This has to do with the Yellow Kid's liminal status.

The previous chapter explained how the Yellow Kid is a comic figure that is situated between different media; that is, he is a serialized comic figure printed in the Sunday supplement of the mass newspapers, a comic figure that appears in the form of several (three-dimensional) merchandise wares, a comic figure that is translated into the poster form, a comic figure that is reshaped in the form of various caricatures in the humor magazines, a comic figure that is adapted as a character in several theater plays, and a comic figure that is transformed into an advertising tool for all kinds of purposes. As I furthermore explained, this medial liminality is also a recurrent topic, and a technique of self-observation in the Sunday supplement pages themselves. The Yellow Kid is a malleable figure in the newspaper comic-tableaux, too. According to Soper, artists "depict[ed] characters that alternated between being the butt of the joke, the sympathetic underdog or everyman, or the unapologetically ethnic trickster who reveled in his outsider status" ("From Swarthy" 272; see also 275–76; furthermore, see Mintz; Conolly-Smith). This is probably most obvious in the early *Hogan's Alley* episodes published in Pulitzer's *World* in 1895, and those printed in the first half of the year 1896, in which a long shirt did not yet hold any words that would convey a specific concern. The Yellow Kid invited readers to project their desires into, or rather onto, the kid. But this holds true for the episodes that were published from mid-1896 onward, too, in which the Yellow Kid's shirt is endowed with commentaries. There are at least two reasons for this, I believe.

For one thing, this has to do with the fact that the Yellow Kid is a mixture of child and adult. And, the comic figure's "messy colloquial street language . . . made him appear both simultaneously ignorant (by standards of assimilation and conventional education) and worldly wise" (Soper, "From Swarthy" 277). For another thing, the ambivalent nature of the Yellow Kid also has to do with the fact that the comic figure oscillates between different narrative levels: More often than not, the Yellow Kid stands in tension with himself, that is, between his status as fictional part of the weekly adventures, his metafictional status as commentator on his own fictionality and popularity, and his intermediatory status as channel for plot-related or content-level remarks as well as remarks on some extratextual, topical issue. The liminal quality of the Yellow Kid is thus not only defined by the figure's plurimedial proliferations; the volatility of the Yellow Kid is related also to the figure's interserial status between the two rival newspaper supplements (an issue I will revisit in the next chapter). And, it is explained by a certain narrative instability of the Yellow Kid in the comic-tableaux.

Just as the figure's openness in the comics series allows for different degrees of engagement, the Yellow Kid's surroundings—the *serial props*, as I call them, of *Hogan's Alley* and *McFadden's Row*—invite different consumption practices. The questions of how these recurrent components function within the individual episode as well as between the episodes in a series and between the competing series and which reading options they trigger are the main points of inquiry in the next section.

TEXTUAL SERIALITIES: THE YELLOW KID'S ENTOURAGES

As I have indicated in the introduction to this study, Richard Outcault created such Hogan Alleyites as Molly Brogan, with her memorable face of astonishment; Slippy Dempsey, who always falls from some kind of building (or any other high spot); Vincent Farrell; Kitty Dugan, with her big hat and fancy dress; or the beautiful Liz, with her two braids—her real name is Delia Dunnigan, but the Yellow Kid calls her Liz. Names, however, do not play such an important role in the comics series. To make the surrounding stock characters easily identifiable for the readers, Outcault endowed them with specific traits such as facial expressions (always in awe, always in shock, etc.), or the reappearance of the same clothes, or, for instance, a particular—falling—position in the tableaux. When George Luks took over the *Hogan's Alley* series in October 1896, he kept only a number of the "original" members of the cast. Instead he introduced new recurrent props to the Yellow Kid comic-tableaux. These included, among others, a nameless boy in a flying machine, who started to appear regularly from October 25, 1896, onward, and the handstand acrobat, or "DE HARLEM ACTUR," named Alfy (Luks, "A Genuine"), who after a couple of episodes is endowed with a regular, recognizable attire, a "BLEW SAILURE SUIT" (Luks, "Thanksgiving Day"). Luks furthermore implemented an unnamed journalist with a "HED PATENTED" (Luks "A Hot Election"), who works for the fictive newspaper titled "JIMMIES PAY PUR" (Luks, "A Seeley Dinner"), which is under the editorship of the fictive editor named Jimmie Jones. A previously unnamed policeman was given the tag "Nelse" (Luks, "A Snowball") and a sword-swinging "BUSTER DE CONEYS iSLE BANDiT" (Luks, "President-Elect") joined the crowd of Alleyites. Luks also introduced an unnamed young man who calls himself "DE PROFESOR" in striped pants, a green shirt, a hat, and a coat with "BALDY SOURS" sleeves (Luks, "A Snowball"), and he added the "RANEMAKER" (Luks, "President-Elect"), an unclaimed green umbrella whose owner—a clown—is only later revealed.

In the scholarship about the Yellow Kid, Luks's *Hogan's Alley* comic-tableaux are very often labeled as inferior to Outcault's Yellow Kid comics pages—they allegedly lack the aesthetic refinement of Outcault's drawings, and Luks is very often described as having "felt a certain lack of fulfillment in perpetuating another artist's work" (Gambone 115). I would argue quite the contrary. When one looks at Luks's comics and especially the serial props he introduced to the *Hogan's Alley* series, one sees that he created a fascinating ever-expanding and elaborate comics network of interweavings and cross-infiltrations. The most prominent serial props that Luks implemented in the *Hogan's Alley* series are two recurrent figures dressed in yellow named Alex and George, who are visual excrescences of the Yellow Kid (see figures 2.1–2.4). Luks established the yellow twin figures in his first *Hogan's Alley* episode (October 18, 1896) but gave them proper names only later. The bold, blown-up round heads of Alex and George and the expansive grins on their faces mirror, in duplicate parody, the two recognizable facial markers of the iconic Yellow Kid (see Luks, "Hogan's Alley Kids").

In 1896, Alex and George evolved as regular twin replicas of the Yellow Kid in the *Hogan's Alley* series, and then "grew" in size and transformed—or mutated—into caricaturesque versions of the Yellow Kid to ultimately become the (mischievous) protagonists in a series titled the *Little Nippers* (1897–98).[6] The grimacing "mutants" were established in the *Hogan's Alley* series and interfered with the Yellow Kid's adventures before they migrated into their own serialized narrative. While Alex and George were stripped of their yellow dresses in the *Little Nippers* series and changed their attire according to the setting (e.g., wrestling outfits in a box-fight episode, military garments), they popped up again in their original yellow shirts and with their grimaces and seeped into other comics series. For instance, in

---

6. The *Little Nippers* series began in September 1897 and ran until May 1898; the first episode bears the caption "The Little Nippers Start a Colony" (printed in Pulitzer's *World* on September 12, 1897), and as far as I can discern, the final episode was printed on May 15, 1898.

FIGURE 2.1. George Benjamin Luks, "The Open-Air School in Hogan's Alley," *The World*, 18 Oct. 1896, Comic Weekly, p. 3 (Alex and George, detail). San Francisco Academy of Comic Art Collection, The Ohio State University, Billy Ireland Cartoon Library & Museum.

FIGURE 2.2. George Benjamin Luks, "The Great Prize Fight in Hogan's Alley," *The World*, 6 Dec. 1896, Comic Weekly, p. 4 (Alex and George, detail). San Francisco Academy of Comic Art Collection, The Ohio State University, Billy Ireland Cartoon Library & Museum.

FIGURE 2.3. George Benjamin Luks, "Thanksgiving Day in Hogan's Alley," *The World*, 22 Nov. 1896, Comic Weekly, p. 4 (Alex and George, detail). San Francisco Academy of Comic Art Collection, The Ohio State University, Billy Ireland Cartoon Library & Museum.

FIGURE 2.4. George Benjamin Luks, "President-Elect M'Kinley Visits Hogan's Alley," *The World*, 29 Nov. 1896, Comic Weekly, p. 5 (Alex and George, detail). San Francisco Academy of Comic Art Collection, The Ohio State University, Billy Ireland Cartoon Library & Museum.

Luks's "Porkville's Four Hundred in the Merry Waltz," Alex and George are guests and perform as musicians who seem to interrupt the "Merry Waltz" and annoy the attendees of the event rather than bring delight. In addition to that, the two reappeared in a comics series titled *Mose's Incubator*, which Luks started in January 1898—this series is structured on the twin or doubling motif. In the *Incubator* series, a long-necked "Trained Chicken" named "Mose" is the recurring protagonist (Luks, "Mose's Incubator—New Twins" and "Mose's Incubator—More Twins"[7]). In the *Incubator* series, Mose tends a wondrous replication machine, which is able to generate a seemingly unending series of products in duplicates—animals, babies, children, objects, and more (see Gambone 120).

The longer *Hogan's Alley* ran in Pulitzer's *World*, the more George Luks seemed to exhaust or probe the limits of serial repetitions and variations. The twins Alex and George not only spun out of their own original *Hogan's Alley* setting; they also exited their own spin-off series—the *Little Nippers*—and percolated into other parts of the Sunday comics supplement. These operations of branching out can be understood as parodic comments on the Yellow Kid's proliferation. Alex and George were implemented as recurring elements in the *Hogan's Alley* series, and once established as immediately recognizable figures, they moved into other textual forms and, as a matter of fact, also across media. The twin replica imitated or repeated the narrative of the Yellow Kid's serial life. Among other things, the twins appeared in newspaper advertisements and functioned to promote the Sunday editions of Pulitzer's *World* (see Luks, "8 Funny Pages"; McCarthy, "The Great Sunday"). And, the two were also appropriated to the theater stage, in a new version of the popular *McFadden's Row of Flats* show—thus they migrated from the "original" Hogan's Alley settings to a McFadden setting on the theater stage.[8] As a contemporary of Outcault wrote about these two,

---

7. Regular readers of Pulitzer's Sunday *World* would have noticed that this fabled creature had been established in Luks's comics called the *Pickaninnies*; the long-necked chicken was also interspersed in a series titled *Kalsomine Family*, which Luks began to draw in autumn 1897 (see Luks, "A Genuine" and "The Kalsomine"). This short-running *Kalsomine* series shows a family of grinning and craps-playing characters in an unspecified rural area; a white-bearded man with the telling name of Uncle Remus is the head of this family (see Gambone 115–16; on "racially coded imagery" in Luks's comics, see Gambone 117–18).

8. The new *McFadden's* musical comedy toured through the states from 1898 onwards, in which Gus Hill adapted Luks's twin characters to the stage; they were first impersonated by Bobby Ralston and W. A. Robinson, and later by Jerry Sullivan, who played George, and Walter Bramblette, who played Alex (see "Star—McFadden's Row of Flats"; "Plays Piano Though Blind"). Together with the famous actor Tom Thumb, Ralston also performed in a vaudeville sketch titled *Hogan's Kids*, produced by Owen

they "had a popularity only second to that of their jaundiced and cynical elder brother" (McCardell 764).

Outcault took notice of the twins and integrated them in his comics as a means of bantering. Alex and George had cameo appearances in Yellow Kid episodes set in Ryan Arcades, which Outcault penned for Hearst's *Journal* in 1897. For instance, in Outcault's "A Christmas Festival in Ryan's Arcade," published on December 5, 1897, we see versions of Luks's yellow twins, laying flat in front the Yellow Kid. In other installments, Alex and George are "roasted" or hanged—in brief, they are tortured in all kinds of ways by the artist (Outcault, "The Crowd Gets Up," "The Ryan's Arcade Gang," "The Yellow Kid Treats the Crowd," and "Thanksgiving Day in Ryan's"). Outcault's colleague at Hearst's *Journal,* Jimmy (James Guilford) Swinnerton, also offered his parodic take on Luks's and Outcault's representations of Alex and George and the serial exchange of teasing comments in the comics of these two artists. In one of the episodes in Swinnerton's popular *Tigers* series, two grim-looking characters named "Mr. Alexander" and "Mr. George" sit at separate working desks observing each other. The caption suggests that these two "sign articles for a match race" (Swinnerton; see figure 2.5).

In Outcault's comics for Hearst's *Journal,* Alex and George are a running gag, and they are entertaining because they sarcastically comment on the scenes depicted in the respective installments as well as on their own desperate situation (they suffer pain repeatedly and explain the cause of their anguish via the words printed on their shirt). But, the fact that Alex and George operate as elements of interserial observation is obvious only when one is familiar with the development of the Yellow Kid comic figure and the competition between the two newspapers and their rival comics series. That they furthermore function as self-ironic references to transmedial expansions of mass-cultural products is only understandable when the spreading of the Yellow Kid and the proliferations of Alex and George in theater and advertising are known.

In early 1897, more recurrent stock characters joined Luks's Hogan Alleyite crowd while others left the scene. For example, Kitty Dugan, with her easily recognizable big theater hat, disappeared from Luks's *Hogan's Alley* series on December 13, 1896, and was replaced by a female couple with big Kitty Dugan–like hats, watching and commenting on the scenes via the words printed on their hats and big dresses; one of them is named

---

Davis and John Fowler, which premiered in New York in the season 1896–1897 ("The Big Comedy Boom"). It ran regularly in New York at Tony Pastor's in the seasons to come, with Dick McAvoy and Alice McAvoy as the leading performers.

FIGURE 2.5. Jimmy Swinnerton, "Is It Possible That Messrs. George and Alexander—Put Up a Job on the Journal Tigers?" *New York Journal and Advertiser*, 27 Feb. 1898, American Humorist, p. 5 (detail). San Francisco Academy of Comic Art Collection, The Ohio State University, Billy Ireland Cartoon Library & Museum.

Em, the other is called Jen, and the latter of the two always holds a lorgnette to observe the others. The first time this Em and Jen couple is mentioned (in a speech balloon) is the Yellow Kid episode from November 29, 1896; the first time the two are visually included in the Hogan's Alley setting is December 6, 1896. After only two episodes, Luks changed their initially Puritan attire into conspicuous fashion fads: big hats, long capes, gored skirts and dresses, fur collars, and so on. Em and Jen gradually shrink in size (except for their hats) and turn into child versions of their adult models and thus reverse and transform back into twin Kitty Dugans (Luks, "Santa Claus," "A Snowball," "New Year's," and "The Victoria Jubilee"). Similar to the recognizability of the Yellow Kid, the supporting cast in Luks's *Hogan's Alley* series is created in a fashion that would make it easy for the readers to identify them in each episode, and to find them in the tableaux is one of the pleasures. In the following, I discuss a selection of Luks's serial props and the interactions and gratifications they afford (see also Meyer, "Serial Entertainment" 80–81, for a discussion of the recurring character named Fatty).

Serialized background characters such as Alfy and the boy with the flying machine serve as playful modes to refer to previous and future episodes, and thus to create interlinkages between the installments of *Hogan's*

Alley (see figures 2.6 and 2.7). In "A Hot Election Day in Hogan's Alley," we see the sailor-acrobat Alfy in a handstand position, saying that he has "BEAN IN DIS SAME POSISSHUN EVER SINCE LAST SUNDAY" (Luks, "A Hot Election"). In the episode that was printed on the cover page of the Sunday Comic Weekly the week before, there was in fact this boy in the exact same acrobatic pose in the left-hand corner of the newspaper page (Luks "The Great Baby Show") — as if Luks had simply copied and pasted the figure into the next episode. Whereas Alfy's handstand act is the same in both episodes, the setting is slightly different, and so is the time of day. In "The Great Baby Show in Hogan's Alley" (October 25, 1896) it is daylight, and the freak-show-like event takes place in a backyard surrounded by a tall fence[9]; in "A Hot Election Day in Hogan's Alley" (November 1, 1896) it is nighttime, and we find ourselves on the street (in the middle of a political parade) in a different corner of Hogan's Alley, and Alfy the acrobat does his handstand on a wall instead of on a fence. Because of the frameless text segment placed in the vicinity of Alfy's head (in the "Hot Election" episode), this element in the comic-tableau is also intelligible to the reader who did not read or engage with the "The Great Baby Show in Hogan's Alley"; the words inform the reader who had missed the previous episode that Alfy has not changed his "POSISSHUN . . . SINCE LAST SUNDAY" (Luks, "A Hot Election"). Alfy comments on his actions in a single episode and his existence in the *Hogan's Alley* series, namely to be in a handstand and to go through the series in a handstand. Similarly, in the "Horse Show" episode, to which I will come back in the next chapter, Alfy tells the reader: "WAIT TILL YOU SEE ME IN ME SAILOR SUET!" (Luks, "A Genuine"). Two episodes later, Alfy is presented in his new "BLEW SAILURE" suit (Luks, "Thanksgiving Day"). I use Alfy here in order to explain the double function of, and double reading modes implied in, this background character in the *Hogan's Alley* series: He functions both to refer to a previous episode — on the structural level of the *whole series* — and to self-reflexively comment on the acrobatic performance (on the plot level of the *individual episode*). In Luks's "A Snowball Battle in Hogan's Alley," this double function is made explicit: There, Alfy is shown in an upright position instead of

---

9. One may read Luks's Yellow Kid episode as a satirical, visual-verbal response to exhibited infants in baby shows — a popular entertainment form in the nineteenth century — and the baby prize contests, which were regularly printed as Sunday features in the Sunday Magazine of Pulitzer's newspaper. The first baby contest took place in Springfield, Ohio, in 1854. On baby shows in nineteenth-century America, see, for example, Pearson. Time and again, the artists in the Sunday supplements addressed this topic in their comics.

his typical, continual handstand position (with his back facing the reader); he addresses the reader through a speech balloon attached to him, in which the words explain the "mistake" in the picture: "SAY! I OUTER BE STANDIN ON ME HED." By stressing that he should be "on his head," the Alfy figure exposes his own role as an element in and the intrinsic serial dynamics of the *Hogan's Alley* comics series; he marks his own variation from the otherwise fixed (established) handstand act and the position in the comic-tableau. The serial, joyful, pleasurable consumption of the pages, then, implies also, or in particular, to recognize the difference in the repetition (see also Meyer, "Noch besser").

A second example occurs with Luks's boy with the flying machine (see figures 2.8–2.10); this recurring prop works slightly differently compared with Alfy. After having introduced the boy and his "NEW FLYIN' MACHINE" in the episode titled "The Great Baby Show in Hogan's Alley" (October 25, 1896), Luks reduced the *size* of the boy and the machine in the following installment, titled "A Hot Election in Hogan's Alley." The words—"SAY!! I'M COMIN"—printed next to him, in relation to the smaller size of this serial prop serve to suggest that he has moved away (from the "Great Baby Show" scene) and is now entering a new scene (the "Hot Election").

Both Alfy and the boy with his flying machine make visible, albeit in different ways, the temporal quality of the serial comic-tableaux. This is echoed also in the utterances composed of the deictic of time (e.g., "since," "till," "dese days," etc.). While the size of the handstand acrobat Alfy stays the same in each individual episode (a means also for Luks to facilitate his work), the boy with his flying machine seems to move around from one episode to the next, which is suggested by the difference in size of him and his flying device in each installment. Alfy is a predominantly *static*, repetitive element (same handstand act, with only slight variations from episode to episode), and the flying-machine boy is a *moving* element (from left to right, from background to foreground, from small to large).

In "A Genuine Horse Show in Hogan's Alley," the boy with his flying machine is placed a little farther to the front; he proudly announces to the reader: "I'M IMPROVIN DIS FLYIN MASHIN ALL DE TIME." This improvement, however, seems unsuccessful, for in the following episode in the next Sunday Comic Weekly edition, the flying machine looks broken, and the boy falls out; he makes the promise, however, that, "I'LL PERFEKT DIS MACHINE ONE UV DESE DAYS YET" (Luks, "The Masquerade"). The reader would find the boy back again in his flying machine in the following Yellow Kid comic-tableau (in the upper right corner of the page). At one point in this kind of serialized, visual mise-en-abyme narrative within the larger *Hogan's Alley* comics series, the recurrent boy with the flying machine drops out of sight / off the page (December 20, 1896), only to reappear a week later in the form of a tiny visual black "spot" in the back of the scene. In "New Year's Celebration in Hogan's Alley," the boy is placed in front of the yellow shining moon, in a V-shaped flying machine, which is hard to see or find but still recognizable for the reader familiar with this recurrent element, because of the balloons (see figure 2.10).

As suddenly as the boy with the flying machine had appeared in October 1896, so too did he disappear from *Hogan's Alley* (three months later)—only to reappear again on May 16, 1897 (he now moves around in an umbrella that is lifted up with the help of many balloons, and the flying machine is actually capable of holding a crowd of children). Both components—the boy in his mechanical device, with which he navigates through space (and virtually through time), and the handstand acrobat Alfy—are elements that generate pleasure individually in the respective installments because of their appearances. But they also function intraserially: Alfy and the boy with the flying machine elicit weekly gratification through the recognition of differences with respect to size or place in the overall arrangement of the respective episode. Yet while one component puts greater emphasis on the sequentiality of seriality—that is, the linear, chronologic, progressive dimension (in the case of the boy with the flying machine)—the other draws attention to the spatially iterative quality of seriality, intrinsic in the Yellow Kid comic-tableaux (in the case of Alfy, the falling boy named Slippy Dempsey who appeared in both *Hogan's Alley* and *McFadden's Row* functions in similar ways in the comics series). I would say that these and other recurrent, formulaic props in Luks's *Hogan's Alley* series engage readers to peruse the individual episode and to search for—marginal—details in the pages; in other words, these serial props help establish an expanding memory of the *Hogan's Alley* series, which is activated in the reading process, and which can then be applied to future installments (belatedly). This holds true, of course, for regular consumers/readers only; one-time readers will presumably regard Alfy and the boy with his flying machine as visual gimmicks that are funny to look at.

One more serial prop from Luks's *Hogan's Alley* series also shows the serial dynamics of the Yellow Kid comic-tableaux: In the following, I explicate the status of the unnamed journalist figure with his bubonic head, who works for the fictive newspaper "Jimmie's Paper," which is edited by a man named Jimmie Jones. This recurrent bald-headed, grotesque-looking figure with "GOLDRIMMED SPECKS" (Luks, "The Great Baby Show"; see fig-

FIGURE 2.6. George Benjamin Luks, "Thanksgiving Day in Hogan's Alley," *The World*, 22 Nov. 1896, Comic Weekly, p. 4 (Alfy, detail). San Francisco Academy of Comic Art Collection, The Ohio State University, Billy Ireland Cartoon Library & Museum.

FIGURE 2.7. George Benjamin Luks, "President-Elect M'Kinley Visits Hogan's Alley," *The World*, 29 Nov. 1896, Comic Weekly, p. 5 (Alfy, detail). San Francisco Academy of Comic Art Collection, The Ohio State University, Billy Ireland Cartoon Library & Museum.

FIGURE 2.8. George Benjamin Luks, "The Great Baby Show in Hogan's Alley," *The World*, 25 Oct. 1896, Comic Weekly, n. pag. (Flying Machine Boy, detail). San Francisco Academy of Comic Art Collection, The Ohio State University, Billy Ireland Cartoon Library & Museum.

FIGURE 2.9. George Benjamin Luks, "President-Elect M'Kinley Visits Hogan's Alley," *The World*, 29 Nov. 1896, Comic Weekly, p. 5 (Flying Machine Boy, detail). San Francisco Academy of Comic Art Collection, The Ohio State University, Billy Ireland Cartoon Library & Museum.

FIGURE 2.10. George Benjamin Luks, "New Year's Celebration in Hogan's Alley," *The World*, 27 Dec. 1896, Comic Weekly, p. 4 (Flying Machine Boy, detail). San Francisco Academy of Comic Art Collection, The Ohio State University, Billy Ireland Cartoon Library & Museum.

FIGURE 2.11. George Benjamin Luks, "A Genuine Horse Show in Hogan's Alley," *The World*, 8 Nov. 1896, Comic Weekly, p. 5 (Journalist, detail). San Francisco Academy of Comic Art Collection, The Ohio State University, Billy Ireland Cartoon Library & Museum.

FIGURE 2.12. George Benjamin Luks, "President-Elect M'Kinley Visits Hogan's Alley," *The World*, 29 Nov. 1896, Comic Weekly, p. 5 (Journalist, detail). San Francisco Academy of Comic Art Collection, The Ohio State University, Billy Ireland Cartoon Library & Museum.

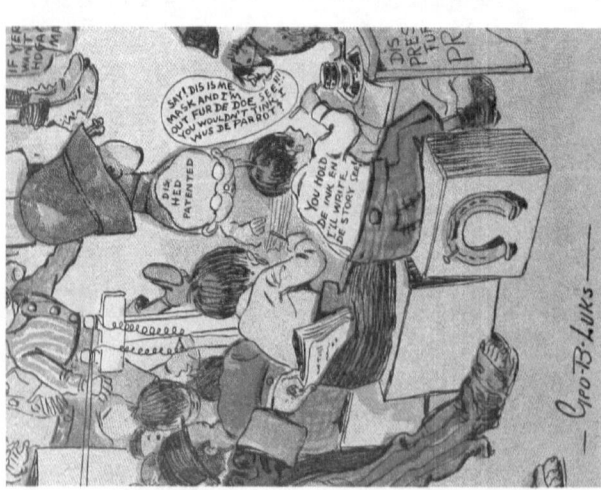

FIGURE 2.13. George Benjamin Luks, "A Snowball Battle in Hogan's Alley," *The World*, 20 Dec. 1896, Comic Weekly, p. 4 (Journalist, detail). San Francisco Academy of Comic Art Collection, The Ohio State University, Billy Ireland Cartoon Library & Museum.

ures 2.11–2.13) is interesting with regard to the serialized reading options inscribed in the comic-tableaux for two reasons: first, because of the figure's implied addressees in the respective installments, and second, because of the functions of the journalist figure, not just within the individual episode and in relation to other episodes in the series, but also with regard to the other features in the comic supplement, in which the comic-tableaux appeared.

Concerning the first point, one of the implied addressees of this journalist figure with a patented head is Richard Outcault, who had attempted to gain control over the Yellow Kid by sending in a copyright request to the Library of Congress in September 1896, and who had made this obvious also in his drawings by adding the information "copyrighted 1896" to the Yellow Kid figure. In other words, the recurrent journalist figure, with his exaggerated head and the iterative "DIS HED PATENTED" printed thereon (Luks, "A Hot Election" and "A Genuine"), serves as a kind of serial visual-verbal pun to parody Outcault's strenuous efforts to copyright the Yellow Kid and to "claim" the comic figure—here it is the specific shape or form of a head that is supposed to be patented. The journalist with his patented head is an excellent additional channel to voice issues concerning ownership and originality. To understand the significance of the journalist figure in the Yellow Kid comic-tableaux relies on knowledge about the medial context in which the comic figure evolved. This means that through the implementation of the recurrent journalist figure, different readerships get their gratification in different ways: For the one-time reader of Pulitzer's Sunday newspaper, the journalist figure is probably just a funny-looking visual gimmick that may or may not elicit humor; for consumers who regularly bought Pulitzer's Comic Weekly, the scanning of the respective page each Sunday and identifying the journalist figure in each episode can cause satisfaction (similar to the satisfaction when finding a hidden object in a picture). Furthermore, the "patented hed" journalist in Luks's *Hogan's Alley* effects a serial pleasure of recognition for an "insider"—or exclusionary—group (of artists, newspaper owners and staff members, and an unspecified number of attentive and informed readers), who followed the competitions between the Yellow Kid series in the two rival newspapers, and who knew about the copyright request.

The journalist figure is an interesting case in point also because it connects the Yellow Kid comic-tableaux with other parts of the Sunday supplement, or to phrase it slightly differently: The serialized *Hogan's Alley* comic-tableaux fold back onto other parts of the Comic Weekly and thus create fascinating serial interweavings between the diverse features in the newspaper supplements, suggesting that they inflect and inform each other. On December 6, 1896, Pulitzer's staff began to serialize a feature titled "Jimmie's Paper" in the Sunday Comic Weekly, which is a carnivalesque version of a sensationalist newspaper with "EDITORiULS," "iTems of INterezt," short announcements, pieces of poetry, a "giRL's KoLUm," and more (all of which is written in dialect spellings), as well as illustrations ("Jimmie's Paper," 6 Dec. 1896). The editorial information in the left columns of "Jimmie's Paper" conveys that the imagined target audience of this fictive newspaper is "uz kidz"—the young "boys AND GirLs." Taken together, one may read the journalist figure with his patented head in Luks's *Hogan's Alley* series, and the content and layout composition of the serialized "Jimmie's Paper" feature in other parts of the Sunday supplement, as an ironic comment on the making, the selling, and the circulation of a mass newspaper. The journalist figure of *Hogan's Alley* and the fictive newspaper that is printed in other pages of Pulitzer's Sunday *World* demonstrate that the newspaper medium can serve as the breeding ground for serial unfoldings—not only of the serial Yellow Kid but of everything related to the comic figure.

What I find particularly fascinating is how Luks and the artist(s) responsible for the creation of the fictive "Jimmie's Paper" create an expanding web of references by "planting" visual cues for the attentive reader to find and puzzle together.[10] On December 13, 1896, for example, the reader of Pulitzer's Comic Weekly would find two (black-and-white) portraits of the Yellow Kid in "Jimmie's Paper." One shows only the face of the comic figure, subtitled "SANTY WITHOUT A BEERD & HARE"; it has the typical features of the Yellow Kid: a bald head, a round face (and a smile on the face), extremely big ears, high eyebrows, and round eyes. The other is a full-body copy of the Yellow Kid, inserted in a framed one-panel cartoon that carries the caption "CRYSMUS KARTUNE—SANTA GITS STUCK IN THE SNOW IN HOBOKEN." That versions of the Yellow Kid populate the fictive "Jimmie's Paper" is in itself an interesting point, bespeaking the ubiquity of the popular comic figure in the newspapers at that time, on the one hand, and testifying to its spread outside the original Sunday comic-tableaux, on the other. What is more, "Jimmie's Paper" folds back into Luks's *Hogan's Alley* series, not only in the form of the recurrent journalist figure. Luks also inserted the office building of the fictive newspaper in his

---

10. This feature was unsigned; it is unclear whether it was just one or many artists who worked on the serialized "Jimmie's Paper" feature. Because of the way in which the illustrations in this fictive newspaper are drawn, I am guessing that it was George A. Beckenbaugh.

comics series: In Luks's "Valentine's Day" episode from 1897, for instance, the reader would find a note about the "GRATE JIMMIE'S PAY PUR" and a house designated the "OFIS UV JIMMIES POIPER"; in one of the windows of this building, one sees a person named "PERCY WINTERBOTTOM," who is working at a desk. If one turns back to the previous page in Pulitzer's Sunday comic supplement, one would find the name Percy Winterbottom listed in the editorials of "Jimmie's Paper," and the information that he is the leading artist of this newspaper. That Percy Winterbottom is the pen name of one of the *World*'s Sunday comics artists, George A. Beckenbaugh, is only later revealed to the readers of Pulitzer's newspaper ("Father Puncherbocker").

If this weren't enough already in terms of things branching out, illustrated rhymes by Percy Winterbottom started to spread outside of "Jimmie's Paper" into other sections of Pulitzer's Sunday supplement in January 1897, and later during that year, colored half-page comic-tableaux signed by Percy Winterbottom would also be found outside of "Jimmie's Paper" in other parts of Pulitzer's Comic Weekly (see Winterbottom, "A Romantick," "It Worked," and "Wie Trane") and in other comics, as for instance, Winterbottom's colored *Klondike* series published in Pulitzer's Comic Weekly in August and September 1897 (Winterbottom, "Wee Are Off" and "Our Klondike" 4).

In view of this, there are two things I would like to point out: First, it seems that popular serial texts are, to use the medical rhetoric of the 1890s, "contagious"—as if they, once they start to circulate, become uncontainable and expand in all kinds of directions. In this case, it is the serial Yellow Kid that "infects" other newspaper supplement features, which, again, are generative forces in themselves (see Mayer, *Serial* 12–13). Second, the props in the Yellow Kid comic-tableaux are not, or rather cannot be, defined simply as formal redundancies to accommodate fixed expectations. The surrounding cast in Luks's *Hogan's Alley* episodes (and this holds true for the cast in Outcault's drawings in the *McFadden's Row* series) generate meaning in diverse ways—on the structural level of the whole series, on the structural level of an individual episode, and on what you might call a meta-level—and contribute to spinning an expansionist web of references and loops within which the Yellow Kid "lives" and grows. Thus, to look at the serial surroundings allows for insights into the intraserial, interserial, and transserial workings of the comics.

The examples provided in this chapter demonstrate the different dimensions of seriality—that is, the temporal dimension (the cyclic, periodic repetition of something, and the difference between each reoccurrence, which becomes apparent only belatedly) and the spatial dimension. By the latter, I mean the repetitive elements that organize the space in the newspaper page and the acts of consuming—perceiving and processing—the Yellow Kid comic-tableaux, which are spatially serial, too. Furthermore, the examples discussed throughout this chapter offer perspectives on both the iterative mechanisms with which the comics are informed and the expansionist dynamics. Building on these observations, the concluding part of this chapter explores the dynamics of serialization in the text narrative columns in the *McFadden's Row* series.

READING OPTIONS IN THE NARRATIVE COLUMNS

One of the most obvious differences between the *Hogan's Alley* and the *McFadden's Row* series is the page layout: The comic-tableaux in *McFadden's Row* are divided into illustrations (penned by Richard Outcault) and narrative columns (written by Edward Townsend). To make generalizing claims about the narrative columns in the *McFadden's Row* series proves difficult, if not impossible. This has to do with the fact that each of the narratives by Townsend functions in different ways in relation to the illustrations by Outcault each week. For instance, whereas the narratives in the second installment as well as in the seventh serve as a kind of framing prologue to Outcault's illustration, the story of the third episode does not explicitly relate to the drawing of Outcault, except for the fact that the central theme in both the penned version and the written version of the "Election Night" is the presidential election of 1896 (*McFadden's* E3). In this episode, there are only three indirect references between what is narrated in Townsend's columns and what is shown in Outcault's illustration. In the fourth installment of *McFadden's Row*, the short text by Townsend serves as an introductory—and satirical—commentary on a topical real-life event: the horse show at Madison Square Garden, which took place in the first weeks of November 1896. The narrator calls it an "opening speech," which complements what is depicted in Outcault's illustration. At other times, the narrative in Townsend's columns serves as a background to give readers further information about, and interpretative guidance for, the depicted scene on the page (see *McFadden's* E12).

The "chapters," as the narrator calls the texts in the individual installments (*McFadden's* E10), are conceptualized both as stand-alone stories and as consecutive chapters—with causal developments—that interconnect via their recurrent cast of characters. What makes the chapters so interesting for my study on serial dynamics are not just the ways in which they relate to the penned scenes in the respective episodes and how tensions are generated; I consider them conducive for the purpose of my study also because each of the altogether thirteen chapters in the *McFadden's Row* series provides reader engagements that are evoked through a volatile narrating agency, multivocalizations, and different focalizations. The narrator in the text columns is at times an extra-diegetic/homo-diegetic agency, at other times an intra-diegetic/homo-diegetic narrative instance, which oscillates between zero-focalization and external focalization. In some of the episodes, the story line of the fictional universe in which the flats' inhabitants interact is explicitly interrupted by such authorial insertions as "these are but preliminary" (*McFadden's* E12) remarks, "but that is anticipation" (*McFadden's* E8), or "that's ahead of the present stage of the story" (*McFadden's* E9). At the end of the narrative in the first *McFadden's Row* installment in which the central theme is the Yellow Kid's move from Hogan's Alley to McFadden's Row (and, implicitly, from Pulitzer's *World* to Hearst's *New York Journal*), the unnamed first-person narrator announces that "the joined communities will be observed from time to time, for the benefit of the readers of this page, by the present historian and artist" (*McFadden's* E1). Here, Townsend stylizes himself as the "recording" agency, the chronicler of the events happening in the fictional, diegetic world of the Yellow Kid; the columns are also signed by Townsend to suggest that he is the authoritative narrator or reporter of the events. Apart from the fact that the first-person narrator is the only narrating voice that conveys the information in standard English, as compared to the dialect spelling by the inhabitants of McFadden's Flats, what strikes me as noteworthy is how this ending in the first installment invokes the idea of serial enjoyment both as thematic leitmotif of the *McFadden's Row* series (which is expressed in "from time to time" and "for the benefit"), and as meta-reflexive folding back onto the series' place inside the Sunday supplement, which is mediated through the deictic expression "this page" (*McFadden's* E1).

The artists stylize themselves also as participants in their own stories, both in *Hogan's Alley* and *McFadden's Row*. In the "Football" episode of Outcault and Townsend, for example, the narrative voice in the text columns explains: "Outcault was there with me, and his pencil caught the scene just at that exciting moment when the Kid finished a run . . . and made a touchdown, which won the game. The picture shows the glory of that moment" (*McFadden's* E5). The narrator continues that he will explain in words what "the picture shows," and then addresses the readers directly, telling them that even though "no mere words can describe that game," they still can be part of the scene: "You should have seen the girls on top of the coach! But you do—in the picture" (*McFadden's* E5). One might say that Townsend's narrator functions as a kind of viewing aid, similar to a museum guide explaining to visitors what a particular work of art depicts. Readers that had first looked at the illustration and subsequently read the columns are now invited to rescan the page, to repeat their engagement with the page, and to search for the details that the narrator talks about.

This episode proves worthwhile to consider for yet another reason: When Townsend puts the words "the game was between the *Tim McFadden Flatters* and an *unclassed* gang formerly belonging to the *defunct Hogan's Alley*" (*McFadden's* E5; my emphasis) in his narrator's mouth, he implicitly pokes fun at Pulitzer, whose Sunday supplement's comics series is now— that is, with the appearance of the Yellow Kid in the *McFadden's Row of Flats* series—outdated and obsolete. It is specifically the last part of the sentence, the designation "defunct Hogan's Alley," that makes this clear: The metafictional reflection, which compares the newspaper supplements' Yellow Kid series, is enfolded into the imagined, fictive world of the episode, in which the Yellow Kid interacts with other participants of the football game; the "Tim McFadden Flatters" team plays against "an unclassed gang" of youths from Hogan's Alley (*McFadden's* E5). With this utterance, Townsend addresses a "knowing" audience; he appeals to readers' memory of Outcault's previous Yellow Kid series in Pulitzer's Sunday Comic Weekly. This enfolded mockery is played out also on another conceptual level: Townsend's nominalization of the tenement's inhabitants as "Flatters" in the *McFadden's Row* series, as compared to the adjective "unclassed," which serves to designate the tenants in Hogan's Alley, is no accident, I believe. Rather, it echoes a public discourse about the tenement buildings, as brought forward by, for example, William T. Elsing, who claimed: "The word *tenement* is becoming unpopular down-town, and many landlords have dubbed their great caravansaries by the more aristocratic name of 'flat,' and the term 'rooms' has been changed to 'apartments'" (49). By comparing the two rivaling teams, and by describing the tenants in McFadden's Row as the "Flatters" and those in Hogan's Alley simply as an "unclassed gang" (in other words, an unspecified crowd gone astray), Townsend inscribes—for humorous purposes, of course—a social hierarchy into the evaluation of the two teams, and thereby implicitly also of the two different newspapers in which the comics series were printed, with a higher or better standing of the new neighborhood in which the Yellow Kid now lives and the *Journal*'s Sunday supplement, in which the *McFadden's Row* series is printed, and a devaluation of the Hogan's Alley inhabitants and the newspaper these appeared in.

Yet, it is not just the mixing of different levels of narration that causes interesting reader engagements each week. When we speak about the reading options in Townsend's narrative columns, something else stands out, which can best be described as focal tensions. This can be illustrated exemplarily with Townsend's narrative in "The Studio Party in McFadden's Flats," in which Townsend not only changes the degree of subjectivity and objectivity but also the tone of his narrator (*McFadden's* E12[11]).

The opening remarks stage the narrating agency as a knowing, historically, politically, and scientifically informed person, giving the *McFadden's Row* audience a lesson in the architectural history of the city: "As every one knows, or should know, certainly, Tim McFadden's row of flats were, many years ago, the home of rich and fashionable people. Not far from them, and *on the very spot where this paper is printed*, was, until within a couple of years, an old family mansion" (*McFadden's* E12; my emphasis). This is, quite obviously, a metafictional comment on the newspaper and the supplement the comic-tableaux were published in. The next lines add to this pedagogical tone a philosophical stance, which complies with the positivist credo of determinism and social Darwinism prevalent in the nineteenth century: "To me, who believes we receive strong mental impulses from our inanimate environments, the facts are chiefly interesting as offering the probable explanation for the notable social bias lately observed among the Flatters" (*McFadden's* E12).

The narration in this particular episode allows for the reader to take on different attitudes in regard to the things and occurrences described, in regard to the characters represented, and in regard to the opinions expressed in the episode. The philosophical treatise prefacing the actual story in the "Studio Party" episode leads into the description of the inside of the studio and what the Flatters undertake on that day. Some paragraphs in the narration serve to complement what is represented in Outcault's drawing—as, for instance, when we read about what Tim McFadden sees: "He saw uncouth wooden figures with legs and arms in wild disorder, . . . old frames, rugs, outlandish tables and what not," or when the text says that "the cat knocked a plaster figure over" (*McFadden's* E12). The details that are mentioned here are also made visible in the illustration, but there are other parts that do not resonate with what is depicted in Outcault's drawing. Readers who invest in both reading the columns *and* reading the pictorial parts will notice that the columns offer not only further descriptive

---

11. The comic-tableau is available online via the digital cartoons catalog at Ohio State University (http://cartoons.osu.edu/digital_albums/yellowkid/1897/1897.htm). See also Meinrenken's readings of the page ("Ver-rückte" and "Künstlermythen").

details of the art elements and people in the studio but also historical background about the former owners of the building.

That meaning-making of Townsend's narrative columns in the *McFadden's Row* episodes also hinges on what might be termed *serial knowledge* about the Yellow Kid's entourage is an argument I wish to engage with in the next paragraphs. Previously, I analyzed how recurrent visual props operate in the comic-tableaux; in what follows, I intend to look at how intraserial reading options are enabled in the chapters by Townsend. I do this with the help of a short passage from the final episode in *McFadden's Row*.[12] The events take place inside a theater, and all Flatters are part of a vaudeville show—there is a dance act, an acrobat act, a singing act, and other performances. While in the illustration the various skits all take place simultaneously for the reader to peruse, the text columns narrate the chronological order of the show. The passage I wish to focus on tells of an incident between two girls who argue about what they would like to perform on the stage.

In the narrative, the Yellow Kid remembers the following dialogue: "Liz sed she wuz gaw'n t' sing Looziana Loo an' Maggy sed dat wuz jest wot she wuz gaw'n t' sing. I sed it foist sed Liz but I wuz t'inkin' uv it foist sed Maggy" (*McFadden's* E13). The argument between Mary Ellen (nicknamed Maggy) and Delia Dunnigan (named Liz by the Yellow Kid) continues a while, until they conclude: "Liz ye t'ink ye're a Melba o I dunno sed Maggy you aint no Kalvay" (*McFadden's* E13). The metonymic references to Emma Calvé (a well-known French opera singer, who also performed in vaudeville shows) and Dame Nellie Melba (an Australian-born opera singer who performed in New York during the mid-1890s) elicit laughter because they indicate that the two young girls don't have the vocal skills to be opera singers. Readers who do not know the opera stars Nellie Melba and Emma Calvé can still enjoy these text passages because of the way in which the girls' fight for the attention of the Yellow Kid is represented. The dialogue between the two is reminiscent of a vaudeville slapstick skit; here the narrated fight between Mary Ellen and Delia Dunnigan over what they are going to perform on stage in the Yellow Kid's show is a funny act on its own.

The competition between the two girls is also depicted in Outcault's illustration, and thus readers who skip the columns by Townsend can also find delight in the visual representation of two young actresses on the stage

---

12. The page is viewable online (http://cartoons.osu.edu/digital_albums/yellowkid/1897/1897.htm).

platform. One (Maggy) plays "ROSEMARY" and the other (Liz) is impersonating the French songstress "YVETTE" Guilbert (*McFadden's* E13); regular readers of the comics series would know by then how these two girls look and would be able to identify them in the comic-tableau. Mary Ellen wears a red dress decorated with red roses and her mouth is wide open. Her depiction is built on a mixture of media images and literary genres; it is a combination of the character Dorothy in the play *Rosemary* (a comedy by the English play writers Louis N. Parker and Murray Carson that had premiered on Broadway in August 1896, starring Maude Adams and John Drew), Rose-Red of the Brothers Grimm's fairy tale, and the female version of the miller's son in Charles Perrault's *Puss in Boots* (note the booted cat sitting in front of her), who laments "COULD I BUT SEE MY DEAR OLD MOTHERS CASH" (*McFadden's* E13). Liz ("YVETTE") wears long black gloves (media images of these accessories had been circulating ever since Henri de Toulouse-Lautrec sketched Guilbert and the black gloves in 1894). In Outcault's drawing, it is in particular how the individual postures of Mary Ellen and Liz are depicted, that is, the hands and arms, that may arouse laughter: Mary Ellen stretches out her empty hands as if she is begging for money, and Liz attempts to imitate a gesture (and facial expression) of the real-life stage performer in gloves that are a little too big for her hands.

Coming back to the narrative passage quoted above, the name "Looziana Loo" (*McFadden's* E13) refers to the musical song "Louisiana Lou," which is a song about the courtship of a young man to a woman and the love between the two, sung by a man to his beloved.[13] The reference is used as a means to describe how the two girls who are both in love with the Yellow Kid (as the regular and attentive readers of Townsend's columns would know) argue about who is going to perform the song about two lovers. The steady reader of the *McFadden's Row* series would be able to remember the recurrent fights between these two girls. In "Receiving the Returns" (November 1, 1896), for example, Delia Dunnigan (Liz) and Mary Ellen (Maggy) are represented as jealous of each other and fighting over who belongs to the Yellow Kid. The narrator recounts: "Two sweet girls fall against one another with rage, folly and contumely in their hearts. It's the Yellow Kid" (*McFadden's* E3). In another episode, Delia/Liz muses: "Ah, Kid . . . if youse will only be me steady"; she would do anything "to win de

---

13. This was a popular song by Leslie Stuart, which was inserted into the musical by Ivan Caryll and H. J. W. Dam titled *The Shop Girl—A Musical Farce* (1894). Louisiana Lou is not to be confused with William West Winter's 1922 Western story by the same title.

Kid for me own, and trow down [the other] goils all to onct" (*McFadden's E5*). Knowledge about the content of the song as well as about the previous installments in the *McFadden's Row* series is necessary to recognize the multilayered irony in the narrative passage. Eventually, the fight between the two is resolved when Mary Ellen turns her attention to two other boys living in the Flats.

In light of these observations, I wish to conclude my analysis of Townsend's narrative columns by inquiring into how the individual Flatters trigger different patterns of engagement. In Townsend's text passages in the *McFadden's Row* series, each of the surrounding stock characters offers a lens through which readers of the comic-tableaux may access, and apprehend meaningfully, the complexities of urban modernity that are depicted in the pages. Via the heterogeneous crowd of Flatters, different concerns, attitudes, ideas, and opinions are voiced to readers. Townsend ascribed to each of these Flatters specific traits, behaviors, and habits and endowed them with idiomatic expressions, which are repeated each week and which make them identifiable for the reader: The Riccadonna girls, for example, are presented to readers with the same formula each week, namely, *the Riccadonna Sisters (four)*.[14] On the one hand, the formulaic depictions of the Yellow Kid's supporting characters in Townsend's narrative serve as memory cues for those—literate—readers willing and curious to follow Townsend's narrative texts and familiar with the cast to actualize their knowledge about the network of characters; the readers can derive pleasure from their repetitive behaviors and predictable doings. On the other hand, such formulaic elements function as guiding aids for those readers not yet familiar with the cast, in order to acquaint them with their "profession," typical behavior,

---

14. In Outcault's drawings, the Riccadonna Sisters are a mixture of pavement princesses, pre–Ziegfeld Follies dancers, and a kind of pre–Walt Disney Tinkerbells in ballet dresses. The depiction of the Riccadonna Sisters draws on the real-life Danish-born Barrison Sisters, who were five sisters performing in many variety shows, first in New York, then nationwide (as, for instance, at the Columbia World Exposition in 1893) and also in Canada. In 1894, they toured through Europe, with stops in the Folies Bergère and the Moulin Rouge in Paris, as well as in such cities as London, Vienna, and Berlin (a Folies Bergère poster by Alfred Choubrac, 1896, shows them in frilled dresses and black stockings, with legs crossed, smoking cigarettes). The Barrison Sisters were known for their provocative cakewalk dances and sexually suggestive song texts, calling out to the audience whether or not they would like to see their "pussies"; when they raised their dresses, they exposed real kittens to the audience. In summer 1895, one of the five sisters quit the troupe and performed solo. In October 1896, all five of them returned to the US and had a number of guest performances in two theaters in New York again. In Townsend's narrative, they are also described as the "naughty Riccadonna Sisters" (*McFadden's* E4) dressed in "fairy costumes" (*McFadden's* E5).

motives, states of mind, and actions. In what follows, I will explicate this in further detail, beginning with unpacking the reading possibilities inscribed in the female figure Mrs. Murphy and the landlord Tim McFadden (in Outcault's drawing, he is a gray-haired, pipe-smoking man).

Tim McFadden is described as the "most excellent landlord" there is and "a man of means and substance" (*McFadden's* E11). He is a well-tempered, good-hearted elderly man, the proprietor of the flats and philanthropist tenement landlord, who gets along well with everybody and who "cannot abide a strife to stand between his tenants" (*McFadden's* E10); he does everything "for the benefit of the McFadden Flatters," including the organization of game tournaments and other leisure activities, the giving away of Christmas presents, and generosity when it comes to the deadlines for paying the rent. Tim McFadden is a longtime New York resident who is acknowledged by his tenants as a well-informed authority: "What Tim says usually 'goes' with the Flatters without argument or dissent" (*McFadden's* E3; see also *McFadden's* E7). He is also the only one who is able to speak and write in standard English and to speak—at least rudimentary—words in French and Latin (see *McFadden's* E11), which are inserted for humorous purposes. The weekly chapters in the columns gradually develop this character. With the Tim McFadden figure, Townsend creates a tenement landlord who not only cares about the tenants and their personal needs and longings but also looks after the maintenance of the buildings, and someone who has enough money not to be dependent on the on-time rent payments.[15] However, this conception of the Tim McFadden figure is available only to those readers of the comic-tableaux who not only invest in the pictorial parts of Outcault's drawing but put in an effort of continuously reading the Sunday episodes and of connecting the contents of the individual story chapters of the comics' narrative.

Townsend's educated Tim McFadden may elicit humor for the simple reason that even though he speaks "elegant langwudge," as Mrs. Murphy would say (*McFadden's* E11), his sentences are more often than not composed of fillers instead of substantial information. "Let me discourse to you on the standing and situation of this status" (*McFadden's* E3), he announces in one episode; in another he exclaims how satisfied he is with

---

15. Progressive reformers repeatedly denounced the greedy landlords in the tenement districts—in other words, the "absentee landlord" (Riis, *How the Other* 156), which seemed to be the rule rather than the exception (on the "tenants uncared for" by the proprietors and the allegedly concomitant moral decay, see Riis, *How the Other* 155–57). Very often, agents instead of the owners of the tenement houses managed the buildings.

"the evening['s] termination, end and conclusion befitting all social functions in McFadden's Row of Flats" (*McFadden's* E7). Tim McFadden is described as a "greata oratory dan deese Garibaldi. I second da motion to elect heem" (*McFadden's* E1). In "The Season Opens with the Horse Show in McFadden's Row of Flats" (November 8, 1896), it is told that "in his opening speech Tim had only got as far as: 'Twas Napoleon said at the battle of the Nile, 'On with the dance; let joy be undefined,'" for it was then "when Mrs. Murphy's growler dropped on his head. Speaking was not what the Flatters wanted" (*McFadden's* E4). Townsend thus also playfully mocks Tim McFadden's style of conversation, his custom of being a smart aleck, and his seemingly higher social standing.

In a similar vein, the longtime friendship between Tim McFadden and Mrs. Murphy is evident only to the steady reader of the series. Mrs. Murphy, whose maiden name is unknown, is an elderly woman of approximately the same age as Tim McFadden, "an old and loyal Flatter," who lives rent-free in one of the flats (*McFadden's* E10)—we are told that she has not paid any rent since her husband died (see *McFadden's* E9). She is a widow, and the mother of Mary Ellen. In Townsend's chapters, Mrs. Murphy serves as a recurrent gimmick to arouse laughter. Anything she does—be it observing what is going on outside of the flat she lives in, be it ironing, be it participating in a sports game, be it thinking about her deceased husband—gives her a "terrible awful thirst" (*McFadden's* E6). She is always introduced to the reader with the same idiomatic expression, *hasten quickly,* and she elicits humor also because of her own ignorance concerning her drinking habits: "It's little I care for the beer . . . I likes tea much more betterer" (*McFadden's* E8). But there is something in the descriptions about this formulaic Mrs. Murphy character that makes them an interesting case in point: In passages that focus on Tim McFadden and his perception of the happenings, Mrs. Murphy is presented to the reader as a likeable, well-mannered "lady" with whom he shares a past and whose knowledge about the other tenants and advice he appreciates (*McFadden's* E8; see also *McFadden's* E9). Yet, in other parts of Townsend's columns, Mrs. Murphy is presented to readers as a lower-class, hard-drinking woman and quite a rude person, who voices anti-immigrant sentiments (see, for instance, *McFadden's* E1); she is also described as an uneducated person, who does not know who Jefferson Davis was, who does not know what a "chaperon" is (*McFadden's* E3), and who thinks that a studio filled with artwork is a "Joss house" (*McFadden's* E12). In still other chapters of Townsend's narrative, she is a person who pretends to know how to behave in a classy manner and how to avoid "terrible awful mistylish" habits (such as riding in a street car; see *McFadden's* E5); then again, she is depicted as an inexperienced, indifferent person, who "[does not] believe much in going in foreign parts" (*McFadden's* E8). One might say that even though Mrs. Murphy is part of the Flatter community and gets along with most of the tenements' inhabitants (in particular with those who serve her with refills for her beer can), she seems at the same time isolated by her illiteracy, her ignorance, and her constant, predominant concern about and excessive consumption of beer.

Each week, the descriptions of Mrs. Murphy offer to readers both a repetition of the representation of her excessive drinking and a new aspect about her life and her attitudes. As the first-person narrator in Townsend's story claims, the way you interpret a scene or incident, or the way you look at the Flatters such as Mrs. Murphy, "depends upon the viewpoint" (*McFadden's* E7). This holds true for the other inhabitants of the Flatter community. In Townsend's chapters, Mrs. Dunnigan may be regarded as Mrs. Murphy's moral counterpart and the impersonation of the temperance movement, who time and again tries to missionize Mrs. Murphy and convince her that to reduce or give up alcoholic beverages would do her good. In one of the episodes, Mrs. Murphy announces, "I'll be having to give up drinking beer and take to mixed ale to be in the swim," upon which "Mrs. Dunnigan had the poor taste to reply: 'You'd be doing yourself no harm, Mrs. Murphy, if you took to drinking water when you give up beer—soon come the day!'" (*McFadden* E10). In a similar vein, Mrs. Dunnigan's daughter, Delia, mocks Mrs. Murphy's excessive drinking: "'Mrs. Murphy has de only cup here,' murmured Delia, 'and dat is never filled but it's empty, and besides it's a can'" (*McFadden* E11). To those readers of the *McFadden's Row* series who disregard the narrative columns, these traits and habits of the surrounding figures such as Mrs. Murphy do not become apparent immediately. Readers focusing exclusively on Outcault's drawings of the *McFadden's Row* series will only know that there is an elderly, gray-haired woman who often stands alone at a window or near a door and looks outside, and who drinks something from a can (see *McFadden's* E3 and E4).

Townsend's serialized narrative in the text columns works with multiple perspectives and layered descriptions of the characters, which often generate competing meanings. This becomes manifest also in the ways in which Townsend establishes the other characters of the Flatter community. Mrs. Murphy's daughter, Mary Ellen, is introduced to the readers of Townsend's columns as "a good child" (*McFadden's* E1), obedient to her mother, and one taking care of the Kelly baby, as a child who "has a great eye for the main chance," (*McFadden's* E1), yet also as a child that is "haughty" and that is more often than not fighting with the "proud" Delia Dunnigan, even punching her in the face (see *McFadden's* E7). She is ill-mannered, rampant, while at the same time imitating Shakespearean syntax: Macbeth-like, she announces in one of the episodes: "Couldst thou but relieve dis o'erburdened bosom, den would I be thinest" (*McFadden's* E6). She cannot decide on whom she wants to love, the Yellow Kid, Marty Dunnigan (the newspaper boy), or Terence McSwatt (the poet). Since money is really important to her, and because she regards diamonds and sealskin as "necessaries of life," her decision about love depends on income, and because the Yellow Kid does not have any money, the only two suitable caretakers seem to be Terence McSwatt and Marty Dunnigan (see *McFadden's* E3). Mary Ellen is interested in "how much each one earns," because, as she continues to reason, "a lady has a right to look out for de main chanst when she's moving in fashionable society." Thus, she advises herself to "steel your heart till you is sure which of does two mugs is winning de most long green" (*McFadden's* E10). Quite obviously, Mary Ellen impersonates the idea of a young woman trying to escape poverty and the "dead sore and weary of life," and to move upward in society, through marriage—in this case, a possible relation to either a mischievous newspaper boy or a cynical poet (see *McFadden's* E6).

The words uttered by Mary Ellen compete with the narrator's patronizing view of her; he implicitly mocks her longings and her need for recognition and admiration and directs attention to her exposure of bad manners (her quick-temperedness, her readiness to use physical violence, her inability to take criticism, her jealousy and rage, her contempt for other girls, in particular the four Riccadonna Sisters, whom she tries to outshine with her beauty). Moreover, Townsend's other female figure, Delia Dunnigan, time and again pokes fun at Mary Ellen and her at times violent, unladylike behavior: "'Goodness gracious, Mary Ellen, be a lady!' giggled Delia Dunnigan, who wickedly rejoined at Mary Ellen's discomfort. 'Be a lady, whativer you be, Mary Ellen! Even if youse hasn't a powder rag like I has, be a lady!'" (*McFadden's* E3).

Mary Ellen Murphy and the other two girls in Townsend's columns—Delia Dunnigan on the one hand and Kitty Dugan on the other—offer to the reader different idea(l)s of womanhood in society. Delia is a free-spirited, at times rebellious child, who is always voicing what she thinks, who is smart, "in love, and consequently giddy," and a child who likes to perform as an actress, knows how to behave like a "lady," but who also likes to plot against others, to name but a few of the traits Townsend ascribed to her (see *McFadden's* E10). Kitty is the mute "angel" and "wonderful maid with a much more wonderful hat" (*McFadden's* E1) who seemingly successfully imitates the manners of bourgeois society and European fashion fads (this resonates in the representations of Kitty in Outcault's illustrations). And Mary Ellen seems somewhat lost or torn between these two "models." Each reader can decide whether to assess the orientation of Mary Ellen Murphy—love is money, money is love—or value it as wrong; adopt her indecisiveness or consider it a weakness of her character; laugh at her pretentiousness or approve of her efforts to escape a life in poverty.

To refer to Lisa Yaszek: "Audiences coming from various discursive formations may all laugh" not only at the serial comic figure but also at or with the surrounding cast of characters, yet "the joke may be different for these various readers, depending on their socio-historical positions" (30). In Townsend's narrative columns, the McFadden's Row inhabitants are sites of ideological contestations and projection screens for the cultural fears, anxieties, desires, longings, tastes, and prejudices of modern urban America. Each Flatter is a kind of prism through which readers may read and understand cultural diversity, class differences, and the chaotic urban world. The Flatters offer multiple interpretive choices to the readers. As a reader, you may adopt a particular viewpoint and assess an ideological orientation, while distancing yourself from others.

What is more, the heterogeneity of voices and multiple perspectives in the narrative depictions of each Flatter are complicated through the representations of each of the Flatters in the illustrations. Verbal representations are either complemented or contrasted by, or completely excluded from, the pictorial representations in the illustrations by Outcault; the father of the four Riccadonna Sisters, for instance, is not present in Outcault's drawing, and neither is Kramer (the grocer), nor Kelly, the barkeeper. So, there are still further possibilities for reader engagements inscribed in Townsend's and Outcault's *McFadden's Row* comic-tableaux. For example, while Outcault's drawing in the first episode in Hearst's American Humorist shows a representation of the colored White Wing street sweeper named Tempy (in all-white uniform and cap, with a broom in his hand), the illustration in the second episode, which first introduces the name Tempy and the profession of the street sweeper to the readers of Townsend's columns, does not include a representation of this male figure. In Townsend's narrative of the second episode, we find the description of "Tempy, who paraded with the White Wings[16] before Li Hung Chang" (*McFadden's* E2). It seems

---

16. The so-called White Wings were a street-cleaning brigade that was established by George Edwin Waring, Jr. in 1895.

as if Townsend wanted to retroactively create a verbal image that would fit Outcault's pictorial representation. What the example of Tempy also demonstrates is that Townsend provides his readers with a number of reading options that hinge on, and would confirm, ethnic and racial stereotypes. Signor Riccadonna is modeled after the ethnic stereotype of the Italian immigrant, who "in his younger days played a street organ," (*McFadden's* E11) who is now "the pushcart man" in the area, and who is "dumb with amusement" when there is something exciting going in McFadden's Row (*McFadden's* E1). The flats' owner, Tim McFadden, addresses him with the abbreviated version of his name, Ricca, and thereby conveys a condescending manner with regard to the Italian inhabitants in the tenements (*McFadden's* E1).

In addition to this, Townsend offers to the readers stereotypical representations of African Americans—in the form of the Sambo blackface stereotype known from and perpetuated in popular minstrel shows and vaudeville, which targeted a white middle-class audience (see Jenkins, *What Made* 70–71 on "the system of typage," the profitability of stereotyping, and the racist implications of stereotyping in vaudeville; see also Bentley, esp. 15–17; Rogin; Byrne; Hodin). In the first installment of the *McFadden's Row* series, the reader meets a child that carries the derogatory name Congo and that is teased by two other children on the streets; as the narration continues, he "jump[ed] high in the air when he first caught sight of [the] radiant brightness [of Liz's red hair]." In Townsend's narrative, the outer appearance of Congo is reduced to a description of his bulging eyeballs, his "eyes looking like two hard-boiled eggs, spotted with ink" (*McFadden's* E1; in this particular episode, readers would find a representation of a blackface child right behind Kitty Dugan). The first episode concludes with a brief mentioning of "disturbances" between Congo and the Yellow Kid. Only in the second episode do readers get more information about this child and his family background (*McFadden* E2). What Townsend delineated in words, Outcault complemented in the visual representations—his depictions of African Americans were limited to inflated lips, an open mouth, bulging eyes, and kinky hair, and by so doing, he confirmed discriminatory images of blacks.

In the end, the kaleidoscopic view on immigrant city life, the urban heteroglot, the disintegrating forces of modernity, and the different lines of conflict that Outcault and Townsend (and, of course, Luks as well) inscribed into the comic-tableaux is still very limited. Even though the artists present a heterogeneous crowd in the *McFadden's Row* series, this crowd is constructed as a predominantly white urban community. With the exception of one episode, in which we find a stereotypical, discriminatory representation of a pigtailed Chinese character with slanted eyes, dressed in yellow (*McFadden's* E7), there are no visual or verbal representations of Asian immigrants, and the diverse indigenous people are omitted, too (again, with the exception of one episode, namely, *McFadden's* E5). The Yellow Kid comic-tableaux, then, while offering a heterogeneity of voices and perspectives, and while instigating multiple readings, clearly convey specific lines of conflict—power versus powerless along the lines of race, class, ethnicity, and gender—and especially in terms of inside and outside, or inclusion versus exclusion.

As the next chapter will show, this takes place not only on the narrative plane of Townsend's chapters but also on the visual plane of Outcault's as well as Luks's illustrations in the individual episodes, in the form of the spatial relations of the respective figures (and the walls, fences, and other "lines" that include them in the scene or prevent them from participating). In view of the conceptual, thematic, formal, and narrativized dichotomy of inclusion and exclusion, the following chapter will provide case studies on the questions of which specific areas of knowledge are produced in the Yellow Kid comic-tableaux and how and with what implications for meaning-making.

CHAPTER 3

BRANCHING AREAS OF INTEREST IN THE COMIC-TABLEAUX

IN THE PRECEDING CHAPTER, I focused on the cultural work the Sunday comics performed in the context of other media options and cultural practices of the same time period, and explained the aesthetic principles that enabled this work. I mapped out the patterns of repetition and variation intrinsic to the weekly comic-tableaux, the liminal status and protean quality of the Yellow Kid, the interpretive modes offered in the narrative columns in the *McFadden's Row* series, and the functions of the immediately recognizable, formulaic inventory in both the *Hogan's Alley* series by Luks and the *McFadden's Row* series by Outcault and Townsend. One of the things I have argued is that serial props such as the twins Alex and George embody dynamisms of serialization—of replication, spinning out, and spread. They illustrate that the series' aesthetic operations are also marked as such in the comics.

Building on these observations, this chapter will argue that the aesthetics of branching out also pertain to the manifold areas of interest and knowledge in the Yellow Kid comic-tableaux. Both *Hogan's Alley* and *McFadden's Row* operate with, to use Shane Denson's expression, a "wide spectrum of docking points" (n. pag.). He makes this argument in regard to the contemporary television show *The Simpsons,* and stresses that the series "manage[s] to speak in several tongues at once, addressing a variety of disparate audiences with messages, allusions, and references [that] speak to their various interests and areas of knowledge." In very similar ways, the serialized Yellow Kid comic-tableaux are tailored to a diffuse audience. The areas of knowledge and interest that are inscribed into the pages include references to current events, political issues (local, national, and foreign), and topical debates. Moreover, the areas of interest in the Yellow Kid comic-tableaux include explicit references and allusions to popular entertainment forms of that time, especially to vaudeville, and to popular songs, performers, plays, nursery rhymes, and more. Last but not least, visual and verbal humor in both *Hogan's Alley* and *McFadden's Row* does not work on one single level and does not hinge on bottom-up demarcations but branches into different directions in order to serve different "tastes" of a heterogeneous readership. While the doings, customs, and leisure activities of the upper classes are the predominant issues for satire and parody in both Luks's and Outcault's Yellow Kid series, to say that they direct their humoristic attacks exclusively toward the high-society members so that lower classes may laugh *at* them does not suffice. As Mary Wood states in her introduction to the Yellow Kid comic-tableaux: "Much of the humor . . . mocks the rich and at other times it appears to highlight gross caricatures of the poor" (n. pag). According to Wood, the pages generate pleasure for a diffuse audience because, for one thing, they "[subvert] the increasingly codified roles assigned to the rich and the poor." For another, the Yellow Kid comic-tableaux also elicit pleasure because "we can also see *hints that some readers* might be laughing *at* the Yellow Kid and his mischievous gang" (my emphasis). While I would endorse Wood's claim about the multiplicity of perspectives, I am hesitant to go along with her in regard to the subversive potential of the comics pages. The Yellow Kid episodes are filled with class-inflected parodies, and mockery diverges into different directions; yet while the pages destabilize hierarchies, they also reinforce hierarchies along the lines of social, racial, ethnic, class, age, and gender differences.

The present chapter will examine the areas of interests and knowledge in the Yellow Kid comic-tableaux and the ways in which they encourage manifold readings. To study each individual episode in the two competing series, and to test all the docking points for their reading options is impossible. So, specifically, I wish to go through the ways in which the notion of *imitation*—and kindred notions of copy, counterfeit, replication, make-believe, emulation, or simulation—is negotiated in the pages, and how readers are invited to take part in the various profusions. This is not a random pick, of course. There are reasons for this choice of focus for the examinations in the present chapter.

When Miles Orvell speaks about American culture in the closing decades of the nineteenth century as a *culture of imitation,* or alternatively a *culture of replication,* he is not particularly thinking about the newspaper comics in the mass papers and the ways in which these were enmeshed in this context. Rather, Orvell focuses on the areas of literature, art, photography, and material culture; the conditions under which the various cultural forms were produced and consumed; and the implications the acts of imitation entailed (see also Glenn). Yet, popular media such as the Sunday newspaper comics were also woven into this "fabric" while simultaneously fueling the idea of a competitive market and imitative culture.[1]

Competitions and replications pervaded the serial life of the Yellow Kid. In this chapter, I show that these processes also penetrate the pages' *form* and the pages' *contents;* discourses of originality, genuineness, authenticity on the one hand, and copy, imitation, and fakeness on the other infuse the comics series. As I will be arguing in two distinct, yet related approaches, it is not just topical questions about cultural forms and objects ready for imitation, and questions about the value of artistic production and creativity in times of mechanical reproduction that are negotiated in the Yellow Kid comic-tableaux. The series' episodes also articulate, visually as well as verbally, social issues about the emulation of styles, clothes, behaviors, and customs of "others," which then again are linked to questions about the participation in or exclusion from urban life. I furthermore argue that the notion of imitation refers to techniques of copying skits and formulaic expressions from other media formats, especially vaudeville—in other words, the comics are filled with issues related to the imitation of "older" forms of entertainment and leisure. The notion of imitation is played out not only on the plot level of the comic-tableaux—referring to elements in the diegetic world of an individual episode in either *Hogan's Alley* or *McFadden's Row*—but also and on an extratextual level referencing elements outside of the diegetic worlds. Because of this, knowledgeable as well as less educated readers, interserial readers as well as intraserial readers, regular readers as well as one-time readers can find delight; gratification and reading pleasure may differ, but the prismatic docking points allow for a diffuse audience to participate in the meaning-making.

---

1. Several book reviews of Orvell's *The Real Thing* engage with his deliberate exclusion of popular cultural products and practices (see Green).

The analysis in the second part of this chapter ties into these observations. I use the examples of George Luks's as well as Outcault and Townsend's "Horse Show" episodes (Luks, "A Genuine"; Outcault and Townsend, "McFadden's Row of Flats—The Season"; see figures 3.3 and 3.4). The horse-show episodes from *Hogan's Alley* and *McFadden's Row* are conducive for my purpose here because the reference to an extratextual, actual real-life event—the equestrian fair at Madison Square Garden—invites us to inquire into how the comic-tableaux construct alternative spaces and possibilities for participation, or nonparticipation, for that matter. In the horse-show episodes, fake inclusion and class mimicry are the axiomatic subtexts along which the artists visually and verbally formulate the inequalities of modern urban life. Whereas Luks's horse-show episode is predominantly concerned with questions of accessibility to and participation at the Madison Square Garden event, Outcault and Townsend's installment of the same day focuses especially on the question of conspicuous imitation. One question I wish to pay special attention to is how spatial relations and other visual modes such as gestures, positions, facial expressions, and other factors generate reading options. Before I come to that, I first discuss how the notion of a real/genuine/original Yellow Kid and copies, imitations, and "fakes" of the comic figure are negotiated in the series and with what implications.

REAL/FAKE

With the emergent new possibilities of cheap and fast mass-productions, mechanical reproducibility, and the rapid and wide diffusion of commodity products, worries about piracy, theft, (unauthorized) copies, fakes, simulations, doublings, and imitations were not far behind. Technological advances triggered anxieties about distinguishing "the real" and imitations (see Ewen and Ewen 124–29; Lears, esp. 268–70). Concerns about the impact and consequences of reproductive technologies also become recurrent "story" units in the Yellow Kid comic-tableaux in both Pulitzer's Comic Weekly and Hearst's American Humorist. For instance, in Outcault and Townsend's "Studio Party," one of the framed pictures presented in the comic-tableau is endowed with the following caption: "DiS iS a REAL ETCHING PRiCE 3 CENTS" (*McFadden's* E12; see figure 3.1). In conjunction with the framed picture, this expression, which is "etched" onto the surface of a painted picture within a comics page, humorously attends to the anxiety of differentiating between an "original," or real piece of art, and an artful copy at a reduced price. In the background of the "Studio Party," there looms a copied version of Sir Frank Bernard Dicksee's famous *Romeo and Juliet* (1884); tagged to it is a note with an ironic comment about the relation between the value of this artwork and its price: "BREAK AWAY ROMEO DiS CELEBRATED PITCHER HAS BiN MARKED DOWN TO $4,89" (*McFadden's* E12). That this is implicitly referring to the legislative situation of art in the 1890s (including the taxed imported foreign art), which was discussed in the periodical press of that era, is only meaningful for those who knew about the trade law—a law that "drew a clear distinction between art and its commodity-form on the basis of public and private ownership" (Meixner 183). Furthermore, one finds a copied version of Alf Cooke's 1895 chromolithograph *"Trilby" (Miss Dorothea Baird)*, which presented a moment of Dorothea Baird's performance of a theater adaptation of the character Trilby in George du Maurier's popular novel by the same title. Baird's impersonation of Trilby, entering the stage barefoot and smoking, wearing a striped skirt and a uniform jacket, became a famous moment that Cooke represented in a chromolithograph poster, which Outcault copied into this Yellow Kid comic-tableau. The narrator in Townsend's columns informs the reader that it is Delia Dunnigan who "was dressed for the part" (*McFadden's* E12) of Trilby. In the illustration by Outcault, Delia imitates the posture of a real-life actress that was captured in a chromo, and Delia's imitative act is reproduced in the form of a sketch on a white canvas (see figure 3.2). For readers who are not familiar with Dorothea Baird's enactment of du Maurier's Trilby character or Cooke's chromolithograph of Baird's stage performance, and are thus unable to recognize and make sense of the mise-en-abyme narrative, Outcault's representation of the sketch of a female person might still elicit humor because of the way in which it references and ridicules the female figure standing in front of the canvas.

From the moment that the Yellow Kid started to spread extensively, it was the comic figure that became the site for struggles over and tensions between original, real, genuine, authentic and copy, fake, replica, imitation, counterfeit—and these struggles were contended in the comic-tableaux, and marked visibly either in a self-ironic manner or in the form of open accusations of copyright infringement. More than once did Outcault make use of the notion of imitation in order to voice the theft of "his" ideas and the copying of the Yellow Kid. In the "Opening Night" episode, for example, a framed panel placed onto a wall—much like an advertisement or an important public notice—carries the exclamation: "IMITATION IS DE SINCEREST FLATTERY ALL RITE EVEN IF IT IS STEALING—BUY ONLY DR.

FIGURE 3.1. Richard Felton Outcault and Edward Waterman Townsend, "McFadden's Row of Flats—The Studio Party in McFadden's Flats," *New York Journal*, 3 Jan. 1897, *American Humorist*, p. 4 (detail). Library of Congress, Serial and Government Publications Division.

FIGURE 3.2. Richard Felton Outcault and Edward Waterman Townsend, "McFadden's Row of Flats—The Studio Party in McFadden's Flats," *New York Journal*, 3 Jan. 1897, *American Humorist*, p. 4 (detail). Library of Congress, Serial and Government Publications Division.

PAINS PINK PILLS FER PIMPLES" (*McFadden's* E10). This announcement has no thematic relation to the happenings that are described in the narrative columns and that are shown in Outcault's drawing. What makes it relevant for my discussions here is how different reader engagements are stimulated through the mixing of mockery of advertising strategies and advertising contents with an insinuation of plagiarism. While the first half of the phrase operates as an implicit warning directed toward all those who copy someone else—one is tempted to say that the words blare out to informed readers the thoughts that had been bothering Outcault ever since he had lost control over the proliferation of the comic figure—the second half reflects and mocks the advertisements for medical health that populated the print culture of that time period.

This notion of copying is reiterated in a number of episodes in *Around the World with the Yellow Kid,* too. In the installment titled "The Yellow Kid Shakes His Trotters in Old Madrid," one of the boxes in the illustration carries the announcement that "DE PIRATE BISNESS IS A HOT SUCCESS IN NEW YORK" and that those who play in this business know very well what they are doing and are known to everyone—thus, there is no need "TO MENTION NAMES" (AW E9). In another episode, the effects of plagiarism are visually-verbally negotiated as follows: In the third installment of *Around the World,* Outcault and Block evoke the so-called Poe-Longfellow controversy—in parodistic manner.[2] The Yellow Kid quotes the lines from the first stanza of "The Bridge," a poem by Henry Wadsworth Longfellow: "I stood on de bridge at midnite an de clox wug punchin de hour. an de moon got scared an hid hisself behind de dark church tower" (AW E3). Not only does the Yellow Kid pervert Longfellow's poem but he also forgets to provide the source reference, and instead signs the passage with his name, Mickey, thus pretending that he is the original author of the piece.

Even before Outcault sent out his letter for copyright registration for the Yellow Kid, attempting to claim exclusive rights to and economic control over what he considered his solitary, creative artwork, and prior to his move to Pulitzer's rival Hearst, discussions about the status and value of the comic figure had already started in the comic-tableaux. To convince the readers of the Sunday *World* that his is the only true Yellow Kid, Outcault, for instance, had strategically placed a substitution warning in one of the other *Hogan's Alley* episodes—directing the readers' attention to his

---

2. In simplistic terms, Poe accused Longfellow of imitating and stealing from other poets, implying a lack of originality; see Piacentino.

signature as a sign for authenticity and credibility.[3] On September 6, 1896, Outcault asked the readers of the *Hogan's Alley* series to search for his signature. A box situated at the bottom of the page, to the left, presents the exclamation "DO NOT BE DECEIVED NONE GENUINE WITHOUT THIS SIGNATURE" ("Li Hung Chang"), which is followed by Outcault's signature; this is an illoctuionary request addressed to the readers of Pulitzer's *World* to look out for, and avoid, imitators. It suggests that there might be other artists copying something that Outcault penned. The exclamation functions as a means to inveigle readers to remain faithful to and exclusively focus on his artworks, meaning the artworks signed by him, which are, as the evaluative adjective "genuine" makes clear, of no significance and value without the authenticity feature. The framed exclamation also conveys the value Outcault ascribed to the Yellow Kid and his other creations and mediates an implicit fear that others would make money with ideas he originated. It is hardly surprising that Outcault added the indication about copyright registration in the episodes of the *McFadden's Row* series in Hearst's *Journal*.[4]

Attempts to claim ownership over the Yellow Kid recur time and again both within the diegetic world of the McFadden Flatters—in the form of explicit remarks printed on the kid's shirt, through implicit or explicit utterances spoken directly or indirectly by other characters in the comic-tableaux, or through the narrator in the text columns—and outside, in the form of paratextual references. Outcault's first "McFadden's Row of Flats" installment for Hearst's *Journal* shall serve as a case in point here. At the top of this episode, next to the announcement that "E. W. Townsend, Author of 'Chimmie Fadden'" (*McFadden's* E1) produces the narrative passages in the columns, the reader is notified that the series is "Illustrated by R. F. Outcault, Originator of 'Hogan's Alley'" (*McFadden's* E1). The declaration "originator" was surely meant to establish Outcault as the sole comics artist to produce the Yellow Kid comics; yet, apart from this, the announcement that the *New York Journal* now had under contract the artist who invented "Hogan's Alley" was also a clever strategy by Hearst to lure those readers who were familiar with the series and who bought the Sunday *World* for

---

3. Here see also Susan Strasser's interesting discussion of substitution warnings in advertising at the turn of the century in her study *Satisfaction Guaranteed* (esp. 83–88).

4. In March 1897, the False Notice of Copyright Act was passed, which would impose a penalty of $100 for purposely issuing, selling, or importing articles bearing a misleading copyright notice (see Hamlin 84); exceptions to this were trade journals. Interestingly enough, Outcault printed "Yellow Kid copyrighted" notices in the 1896 *McFadden's Row* comic-tableaux, but none of these are to be found in the comics he drew in 1897 and 1898.

the precise reason that this newspaper held the popular Yellow Kid pages, to switch to the *Journal*.

The question of who the original and authentic kid is is also discussed in the Yellow Kid comic-tableau's diegetic world. On the Yellow Kid's shirt, we read: "SAY! WHEN WE GiTS IN OUR NEW HOME WE'RE GOiN TER BE DE REAL TING" (*McFadden's* E1).[5] It is not just the Yellow Kid that Outcault fashions as authentic, but the entire entourage ("we") that he sets out to establish as the only "real" crowd. This is further verbalized and visualized by the words printed on the travel bag the kid carries: "DE KID HOGAN'S ALLEY MCFADDEN'S FLATS" (*McFadden's* E1). Through the crossed-out words, and through the mentioning of a "new home," Outcault explains to the readers of the newly established *McFadden's Row* series in Hearst's newspaper that the Yellow Kid and his entourage had formerly populated a distinct corner of New York and are found under a new address now. He also suggests that the readers who are acquainted with the Yellow Kid (from Pulitzer's paper or via billboard posters, ads, and placards on the streets) will find the same kind of pranks and mischievous doings in the new setting; all that has changed, the remarks explain, is the background, the new "home." This is echoed in a statement printed on one of the boxes in the background of the page, which is held up by an unnamed boy: "A FOXEY MOVE—BE GEE / FROM DE ALLEY NOW WE GO DOWN INTO MCFADDEN'S ROW . . . BUT WE'LL BE DE SAME OLE CROWD WHERE QUIET AINT ALLOWED AN TE MAKE YE LAFF WE'LL ALLUS DO OUR BEST" (*McFadden's* E1). The pronoun *we* in this announcement is ambiguous; it not only refers to Mickey Dugan and his move to another place together with "DE REST OF DE GANG" but it can also be understood as a playful strategy—with Pulitzer as the implied addressee—to mockingly refer to Outcault's "foxey" maneuver to work on a Yellow Kid series for another newspaper while still continuing to draw cartoons for Pulitzer's Sunday supplement (see Meyer, "Urban"). The remark also conveys that there is nothing to fear; those readers who are familiar with the Alleyites—that is, the series' protagonist and the other recurrent characters and animals—and who have decided to switch the newspapers do not have to get accustomed to anything decisively new or different. There is comfort, for it is the "same ole crowd," just moved to another section in the city. The Yellow Kid and his entourage simply found, the text continues to proclaim, "A BETTER PLACE TE STAY." This resonates with a statement printed on

---

5. Questions about originality and authenticity also pervade previous episodes, in which the Yellow Kid announces to the readers that he, and only he, is "de real ting" (Outcault, "Hogan's Alley Folk Have a Trolley Party").

another box in the background of the page: "SAY! HOGAN'S ALLEY ... WE WAS GITTIN TIRED OF IT ANY WAY" (*McFadden's* E1). In Townsend's narrative columns, the "move" to another place is made a topic, too: The third-person narrative voice explains to readers the "procession" of a crowd "down the streets from up Cherry Hill." In addition to that, various McFadden Flatters give their respective impressions of the newcomers and of the "aforetime flower and pride of Hogan's Alley" (*McFadden's* E1). Similar to the example mentioned before, these statements can be meaningful in two ways: as an interserial reference and inter-diegetic comment on the move from one place to another, and as a metatextual pun alluding to the move of former *World*'s staff members to Hearst's newspaper.

George Luks's Yellow Kid comic-tableaux in Pulitzer's *World* likewise had a part in the discussions over the originality and authenticity of the Yellow Kid, and in the debates about imitation and copyright ownership.[6] In his episodes there are, I would say, two prevalent strategies with which he negotiates the status of the Yellow Kid and conveys it to the readers of the Sunday Comic Weekly: Luks shifts the focus from the notion of stealing of intellectual property based on the idea of individual, genius creativity and single authorship to the lack of inventiveness of the rival newspaper—and implicitly of the artist, Outcault. Furthermore, Luks puts emphasis on the newspaper in which the Yellow Kid rose to fame and reached popularity and delineates the *World* as the legitimate owner of this product. Two brief examples shall illustrate this. In Luks's first installment of the *Hogan's Alley* series (published on October 11, 1896), readers are informed about that the fact that a new "parent"-artist had adopted the familiar Yellow Kid—the words on the Yellow Kid's dress convey: "i GOT ME MUDDERS SWITCH SEE?" (Luks, "Training for the Football"). While this remark announces that there will be another "mother" from now taking care of the Yellow Kid (and implicitly of all the other Alleyites), it also reassures the readers of Pulitzer's *World* that this switch is nothing to be afraid of; the "mudders" may have changed, but apart from that nothing is really different, and nothing will considerably change.

This trope of parenting is reiterated in another episode. In "Thanksgiving Day in Hogan's Alley" (November 22, 1896), the journalist figure (which I have thoroughly analyzed in the preceding chapter) hides on a roof, with a scroll hanging down in front of him; the words proclaim, in rhyme: "HE'S HIS MUDDERS ONLY BOY, HOGAN'S ALLEY'S PRIDE EN

---

6. Other newspaper (and magazine) artists participated in the debates, too (see, for instance, McCarthy, "The Popular Disease").

JOY ODER YALLER KIDS DAN HE ARE FAKES AN IMATASHUNS SEE." Here, the joke is targeted toward Outcault—Luks is fashioning Outcault as the "mother" who has given birth to "ONLY" one child, suggesting that Outcault doesn't do anything else than draw the same "BOY" each week. But that is not all: Masked as parody, the rhyme also mediates that there are other versions of the Yellow Kid out there, but that the only true and original Yellow Kid is to be found in Hogan's Alley, the place where the kid belongs. The remark is a warning and a plea for established readers of Pulitzer's Sunday Comic Weekly to remain faithful to the original Yellow Kid in the *World* and not to turn attention to another place—that is, to the "other" newspaper printing imitations of the original Hogan's Alley kid (see Luks, "Training for the Football").

Similarly, in the "Open-Air School" episode, Luks presents the following commentary on the Yellow Kid's shirt: "SAY! THEY'RE IMiTATIN' ME ALL AROUND TOWN! I'M THE SUNDAY WORLD'S KID AND AND HAVE BEEN FUR A YEAR & A HALF! ALL OTHERS ARE FAKES" (see also Winchester, *Cartoon Theatricals* 65–66). What is voiced here in this self-referential comment is not so much a critique about unauthorized copies and copyright infringements; rather, he suggests that the newspaper is the place of the kid's birth and thus the legitimate "parent" (and genuine owner) of the comic figure. So, Luks's formulation in this episode does not tie questions of originality and authenticity to artistic creativity and to the genius of one particular individual author but to the place in which a specific object emerged.

The repeated and varied negotiations in the Yellow Kid comic-tableaux in both Pulitzer's *World* and Hearst's *Journal* about imitations invite readers to select—that is, to decide which of the two comic figures is "the real" and "the authentic" and implicitly, also, which of the two is the more valuable, the superior one. As such, readers are immersed in the reflections on original/real/authentic and copy/imitation/fake and are asked not only to ascribe an aesthetic value to the Yellow Kid but also to submit a judgment and to class themselves according to their preferences and interests, with either the *Hogan's Alley* or the *McFadden's Row* protagonist.

This decision-making inscribed into the pages is not only or exclusively directed toward those readers who are acquainted with both series and would be able to compare and distinguish the versions of the Yellow Kid comics series. Those readers not familiar with the medial context and the competition between the newspapers, and one-time consumers of either a *Hogan's Alley* or *McFadden's Row* episode are also part of the negotiations about originality and imitation, yet in different ways than those described above. Outcault's "Horse Show" episode, to which I will return in greater detail in the next section, proves a case in point in this regard (see figure 3.4). To the left of the drawing, right below the first text column by Townsend, there is a boy who is wounded—he is shown with bandages and first-aid equipment, and some scratches. In the accompanying speech balloon, we read: "I GUESS I WONT TRY TER IMITATE FALLIN OFF DE HOUSE ANY MORE I'LL IMITATE DE YALLER KID HE IS EASY" (*McFadden's* E4). First of all, this enunciation bespeaks the iconic simplicity of the Yellow Kid—in other words, it is easy to copy the comic figure. This can be understood in different ways: On the one hand, the boy's remark refers to the fictional world of this particular episode, suggesting that he will emulate what the Yellow Kid is doing, who is at the center of McFadden's courtyard pretending to be the ringmaster of the horse show. On the other hand, the idea of the imitability of the Yellow Kid serves as an allusion to the extratextual world in which the comic figure was reproduced numerous times and proliferated widely.

At the same time, the phrase in the speech balloon and the representation of the wounded body serve to comment on the unnamed boy's doings in the past weeks. First, this boy had imitated Slippy Dempsey's falling act and fell off a building (*McFadden's* E2), and then, in the following week, he was described as "NEAR DEAD" (*McFadden's* E3). What is thus interesting about the representation of the unnamed boy is that while the remark "imitate de yaller kid" can be meaningful for any reader in different ways, the visual depiction of the bandaged boy, and the remark that he intends to quit the imitative falling act, are only meaningful as a reference to previous episodes for those regular readers who had been attentively following the boy's actions.

In another *McFadden's Row* episode, the recurrent Slippy Dempsey figure also comments on the unnamed boy and his falling act: "DERE'S A KID IMITATING ME HE'LL KILL HISSELF IMITATORS ALWAYS DO" (*McFadden's* E2). Similar to the speech presentation just mentioned, this statement evokes two possible readings: Dempsey's remark is related to the depiction of another boy falling down, and it thus operates on the plot level of the specific episode; the last three words of this comment can also be meaningful as a reference to the many imitators of the Yellow Kid comic figure in the real-life world. While the unnamed boy serves as a self-ironic element in altogether three episodes to comment both on his own failed attempts to copy another boy's action and on the multiple—fictional and real-life—copycats replicating the Yellow Kid, Slippy Dempsey's remark about imitators always killing themselves also carries an undertone. The words are strategically imprinted to voice critique, and a tongue-in-cheek warning, which Outcault directed toward all those artists—in particular George Luks but also all the other anonymous artists—who did copies of the Yellow Kid. Implied are also, I would say, Outcault's frustrations about his loss of control over the Yellow Kid comic figure.

In the next section, I will further develop the idea of the diffusion of interpretative possibilities, with a special focus on the question of how the notion of imitation is intricately tied to questions of participation. My goal in the ensuing analysis is to demonstrate how artists develop class-inflected parodies that branch out to various readers, on the one hand, and to go through the ways in which the aspects of inclusion and concurrently of exclusion pervade the respective installments, on the other. What interests me in particular is how *spatial relations* and other visual modes generate reading options, and how knowledge hierarchies are inscribed in patterns of humor.

IMITATION AND PARTICIPATION—THE HORSE-SHOW EPISODES

On Sunday, November 8, 1896, both Hearst's American Humorist and Pulitzer's Comic Weekly printed a Yellow Kid comic-tableau, in which Mickey Dugan and his friends are part of a "Horse Show." With their horse-show installments, the Sunday supplements' artists George B. Luks and Richard F. Outcault and Edward W. Townsend foreshadowed a topical, annual (media) event—the National Horse Show at Madison Square Garden—which was to open on Monday, November 9, 1896.[7] The newspapers (not only those printed and distributed in New York but also papers printed in other cities across the country) were saturated with articles about the upcoming equine exhibition and horse competitions, and while it took place, the main sections during the week and the following Sunday editions covered the "glittering social drama" ("High-Class Horses") in the form of brief reports about the blue ribbon and rosette winners, editorial commentaries and short essays about the meaning and importance of this event for New York City and its citizens, elaborate listings about the attendees of the show (spectators as well as horse dealers), illustrated articles about the fashions worn by the elite "pillars" of society (such as, for instance, the

---

7. The National Horse Show took place annually in November and was a mixture of festival, show, fair, trade, and judged competitions; in 1896 it opened on November 9 and closed on November 14.

family members of the Belmonts, the Astors, the Vanderbilts, and the like), caricatures penned by the newspapers' leading artists, and printed gossip talk about the so-called social 400.

In Luks's "A Genuine Horse Show in Hogan's Alley" and Outcault and Townsend's "The Season Opens with the Horse Show in McFadden's Row of Flats," respectively, the upcoming event is depicted as a colorful, energetic spectacle, an outside-street equestrian circus, in whose central ring animals and "humans" gather together to interact and perform a joyful show for readers. They are quite "congested" pages, filled with riding crops lying on the ground, horseshoes, dice (in Outcault's *McFadden's Row* episode), a mattress from which the batting oozes out (in Luks's *Hogan's Alley* episode), a number of animals—cats, dogs, parrots, goats—a heterogeneous group of participants and onlookers, a music band, action (such as a fistfight, in Luks's comic-tableau), the press, and lots of banners, billboard-like signs, and placards. There are vaulting acts—Liz performs a vaulting competition in Outcault's horse-show episode; in Luks's episode, it is the Yellow Kid who "vaults" in front of the readers. There are rodeo acts (in Luks's installment), stunts, jumping competitions, and more.

The artists frame their respective horse-show episode with different captions ("*A Genuine* Horse Show" on the one hand, and "*The Season Opens* with *the* Horse Show" on the other), and by so doing put emphasis on specific aspects that are related to the equine exhibition. Whereas the indefinite article in Luks's title does not immediately trigger an extratextual reference or invoke Madison Square Garden's fair, and while the term *genuine* suggests that questions of authenticity, originality, or imitation play a more important role than other issues, the definite article in the title of Outcault and Townsend's *McFadden's Row* episode at least implies a reader who would recognize the specific horse show that is referenced. Although they both deal with the same topical event and bring it into the rows and alleys of Lower Manhattan, the artists chose different compositions for their horse-show scenes, such as the placement of the Yellow Kid in relation to the other elements.

The horse-show episodes—and the Yellow Kid comic-tableaux in general—allow for *associative viewings* that evoke interpretative ambiguities. The crowded layouts of the comic-tableaux, in which the Yellow Kid functions as the eye-catching device, prompt readers to engage in a back and forth, up and down, crisscross viewing of the individual episodes. In his insightful study *The Origins of Comics*, Thierry Smolderen identifies William Hogarth's graphic narratives as precursors and inspiration to the Yellow Kid comics, in that Hogarth's "engravings invite a variable, zigzagging circulation of the reader's gaze" (5; see also 57). Jens Balzer speaks about a perceptual process of *dispersed looking* to grasp the profusions of signs on the pages ("Hey, schau" 28, 33; see also Duval 106 on the "invitations à glisser" and 109 on how the comics pages afford to "fait glisser le regard et bouleverse la composition échelonnée"[8]). This is different in the Yellow Kid comic strips that were printed parallel to the comic-tableaux series in Hearst's *Journal,* in which panels function as a structuring device in the reading process[9]; they determine the order with which the images in sequence are supposed to be read in order to establish meaningful coherence.

In the comic-tableaux, the mode of zigzag viewing of the individual episodes extends to the serial props that recur week after week, and that the consumers of the respective series are invited to locate. Such dynamics of proliferating perception cued by the erratic arrangement of the visual elements resonate with the profusions of verbal remarks—that is, the dialogues between characters, between animals, and between inanimate objects; the captions that are scattered here and there; and the different narrative voices—which enable the Yellow Kid comic-tableaux to accommodate the different reader interests. What I will be doing in the ensuing pages is to explore how specific competencies are prompted in the horse-show comic-tableaux. I begin by investigating how the Yellow Kid comic figure operates in the respective episodes.

In George Luks's "Genuine Horse Show," the Yellow Kid is placed in the geometric center of the page, standing on top of a brown horse, holding up his arms and holding the reins that are knotted to the horse's ears. As usual, the Yellow Kid is barefoot, and wears his long yellow dress (in this episode, it is additionally endowed with a prize-winner blue ribbon); also as usual the kid smiles at the viewer, and announces something via his long yellow shirt: "DIS IS DE ONLY GENUWiNE HOARSE SHOW BUT ES USUAL I HERE DAT DERE GONTO IMITATE US AT MADISON SQUARE GARDEN—JUST FOR SPITE I'LL GO UP DERE EN TAKE DE FURST PRISE FUR DE BEST KOMEDIAN HOARSE IN DE BISNESS." Apart from the fact that this comment carries word plays, based on the homophony of words (*hoarse* and *horse* as well as *here* and *hear*) to evoke laughter—for literate readers with basic linguistic knowledge—it is composed of dichotomous deictics (*they/us* and *up/down*), which serve to indicate class differ-

---

8. Here is a paraphrasing translation of Duval's argument: The comics pages afford the gaze to slide down, over and across the staggered composition. My thanks to Nicolas Labarre.

9. In my conclusion to this study, I say more about the Yellow Kid comic strips.

ences between the inhabitants of the tenement houses in "Hogan's Alley" and the richer citizens of upper New York. The Yellow Kid's shirt might be understood as a platform and channel for Luks to write himself into the page; in satirical manner he comments on the—alleged—emulating of the behavior of upper-class people by socially lower-classed groups. By suggesting that the horse show at Madison Square Garden is but a fake, a copy of the "genuine" or authentic, real horse show that is taking place in the (fictional) "Hogan's Alley," Luks mocks the social elite; the remark on the kid's shirt, implying a lack of originality among the upper classes, suggests that they can only find enjoyment in their constrained, rigid, reserved lives by imitating the—joyful, lively, and spectacular—tenement districts' leisure activities.

In addition to this, the words on the Yellow Kid's shirt reflect on the status of the kid as a humorist element in the comics series: "I'LL GO UP DERE EN TAKE DE FURST PRISE FUR DE BEST KOMEDIAN HOARSE IN DE BISNESS" (Luks, "A Genuine"). What is interesting here is that because the term *business* has no fixed relation to one particular semantic field, the remark on the kid's shirt generates ambiguity and triggers three—interrelated—readings: First, it is a pseudo-economic comment on the *horse trade business* "up there" at Madison Square Garden, which is more of an entertainment or comedy show than a serious business venture. Second, it functions as a comment on the *entertainment business,* of which the Yellow Kid is a part—on the diegetic level, it is also a visual-verbal comment on the kid's own doing as a "komedian horse" performer who stands upon the horse's back to entertain the onlookers. And third, it is also a meta-reflexive comment on the Yellow Kid, which was, as the informed reader would know, a prize-winning, best-selling device in the "hoarse" (in the sense of harsh, severe, or rough) *newspaper business.* The different readings are made possible through the lexical ambiguity in the remark on the kid's shirt.[10] It is a playful strategy—similar to the double and triple entendres in variety shows[11]—to arouse delight in various ways: The interpretation of the term *business*—that is, the way you frame the remark—largely depends on the reading context, the degree of literacy, and different degrees of knowl-

---

10. Lexical and syntactical ambiguities, deriving very often from unknown referents, are two of the most prominent strategies that both Luks and Outcault make use of—inviting word associations during the reading act.

11. The effect of double and triple entendres is that people not familiar with the alternative meanings of a word or a sentence may not understand the allusions and may thus be excluded from laughter. On the tradition of double entendres in variety shows, see Erdman.

edgeability about current events and the larger social issues.[12] Luks writes himself as a well-informed reader into the page, and allows other knowledgeable readers to distance (and distinguish) themselves from other, let's say, less sophisticated readers. As Soper would say, the pages "inevitably splinter into multiple meanings in the hands of various readers" ("From Rowdy" 152). If read out loud, the words *horse* and *hoarse* also call to mind the colloquial term *whores*[13]; in relation with the second term, *business*, the expression on the kid's shirt has yet another connotation, adding to the previous reading options the idea of the Yellow Kid (the "komedian hoarse in de business") as offering to display, or prostituting himself and his talents to please potential consumers.

The point here is that ambiguities also emanate from what you might call an auditory dimension of and in the comic-tableaux. Although I am not able to produce empirical data that would confirm that the written enunciations in Yellow Kid comics pages were not only quietly consumed but actually repeated aloud as well, explained or read to other nonliterate readers, it seems reasonable to suggest that the phonetic spellings of the imagined dialect that the comic figures and inanimate objects speak, and in particular the orthographic misspellings of the English language and the typographic specificities, invite a phonographic reading—in other words, an imitation of the pronunciation—of the remarks in the respective episodes. In this sense, reading experiences and pleasures are multiplied, hinging both on the silent and acoustic reading ("hearing") of the words and phrases that are framed in the illustrations by Luks and Outcault. It is not only the production of an "inner speech" that I am thinking of—an inner speech that forms in the process of deciphering the letters and words and then rehears-

---

12. In this context, see also the comment printed on a broken collar, which is placed around the tail-docked, prize-winning brown horse in the middle of Luks's horse show page: "DIS IS ONE OF DE SHINIEST COLARS AGONE AND I'LL BET DEY TINK ITS SILVER." This announcement is doubly connoted: For one thing, these words poke fun at the parading of jewelry at the horse show, which interrelates with articles in the main section of Pulitzer's paper on this day and throughout the week. For another, the words *colar* and *silver* relate to the conflictual money issue during the presidential campaign in 1896 (goldbugs versus silverites), which had just ended with Republican McKinley's victory over the Democrat Bryan on election day, November 1, 1896. This visual-verbal detail of the page can thus be read both as a satiric commentary on the pretentiousness of the "other" half of New Yorkers and as commentary on the Democratic party program during the elections of 1896; while Pulitzer's newspaper had a Democratic leaning, it was reluctant to assist the Democratic candidate William Jennings Bryan and his silver coinage program (see Wood n. pag.; on these matters, see also Gambone 165f and 203f).

13. My thanks to Jana Wachsmuth for pointing this out to me.

ing them, processing them, without actual vocal output for others to hear; this is something human beings do all the time when reading or thinking.[14] I mean also an overt articulation of sounds in the reading acts. And very often the phrases in the Yellow Kid comics have to be read out loud in order to make sense.

In Outcault and Townsend's horse-show episode from the same day, something else happens with respect to the Yellow Kid. The words on his dress announce to the readers: "DE MADiSON SQUARE GARDEN SHOW MAY HAVE MORE FiNE CLOSE BUT DEY AINT IN IT WiT US FER LOOKS AND WiTS" (*McFadden's* E4). These words cue a parodistic reading: In this sense, the horse show is a (conspicuous) parade for bourgeois society to show off their luxurious fashion fads rather than a platform to present horses. In other words, the ingredients for a successful horse show are lots of fashion, lots of affectations, and no horses, and that is exactly what the horse show in McFadden's Row looks like (see also McCarthy, "The Horse Show"). This is reflected in the illustration as a whole: There is only one meager horse in Outcault's drawing, placed right behind the Yellow Kid; all the other horses are made of wood—two rocking horses to the left of the page, and a hobbyhorse to the right. In one of the poster-like, framed text passages in Outcault's illustration, we read that this horse had been "SECURED [BY DE MANAGEMENT . . .] TO MAKE DE SHOW CONẑiSTENT" and had been awarded with "DE PRIZE FER BEIN ALIVE" (*McFadden's* E4). It is quite a grim sense of humor that Outcault writes into his drawing here, alluding to the short life-spans of city horses in service working both as transportation vehicles for passengers and delivering goods—and who fairly often died of exhaustion on the streets (see McShane and Tarr, esp. 27). Outcault mediates the contrast between the prim and proper horses at the national horse show, strutting around in the ring to impress and entertain the patrons, and the harsh life that working horses in the cities actually had.

The clothes (of those in the front and also the onlookers of the scene in the background) are the central issue. And, this idea is further substantiated by means of the conversations in the narrative columns of *McFadden's Row* horse show, by Edward Townsend: "'De graft of de Horse Show isn't de horses,' said the Yellow Kid, as he and the Dunnigan Twins were discussing it. 'De show is de folkses.'" As the narrator then continues, in an equally ironic tone, "The naughty Riccadonna Sisters (four) supplied the

---

14. For further information, see Rosenblatt (on transactional reading) and Ridgway (on the "inner ear" in the reading process).

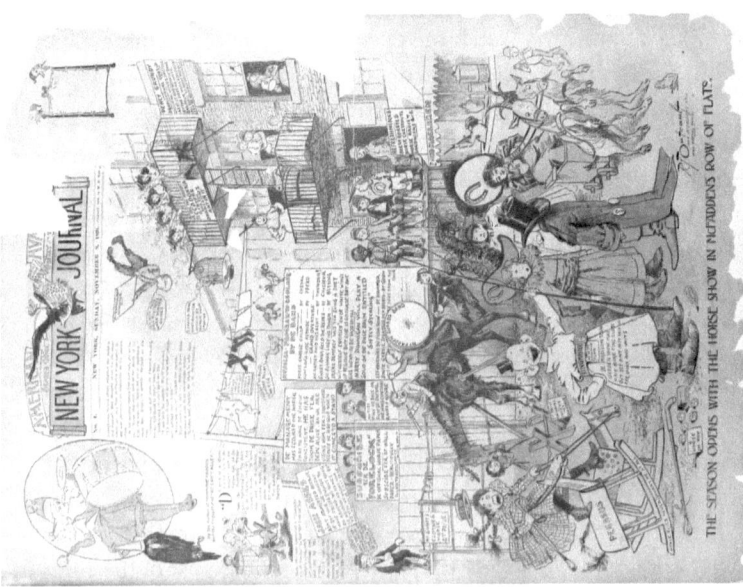

FIGURE 3.3. George Benjamin Luks, "A Genuine Horse Show in Hogan's Alley," *The World*, 8 Nov. 1896, Comic Weekly, p. 5. San Francisco Academy of Comic Art Collection, The Ohio State University, Billy Ireland Cartoon Library & Museum.

FIGURE 3.4. Richard Felton Outcault and Edward Waterman Townsend, "The Season Opens with the Horse Show in McFadden's Row of Flats," *New York Journal*, 8 Nov. 1896, American Humorist, n. pag. Library of Congress, Serial and Government Publications Division.

fashion, and scandal . . . and Tim McFadden represented the wit and eloquence so noticeable at the Garden show" (*McFadden's* E4). In Outcault's drawing, the Riccadonna girls watch the events from one of the fire escape balconies to the upper right of the page, dressed in their regular tutu attire, leaning onto the rail, legs crossed, and smoking cigarettes. Attached to the balcony is a framed sign, announcing: "WE ARE THE NAUGHTY RICCADONNA SISTERS AND THE BARRISONS AIN'T IN IT" (*McFadden's* E4). As mentioned before, the Barrison Sisters were five real-life sisters who performed provocative dances and sexually suggestive song texts. The metonymic reference serves as a cue for readers familiar with this context and will bring enjoyment because of the (connoted) associations it gives rise to.

Humor in the *McFadden's Row* horse show is geared toward what Outcault and Townsend identify as follies of the social upper class (i.e., falseness, hypocrisy, and the importance of outer appearance at social events). This is echoed also in the way the Yellow Kid is dressed in this particular show. First of all, the kid wears a tin-cap (a miniature version of the black cylindrical gentleman's hat) and oversized jackboots, and instead of the typical, loosely hanging long yellow dress, here the protagonist of the comics series is shown wearing a dress laced up with a "RINGMASTER" belt and ornamented with an appliquéd piece of "ME CONSUELLO PLAIT" (*McFadden's* E4). This is a misspelled reference to the real-life socialite Consuelo Vanderbilt, member of the well-known Vanderbilt family (she was frequently referenced in accounts of the ladies' toilette in the nineteenth century). In Outcault's drawing, the Yellow Kid's gored garment and the "Consuello plait" reference function as a visual-verbal parody on the so-called Consuelo skirt, a "Ladies' Seven-Gore" skirt that, according to the sewing pattern in the *Tailor System* instruction manual (1896), is side-plaited at the back, with under-folded plaits forming flutes at the side seams below the hips (H. P. Evan Co. 42–43; see also 50). By representing the Yellow Kid as a kind of caricaturesque clotheshorse, Outcault pokes fun at the high society's affectations, and in particular at the female members of the upper classes who follow European (aristocratic) fashion fads and turn themselves into trophy women, on display for admiration by others.[15] Yet, Outcault

---

15. Dress codes and the display of fashion at the National Horse Show had already concerned Outcault the year before, when he drew oversized hats, buttoned coats, and immensely big puffy sleeves (to name but a few visual elements here) for the comic-tableau titled "The Horse Show as Reproduced at Shantytown" (printed in the *World*'s Sunday supplement on November 17, 1895). A week earlier in the same year, the *World*'s other famous artist, Walt McDougall, had illustrated the upcoming horse show, and had put center stage the pretentiousness of the show's attendees (see McDougall, "What Our Annual"). Dress codes, fashion display, and especially the question of how

also formulates his parody in the direction of those—lower-middle-class—women who copy certain sewing patterns and attempt to imitate the dressing styles of the upper-class women.[16]

Through the representations of the various pieces of clothing in the Yellow Kid comic-tableau, Outcault echoed the predominant line of argument (and complaint) in the numerous accounts of the horse shows at Madison Square Garden, namely, that it had in recent years turned into a (conspicuous) practice of a display for fashion and wealth of the social elite, and that the focus had shifted from the central arena to the surrounding boxes, from the horses (the "beasts") to the—female—attendees (the "beauties") of the show (see Saltus; see also Charlotte Smith). Yet, again, the social satire is not only directed toward New York's upper classes; Outcault's irony cuts both ways: to the upper class, and more generally, to Anglo-Saxon dominant culture (customs and conventions). The satiric view inscribed into this particular Yellow Kid comic-tableau is, by extension, directed toward, and includes, all those who ape older traditions or try to imitate Victorian dress conventions, decrying the New York upper classes, and more generally the American "aristocracy" as "fakes" of the original. It is not just the members of the upper class and British aristocracy that face mockery, but also the middle class, whose attempts to emulate (and sham) aristocratic, Victorian modes of style and behavior are lampooned. That Outcault simply, and exclusively, pokes fun at New York's high-society's habits, clothes, and behaviors is thus too reductive a view of the page. There is no one single level of humor serving one single reader gratification. Laughter is evoked in at least two ways in Outcault's illustration: top-down and bottom-up. On the one hand, readers may smile at the visual exaggerations of the clothes and postures presented in the horse-show comic-tableau, or they may laugh *at* the kid and the others' failed imitation of upper-class dress codes—nothing really fits together, including the attached sign "ME CONSUELLO PLAIT." On the other hand, or in addition to this, readers may laugh with the kid and at the ridiculous upper-class doings.

In Outcault and Townsend's horse-show comic-tableau, it is not only the protagonist's ragtag clothes that serve to mock upper-class fashion

---

to choose the right garment are also the key issues in other newspapers; the target audiences, however, differ. The *New York Herald,* for instance, catered to an upper-middle-class audience, as compared to the working- and lower-middle-class audiences of Pulitzer and Hearst (see Roeder 59).

16. One might argue that the visual insertion of the appliquéd plait on the Yellow Kid's "self-made" dress is an allusion to the practice of "[giving] away dress patterns and sewing kits" (Barth 213) to women attending vaudeville shows.

fads and the lower classes' attempts to imitate the "pomps." Molly, who is standing right next to the Yellow Kid, is wearing an overlarge feather hat and a green dress with an oversized sash and ruffled collar covering her neck and shoulders, and another boy right next to Mickey Dugan is wearing a black top hat, boots, and a blue-colored tailcoat, all of which are too big for him. Brought together, these elements in Outcault's drawing not only parody dressing codes and fashion displays but also serve as an ironic, self-reflexive comment on the comics page's characters and their clothes and behavior, turning them into ridiculed versions of themselves. Viewed in this way, the kid's remarks about the "FINE CLOSE" and the "LOOKS AND WiTS" are thus doubly encoded, and humor is inscribed in two ways: as strategically guised (social) satire about emulating clothes and behaviors and as playful self-deprecating humor. The recurrent Kitty Dugan figure is another interesting case in point here: In Outcault's horse-show episode, Mickey Dugan's sister is endowed with a big hat (emblazoned with a horseshoe), a puffy dress (or at least a dress that is too big for her figure), and gloves. She pretends to be riding in an open harness carriage: She sits in a simple, wooden curricle, and this wooden curricle is drawn by two prancing goats (if readers move their eyes a little farther down, they recognize that the goats prance because there is a frog sitting in their way). This depiction of Kitty is ambiguous: For one thing, the goat-drawn carriage can be read as a caricaturesque representation of the obstacle-driving competition at an equestrian exhibition (this interpretation is triggered when the focus is put on the two goats prancing in front of the obstacle—the frog). For another thing, the riding calls to mind the leisure driving of a woman, and might be understood as a caricature of an upper-class woman's appearance in public space (here, in the form of the children's goat-carts attraction at Coney Island). This reading option emanates when readers focus on Kitty's attire and posture and when knowledge about boulevard harness driving is applied; it is also triggered when (regular) readers actualize their (serial) knowledge about Kitty's recurrent emulative acts, that is, her efforts to imitate high-class habits and fashions.

With respect to the interpretative possibilities in the horse-show comic-tableaux, the different patterns of humor, which are built on quite distinct forms of knowledge, bring to light how different degrees of engagement are generated in the pages. Apart from predictive slapstick or gag situations that readers familiar with vaudeville acts would recognize immediately, and expect and enjoy (such as characters hitting each other, "by accident," with all kinds of devices, or people stepping on another person's—unfitting—clothes), humor in the comic-tableaux also intricately draws on extratextual allusions (to, for example, the doings of real-life people). In the following, I wish to unravel the various patterns of humor and show how humor caters to different addressees.

I would first like to draw the attention to a billboard-like box filled with words in Outcault's illustration for the *McFadden's Row* episode. In the background of the horse show arena, one finds a "MUSICAL PROGRAM," which lists what else is going to happen during the day. What is interesting about this program is that the (at times nonsense) jokes that Outcault wrote onto this sign depend on different kinds of knowledge. The first lines of the program, "HORSE A HORSE GALOP—BY CHEVAL" and "HOW LONA RODE ASTRIDE—BY PFERD," for example, can elicit enjoyment in two ways: For one thing, the announcements are readable as verbal gags, when "cheval" and "Pferd" are identified as "foreign" words and then, in the act of reading back, are related to the beginnings of the phrases. Then, the lines will become apparent as gags based on language games—a fictive composer named "cheval" playing a musical composition that follows the rhythm of a horse gallop, and, in the second case, a horse composer playing a horse rider in astride position. For another thing, the remark about Lona riding astride is an explicit reference to Lona Barrison, who caused a great stir at the real-life Madison Square Garden event when she entered the arena on her horse—Pulitzer's *World* published detailed (and illustrated) accounts of Lona Barrison's entry at the horse show. The remark is thus a verbal cue for readers familiar with reports about Lona Barrison's appearance at the horse show, and her usually sexually provocative performances on the stages of New York's variety theaters.

Meaning-making often rests on the level of education, on literacy, and on extratextual knowledge about specific persons. The child Kitty Dugan—whose recognizable feature is her large hat—and the male figure who is placed next to her (in the right-hand corner of the Luks's horse-show comic-tableau), dressed in a yellow buttoned coat, yellow gaiters, yellow pants, a yellow shirt, and a yellow hat, shall serve as examples to illustrate this. Kitty Dugan shakes hands with a boy dressed as an adult, and "converses" with him via her hat; similar to the Yellow Kid and the surrounding characters, Kitty Dugan uses her clothes to communicate with the reader. The words on her hat display the following question: "HOW DYE DO FATTY YOU ALWAYS TURN UP AT DE SHOW DON'T YOU?" (Luks's "Genuine Horse Show"), a question to which she does not receive a response. One can read this interaction between Kitty Dugan and Fatty as a visual-verbal mockery of small-talk pleasantries at social events, as a means to make fun of introducing habits and the exchange of greetings in public spaces, as, for instance, between men and women. Yet, for those readers who were familiar with the reports about the regular attendees of the horse show, this Fatty whom Kitty Dugan mentions, carries a different meaning: Fatty is Luks's ridiculed, infantilized version of Charles (Fatty) Bates, who won in the harness horses category that year, and who had won a number of blue rosettes in previous years.[17] In the "Horse Show" episode, Luks addresses both the readers who knew about the real-life stable owner and who would consider the caricature of Bates humorous and the readers who did not know and who would simply enjoy the interaction between two funny-looking children dressed in red and yellow.

The representation of a group of figures placed in the lower left side of the page is another interesting case in point in this regard. In the corner that is "PRESERVED FUR DE PRESS" (Luks's "Genuine Horse Show"), one finds not only a number of unnamed male characters sitting on boxes in front of a bench, telegraphing (there are two wires, invoking the idea that there is a telegraph connection to an office), drawing, or taking notes, but also the recurrent "HED PATENTED" journalist figure and the green parrot, with which regular readers of the *Hogan's Alley* series were familiar. The parrot announces, via a speech balloon: "SAY! DIS IS ME MASK AND I'M OUT FUR DE DOE SEE!!! YOU WOULDN'T TINK I WUS DE PARROT?" The mask the parrot references is a human-looking face, which upon closer inspection reminds us of Luks's caricaturesque portrait of Outcault printed earlier that year in Pulitzer's *World* (see "Cartoonists on the Staff"). Luks included visual parodies of Outcault in many of his *Hogan's Alley* comic-tableaux as a means of implicit teasing. This bantering is, however, only fully understandable, and only arouses laughter, for those who knew how Outcault looked, and the remark "OUT FUR DE DOE" (see also Luks, "President-Elect") only makes sense as an allusion to Outcault for those who knew about his departure from Pulitzer's paper and move to

---

17. A caricature of Bates is also displayed in McCarthy's paneled comic on the horse show, which was printed on the same day in Pulitzer's comic supplement. There, Fatty is placed in the upper left part of the page, where he performs "The Horse Show Shake" with one of jockeys (McCarthy, "The Horse Show"). The equestrian fair was one of the leading topics in the November editions of the newspapers (and not just those of Pulitzer and Hearst), and pictures of the participants appeared in the different sections of the papers; one of the most often portrayed people was Charles Bates. Ever since he started exhibiting horses at the Madison Square Garden horse show in New York in 1890, pictures and caricatures of Bates had been printed in diverse magazines and newspapers, and advertisers and clothing manufacturers played a role in circulating images of the stable owner, too. One can assume that readers knew about Bates and how he looked.

Hearst's *Journal* because of the larger paycheck he received from the latter for doing Yellow Kid comics.[18] These elements, then, are visual-verbal "codes" or playful inscriptions (in-jokes) that Luks writes into his page, which are unintelligible for those not familiar with Outcault's looks and his leave from the *World*.[19] This further explains, then, the diffuse audiences addressed in the pages, or the different—imagined—reader group formations that are inscribed into the Yellow Kid comic-tableaux in both comics series, I should say.

While the previous example helped illustrate how some of the elements in Luks's horse-show episode are geared toward Outcault as implied reader as well as toward readers who are well informed about the competition between the two leading New York City newspapers, there are other elements in the "Horse Show" episode that demonstrate how Luks speaks to both a one-time consumer of Pulitzer's Sunday *World* and a regular reader, and by so doing generates different ways of gratification. To explain this, I would like to draw attention to the two grinning babies dressed in yellow, sitting on the ground, placed in between the center-stage prize-winning horse and the goat pulling at the blue ribbon tied to the brown horse; each of them wears a white hat with the exact same wording: "DE FURST PRIZE BABY SHOW" (Luks, "A Genuine"). That these two evolve as regular, serialized, twin replicas of the Yellow Kid and then transform into the protagonists Alex and George in a separate comics series is an aspect I have explored in the preceding chapter. In the "Horse Show" installment in the *Hogan's Alley* series, the yellow twins and their accompanying twin toys are endowed with at least two functions: First, the grotesqueness of these two babies (extremely large heads in relation to the rest of their bodies, their attire, and their broad grins) invites readers to laugh and enjoy them as a visual gag. Second, for the regular reader of Pulitzer's Comic Weekly, the two babies are memory cues, triggering an intraserial reading of the Yellow Kid comics. In Luks's "Horse Show," the formulaic, serialized twins serve to activate the readers' knowledge about the "Baby Show" episode, which Luks had penned two weeks before. There, the Yellow Kid had announced

---

18. The remark "out fer de doe" appears in many ways in Luks's *Hogan's Alley* comic-tableaux. While the expression serves to allude to Outcault here, the words were placed in other corners of and in relation to other characters in the pages, too, and thus function differently. To be "out for the money" was a well-known expression that was perpetuated in many songs performed in variety shows (see Barth 219).

19. The idea that the Yellow Kid comic-tableaux were endowed with secret codes or messages, directed toward very specific readers (in this case Outcault), is articulated in Tom De Haven's novel about the nineteenth-century newspaper world, too (see De Haven 288, 318).

via his shirt: "DEM LiTEL YALLER KIDS iS DED SURE WINNERS" (Luks, "The Great Baby Show"). The child in leapfrog position a little farther to the front of the horse-show episode is likewise a visual echo of a visual element in Luks's "Baby Show" episode.

Through such elements as the yellow twins Alex and George, humor in *Hogan's Alley* is serialized. Laughter that is elicited in one episode is reactivated and carried to another episode. For the regular reader of the Comic Weekly, the yellow twins with the remarks printed on their hats provide a form of belated reward for the reading of the past installment, a reactualization of the past in the present—one might call this retroactive reading pleasure. One-time consumers of Pulitzer's Sunday *World* are excluded from this kind of "extra" delight—readers who only started to buy and consume either Pulitzer's *World* or Hearst's *Journal* (or both) in, let's say, 1897, did not have at their disposal the foils of preceding issues against which to read the current episode. Reading pleasure, however, can also be derived instantly from the yellow twins, as an element of quick—visual—slapstick. Laughter is generated immediately as well as retroactively, with the consumption of the next episode.

Such props as Alex and George illustrate that humor works both "inwardly" (*within* one episode and in multiple directions) and "outwardly" (*between* and as a continuation of different episodes). What we can observe from those examples is that the network of references spans extensively within the episode (in words and pictures) and beyond the individual installment. In view of these observations, the remainder of this chapter intends to examine how spatial relationships generate interpretative options. My contention is that in all their openness for projection, both comic-tableaux offer what might be called middle-class perspectives on urban life.

In the top left corner of Luks's horse-show page, a scared-looking horse with its mouth wide open and tongue sticking out, which had been "SKIED BY DE HANGON COMMITTEE" (Luks, "A Genuine") dangles helplessly on a wooden stake with clotheslines. To the left of this horse, there is a boy in his "FLYIN MACHIN" (created by Luks as another recurrent element in the *Hogan's Alley* series, as I have indicated in the previous chapter), who holds a feather duster, and announces via his metal tray: "DERES NO FLISE ON DAT HOARS." The visual-verbal interaction between the boy with the flying machine and the horse is cued not only by the referential remark of the boy ("that horse") but also by a feather duster held in the direction of the horse, and the viewing direction (as well as the facial expression) of the horse. For those readers who browse the page without paying attention to the words or to the various lines in the page, the two interconnected visual elements may arouse laughter (the boy with the flying machine, in itself already funny to look at, who is wiping the terrified-looking horse with a duster; a horse that finds itself in the most uncomfortable position possible, with legs stretched in all directions). Similarly, the look and the pose of another horse can elicit humor: A tongue hangs out of the horse's mouth and the front hooves are hanging above the fence. The horse seems to be panting due to the effort of trying to come in and participate in the happenings inside; the horse's request, "LET ME IN?" is not heard, though. While these elements are certainly funny to look at, both horses and the ways in which they are positioned also invoke the idea that not every horse is allowed into and has access to the arena. One horse cannot come in due to the erected barrier; another horse is banned from the show ring because it was not able to jump high enough in the high-jump competition at the horse show. An unskilled horse brings no prizes, and is, consequently, pushed to the margins of the show. As a result, "DEY'VE BEEN STRiNGiN' HIM." This is echoed in the representation of an "OLD SKATE" placed in the left in Luks's comic-tableau. This "old skate" is a pale, meager, unhealthy-looking horse (bones show, giving the impression of the horse being ravenous), which kicks a group of people to the ground (and out of the picture frame, for all that is seen is a pile of feet and legs), thus expressing the contempt about the disqualification and elimination from the show by the judges because of age.

All this is certainly entertaining, but I think that these elements carry a subtext. The elements in Luks's comic-tableau are filtered through an ideologically inflected anthropological lens: The boy's cleaning of the "skied" horse with the feather duster, for example, can be understood as a commentary on the hygienic problems in the tenement areas. It is a middle-class-filtered view that conveys anxieties about the filth, dirt, smell, and contamination coming from the housing congestion in the tenements—including the stench of the manure and urine caused by horses in a horse-powered city, and the potentially disease-carrying flies (see McShane and Tarr). In Outcault and Townsend's horse-show episode of the same day, it is the words printed on the clothes that convey the olfactory experience and expose one of the serious problems in the densely populated tenement districts. On a shirt tied to the clothesline, we read the following remark by an unidentified first-person voice: "I WISH THE OLE MAN WOULD GET A NEW SUIT OF UNDERWEAR WE NEED A REST—BADLY" (*McFadden's* E4). Outcault is quite skillful in guising a critical comment about the smell in the tenements with a visual-verbal pun: On the one hand, the pronoun *we* refers to the inhabitants of the flats in McFadden's Row. This reading option is made possible by the visual connection between the clothesline, the building to which it is tied, and the people in the building. On the other hand, the deictic term can mean in reference to the clothes that hang together in a row on the laundry line. Read in this way, inanimate objects are turned into fabled, speaking beings that converse with each other through words and gestures (as, for instance, the position of the two black stockings right next to the shirt). Clothes and other nonliving objects operate as speaking parts in the scenes to comment on the smells in their environment.

The argument about a filtered view and class-inflected readings can be further illustrated with the help of a smiling "WESTURN KID" in Luks's horse-show episode (located a little above the head of the brown horse). The kid performs a Wild-West-show-like rodeo act on a wildly snorting saddle horse; two green birds, placed in a cage to the right of the rough rider, comment on this, in tandem: "DAT WESTURN KID'S A HIGH FLIER EN HE HAINT GOT NO WINGS" (Luks, "A Genuine"). This gun-wearing male rider with rumpled, chin-length red hair and in fringed pants successfully lassoes the "OLD SKATE" below. Once again, this acrobatic act (of a horse that seems to be walking a tightrope, which is held by another boy) and the lasso skills of the rider are funny to look at. Luks draws on an entertainment genre familiar to most of the readers of the Sunday papers, namely the Wild West shows that toured through the country (and worldwide) in the second half of the nineteenth century, implementing and spreading clichéd images and formulaic narratives of frontier experiences and the westward expansion.[20] This detail in his *Hogan's Alley* installment—the rough rider on a snorting horse—is also amusing because Luks's visualization of the "flying" rider on a tightrope parodies the rodeo act in the popular Wild West show. Usually horsemanship and lassoing skills are performed and shown to the audience by actors, capturing a wild steer or horse in the quickest time; here, however, all the grinning bronco rider is able to lasso is an "OLD SKATE." Furthermore, the figure is endowed with a speech balloon, which holds the words "I'M A ROUNDIN' EM UP!!" What is interesting about this enunciation in regard to the tensions in the comic-tableaux is that the denotational meaning of the words in this speech balloon (the verb to "round up" and the deictic expression *them/em*) coming from the boy's

---

20. Ten years earlier, in December 1886, Buffalo Bill's Wild West show had performed indoors for two weeks at Madison Square Garden in New York. In 1894, a new, extended version of the show was played outdoors in South Brooklyn's Ambrose Park (see Kasson, esp. ch. 2; see also Stoeltje).

mouth is, I would say, not fixed. One may read the words as a comment on the boy's own rodeo act, and in this "literal" sense, the expression serves to describe the cowboy activity of driving and herding up the cattle, or of bounding and lassoing a steer (in this case, *em* stands metonymically for the animals the rider catches). Because the rough rider and his bronco are visually and explicitly connected to the eliminated "old skate," the expression "round up" can also be understood in another way, namely as "to add up"; in that sense, the deictic *em* would refer to the unwanted, the excluded classes of horses—those put on the fringes of the show.

In Luks's "Horse Show" episode, then, the notion of imitation (along the line of class) and issues of participation are negotiated in dichotomous ways—deictics of us and them (in words), up and down (in words and via spatial modes), old and young and fit and unfit, as well as eligible and not eligible, and more, operate in the page, encouraging readers from different classes and with varying educational backgrounds to laugh with or at the crowd in Hogan's Alley. In this regard, there is one more aspect to point out: In the middle of the page, behind the Yellow Kid, who is standing on the prize-winning horse, we see two thick-red-lipped blackface figures riding on a mule (marked by the very long ears and the short-cropped mane). On top of the mule, one of the figures is neatly dressed in red stockings, a pair of short green pants, a red long-sleeved shirt, and a red cap, grinning broadly at the reader with eyes wide open; sitting behind this grimacing male character is a barefoot, infantile, round-faced, puppet-like figure dressed in white, with equally thick, red lips and kinky hair.[21] The position of the two (placed behind the Yellow Kid), and the utterance "ISE JUST KOMPETEIN FUR FUN" (Luks, "A Genuine") in the speech balloon accompanying the older of the two characters indicate that while the two are inside the ring of the horse show, they still remain outside, in the sense that they do not have access to the prize competitions. Put differently, while the two are in the arena and are placed together with the other participants and onlookers, they are still represented as unequal in relation to the "others," with no "rights," one might say, to seriously compete—underlined also through the phrase "just for fun." I think that the representation of

---

21. Older generations of newspaper readers would presumably recall the tradition of the immensely popular baby shows organized by P. T. Barnum, and in particular the blackface baby shows, which are echoed in Luks's representation (see also fn 9 in the previous chapter). On the perpetuation of the derogatory *pickaninny* in visual print culture, see Holt; Santiago-Valles. In early 1897, Hearst's *Journal* began to print E. Kemble's *Blackberry Sisters* comics series, with recurrent *pickaninny* figures in all kinds of—mainly rural-life—situations. See also Kemble's *Coon Alphabet* series, published in Hearst's American Humorist in 1897.

these two, sitting on a mule, gives Luks's comedic version of an equestrian show another twist in regard to the inclusion in and exclusion from urban (leisure) activities, and it endows the term *genuine* (in the episode's caption and on the Yellow Kid's shirt) with a subtext. Blackface minstrelsy, simply put, was based on masking, pretending, mimicking to "be" someone else for entertaining reasons—that is, white persons fashioning themselves as black in order to "pass" as "authentic" African Americans. Blackface figures are masked allegories to give the audience a simulation, a fake idea of African American cultural life.[22] The fact that Luks presents the two unnamed blackface figures on a mule, a hybrid animal race that is commonly conceived of as inferior compared to a thoroughbred horse, conveys power relations in the horse-show episode, which hinge on an awkward mix of racial and ethnic superiority/inferiority (the blackface figures are shown as noneligible for the prize competition, and the mule is inferior to the thoroughbred). This dichotomous scheme of inferiority/exclusion and superiority/inclusion is inscribed not just on the plot level of Luks's comic-tableau but also on the compositional level (the spatial arrangement of the page). The ability to participate for those two is limited to entertainment purposes for others. In the end, Luks's comic-tableau does not, however, structure power relations in order to generate a critical reflection.

Thus, in all their openness, the pages also move toward the exclusion of full participation in modern urban life based on categories such as race, and, as I will now further elaborate on, also on class.[23] One thing that the two horse-show pages have in common is that neither of them conveys to readers the option to actually walk up to Madison Square Garden and participate in the real-life event—this movement in urban space is not imagined in the horse-show episodes. In a different context, Sabine Haenni speaks about "the heavy restrictions on many people's actual mobility" and argues that "spaces of leisure provided forms of virtual mobility" (23). This is applicable to those Yellow Kid episodes in which the crowds travel to an imagined Coney Island, for example, or visit the aquarium. But for some reason, "virtual mobility" is not offered in the horse-show episodes.

---

22. Luks exploited racial stereotypes in both the *Hogan's Alley* series and the *Incubator* series, mentioned previously. On the ways in which Luks "referenced segregationist practices," see Gambone 118. As Gambone has furthermore pointed out, Luks was familiar with minstrelsy: He himself performed as blackface imitator (see Gambone 6–7). The wide appeal of minstrel shows is discussed in Rehin, who also traces how minstrelsy was adapted to British music halls in the nineteenth century (689–96).

23. For a broader perspective on and thorough discussion of racial nationalism exercised in the cultural imagination at the turn of the century, see Gerstle, especially the introduction and ch. 1.

Neither the Hogan Alleyites nor the McFadden Flatters can move *inside* the Madison Square Garden building and look at the high-class horses presented in the ring. The inside event is taken outside, into the streets of the respective street corners, that is, Hogan's Alley and McFadden's Row, and the inhabitants do not disturb the city grid of segregated sections (economically/socially/ethnically) but remain in "their" district, geographically separated from other parts of the city.[24] Readers of the horse-show episodes in Pulitzer's *World* and Hearst's *Journal*, respectively, are not given the practical option of "going up there" and entering the public realm of leisure and business of the upper classes.[25] While in the main sections of both newspapers, readers are endowed with information about ticket prices, venues, and brief accounts of what to wear and how to behave (or rather, how to imitate the manners of the higher classes), the comics pages by Outcault and Townsend as well as by Luks offer restricted participation in their alternative, imagined versions of the horse show. What the episodes suggest, then, is that there are class-specific activities that remain inaccessible to the lower classes (see Guarneri 136; see also Soper, "From Rowdy" 157).

To conclude, to say that the "Horse Show" episodes exclusively mock the upper-class members and their pretentious doings, their lack of creativity and ingenuity, and that they poke fun at the exhibition at Madison Square Garden by turning it into an anarchic, rowdy circus-like event, tells only half the story of the humor inscribed in the page. While Outcault and Luks mock, criticize, attack, and parody certain high-society habits and mores (such as Victorian codes of polite behavior, gentility, and respectability), these two pages also reassure and uphold middle-class ideologies (including social hierarchies), and articulate, or better reproduce—in implicit and explicit ways—racial and ethnic prejudices.

---

24. McCarthy's full-page horse show comic, printed on the final page of Pulitzer's Sunday Comic Weekly, picks up the theme of the National Horse Show again, offering, however, an entirely different perspective on the event: His tableau is a collection of fragmentary—and caricaturesque—glimpses of the "inside" of Madison Square Garden, in comparison to the "outside" presentations of Luks's and Outcault's illustrations. One might say that McCarthy's horse-show episode serves as an addition to Luks's installment, so that the readers of the eight-page newspaper supplement are given the possibility to "enter" the fairground.

25. In another episode by Outcault and Townsend, the Yellow Kid and the other tenants set out to parade to Fifth Avenue to take a look at the "glass houses" the rich people live in, or so the McFadden Flatters think. Yet they never arrive there because they are stopped by a police officer; class hierarchies remain intact in the comics series—the tenants never actually infiltrate the spheres of the upper classes (see Meyer, "Topographien").

In the Yellow Kid comic-tableaux in both the *Hogan's Alley* and the *McFadden's Row* series, playful humor and criticism are pitted against affirmative messages (concerning class distinctions, for example). In the respective episodes, we find tensions and competing messages at work: They alternate between class mockery and maintaining class hierarchies, social satire of vices and follies and carnivalesque representation of the tenants, ethnic humor and stereotyped representation of the ethnic other, and visual slapstick gags and verbal expressions inflected with severe undertones, and different modes of address, different voices (and forms of speech presentation), and different styles intermix with multiple viewing directions. Within each installment, mockery is played out in all kinds of ways. Furthermore, tensions emanate from the different implied addressees that the comic-tableaux operate with. The comic-tableaux are replete with competing "forces," which allows for multiple readings of the pages. This seemingly paradoxical nature of the Yellow Kid comics turns out not to be so paradoxical, for the areas of interests in the pages are tailored to different individuals and groups of readers and generate different ways of gratification. This scheme of diverging interpretations, and competing forces, is operative in each and every Yellow Kid comic-tableau.

Against this backdrop, my next chapter engages with a selection of episodes from *Around the World with the Yellow Kid*, which imagines mobility in a transatlantic space. The aim is to examine how *Around the World with the Yellow Kid* probes into this scheme of strategic and playful inscriptions, on the one hand, and to investigate the serial status of the travel narrative in relation to the *Hogan's Alley* and *McFadden's Row* series and in relation to the Yellow Kid's career, on the other.

CHAPTER 4

SPAWNING CONTINUATION?

Dynamics of Repetition and Variation, Once More

JUST THREE MONTHS after Richard Outcault and Edward Townsend had started the *McFadden's Row* series in Hearst's *Journal*, the recurrent New York setting of the full-page comic-tableaux was deleted from the Sunday supplement again. On January 10, 1897, the Flatters "give," as the narrator in Townsend's columns declares, "a farewell bennyfitt" vaudeville show (*McFadden's* E13). It is the final part to the *McFadden's Row* series—though not all is solved with the termination of this series—and marks the end of the collaborative work of Outcault and Townsend. That the vaudeville episode would be the last Yellow Kid comic-tableau set in New York became evident only for those who read the columns by Townsend. Readers who exclusively focused on Outcault's drawing would not have recognized the status of this episode as the end of the *McFadden's Row* series and the transition to a new series, or they only noticed this in retrospect, with the consumption of the next Sunday edition, in which the familiar, recognizable Yellow Kid figure reappeared in a new setting in *Around the World with the Yellow Kid*.[1] The shift to a new Yellow Kid story is revealed to readers in the

---

1. The Yellow Kid continued to show up also in various multipaneled comics that Outcault created parallel to the new graphic narrative.

concluding lines of the narrative columns: "De hole gang's gaw'n t' Yoorup nex' weak. . . . [W]e're gaw'n t' Lundn an' Parris an' Boilin an' if d' Moolang Rooj doesn't brake us we're gaw'n t' stakk up aggenst Monty Karlo. . . . I letche no what we do" (*McFadden's* E13). These sentences, while closing the *McFadden's Row* series, simultaneously anticipate the sequelization, or predict a continuation of the Yellow Kid's adventures and the surrounding Flatter crowd's doings in another serially progressing narrative—suggested by the enumerative "an' . . . an'"—with a new and different location outside the tenements of New York. The last paragraph announces to readers that the Flatters will be going on a journey abroad, which is an invitation to come along and follow the new serialized narrative with the Yellow Kid.

Around the World with the Yellow Kid was collaboratively sketched and written by Richard Outcault and Rudolph Edgar Block, who was the editor of the Sunday American Humorist at that time, and who contributed the first-person narrative passages in the framing columns.[2] *Around the World* is a travel narrative, consisting of altogether seventeen full-page comic-tableaux that appeared weekly in Hearst's American Humorist in the first half of 1897 (from January to the end of May). If we follow Roger Hagedorn's distinction between series and serial,[3] *Around the World* is a kind of hybrid mode of serial storytelling, combining a pattern of unrelated, self-contained episodes with recurring elements to create cohesion, and the form of a continuous, chronological storyline with breaks in between. It is serial, with a clear beginning (the departure); a chronological, linear development (the individual stops along the route); and an explicit ending. *Around the World* has an overarching narrative structure—the journey from, and back to, a specific point of departure: New York City. The return to New York is implied from the outset of the narrative.

Each episode usually holds two Yellow Kids—one is the recurring protagonist in the illustration. In addition, a miniature Yellow Kid is placed at

---

2. Before Rudolph Block (1870–1940) was in charge as editor of the *Journal*'s Sunday comic supplement, he had worked as a reporter for the *New York Sun* and as features editor for Pulitzer's *World* (see Benington 36–37). Block is known for his serialized newspaper travel chronicles *Vagabondia*, which he published under his pen name Bruno Lessing.

3. Hagedorn distinguishes between a "serial proper" and a "series proper." According to Hagedorn, a "serial proper" is a mode of serial storytelling defined by "breaks" in between the respective episodes or chapters of a narrative that leave the consumers in a moment of suspense or tension (relieved only with the next or any future episode). In comparison, a "series proper" is a mode of serial storytelling defined by self-contained, unrelated episodes that generate cohesion through recurring characters and a "basic diegetic situation" rather than through chronological, linear development within an "extended narrative" ("Technology" 7–8).

the top of the respective page right next to the columns; this Yellow Kid is dressed "according" to the country he visits and serves to direct attention to the narrative text in the columns. Some of the installments of *Around the World* stand out in the eight-page Sunday supplement because they are printed vertically, so that in order to be able to read or look at the landscape spectacle, one had to adjust the page, or rather rotate the newspaper by ninety degrees. The rearrangement of some of the pages or the spaces of the newspaper page from the vertical to the horizontal reflects the recontextualization of the Yellow Kid and his entourage to the broad, transatlantic space.

The title of the Sunday travelogue by Outcault and Block fuels expectations; yet, hopes to find a narrative about a global circumnavigation with the Yellow Kid at its center are not satisfied. Despite the title's suggestion and the two representations of the globe framing the title, the *Journal*'s serialized *Around the World* is not a narrative about a world tour. Instead, it tells of a tour to the European continent—the old world. *Around the World* is a playful parody of the Grand Tour. With each new installment of this journey, readers enter a new space—a funny visual-verbal representation of the "obligatory" spots of the Grand Tour, which had been repeated in many Anglo-American travel chronicles of the late eighteenth and early to mid-nineteenth centuries. As I will demonstrate in this chapter, the serial mixes common features and topoi of the grand-tour books, as, for instance, a visit to the Louvre, with visual-verbal depictions of foreign places. The artists playfully insert references to all kinds of national literature, such as Scottish, Irish, or French works; paraphrase passages from literary texts; and imitate literary genres, especially poems. The serial furthermore contains numerous references to actual, real-life people (for instance, to political figures such as Queen Victoria or Bismarck), cities (London, Paris, Madrid, and others), and places (such as, for example, Balmoral Castle). Moreover, the weekly installments visually and verbally represent folkloristic symbols and tales in the individual episodes (such as the tale of Wilhelm Tell or the legend of the Blarney Stone), icons of nationality (such as, for instance, the shamrock), images of—alleged—customs and eating habits in foreign countries, and representations of traditional attires (the Scottish Highland dress, for example). The background landscapes in Outcault's illustrations are furthermore filled with all kinds of people, things, and animals and with allusions to vaudeville skits.

Around the World with the Yellow Kid is another form of textual proliferation of the Yellow Kid, which is imbricated in patterns of repetition and continuation, yet also, as I aim to illustrate in this chapter, with patterns of containment. *Around the World* provides a new geographic, territorial space of action and adventure, moving actions beyond the city borders, and reinvents the Yellow Kid comic figure and the entourage of animals and other characters in another context; at the same time, however, the serialized travel narrative hinges on mechanisms of recursivity, folding back as it were, and securing what had been established previously. It works both backwardly and forwardly, triggering, securing, and gradually extending the serial knowledge about the Yellow Kid.

In their introduction to *Second Takes*, Carolyn Jess-Cooke and Constantine Verevis reflect on "the sequel's investments in repetition, difference, continuation, and retroactivity" and argue that a sequel—deriving from the Latin *sequela*, "that which follows"—"recapitulates features of an 'original,' but additionally offers something new to its source" (4–5). Outcault and Block's *Around the World* is a sequel to the *McFadden's Row* series and prolongs, continues, and adds on top of already existing formations, while at the same time it folds back, and validates what had been there already. In what sense is *Around the World* a sequel, or in what sense does it operate as a sequel? Or, to ask with Paul Budra and Betty Schellenberg: "What configuration of 'author,' original narrative, and audience, in what cultural conditions, explains a sequel?" (3). To ask questions such as these is important not least because they direct our attention to notions about the relationships and transformations of texts and meaning of originality and imitation, about audiences, and about, to quote Budra and Schellenberg again, the "intricate relations among author, narrative, and audience within any cultural moment, relations that govern the generation and circulation of all stories" (17). Budra and Schellenberg use the term *tensions* in order to describe these intricacies "between the individual text and its precursors," on the one hand, and the "tensions between the producer of the text and her or his audience, tensions between the aesthetic and the material aspects of artistic production [and] tensions between the ideal of unmediated transmission of meaning and the vagaries of reception," on the other (6–7). To give answers to such questions as what it is that Outcault and Block's *Around the World* continues, resumes, and extends, and in what ways, and with what implications, it does not suffice to deal with the formal and representational level of the serialized travelogue. Outcault and Block's *Around the World* narrative combines, to use the wording from John Frow, a "moment of invention, and [an] integrative moment of assimilation and reproduction" (156). Their travel serial *exploits* structures of the prior series and further *explores* established formulas of the New York series (such as layout compositions, contents, features, recurrent figures, and background props). *Around the World* imitates a textual precursor (*McFadden's Row*), while at the same time it departs from it—with intended or unintended allusions to the *Hogan's Alley* series. The backstory of origin of the Yellow Kid's Irish "4Fadders" (AW E5), for instance, reconfirms what had first been introduced and repeated in the *Hogan's Alley* series in the Sunday supplements of Pulitzer's *World*. While explicit references and allusions may add gratification to the reading (at the moment of recognition), the *Around the World* narrative stands for itself also, and the individual comic-tableaux might certainly be enjoyed without knowledge of past episodes. Not having knowledge of specific precursory texts is no impediment for understanding and enjoying the pages. For those readers who are able to capitalize on serial knowledge, pleasure is elicited through the reiterations of usual gestures, not only by the protagonist but also by the serial props. Enjoyment comes from the certainty that they would re-meet/-see the crowd on a regular basis again, and that narrative affordances are repeated. To explore these serial dynamics of the *Around the World* narrative is the aim of this chapter. With respect to the status of the travel narrative in relation to the two rival series set in New York and to the Yellow Kid's career, my contention is that the serialized travelogue about the Yellow Kid's adventures abroad is but a gesture to expansion, which is, ultimately, yet another effort to manage and control the self-propelling Yellow Kid and an—illusory—attempt to *finalize* the unfolding of the popular comic figure.

This chapter is organized in two parts, which follows a two-part purpose. It positions the narrative's sequentiality in the broader media-historical context: *Around the World* derived from, and tapped into, the practice of transatlantic travel, transatlantic journalism (see Wiener 64, 67–70), and written reports—fictional as well as nonfictional—about travel experiences. Travel is also the structuring principle of the narrative, the serial progression from one spot to the next. Each of the episodes offers to the reader a visual-verbal depiction of a new geographic space and representations of foreign cultures. Second, and in close connection to the purpose just outlined, this chapter analyzes the sequel's intrinsic aesthetic principles and narrative dimensions and their implications for the meaning-making. This investigation helps us also to better understand how the form, structure and content of *Around the World* differ from, while at the same time relate to, the prior series (*McFadden's Row/Hogan's Alley*), and how countervailing forces of expected and expanded reading affordances are at work in *Around the World*. In what follows, I first examine how Outcault and Block's visual-verbal travelogue defines itself against concurrent cultural products, and how it is related to popular cultural practices of the time period—travel and travel writing.

THE YELLOW KID'S GRAND TOUR—INTERTEXTS, CONTEXTS, AND COMPETITIONS

Christopher Endy has argued about "transatlantic travel [and] the voluminous commentary and literature it generated" that it "provided upper- and middle-class Americans with an essential means to understand other cultures as well as the place of the United States in the world" (592). Beckert and Rosenbaum offer a slightly different take on the activity of traveling to foreign places and the practice of recording the various experiences that played a particular role as forms of "cultural involvements" in the "process of bourgeois class formation" (3). In a similar vein, Maureen Montgomery has claimed that "these writings performed the cultural work of class formation and definition" ("Natural" 29; see also 27–28). Thus, one may read travel and travel literature in the nineteenth century as a symptom of "the expansion of the middle class" (Barber 68) and the growing leisure activity, which is grounded in, among other things, technological improvements such as steamships, the improvement of roads, and the expansion of the rail infrastructure. Within this framework, one may regard Richard Outcault and Rudolph Block's serial about the Yellow Kid's journey abroad as a visual-verbal response to these developments. The serialized travel story of the Yellow Kid can furthermore be read as an allegory for the expansionist economy and for the spread of popular culture through tourism and trade of objects. In 1903, Frank Norris stated that "there must exist [. . . a] fundamental connection between this recent sudden expansion of things American—geographic, commercial and otherwise—and the demand for books. Imperialism, Trade Expansion, the New Prosperity and the Half Million Circulation all came into existence at about the same time" (104).[4] The narrative about the Yellow Kid's travel abroad takes the Grand Tour's typical stations as the baseline against which to project the cultural development of a growing commodified tourist business (see Boorstin 86–90; Böröcz, esp. 737).

---

4. Expansionist initiatives—that is, economic, cultural, or territorial—were issues that were widely discussed at that time. Expansion was a trope that also permeated through fiction, art, journalistic articles, illustrated essays, and more (see Howells 241). The most well-known reflections on sociogeographic expansion is probably Frederick Jackson Turner's 1896 lead essay for the *Atlantic Monthly*, titled "The Problem of the West," in which he formulated the belief that the frontier will be extended beyond the borders of America (see also the 1896 essay by George Burton Adams, "The United States and the Anglo-Saxon Future," published two months before Turner's in the *Atlantic Monthly*, in which he engaged with questions about England's colonial expansion and the future of the relations between England and the US).

Outcault and Block's *Around the World with the Yellow Kid* was certainly not the first graphic travel narrative printed in a newspaper, but it was one of the first in the form of colored, full-page comic-tableaux, published serially over a time period of five months, in the Sunday comic supplements of the growing mass-paper market. Whoever eventually decided to produce the travel serial for the Sunday newspaper supplement, it was a clever idea, capitalizing on the previous success of the Yellow Kid comic figure, and also on the popular genre of travel writing. Of course, there might have been creative motivations, too—meaning, the artist Richard Outcault, who had been hired to do Yellow Kid comics, had wanted to draw a new series, not related to the weekly comic-tableaux showing the tenement buildings and street scenes.

There is, to the best of my knowledge, no record available that would prove any of the points above—it seems best to follow Mary Ann Gillies's assumption about literary sequels here. According to Gillies, "the decision to compose a sequel results from a complex interaction of cultural and material forces in which reader, writer, and publisher are involved" (133). With respect to the latter point, what can be said about Outcault and Block's *Around the World* narrative is that it plays a particular role when considered in the context of the competitive press market; it was not a coincidence that next to weekly paneled Yellow Kid strips, the comic figure was placed in another serial format, and was sent abroad on a transatlantic journey.

In light of the competition over market supremacy, Hearst had good reasons to show something new and different in order to outbid Pulitzer and to set his Sunday supplement pages apart from Pulitzer's. While the *World*'s Yellow Kid stayed in Hogan's Alley in New York, the *Journal*'s Yellow Kid left the city and went sightseeing abroad. In the narrative columns in the first episode, the Yellow Kid's voyage is promoted in superlatives, as "d' gratest tripp around d' woild dat evver wuz" (AW E1). The *Journal*'s supplement presented a new serialized Yellow Kid narrative with the same, recognizable crowd so that readers would enjoy something new against the background of the familiar. Since both Outcault and Block had previously worked for Pulitzer's *World* before they were hired by Hearst to produce features for the *Journal*'s supplement, one might consider the publication of the serialized travel narrative another—commercially motivated—strategy to tease the adversary. Seen in this context, Outcault and Block's *Around the World* is thus also materially sequelizing the competition between the rival newspapers that had started prior to Hearst's move to New York.

Though the *World* abstained from printing its own around-the-world-travel serial with the Yellow Kid, the newspaper continued to play the game of outstripping the other paper. Quickly, Pulitzer's Sunday staff imitated the *Journal*'s idea of serialized graphic travel narratives, and the supplement artists would do around-the-world comics series for his Sunday Comic Weekly; among others, there was William J. Glackens's serialized comic-tableaux titled *The Merry-Go-Rounders*, with a recurrent crowd of children who travel to different countries and experience all kinds of adventures.[5] Moreover, Charles Saalburg created a travel series titled *The Dinkies*, and J. B. Lowitz penned *The Captain Kidd Kids*; both series were printed in 1897 (the Kidd Kids' adventures continued into 1898).[6] In January 1898, Hearst's staff of the American Humorist picked up the journey topic again, and from January 16, 1898, onward, Edward Kemble produced a continuous narrative titled *Around the World in 30 Days*—this was a half-page comic-tableaux series with separate text blocks, written in rhymes. And a year later, Jimmy Swinnerton sent his crowd of Tigers away from New York, first to Europe and then around the world; the series *Our Tigers Go Abroad* ran from March 5, 1899, to July 9 of the same year. Once they hit the shore of San Francisco, the Tigers continue their journey through the Union. Other metropolitan newspapers followed the trend, as, for instance, the *Chicago Sunday Tribune*, which printed the *Kin-der-Kids Abroad* series by Lyonel Feininger. In the early years of the twentieth century, the artist Fredrick Burr Opper picked up the tour-to-Europe theme and sent his famous Happy Hooligan tramp to meet European aristocrats; his series, too, serves as a parody of the Grand Tour traveling habits of British aristocrats (see Soper, "From Swarthy" 285–86).

A few years before Outcault and Block's *Around the World* serial was produced for Hearst's American Humorist, Joseph Pulitzer's *World* had printed a very popular stunt by Nellie Bly (Elizabeth Jane Cochran's pen name), which was serialized under the title *Around the World in 72 Days* (see Roggenkamp 25).[7] Bly's story about her voyage relates to Jules Verne's seri-

---

5. Glackens's comic-tableaux of *The Merry-Go-Rounders* were accompanied by text columns, written by R. K. Munkittrick, who also wrote the verse lines for other comics series. Munkittrick furthermore contributed short texts—in verse—to the editorial page of Hearst's newspaper, which commented on topical issues (he, too, worked for both newspapers).

6. Saalburg's short-lived *Dinkies* series was printed in July and August 1897, with adventures set in Venice, Rome, Cairo, India, and so forth. Lowitz's *Captain Kidd Kids*, for which Munkittrick provided the verses, is a serialized narrative of sailor "pirates" around the world; the central character is based on the real-life Captain William Kidd, who was a well-known shipmaster from Mulberry Street in New York.

7. For further information on stunts as a journalistic practice and muckraking reporting as a genre specific to the sensational press of the late nineteenth century, see Adams et al. 85–112.

alized narrative *Around the World in Eighty Days,* and since Bly managed to travel around the world in only seventy-two days, she broke Phileas Fogg's fictional record.[8] Bly's unescorted travel had been serialized while she was still en route; reporters of Pulitzer's *World* would speculate on the incidents, and what adventures she would have, endowed with photographic engravings (see Withey 269–70). In order to engage his readers with Bly's travel, Pulitzer's paper furthermore offered cutout board games, designed for anybody and any size of groups to play, and with the goal to invite newspaper readers to take part in Bly's record-breaking race and "to complete the circuit of the world and reach New York first" ("Round the World" 21). After Nellie Bly had returned to New York, her version of her actual experiences was printed in the Sunday editions of Pulitzer's *World* between January and February 1890 (see Roggenkamp 26–27). The travelogue circulated widely and proved very profitable for Pulitzer—and Bly became one of the most famous and celebrated stunt reporters.[9]

With the publication of Outcault and Block's Yellow Kid travel narrative in installments, the readers of Hearst's *Journal* would now follow a fictional celebrity on the "gratest" (AW E1) journey around the world and experience traveling through the eyes of the Yellow Kid and his entourage. Prior to the publication of the first installment, Hearst's newspaper printed numerous advertisements (and lithograph posters), in which *Around the World* was promoted as a narrative that was based on an actual journey of the two artists—a "personally conducted tour" (*Around the World* n. pag.). However, Outcault and Block did not go abroad for half a year to produce the comic-tableaux, which is also marked in the pages of *Around the World* (see AW E15, in which Outcault adds the street name "PARK ROW" below his signature to indicate the drawing's place of origin). Rather, Outcault and Block's narrative was built on and inspired by preexisting models in

---

8. Jules Verne's narrative about a global circumnavigation of an English nobleman was first printed in serial form in *Le Temps* in 1872 (from November 6 through December 22, 1872); it was translated into English in 1873. A year later, stage adaptations (so-called spectacle plays) began to proliferate in Europe and abroad, first in Paris (in 1874), and then, a year later, in London; shortly afterward (in 1877), theaters in metropolitan cities in Canada and the US scheduled stage productions of *Around the World*.

9. Bly's race against the fictional record of Phileas Fogg attracted magazine editors and publishers, too, and they considered a serialized narrative about a woman's journey a means to compete with the newspapers. *Cosmopolitan*'s editor, John Brisben Walker, sent Elizabeth Bisland (who had previously worked for the *Sun* as well as the *World*) on a sponsored trip abroad to follow Bly and to beat her record, which she did not succeed in doing (see Fahs, esp. 313).

the genre of travel writing, and borrowed from and competed with other formats and modes or representation.

Travel narratives of domestic and overseas journeys were popular in the nineteenth century—fictional and nonfictional alike, and in all their diverse forms (as, for instance, diaries, essays, collections of letters, etc.[10]); these were printed mostly in the ten-cent periodicals and literary magazines tailored to a middle-class readership, but appeared also in book form. In this context, what comes to mind are such instructive travel narratives as William Francis Ainsworth's multivolume, illustrated documentary *All Around the World* (1860–62, reprinted in 1894, with illustrations by, among others, Gustave Doré; see Ainsworth); Thomas Stevens's pictured rendition of traveling around the world on a bicycle titled *Around the World on a Bicycle— From San Francisco to Teheran* (1887); and the fifteen-cent monthly magazine *Around the World: Contributions to a Knowledge of the Earth and Its Inhabitants*, which began publication in 1894 and which was edited by Angelo Heilprin. In addition, there were travel guidebooks—Baedeker, Murray, or Morris Phillips's *Abroad and Home: Practical Hints for Tourists* (1893)— which grew in number; many journalistic reports of continental travel and travel abroad; and numerous literary narratives dealing in diverse ways with travel-related topics, including, for instance, the immensely successful travel books series targeted to youthful readerships.[11]

The sheer number of publications in the 1890s focusing on travels around the world bespeaks the popularity of this genre and writing practice: There were ethnographic, illustrated, narratives of overseas journeys, such as Allen H. Tupper's *Around the World with Eyes Wide Open* (1898), and collections of impressions, such as Charles Parsons's illustrated *Notes of a Trip around the World in 1894 and 1895* (published in 1896) or George E. Raum's descriptive (yet not illustrated) *A Tour around the World* (1895). Other writing included letter-form reports of a family trip (see Floyd) and

---

10. On the practice of (fictional as well as nonfictional) travel writing in magazines, see Endy 568; Buzard, esp. ch. 3. On antebellum travelogues and their legacies, see Lockwood. Written records about travel experiences had existed before the nineteenth century, as Zumthor and Peebles demonstrate (see also Mancall). On the history and genealogy of travel writing in the US, see Ziff; Stowe. Stowe also thoroughly discusses that travel narratives were not exclusively male dominated (see esp. chs. 1 and 6).

11. I am thinking here of such authors as Horace E. Scudder and his so-called Bodley family series (1875–87), a series of travel stories geared toward children; Thomas Wallace Knox and his *Boy Travellers* series of illustrated books, in which two youths experience all kinds of travel adventures at home and abroad (1879–94); and the fictional, illustrated *Vassar* girls series (1883–92) by Elisabeth Williams Champney, in which three college girls travel abroad. All these book series were targeted to middle-class families. On these matters, see Kensinger, esp. ch. 4.

illustrated narrative records by two or more authors (see Clark and Clark; see also Boorstin, esp. ch. 3; Gilbert and Hancock). Some illustrated narratives were serialized in newspapers, too, as, for example, S. A. King's *A Trip to Europe in a Balloon*; the first installment was printed in the *Philadelphia Inquirer* on February 10, 1895, and it ran for several weeks in the paper's Sunday Supplement.

Though "travel book[s] [were] often victimized by [their] . . . simple though flexible formula" of recurring "patterns and themes," as Mark Melton rightly states (23), it is precisely because of the redundancy that the travel genre was so successful. Other precursory texts of the time period by well-known novelists include the two volumes *Collected Travel Writings: The Continent* and *Collected Travel Great Britain and America* (1893) by Henry James (see Rawlings; Montgomery, "Natural"). James published his early travel accounts ("Travelling Companions") in the November and December issues of the *Atlantic Monthly* magazine in 1870 (see Buzard 237–47; see also ch. 5 in Ziff); a couple of years later, he provided "Parisian letters" that were sent to and published in the *New York Tribune* in 1875 through 1876 (James, "Paris," "Parisian Sketches," "Parisian Life," and "Chartres"). Another popular and successful American travel narrative writer in the nineteenth century is Mark Twain, whose illustrated travel books *The Innocents Abroad* (1869) and *A Tramp Abroad* (1880), as well as the written account of his 1895–96 lecturing tour, published in 1897 under the title *Following the Equator: A Journey around the World*, were widely read.[12] One of the most well-known antebellum travel writers who helped popularize the image of a tramp going abroad and touring the continent by foot was Bayard Taylor: He "made his famous two-year pedestrian tour of Britain and the Continent for $500, which he wrote up under the title *Views Afoot*" (Lockwood 374)—this was parodied in George Alfred Townsend's 1870 *Lost Abroad*, "a fictionalized [and 'deromanticizing'] account of a pedestrian tour of Britain" (see Lockwood 376–77). One might say that in Outcault and Block's *Around the World*, the Yellow Kid "imitates," in a sped-up version and with bare feet, the pedestrian Taylor tour through Europe.

Apart from written accounts of traveling abroad, visual-verbal narratives such as Palmer Cox's well-known children's quarto book *The Brownies*

---

12. Twain's *Innocents Abroad* was partly based on travel letters that were serialized in 1868–69, as a Sunday special in *Alta* and in other Californian newspapers; the travel book quickly became a best seller (see Ziff, esp. ch. 4). A reading of Twain's travel writings is offered by Messent.

around the World (1892[13]), and illustrations of transatlantic voyages and of faraway foreign places, as for instance in the form of steel plates, photogravures, or stereographs, were consumed by many people.[14] And, the panoramic lantern slide shows—travel talks or travel lecture series that were mainly geared toward the middle-class—were likewise immensely popular.[15] These offered to the attending audiences "a visual experience," to use Ohmann's wording here, and brought the sites "into imaginative existence" (237, 231). They were, in short, the means of producing and disseminating knowledge about foreign places.

Just as stereographic images and other visual material allowed viewers to "enter" faraway places, the episodes in the serialized *Around the World with the Yellow Kid* virtually placed their onlookers into—imaginative—foreign countries and cultures. The Sunday visual-verbal travel serial by Outcault and Block appropriated transatlantic traveling—a practice of the upper classes at the end of the nineteenth century—as a thematic backdrop and plot device; the artists reframed the writing about traveling and travel experiences, and readapted it for serialized consumption in a mass newspaper. Their graphic travel narrative is a generic mixture of those texts mentioned above. Yet, while Outcault and Block's *Around the World* was influenced by other cultural products and borrowed from other formats, and while it is related to other intertextual referents, the serial is especially in line with such mid-century travel parodists as Artemus Ward (the pen

---

13. The latter was originally published as a serialized visual-verbal narrative in magazines geared toward children, before it was published in book form in 1892 (and reprinted in 1894). The motif of the traveling Brownies is recycled not only in Cox's 1894 *The Brownies through the Union* but also in Cox's sequel to the *Around the World* book titled *The Brownies Abroad* (1899), in which the popular characters visit, inter alia, the ruins of Norham Castle, the Lakes of Killarney, and Mount Vesuvius. Apart from that, musical adaptations of the *Brownies* toured through the US for five years, beginning in 1894.

14. The Library of Congress's Prints and Photographs Reading Room holds a wonderful collection of stereographs of travels, some of which are digitally reproduced and available online. For further information on photogravures, see Walsh.

15. Illustrated travel lectures, or "lantern journeys," and their predominantly genteel audiences are discussed in Barber. One of the most prominent figures at that time giving illustrated travel lectures was John L. Stoddard, whose lectures were later also published in book form (see Barber 70–73; see also Musser, esp. 428–34); the first edition was sold in 1897 (Barber 73). Stoddard's "successor" was Chicago-born Elias Burton Holmes, who rose to fame as a travel "lanternist" after Stoddard's retirement in 1897 (see Barber 78, 81). One should not forget, however, that the costs for seats for travel lectures were fairly high; usually they were advertised in middle-class newspapers such as the *Herald* or the *Tribune*, excluding prices for children.

name of Charles Farrar Browne) and Mark Twain.[16] Ward's panorama lectures were written and performed in the vernacular language; they burlesqued the seriousness and the "pompous" language of the instructive lectures of antebellum times "on morality, religion, and travel" (de Abruña 47; see also Dahl 476, 483; Branch 966–68). In his early travel narrative *Innocents,* as well as in both *Tramp Abroad* and *Following the Equator,* the mode of parody served Twain to expose hypocrisy and social prejudices, and to mock the "false expectations" of travelers (de Abruña 46, 50; see also Melton 141–43; Rowe 111–12, 122). While different in purpose and with different target audiences, the mode of parody in Ward's panorama lectures as well as in Twain's travel narratives and their writing styles—the vernacular, and the associative, anecdotal diary style—reverberate in Outcault and Block's Sunday newspaper narrative.

Around the World with the Yellow Kid is a serialized illustrated slide show—giving readers an idea of the (stereo)typical itinerary on a Grand Tour. *Around the World* does not parody one particular fictional or nonfictional travel text; rather, the travelogue refers to, in parody, the principle theme of many late nineteenth-century travel writings about transatlantic voyages, namely, the young adult, bourgeois traveler searching for educational or spiritual, cultural, or recreational input to expand knowledge (see Withey, esp. ch. 1). *Around the World* is a playful parody on the formal-education-finishing Grand Tour of well-educated, privileged young men in the eighteenth and early nineteenth centuries. In Outcault and Block's *Around the World,* the satiric targets are the upper classes, and more precisely still, American nouveaux riches, who were in the pecuniary situation to pursue Atlantic crossings, yet who very often traveled abroad for reasons of social prestige and display of taste—emulating, as it were, the Grand Tour experiences that others had gathered and recorded before them. In other words, many of them traveled on scripted tours and took in "scripted" reactions to oft-visited sites, cities, and places in Europe, striving to accumulate the diverse markers of prestige, the "most desired" aspects of a transatlantic voyage. In the *Around the World* narrative, these leisure tourists are depicted as "RELIC HUNTERS" (AW E2), attempting to gather as many souvenirs as possible (even the "HOUSES" in London that are "BUILT FROM GENUINE LONDON—FOG" [AW E2]). According to

---

16. Here, see Don Carlos Seitz (1862–1935), former managing editor of Pulitzer's *World,* who published a biography on Charles Farrar Browne. On Ward's influence on Twain, see Caron, esp. 183f; Judith Yaross Lee 7–8; de Abruña, esp. 49–50; Branch. Artem*u*s Ward is not to be confused with Artem*a*s Ward, who achieved reputation as advertising copywriter in the 1890s (see Laird 180–81).

Maureen Montgomery, "these new transatlantic travellers (the latest beneficiaries of capital accumulation in industrial America) had come to Europe to relieve themselves of their burdensome wealth in a manner guaranteed to attract attention, arouse envy, and violate the canons of good taste." In short, "they conspicuously spent and conspicuously consumed" (*Gilded* 19; see Veblen 41–60; see also Brodhead 125–26; Buzard 219; De Sapio 57–58). But there are others that are also lampooned in Outcault and Block's *Around the World* narrative, such as the "NO ABILITY OF YOOR RUP" (AW E1), and in particular the British and the Spanish royal families. For example, Prince "Al" (AW E1) and his involvement in the Baccarat scandal in 1890–91—Prince Albert Edward played an illegal card game in 1890—are repeatedly made fun of in the comics pages (see especially AW E2, AW E3).

The setting of the European Grand Tour is the foil against which the artists projected their parodies on the growing number of moneyed leisure class members in US society, imitating an old tradition, and the "old" nobility in Europe and their various facets of pretension and fakeness. In the second installment, for instance, which takes place in the city of London, readers find the familiar McFadden crowd, yet this time they are dressed in formal wear to meet with royalty—"Al" and "d' kween . . . Vicky [who] nearly had a konniptick fit w'en she seen us" (AW E2). All of the male Flatters, including the animals, appear as monocle-wearing visitors, and some of them wear a cylinder hat and tall collars. In the foreground, we see the Yellow Kid, who, even though he looks slightly different in comparison with the usual appearance in the New York series, is immediately recognizable. Instead of his typical long yellow shirt, he wears a long, double-breasted frock overcoat with a boutonnière on the left lapel, trousers, gloves, a stand-up collar and cravat, a top hat, and a monocle, all of which are in the same color: yellow. The Yellow Kid, although dressed in formal wear, is still barefoot, and as always, he grins at the reader, and there are words printed on his clothes—these are all established key elements of the comic figure (here, it is the space below the horizontal waist seam of his overcoat that shows a (political) comment by the Yellow Kid). In one of the banners to the left of the illustration, we are acquainted with the crowd that populates the streets of London. The announcement—obviously parodying an obsession with aristocratic titles—reads: "MiCKEY IS A PRiNTS DEN DERES KOUNTNESS KITTY HOGAN [sic] AN LADY LIZ DERES MOLLY DE MARCHONESS OF WONDERLAND AN MARQUISS MCSWATT AN VICOUNT VINCENT FARELL AN LOTS OF ODDERS" (AW E2). The exchange of money for aristocratic titles, and the prestige and status they brought with them, runs through the serial as one recurrent subject matter.

Moreover, the familiar, recurrent character Liz serves as a site for lampooning the transatlantic "marriage market" between American women and men with hereditary lineage in the European aristocracy.[17] In the course of the first couple of installments in the *Around the World* serial, she is shown linking arms with the Prince of Wales (and later she is also dancing with the Spanish king). In the columns, the narrator time and again tells of Liz's attraction to the prince and the European nobility in general. In the first episode of the *Around the World* serial, it is said that Liz would not mind "t' marry an Inglish lawd or kount" (AW E1). She is presented as uninterested at first, even "kinder bashful an' wuz tryin' t' sneek away" from Prince Albert Edward, but then, "stakked up aggenst de Yoorupean nobility," and to the dislike of the narrator, "she's been gettin' fresh" (AW E5). Ultimately, overcoming all oppositions, Liz and the Yellow Kid return to New York, and the words on his shirt in the last episode announce what is to come: "AN NOW ME AN LIZ IS GOING TO BE MARRIED AN LIVE HAPPY EVER AFTER. SEE" (AW E17). Their implicit future is framed by a conventional fairy-tale ending; the joke is obvious.

In addition to the Sunday comic-tableaux of *Around the World*, Hearst's newspaper printed a *Leaflet from the Yellow Kid's Diary* series, published weekdays as well as Saturday in the editorial page of the *Journal*. These are quarter-page, black-and-white, illustrated snippets of the journey, told in the first person. One of the subnarratives that is established in the diary leaflets is the narrator's self-reflection on the writing process—and progress—of the travel dairy: "I am ony ritin in me diary onct a week now cause de diary is gittin to be a bore—besides diaries is ony fer people wot takes dere self's serious" (AW Leaflet 7; see also AW Leaflet 5). The snippets are framed by either one or two images of the Yellow Kid—endowed with different accessories to indicate the country he has visited or will be visiting. Most but not all of the serialized snippets that were printed parallel to the Sunday *Around the World* narrative were written by Rudolph Block and illustrated by Richard Outcault; there are at least two installments that were done by Outcault only (see AW Leaflet 5; AW Leaflet 6). And, while the first number of diary entries indicate the author and artist of the respective leaflet, the last installments in this series are unsigned, which makes it difficult to determine whether Block was still involved—Outcault continued to do the Yellow Kid drawings. Since Edward Townsend was also working on features for the editorial page of Hearst's newspaper, it is pos-

---

17. For further information on marriage alliances between the daughters of American families and British nobility, see Montgomery, *Gilded*.

sible that he was assigned to write a few of the leaflets. Some of the snippets are even signed by Mickey Dugan, as if the Yellow Kid was the real-life author who contributed to the *Journal*'s editorial pages.

The content of each of the illustrated travelogue leaflets is different, and the narrator points forward to the events in the ensuing Sunday episode of the serial and adds background information in regard to the itinerary of the Yellow Kid presented in the Sunday comic-tableaux, as well as backward to something that had already happened in a past Sunday installment—or both; or the diary leaflets depict something that is not picked up and represented in the comic-tableaux of the Sunday pages. For instance, in one of the illustrated weekday leaflets, the short narrative holds an account of a stop in Greece; this occurrence, however, is not shown or mentioned in any of the Sunday comic-tableaux in *Around the World*. The editorial page of Monday, April 19, 1897, in Hearst's *Journal* shows a framed dispatch from the journey titled "The Yellow Kid in Russia," in which he is depicted (verbally and visually) meeting "Zarry ole spaurt" and "all d' nobility" (AW Leaflet 12). Again, this encounter is not delineated in any of the Sunday pages in the American Humorist (this probably also had to do with the fact that the weekend of April 24–25, 1897, was dedicated to a special Easter holiday edition of the *Journal*). This pattern of additional serialized narration during the week, bridging the interval from one Sunday episode to the next, had been first introduced in October 1896, when Outcault began to work on Yellow Kid comics for Hearst's *Journal*. Similar to the diary leaflets, which were printed parallel to the *McFadden's Row* series in 1896, the *Around the World* leaflets are supplementary resources for knowledge and, at times, more explicit political messages than in the Sunday comic-tableaux of the *Around the World* narrative. But, whereas the leaflets that were printed parallel to the *McFadden's Row* series offer further insights into the "private" life of the Yellow Kid's doings during the week and comments on domestic politics, sports, education, and urban life, the diary snippets that tie into the serialized Sunday comic-tableaux function to voice the Yellow Kid's political stance on American foreign relations and foreign policies. Not following these weekday diary entries does not, however, impede readers from understanding and enjoying the Sunday installments. Against the background of these reflections, the next section will examine the patterns and degrees of engagement that *Around the World with the Yellow Kid* enables, and unravel the mechanisms of expected and expanded reading affordances with which the serial operates; by so doing, I also aim to explain the status of this narrative in the Yellow Kid's serial career.

MODES OF ENGAGEMENT IN *AROUND THE WORLD WITH THE YELLOW KID*

Although traveling in the late nineteenth century was becoming more affordable to a larger group of people, it was still, in the 1890s, an activity limited to the affluent middle class and the wealthy upper class (see "Types of the Tourists"). As De Sapio states, "despite the 1891 assertion . . . that tourists 'hail from everywhere . . . from all the various and dissimilar classes . . . wide apart they are by education, wealth, and social bias!,' the reality was decidedly less democratic and somewhat more exclusive" (55). In Outcault and Block's fictional *Around the World* narrative, it is the Irish American city dweller Mickey Dugan who leaves—or escapes—the overcrowded tenements in McFadden's Row, and the overcrowded city at large, and together with some of the other tenants he sets to "sale fer Yoorup." The Yellow Kid's motivation: to have fun, to seek pleasure, and, as it is announced in the final *McFadden's Row* installment, "t' boin [munny]" (*McFadden's* E13). In *Around the World,* the Yellow Kid is staged as an affluent, leisure-class tourist, traveling to Europe. In the first episode, the Yellow Kid is asked by one of the fellow travelers whether he has "evver been akrawss d' pond befaur," to which the Yellow Kid answers, "o yes," conceiving of himself as "a reg'lar pond lilly" (AW E1). In *Around the World,* the Yellow Kid, equipped with a travel guide and a suitcase full of "LETTERS OF INTRODUCTION," embarks on one of the "RECORD . . . BREAKIN" transoceanic steamships—of the "UNITED STATES S. S. LINE" company—and sets off for the journey. This tour is proclaimed as "d' grates tripp around d' woild dat ever wuz" (AW E1). Letters of introduction—enabling persons to meet with the dignitaries of a foreign country and with "leading achievers in science, literature, and the arts" (Lockwood 350)—were a commonplace (etiquette) practice in the eighteenth and nineteenth centuries. As *Around the World with the Yellow Kid* proceeds, the readers come to know that the Yellow Kid is in no need of such letters. Everybody in Europe knows the Yellow Kid, the narrator in the columns suggests. He is described as a public persona who visits some "ole frends uv d' noability" (AW E17), and who has access to the upper-class circles.

The departure is staged as a sensation; it is celebrated as an important event for the city's inhabitants: On January 17, 1897, the Yellow Kid and his entourage leave New York on board the steamship heading toward Liverpool. In the columns, the first-person narrator tells the reader that a group of reporters attends the Yellow Kid's departure in order to write about it.

In the drawing by Outcault, readers face visual-verbal representations of a number of social-political officials; name tags indicate who the penciled figures are supposed to represent (see figure 4.1): There is "Waring," (George E. Waring), "Doctor" (Charles Henry Parkhurst), "Teddy" (Roosevelt), "William" (William Lafayette Strong), and "Chauncy" (Chauncey Depew). They are lined up on the pier, and they raise their hats and wave good-bye to the travelers. Note that the twins Alex and George (see my discussion in chapter 2) are also present, sitting on the roof of the "BON VOYAGE" terminal building; the flag they are holding up explains that "WE AINT GOIN TOO WE'RE LEFT" (AW E1). On the steamship, among a "huddled" mass of other unspecified travelers, one recognizes further familiar characters of the past Yellow Kid series: Apart from the Yellow Kid, endowed with naval insignia and a jockey cap, one sees Liz with her typically braided hair, who is sitting comfortably in a deck chair, sipping champagne; Molly (with her typical hand gesture and astonished look on her face); Mary Ellen, or Kitty (with her large hat); and others. "If ye'd a been wid our krowd," the narrator tells us, "ye'd a t'ougt we owned d' ship" (AW E1). The Flatters set out to follow the itinerary of a guidebook that the Yellow Kid takes along with him on the cross-oceanic journey. Each of the episodes offers to readers a visual-verbal depiction of a new geographic space and representations of foreign cultures.

The trip brings the barefooted traveling Yellow Kid and the "MOB" to "POOR YOORUP" (AW E1). During the several months-long voyage, he and his companions (and the readers with them) "invade" the British aristocratic society, meet with the monarchs and politicians from different countries, attend sporting events (such as a bull fight), and so forth; their leisure travel includes the sightseeing of famous and oft-visited sites, monuments, and places. In a different context James Buzard speaks about the "series of mnemonic stereotypes" of European cities that travel writers of the nineteenth century helped perpetuate (12); in the serialized newspaper comics of Outcault and Block, these are representations of popular tourist attractions such as Napoleon's tomb, the Sphinx, the lakes of Killarney, the Scottish Highlands, the Rhineland, and others. In the second episode of *Around the World*, published on January 24, 1897, Block includes in his narrative a kind of guided tour through "sum o' d' sites" of London, for example, and the reader is invited to follow along "fer a wauk" (AW E2). While Outcault's illustration does show the sites the Yellow Kid and his entourage visit (in the background, one simply sees the sketchy outlines of such iconic architectural buildings, memorials, and public places as Big Ben, Westminster Abbey, Trafalgar Square, and so forth), the narrative further explains, albeit very briefly, the history or function of these sites.

FIGURE 4.1. Richard Felton Outcault and Rudolph Edgar Block, "Around the World with the Yellow Kid. Off for Europe—Where They Won't Do a Thing to the Effete Monarchies," *New York Journal*, 17 Jan. 1897, American Humorist, p. 4 (detail). San Francisco Academy of Comic Art Collection, The Ohio State University, Billy Ireland Cartoon Library & Museum.

The Sunday travelogue delineates the Yellow Kid and his entourage as a mobile crowd. In the past chapter, I have shown how the inhabitants in both *Hogan's Alley* and *McFadden's Row* do not disturb the city grid of economically, socially, and ethnically segregated sections, but remain in "their" district, geographically separated from other parts of the city. In contrast to the New York series, in which the McFadden Flatters remain fairly static within the cityscape, the *Around the World* serial imagines mobility in a transatlantic space; by so doing, *Around the World* offers to newspaper readers diverse platforms to situate themselves in relation to new settings and contexts of otherness. The travel serial provides structures and makes the world out there legible.

This is mixed with a host of—expected—comical malapropisms, buffooneries, and, hardly surprising, cliché-laden representations of foreign cultures, such as customs, traditions, and national dishes. Stereotypical representations along the lines of ethnicity, race, and gender were common currency in turn-of-the-century visual popular culture forms, feeding into an appetite for fun, and evoking humor at the expense of the other (see Dormon). In the "Ireland" episode, all the older men are depicted in "Paddy" style, a stereotypical representation of the Irish, perpetuated in the vaudeville shows of the turn of the century. The "PADDY-DUFFY[S]" are shown as apelike men, with long muttonchops, smoking corncob pipes and wearing black hats, and some of them either riding on a wagon or playing a "HARP THAT ONCE," or drinking and/or fighting (see AW E5). Some of the representations that are meant for humorous entertainment are outright racist: In the fifth episode of *Around the World,* for instance, the narrator retells how "d' coon went swimmin' an' d' laiks wuz full o' ded fishes d' next day 'caus dey'd never saw a coon befaur. We're havin' grate spaurt wid d' coon" (AW E5). In another episode we read: "KYRO.—On d' midway I hav nevver been, but heer I am, me an' d' hole gang in d' streets uv Kyro, I aint ded stuck on dis town . . . nuthin' but niggers an' doit an' kammils" (AW E15). In the "Scotland" episode, then again, the travelers are "all waerin' kilts"—including the animals—and imitate the traditional Scottish Highland attire. Laughter in this specific episode is evoked through the visual excess. As Timothy Collier has argued with reference to Gerry Beegan's *The Mass Image,* stereotypes that were constructed in and perpetuated through the mass media at the turn of the century "provided 'comforting and partial knowledge,' 'identifying threats and problems and, simultaneously, making them less threatening,' and thereby 'suggest[ing] to the viewer that the urban masses were recognizable and categorizable'" (Beegan qtd. in Collier 493)—in one word: manageable. The visual-verbal representations in the episodes of *Around the World* provided for the reader platforms for projection and negotiations of anxieties.

Outcault and Block's visual-verbal travelogue is furthermore a means of negotiating New York City's—and American society's—relation to the world. The individual episodes in the travel narrative are composed of extratextual references to the city. New York serves as a background and basis of comparison to the comics travelogue. To be more precise, it is the area where the Yellow Kid and his fellow travelers live (the tenements in lower Manhattan) that determines the experiences abroad—all that the narrating Yellow Kid sees is compared to something he knows and remembers from the metropolis.[18] In comparison with the "glaurious metropolis" of New York (AW E1), the British cities such as Liverpool and London turn out to be a "wonderful sitty noated fer its salers' baurdin houses an' its dox," and "d' peachiest sitty wot every cum down d' pike" (AW E2). The quality

---

18. On the convention in many travel writings to compare the status of modern cities in the US and those in the old world, see, for instance, De Sapio 58ff.

of foreign cities, countries, and people is grasped and gauged through comparisons with New York. Madrid, for instance, "is littler n' Brooklin an' it aint got so menny trolly kars" (AW E9). Or, to offer another example from the Yellow Kid's visit to Spain: "Dem buls wot'che c'n see up in d' slauter houses on de East river aint in it wid d' bulls dat fite here [in Spain]. Nit, billy, dey aint in d' saim class, dese buls is jentiemen wile dem East river buls is lofers" (AW E10). The touring, then, is measured against the background of the living conditions in New York. The buildings in European capitals are matched with buildings in the Bowery. When the crowd and the monocled Yellow Kid face Westminster Abbey, the narrator exclaims that it is "a big bildin' say it wuz bigger'n d' peeple's t'eatre on d' Bowerey" (AW E2). Or, when "takin' in d' sites" of Paris, the Yellow Kid explains to his conversing counterpart (none other than Sarah Bernhardt) that "we've got bildins in Noo Yaurk wot's so high dat ye cud put dat [Eiffel] towr in d' basement an' none uv d' tenants wud cumplane" (AW E6). While certainly humorous—"d' krown wot he [the Prince of Wales] waur o it wuz better dan a hole hock shop winder on d' Bowry" (AW E2), or "dem rooms" in the queen's "pallis," they "look jest like d' sho winders in d' furnitcher stores on d' Bowry" (AW E3)—these and other comparisons carry also a bitter subtone, making visible the clash between the wealthy and the poor, and that the things that are displayed in windows remain unreachable.

In *Around the World*, the Yellow Kid is not only the penned, recurring protagonist and commentator but also the witnessing tourist and the "spokeskid fer d' crowd" (AW E6). He is the narrating voice and the author of his travel story, who writes down and sends home his impressions of the journey. The narrative columns framing the illustrations are written in the mode of stream of consciousness—there are hardly any punctuation markers that would help readers identify the beginning and ending of a dialogue or conversation. This mode of speech presentation imitates, in orthographic misspellings of the English language, the way the Yellow Kid speaks, and the ways he hears and understands the words others speak. It conveys how he converses with them and how he perceives himself and those surrounding him.

The first time this mode of narration was introduced to the readers of the *Journal* was the final installment in the *McFadden's Row* series, in which the Yellow Kid gives an account of the events taking place around him and, for the first time, reflects on his own storytelling skills: "If I only cud rite Inglish like dat Laura Jeen Libby 'r ole Kap Kollyer wot rote Out fer a millyun 'r de Mistry uv d' Kabel Slot say I'd rite ye an elligint staury about day perfawmance it wuz a dreem" (*McFadden's* E13). The narrator fantasizes about being as talented, successful, and famous a writer as the real-life Laura Jean Libbey, well-known and widely read female writer of—formulaic—romance novels,[19] or as clever as "Old Cap Collier," the name of a famous dime novel detective figure (and title of a mass-circulated weekly magazine[20]). The Yellow Kid describes himself as a consumer of family story papers (with enough leisure time to pursue the reading), and is conveyed here as a person finding delight and inspiration in, and shaped by, popular culture entertainment forms (popular narratives and detective figures serve as a source of knowledge and improvement for him). Moreover, the narrator, himself a fictional creation in the two-dimensional newspaper page, blurs the lines between fictional detective characters and real-life—female—authors to describe his desire to produce an entertaining and "elligint" account of the variety show performances on stage, while simultaneously directing attention to his own (language and writing) deficiencies, in the form of incorrect English orthography. Furthermore, Libbey was not necessarily considered a "good" writer of high, "elegantly" written literary works by contemporary literary critics but was a successful and very popular writer, catering her stories to a young female audience (see Noel 152; see also 124, 150–53, 290–95). With that knowledge in mind, the utterance of the Yellow Kid, comparing himself to Libbey and considering her a writer of aesthetic superiority—she writes "elligint" stories—is ascribed with an ironic undertone.

In similar veins, the text columns in the *Around the World* serial convey the Yellow Kid's view of the days' events and spectacular occurrences; they endow the visual-verbal travel narrative with a—somewhat—chronological, linear continuity. The narrative parts oscillate between the epistolary writ-

---

19. Her stories were first printed in serialized form in diverse weekly story papers, as, for example, in New York–based, middle-class household weekly papers such as *Family Story Paper* (purchasable by yearly or biannual subscription), the *Fireside Companion*, or the *New York Ledger*. See, for instance, the cover page of the *Fireside Companion—A Journal of Instructive and Entertaining Literature* (No. 1311, December 10, 1892), promoting Libbey's newest story ("Kidnapped at the Altar, or The Romance of That Saucy Jessie Bain"), and printing the first chapter and an accompanying illustration (see Libbey). In the early twentieth century, some of her stories were made into films (such as *A Poor Girl's Romance*, 1926). In the closing decades of the nineteenth century, Libbey was a household name. Today, she is barely remembered; only some scattered publications pay attention to her works (see Petersen; Denning).

20. The illustrated *Old Cap. Collier Library*, established in the 1880s, was sold weekly at the newsstands, featuring all kinds of detective and frontier stories. In comparison with the family story papers such as *Fireside Companion*, mentioned above, this and other small-format magazines did not print chapters of longer, serialized narratives, but single, self-contained stories each week, with no further development.

ing style and the anecdotal style of diaristic writing: The columns appropriate the "letter-from-Europe" practice, and the personal travel-journal or travel-diary mode to chronicle the events.[21] In those episodes of the *Around the World* serial that do not make use of the diary form in the narrative columns, the narrator addresses the letters to members of the McFadden's tenement crowd in New York that do not travel along—the reason for their absence is explained in the final episode of the *Around the World* narrative. Billy and Mrs. Cassidy did not come along on the journey because Billy, so we are told, "had d' meezils w'en I left Noo Yoork" (AW E17). From the fourth episode onward, the names of "billy Cassidy" and "Missus Cassidy" are mentioned as intended recipients of the letters; these are signed, among others, "Rispectibly years trooly, Mickey Dugan" (AW E4), or "Yure luvly frend" (AW E5)—ten installments later, these addressees are missing again. Apart from commenting on what is shown in the illustration, the narrative passages in the individual episodes add further details of past and future actions not visible in the illustration. In the second episode of *Around the World*, the crowd visits London, and the narrative blocks substantiate the scene depicted by Outcault with further details and preliminaries, such as, for instance, of Mickey's arrival at the British shore, his (customs) experience upon the entry in Liverpool, his travel to London, his checking in at the hotel, and the invitation of the royal family (see AW E2).

Similar to the final installment of the *McFadden's Row* in which the Yellow Kid addresses the reader directly instead of the heterodiegetic narrator (who had served as a guiding voice through the events in the previous installments of the *McFadden's Row* series), the events in the columns in *Around the World* are focalized through the Yellow Kid and are mediated in the form of the vernacular that he (or rather his shirt) had been endowed with from his "birth." The autobiographical speaker and the direct speech presentation certainly have the effect of oral immediacy and intimacy; what makes the mode of narration so interesting is that it is difficult to determine or to assign coherency to the speaker. As a result, alignment with the narrator proves complicated, or to put it in a different way, reader engagement is multifarious. Again, I am not interested in making any claims about the

---

21. When I speak about the "letter-from-Europe" practice, I mean not only the widespread convention of private letter correspondences but also those letters that were printed for the public in the newspapers (see Endy 568). Among the many predecessors of such newspaper letter practices, Mark Twain's series published in newspapers on the West Coast as well as in the New York *Tribune* and *Herald* and Henry James's letters for the *New York Tribune* (1875–76), were probably the most widely known (see Ziff, esp. 184–85).

actual meaning-makings of the historical reader; instead I will carve out the different patterns and degrees of engagement that are enabled through the mode of narration in the columns.

That there are various reading options has to do with, among other things, the fact that the intradiegetic-autodiegetic narrator is versatile, shuttling between adult and child perspectives, between informed and knowledgeable and unsuspecting and ignorant attitudes, and so on, oftentimes generating the effect of unreliability and untrustworthiness. Moreover, there are temporal overlappings: Retrospective narration and prospective narration of what is happening at the moment of speaking or writing coalesce—even within one sentence (as, for example, in: "Markwiss I sez... wel Mickey he sed ... Hooze keepin' it back I sed. he guv me d' wink an' sez" [AW E5]). It is an associative, zigzagging course of thought of the narrating Yellow Kid, in which past, present, and future collide. In addition, ambiguities also derive from the different addressees in the columns. In such remarks and questions as "Did'je ever travvil round d' woild? Did'je ever cum t' lundun [?]" or "ye'd orter heard Liz skreem" (AW E2), the referential function of the pronoun *you* is ambiguous, evoking as implied readers not just the "speech community" of the (fictive) Flatters in the diegetic world, in which the Yellow Kid narrator is embedded, but also the imagined readers (the large newspaper audience). In other episodes, the text in the columns oscillates from an unspecified addressee to the explicitly mentioned fictive addressees: Billy Cassidy and Mrs. Cassidy (see above); in these cases, the narrator and the addressee are imagined to come from the same sociolinguistic background.

Furthermore, the narrative columns generate ambiguities because there are tensions between an outward and inward standpoint and subjective view of multiple "personalities" or identities, and because the degrees of overtness and covertness that are inscribed into the narrating figure vary. The "I" in the narrative columns is occasional and liminal. The following text passage—taken from the "Kairo" episode (May 9, 1897)—nicely illustrates the ambiguities offered through the narrative columns, and the ways in which readers are stimulated to change perspectives and to further speculate on (i.e., to imagine) the reactions of the dialog partner:

Wel, we all sashayed back t' Kyro.... Keedy I sed, ware does Fateemer liv, d' keediv smiled jently, we got Fateemers t' boin, dere goes wun uv dem. Wot, dat lay I cride, say Keedy are dey all like dat wun, purty mutch, he replide, wel den if I wuz you I sed, I'd boin 'em. oh she had a fase like ded man's coive.... [B]ut Keedy ole spaurt I sed, puttin' me arm round 'im t' olly 'im, ware does dat little peetch liv wot did d' dants at d' woild's fare? o I know who ye meen, sed d' Keediv, I got her adress in me note book, den he took out his book an' sed, she livs in west Toity-ate street. Heer in Kyro, I askt, no in Noo Yaurk he replied. (AW E15)

The last sentence is, of course, a punchline that provokes laughter (an ironical view is cast here on the autodiegetic narrator). Quickly, the narrator redirects attention to the belly dance, and the passage continues then by recounting the erotic fantasies of the Yellow Kid and his desire to see sexually laden dances by female dancers. What interests me about the passage is the effect of polyphony: The intradiegetic level of narration and the autodiegetic type of narrator that tells what happens are "disturbed" by, or composed of, a diversity of voices: The authorial voice of Rudolph Block shines through the character of the Khedive here, with the help of such adverbs as "jently" in "d' keediv smiled jently" to mediate the Yellow Kid's (mis)conception of the situation; this invites readers to laugh at the Yellow Kid for his inability to understand the Khedive's subtle irony.

Here is another example: Before returning to New York, the Yellow Kid and his companions go back to London to see the queen one more time and bid farewell to her, to her family, to "me ole frends of d' noability" as well as to a number of political dignitaries, all of whom "wuz orfly sorry w'en dey hoid dat we wuz gaw'n bak aggen o stay wid us dey cride, but I sed nit jently" (AW E17). The narrator recounts the meeting, which he uses not only to speak about the traveling experiences of the past months but also to interfere—once more—with the politics, in this case with the role of the British Empire during the Greco-Turkish War of 1897[22]: "W'y did'je let d' poor greaks get soaked?" asks the Yellow Kid, to which the queen replies, "Micky [sic] dere's lots uv t'ings wot yure ignerent uv an' dat's wun uv' em." Here, the queen is criticizing his myopic understanding of world politics, which the narrator, however, does not notice; instead he turns his attention to "saulsburry himself [who] cum in." Salisbury greets the Yellow Kid, "holidn' out his hand," which the Yellow Kid does not accept; "No souly, I sed coldly, I c'n nevver shake d' hand uv a man wot let d' poor greaks geddit in d' neck . . . I aint stuck on d' greaks I sed but I'm ded soar on d' Toiks 'cause dey all smoke siggerets and ware bloomers. Dey're sissies" (AW E17). England, the Yellow Kid suggests, stood aloof and wit-

---

22. The war was widely covered in newspapers and magazines; the *New York Press*'s London correspondent, Frederick Palmer (a well-known war correspondent at the turn of the century), brought to the market an illustrated account of the conflict between Greece and Turkey titled *Going to War in Greece* (1897).

nessed the events instead of becoming actively involved in the conflict. In the passage, there is an obvious switch in attitude of the narrator—moving from criticism of Salisbury's politics and England's passive role in the Greco-Turkish conflict to an aesthetic evaluation of the militaries' uniforms (see also AW Leaflet 9).

What I would like to emphasize is that passages like these convey the perceived interests of newspaper readers. In the months the Yellow Kid's Sunday serial and the weekday snippets were published, the *New York Journal* expressed support in favor of Greece; sympathies were in general with the Greeks. "All the brag and bluster of the rest of Europe have not shaken one whit the splendid determination of Greece to stand firm," wrote one of the editors in Hearst's *Journal,* admiring the "heroism of the Greeks." The anonymous contributor proceeded: "Let them preserve their resolute front, proof against threat and railing, and the end will crown their courage. When it comes to the last the powers will not permit Southeastern Europe to be plunged into war by their backing of Turkey" ("Heroic Stand of Greece"). These and other debates are alluded to in the narrative columns in the Sunday episodes of *Around the World*; they are negotiated in the serialized diary leaflets, too. The diary leaflets are filled with visual-verbal commentary on political issues dealt with in the newspapers—such as the Greco-Turkish War of 1897, or the arbitration treaty, which was proposed in the aftermath of the Venezuelan border crisis.[23]

In the serialized travel snippets, the Yellow Kid is not only a private leisure traveler who narrates his personal impressions and occurrences of the journey ("last night . . . de next day" [AW Leaflet 5]); in a number of the leaflets, he performs as a foreign (war) correspondent, a politician, and a mentor. For example, on March 23, 1897, one of Hearst's editors noted: "The appointment of Prince George to govern the island under the temporary protectorate of the great powers, even with nominal Turkish suzerainty, would probably satisfy the Greeks and the Cretans, and happily settle the dangerous dilemma" ("The Cretan Blockade"). Placed to the right is a travel leaflet in which the Yellow Kid suggests settling the conflict by

---

23. I am referring to the Olney-Pauncefote arbitration treaty (alternately titled the Olney-Salisbury treaty) that was proposed in the aftermath of the Venezuelan border crisis, which had ended in 1895. Richard Olney, who was US secretary of state at that time, corresponded with British prime minister Lord Salisbury and the British diplomat Julian Pauncefote, and in 1896 Olney and Pauncefote negotiated an agreement between the US and Britain that was supposed to help avoid future conflicts between the two countries. The treaty was, however, rejected by the US Senate in May 1897 (see "Arbitration and Manifest Destiny"; see also "Kill the Arbitration Treaty"). Blakeney provides a thorough discussion of the arbitration treaty.

means of "DE PEN" rather than "DE SORD" (AW Leaflet 9). In two of the weekday leaflets printed on the editorial page of Hearst's *Journal*, the Yellow Kid is depicted as having taken part in the war between Turkey and Greece (AW Leaflet 9 and AW Leaflet 13). He goes to and observes "the seat of war" in Greece twice. The first time the Yellow Kid is mentioned to be in Greece is on March 23, 1897 (thus approximately a month before the war had officially been declared); "D' waur wot dey're all talkin' abut is a ded fake," states the Yellow Kid, and adds: "Heer I am Mickey on d' spot an' wot do I see? nuthin'" (AW Leaflet 9). This is echoed in one of the two framing illustrations that show a Yellow Kid; the comic figure's dress holds the following message: "DIS TURKEY GREASE WAR IS A FAKE." Eventually, he does encounter the Greek army. When they inquire, "Are you a fren or an ennemy," the Yellow Kid makes clear that is the impartial spectator who will then "refferee d' skrap" (AW Leaflet 9). Later, he is asked whether he is "a beleever or a infiddle," to which the Yellow Kid replies, "neether . . . I am a mugwump" (AW Leaflet 9). That he does not just observe the situation but actually intercedes is narrated in another leaflet, which was published on May 7, 1897. In this leaflet, it is told that the Yellow Kid intervenes first in favor of Greece, and then, crossing the borders at Maluna Pass to provoke disarray behind the enemy lines, joins the Turkish army—the image of the Yellow Kid at the top of the leaflet shows him holding the Greek flag; at the bottom of the page, the second image of the Yellow Kid shows him holding up a sword with the insignias of Turkey. "Dis fitin' agreeze wid me," says the Yellow Kid at the outset of the narrative, and adds that he only came "t' see d' spaurt an' d foist t'ing dey did wuz t' inwite me t' join in d' gaim. dat wuz d' greaks . . . ye shud see me wid a gun in me hands, it 'd make ye laff. I grabbed me gun an' sed t' d' krown prints . . . sho me a Toik an' I'll murder 'im" (AW Leaflet 13). Shortly afterward, the Yellow Kid tells his readers, he "spide a Toik" and because he shoots his adversary, "d' battil uv Maloney pass wuz commenst" (AW Leaflet 13). In his report, the Yellow Kid summarizes that he "kild nearly a t'ousand." Because he is busy fighting and shooting, he does not realize that he is surrounded by the Turkish army and is eventually captured and brought to the "Toikish genrul." The only way out is to join "d' Toikish army an' dat's how d' battil uv Maloney pass wuz wun." The narrator proclaims: "I kuvvered meself wid glaury an' scratches" (the pun is obvious), and then adds in hyperbolic manner: "I kilt nearly a milyun greaks." When the fighting is over, the Turkish "jenrul took off all his meddils an' handed 'em t' me. Mickey he sed, if it hadn't been fer you we wud hav been likked out uv our boots. yure d' hero uv dis battil" (AW Leaflet 13). The Yellow

Kid caused the fighting at the Meluna Pass, but then by switching sides he is able to end the battle.

To make general claims about the serialized leaflets is difficult. They are structured on the rhetorical operations of malapropism, non sequitur, asyndeton, and anacoluthon, to mention but a few of the devices. The Yellow Kid's impressions in the leaflet follow a scheme of associative thinking, which becomes absurd to the point of being confusing. From leaflet to leaflet the commentary might change in tone; even within one diary entry, from paragraph to paragraph the commentary might change in tone. The attitudes expressed in the leaflets, however, mostly resemble the *Journal*'s political position.

Whereas the Sunday installments stage the Yellow Kid as a leisure-class traveler who imitates the Grand Tour, the serialized dairy leaflets are an illustrated account of the travel abroad in terms of politics. The representations of the weekday business-travel leaflets and the Sunday leisure-travel comic-tableaux are played out in separate sections of the newspaper; through the Yellow Kid's adventures outside of New York, readers of the *Journal* were offered partially divergent yet at the same time complementary perspectives on world views.

Coming back to the Sunday comic-tableaux: Apart from what I have described above, the mode of personal addressing also offers insights into the ways in which the Yellow Kid interacts, in oftentimes supremacist manners, with "dem forriners" (AW E6); more than once does an imperialist rhetoric fuse into the narration. In the "Madrid" episode, for instance, the Yellow Kid states: "Deer Missus Cassidy, spane is a luvly country nit. D' klymit is on d' bum an' I don't speek d' langwij it sounds like chinees only woise" (AW E9; see also AW Leaflet 8). Given the fact that the US and Spain were in a tense relationship at that time period, these and other unflattering remarks hardly come as a surprise. In narrative moments such as these, the ideological orientation of the text columns is mediated, and these are assumptions and formulations that the implied readers were expected to share. The comic-tableaux concur with the newspaper's pro-interventionist agenda.[24] Rhetorics of taking in, invading, and owning are verbal markers or manifestations of the narrator's idea of transatlantic partnerships. The Yellow Kid interferes with politics in foreign countries: Together with

---

24. Hearst's *Journal* approved of America's expansionist initiatives — economical, political, military — and his newspaper promoted nationalism and endorsed imperialist projects. Repeatedly, the contributors to the *Journal* reflected on the importance of international conflicts to national policy, and Hearst's newspaper proposed a more active international role by the US (see Endy, esp. 565).

Albert Edward, Prince of Wales, he wants to, among other things, finally "SETTLE DIS IRISH QUESTION" (AW E2). The Yellow Kid's trip abroad is thus also, or at least partially, staged as travel on official business, with the Yellow Kid, who thinks of himself as a policy maker and mediator between disputing parties, involved in this and other conflicts.

To summarize, throughout the *Around the World* serial, the first-person narrator is fallible but likeable, and also fallible and dislikeable. He is quick-witted and/or naïve, tolerant and/or ignorant. The first-person narrator operates as satirist, openly ridiculing the European aristocracy and upper-class groups (for their pretensions), but he also becomes the object of satire within his autodiegetic narration. Readers are able to take a superior position and look *down* at the Yellow Kid in patronizing fashion, or take the position of the—poor turned (temporarily) rich—Yellow Kid and enjoy the various ways in which he pokes fun at socially *higher* standing people, at "high" art and other cultural products, at rules of etiquette, and so on. The narrative columns prompt different forms of reactions to the way the narrating Yellow Kid presents himself and his world view, and to the ways in which he perceives his surroundings (including his "distorted" self-image, as in, "I don't like to brag" [AW E16], which he actually does quite often), and the ways in which he thinks others perceive him. The Yellow Kid conceives of himself as a likeable person and celebrity, whom everybody knows, and women in particular seem very often to "nearly [have] a fit" when they see the Yellow Kid (AW E6).[25] Readers are able to laugh *with* the narrating Yellow Kid and at the variedly entertaining doings and reactions of others, or *at* the Yellow Kid and his misunderstandings and misconceptions (see Wood). Readers are encouraged to do both to adopt the position of the narrator and distance themselves from him.

Similar to the *Hogan's Alley* and *McFadden's Row* series, which are built on dichotomous deictics (us/them and up/down, etc.) to indicate as well as parody class and spatio-geographic differences, the *Around the World* narrative is composed of recurrent dichotomies of home/abroad, America/Europe, domestic/foreign, and "we"/"they"; the point of departure and the point of return is New York. Because these dichotomous sets are played out on various "levels" of the comic-tableaux, different ways of reader engagement and interpretations are made possible.

---

25. Little has been written about the chauvinist attitude that Block inscribes into the narrating Yellow Kid in the leaflets and in the Sunday comic-tableaux. The use of a dominant voice in terms of gender needs a closer examination. An exemplary reading of the ways in which Kitty Dugan is represented in the *Hogan's Alley* series can be found in Meyer, "Urban"; see also Frahm.

FIGURE 4.2. Richard Felton Outcault and Rudolph Edgar Block, "Around the World with the Yellow Kid—Mickey and His Friends Hobnob with Royalty," *New York Journal*, 31 Jan. 1897, American Humorist, p. 4 (Goat, detail). San Francisco Academy of Comic Art Collection, The Ohio State University, Billy Ireland Cartoon Library & Museum.

FIGURE 4.3. Richard Felton Outcault and Rudolph Edgar Block, "Around the World with the Yellow Kid. High Life in Paris—The Yellow Kid (L'enfant Jaune) Takes an Airing," *New York Journal*, 21 Feb. 1897, American Humorist, p. 4 (Goat, detail). San Francisco Academy of Comic Art Collection, The Ohio State University, Billy Ireland Cartoon Library & Museum.

Taking these observations as a cue, the remaining pages of this chapter will elucidate how expanded and expected affordances are inscribed in Outcault and Block's *Around the World with the Yellow Kid*. The sequel adds to the complexity of the serial mechanisms—the narrative and visual elements of *Around the World* are added on top of existing structures. The serial prompts such questions as how it sustains and capitalizes on intertextual relationships and synergies created after the past series (*McFadden's Row* as well as the serialized diary leaflets) and texts (travel literature), how these relationships are continued, and how certain reading capabilities and expectations have to be developed and are exploited across texts and contexts over time.

While Outcault and Block's *Around the World* offers novelty (in regard to format, background settings, and plot and content—each week—and thus in regard to the reading investments), it is simultaneously informed with moves and strategies toward categorizing, validating, and confirming the known, the familiar, the established. This includes not only the con-

FIGURE 4.4. Richard Felton Outcault and Rudolph Edgar Block, "Around the World with the Yellow Kid. A Bull Fight in Honor of the Yellow Kid," *New York Journal*, 21 Mar. 1897, American Humorist, p. 4 (Goat, detail). San Francisco Academy of Comic Art Collection, The Ohio State University, Billy Ireland Cartoon Library & Museum.

FIGURE 4.5. Richard Felton Outcault and Rudolph Edgar Block, "Around the World with the Yellow Kid. Fortune Smiles Upon the Yellow Kid in Monte Carlo," *New York Journal*, 7 Mar. 1897, American Humorist, p. 4 (Goat, detail). San Francisco Academy of Comic Art Collection, The Ohio State University, Billy Ireland Cartoon Library & Museum.

tinuous reference point in the narrative columns of the text, namely New York City, against which the impressions abroad are measured, but also the serial props of *McFadden's Row*, as I illustrate exemplarily in the following. Each episode in *Around the World* shows a crowd of figures and animals that readers familiar with the New York Yellow Kid series would recognize, such as Slippy Dempsey, Molly, or Liz; readers would also reencounter the animals such as the cat, the parrot, or the goat. They are presented in different, weekly renewed, settings.

In similar ways, the running gags that were established in the New York series are picked up and continued in the Yellow Kid travelogue: One of the running gags implemented in the New York series and taken into the *Around the World* narrative is the goat and the animal's (at times belligerent) behavior and consumption habits (see figures 4.2–4.5). Likewise, Molly's expression of astonishment is reiterated in every episode of the travelogue (see figures 4.6–4.8), and Slippy Dempsey keeps on falling from buildings,

FIGURE 4.6. Richard Felton Outcault and Rudolph Edgar Block, "Around the World with the Yellow Kid. In the Louvre—The Yellow Kid Takes in the Masterpieces of Art," *New York Journal*, 28 Feb. 1897, American Humorist, p. 4 (Molly, detail). San Francisco Academy of Comic Art Collection, The Ohio State University, Billy Ireland Cartoon Library & Museum.

FIGURE 4.7. Richard Felton Outcault and Rudolph Edgar Block, "Around the World with the Yellow Kid. Mickey and His Friends Climb the Alps," *New York Journal*, 28 Mar. 1897, American Humorist, p. 4 (Molly, detail). San Francisco Academy of Comic Art Collection, The Ohio State University, Billy Ireland Cartoon Library & Museum.

FIGURE 4.8. Richard Felton Outcault and Rudolph Edgar Block, "Around the World with the Yellow Kid. The Yellow Kid in Cairo," *New York Journal and Advertiser*, 9 May 1897, American Humorist, p. 4 (Molly, detail). San Francisco Academy of Comic Art Collection, The Ohio State University, Billy Ireland Cartoon Library & Museum.

mountains, and any other high spot. Interestingly enough, however, while Slippy makes it back to New York with a "final" "DOWNFALL" (AW E17) in Outcault's illustration, in the narrative columns by Block he gets killed — in the penultimate episode, Slippy Dempsey, we are told, jumps into the volcano, "slippy slippy I cride don't jump 'cause ye can't tel ware ye'll land. but it wuz too late he had alreddy jumpt an' we will never see poor Slippy aggen" (AW E16); yet, even though he is not mentioned anymore in the columns, the readers are assured in the last installment that he survived (falling headlong from the steamship). After all, the serial is not about plausibility. Slippy Dempsey falls and falls, only to reappear again and again (this established, formulaic serial prop also permeates some of the later self-enclosed Yellow Kid comic-tableaux that Outcault drew in late 1897 for Hearst's *Journal*).

Though the *Around the World* narrative is linked to the New York series, it is first and foremost to be considered an extension of the space in which the individual adventures take place and in which the characters (inter)act. Already the first installment of the travelogue connects the events of the new series to the past series, also informing uninitiated, new readers about where the "gang" had lived prior to their departure from the New York harbor; in rhymes the narrator explains: "McFadden's Flats is busted up / We awl wuz dispersessed / An' now we're gaw'n aroun' d' world / T' giv Noo Yaurk a rest" (AW E1). Moreover, in one of the altogether four installments taking place in the United Kingdom, the queen inquires about "ole McFadden" (AW E2), thus invoking the idea that the flat owner and the queen are in some way acquainted with each other. Such interlinking between the two series also takes place in Outcault's illustration: In the "High Life in Paris" episode, for instance, the readers are informed that "DE GANG FROM LES APPARTEMENTS DE MONSIEUR MCFADDEN" is visiting the French capital (AW E6). Here and on other occasions, the characters of the *Around the World* serial are explicitly linked to the crowd represented in the past *McFadden's Row* series. That this can also be understood as an attempt to locate the Yellow Kid and the surrounding crowd of animals and other iconic characters within the *Journal*, and also a further attempt to lay claim on the popular comics series' characters, is one of the reasons why I consider it worthwhile analyzing the *Around the World* narrative more closely within the framework of principles of seriality.

Outcault and Block's serialized travelogue is another proliferation of the Yellow Kid and textual manifestation of the comic figure's serial unfolding. The travelogue was certainly a means to exploit the success of the Yellow Kid and to offer yet another way of extended reader engagement and gratification. But I think that the publication can also be viewed in the context of reclaiming control and ownership over the comic figure. In a different context, Budra and Schellenberg elaborate on the "tendency of the sequel to serve the interests of consolidation and conservation, manifested variously," as for instance, "in an author's assertion of control over her or his characters" (12). They focus on literary sequels, but their observations on the mechanisms of sequels suggest some of the patterns that I see at work in the *Around the World* narrative, too. Outcault and Block's sequel to the *McFadden's Row* series expands territorially and offers something new to readers; yet it also is informed with recursive dynamisms to retrieve and secure the module (the Yellow Kid), the material, formulas, forms, and contents and an attempt to regain control and reclaim a single author and ownership over the intellectual property.

The *Around the World* narrative, then, while gesturing toward expansion and exploring further the variations of the Yellow Kid, helps reconfirm what had been established, and by so doing consolidates and secures the known. And this refers not only to the protagonist but also to the surrounding serial props, such as Molly, Liz, the goat, and the parrot. The serial operations of and in *Around the World with the Yellow Kid* are defined by innovation and repetition as well as reconfirmation and validation, and these countervailing forces also give rise to expanded, anticipated, and retroactively affirmative reading affordances.

The full-page comic-tableaux series with the recurring Yellow Kid ended half a year after it had started. The Yellow Kid returns to New York and is depicted as a successful "conqueror" of the world, endowed with laurels around his head and two badges for merit on his yellow dress. Dignitaries attend the event, some of the people wear Yellow Kid buttons on their lapels, and other upper-class members greet him with open arms. His return to New York is staged as a spectacular event again, with politicians and celebrities of the theater world attending his arrival at the New York Harbor. Newspapers bring front-cover headlines about the Yellow Kid's journey and return home.

The Yellow Kid's tour came to an end in May 1897. Not all the aspects that are narrated in the columns are solved with the publication of the final episode of *Around the World*—in the "Paris" installment, for instance, it is said that the crowd received an invitation for a dinner with Anna Gould, and "all goin' xcept me. I'll tel ye about dat w'en I get back bill" (AW E6). This occurrence and the reason why the Yellow Kid did not follow the invitation are never explained to the readers; nor do readers get any further information about the affair between the narrating Yellow Kid and a girl named Mamie, indicated in the "Kairo" episode: "It wuz Mamie, say I never told ye about Mamie did I, wel I wont, it wuz beaur Liz" (AW E15). In brief, there are a number of inconsistencies (also in regard to the variant spellings of names) and incongruities that remain unresolved. Outcault and Block's collaborative work ended, and the crowd of traveling Flatters did not repopulate the tenements in the *McFadden's Row* series. This does not mean, however, that the format of full-page comic-tableaux disappeared from the American Humorist; nor did the Yellow Kid comic figure vanish from the Sunday supplement. While *Around the World with the Yellow Kid* is a form of completion—a farewell tour, so to speak—it does not bring an end to the reiterations of the Yellow Kid. He lived on, resisting total narrative closure. The comic figure still appeared in Hearst's *Journal* as well as in Pulitzer's *World* in scattered Yellow Kid comic-tableaux and multipaneled strips—in order to offer satirical views on New York society.

Up until the moment of the Yellow Kid's journey abroad and return home (that is, mid-1897), the Yellow Kid was found in one-panel cartoons and multipanel, sequentialized comic strips and functioned as a recurrent protagonist in half-page and full-page comic-tableaux in rival comics series. All formats had been tried and tested. There is not one route that had not been taken. The Yellow Kid "lived" in the streets of New York (in different parts of the city), and "journeyed" through Europe. The comic figure appeared in vertically printed pages as well as in horizontally printed pages, and in every other conceivable layout both in the Sunday supplements and in other parts of the newspapers. Outside of the newspapers the Yellow Kid proliferated in various media formats and two- and three-dimensional forms.

Then what happened? When did the Yellow Kid leave the New York newspapers and the public sphere for good, or did he actually ever really vanish? Moreover, what happened to the manufactured Yellow Kid items, the theater adaptations of the Yellow Kid comics series, and all the other copies of the comic figure? Mark Winchester writes that the many images of the Yellow Kid inside and outside of the newspapers may have "led to an overexposure for theme and character" (*Cartoon Theatricals* 70), which ultimately led to the comic figure's death in 1898. Though I endorse the claim about overexposure, I am hesitant to sign the death certificate, for the simple reason that the Yellow Kid continued to circulate through consumer culture and the entertainment industry well into the twentieth century. It is true that the comic figure's expansive grin disappeared from the newspaper comic supplements, but the Yellow Kid did not entirely disappear. This brings me to the conclusion of my study.

CONCLUSION

SERIAL RETURNS, OR THE AFTERLIFE OF THE YELLOW KID?

THE YELLOW KID'S emergence, the imitations the comic figure inspired, and the figure's many ramifications in print and other media and in two- and three-dimensional forms across the country instigated heated debates among literary and social critics, temperance reformers, educators, theologians, legislators, medical scientists, and librarians. From the many reactions that were printed in literary and scientific magazines and many newspapers, it becomes obvious that there was a wish to get rid of the Yellow Kid, sooner rather than later (see Guarneri 28–29). One prominent strategy was to use a medicalized rhetoric to describe the impact of the comic figure: In December 1896, the *Philadelphia Inquirer* wrote that it was time to "exterminate" the "yellow kid malady" ("Editorial Clippings"). The Yellow Kid was regarded as a contagious creation. The comic figure "spread over the country like a plague" ("An Unlamented"), like an "epidemic ... more violent than the small-pox, and almost as far-reaching in its results" (Slocum), and this needed to be halted, it was agreed. Discourses of control and containment infused the career of the Yellow Kid, which intersected with larger social discourses of health, civilization, and refinement. In the debates about legitimate reading material, about standards of taste, about refinement and beauty, and about how to spend Sunday leisure time adequately, the Yellow Kid was deemed harmful and inappropriate and denounced as a "low" cultural product.

The main points of criticism were the Yellow Kid's vernacular language, which, because people started imitating certain idiomatic expressions (see "Bogus Yellow Kid Jailed"; "Real Yellow Kid Fooled Cobblers"), threatened to pervert the English language (see Wardman, "On"); the "profanity" ("Favus" 139) and the ugly outer appearance of the Yellow Kid—the "horrible, grinning, toothless, long-eared infant" (Banks 423)—which was considered an intellectual "pollution" (Banks 423) and disgrace; and the fact that the "yellow kid monstrosity" (McDonnell 289) appeared in the mass papers' Sunday supplements, which the critics regarded as "artistic abominations" (Swift 343; see also Warder 259) and especially dangerous for the "lower classes of people" (Banks 423) and children. The comics had a "seductive" potential ("The Descent") on "young imaginations" (Hallock), it was repeatedly argued.[1]

While some scholars would claim that the Yellow Kid had such an ill repute in public discourse because the comic figure symbolized sensational—yellow—journalism (see Mott vol. 2, 526; see also Emery and Emery 247), I would argue that the Yellow Kid was cast with a critical eye first and foremost because the comic figure proliferated so rapidly and extensively (like a plague) and because it leaked into all kinds of spheres and fields of private and public life.[2] In an anonymously published essay for *Munsey's Magazine*, a contemporary of Outcault explained that the danger of the Yellow Kid lies in the fact that the comic figure spread so widely through the country and "even threatened to become the central figure of a *legitimate* drama" ("An Unlamented").[3] The comic figure was harmful not only because it infiltrated the private lives of the lower classes of people that bought and read the cheap newspapers but also because it invaded the upper-classes' leisure space: The Yellow Kid "actually appeared, too, . . . within the *sacred* precincts of the four hundred" ("An Unlamented" 473). The Yellow Kid posed a threat to status and exclusivity.

---

1. The anticomics voices that so prominently heralded the delinquency and the stultification of the innocents during 1940s and 1950s may have been louder in those two decades, but deprecatory gestures toward the comics medium were uttered a lot earlier.

2. In a separate project still in progress, I show that the term *yellow journalism* does not derive from the Yellow Kid, as it is commonly maintained.

3. For further information on the distinction between legitimate and popular theater, see Lehuu 34–37; see also Levine, esp. 59–62.

Moreover, the Yellow Kid saturated the public environments of the cities in the form of billboard posters, cardboard cutouts for window display, and advertisements. In an article for the scientific magazine for children titled *The Great Round World* in 1896, the anonymous author expressed his or her concern that the Yellow Kid will also soon populate the nightly cityscapes: "Some clever person has thought of a very novel advertising scheme. It is for use at night, and [. . . if] it proves a success, the glaring announcements of the bill-boards, which annoy us by day, may be repeated in the sky at night; . . . and the obnoxious 'Yellow Kid,' with a hideous electric toe, will parade among the stars undaunted and unchecked" ("Invention and Discovery" 807). The many reactions against the Yellow Kid comic figure in the 1890s and in the early twentieth century had to do with fears of uncontrollable proliferations, and these fears were rooted in anxieties over the changes in social relations brought by new economic structures and the disorders brought by new mass-cultural products. Central to the debates over the Yellow Kid were the uncontainable energies emanating from this product and its unprecedented reach.

The Yellow Kid is the epitome of a burgeoning mass culture in the nineteenth century; the comic figure multiplied in seemingly infinite ways inside and outside of the original newspaper carrier medium. The Yellow Kid was propelled to stardom across the continent. Outcault himself talked about this in the essay "How the Yellow Kid Was Born," which I mentioned in the introduction to this study. Accompanied by a short comic strip titled "The Bud and Blossom of the Yellow Kid—His First and Latest Appearance," the essay conveys how Outcault had envisioned his creation and how he had lost control over it soon after its implementation in the Sunday Comic Weekly of Pulitzer's *World*. In the essay, Outcault describes how the comic figure affected his own life. It "had overwhelmed me" (7), and started to haunt him. It is not that Outcault had intended to create an item designed to be spread; he himself was quite surprised by the sensation the Yellow Kid caused. In his account of the Yellow Kid's rapid rise to prominence, the comic figure's huge success as a fast-selling item (textual or otherwise) with its own, uncontrollable, dynamics, Outcault compares himself to the author Mary Shelley, who "had brought forth a Frankenstein" (7).[4] Outcault admits that he "cursed the day that he came into existence" (7) because he had no power over the Yellow Kid and the comic figure's dispersal.

---

4. In the 1831 introduction to *Frankenstein*, Mary Shelley compares her book to a monster over whom she had lost authorial control. I have to thank Shane Denson for drawing my attention to this.

This study has traced how, why, and in what ways the Yellow Kid became the "reigning fad" in the 1890s ("Yellow Kid Schottische"). Seriality has provided me with a conceptual lens through which I read and analyzed the iterative and expansionist processes of the Yellow Kid. The central argument around which I have developed my investigation is that the Yellow Kid's career was predicated on operations of repetition, multiplication, and spread, and these accrete mechanisms were embedded in and spawned by the economic structures, technologies, and ideologies of capitalist culture. The concept of seriality has also helped me to understand the aesthetics of the comic-tableaux the Yellow Kid appeared in, and how the Yellow Kid comics series—*Hogan's Alley, McFadden's Row,* and *Around the World*—catered to a diffuse audience. In the concluding pages of my study, I will take the central idea about the Yellow Kid's serial life in order to reflect on the comic figure's "returns" in the twentieth and twenty-first centuries, arguing that the seriality of the Yellow Kid may also be understood in the sense of residual continuities, on the one hand, and to reflect on the significance of the Yellow Kid's career in the scholarship on comics and on media and forms of serial narratives today, on the other.

As indicated at the end of chapter 4, the Yellow Kid's life in the comics series in the supplements of both Pulitzer's *World* and Hearst's *Journal* ended, but the comic figure continued to be utilized in various advertising campaigns in the twentieth century until at least the 1920s (see Brittain & Co.; Chapman, "Wire," "Builders," "Heating," and "Ammunition"; The Filbert Grinding Co.).[5] Outcault himself played a crucial role in this regard: In 1907, he founded the Outcault Advertising Company (located in Chicago), and until his death his advertising company sent out printing blocks and cartoon ads (see Marschall and Bernard 27). Many of these advertising blocks included pictures of the Yellow Kid in different situations, such as gardening, hunting, crafting, or hammering. The production and distribution of Yellow Kid printing blocks from 1910 onward can be understood as yet another effort by Outcault to reclaim authorship over the comic figure.

Outcault had announced in 1898 how tired he was of producing Yellow Kids (see Outcault, "How the Yellow Kid"), but he continued to exploit the comic figure's success. In this context, it is also worthwhile noting that both the Yellow Kid and the emblematic Buster Brown comic figure that Outcault created in 1902 were printed in joint company in a number of advertisements and souvenir consumer items (see Outcault, "Buster Brown and

---

5. During my research, I stopped looking for Yellow Kid advertisements after these dates, but I am convinced that the comic figure continued to exist in ads in the years to follow.

His Bubble"). And, Outcault placed the Yellow Kid in some of his Buster Brown installments as a means to pay homage to a popular comic figure of the 1890s, to reflect on the Yellow Kid's role in the comics business, and to address the comic figure's place in a competitive media environment (see Outcault, "Buster Brown Meets").[6]

Furthermore, Yellow Kid ephemera persisted and continued to circulate through culture. "Stuff" such as the Yellow Kid papier-mâché masks were stored and then reused at later moments in time and for various purposes ("James M. Hamilton and Others in Costumes"). As the 1915 *Illustrated Catalogue of Papier Maché, Linen, Wire, Gauze, Wax and Show Masks—Large Heads, Noses, Wigs, Beards, Dominos, Etc.* by the American Mask Manufacturing Company discloses, Yellow Kid masks continued to be produced twenty years after the comic figure's initial success—for parade floats at Halloween, for instance (up until at least 1918, as photographic images prove; newspaper reports suggest that Yellow Kid costumes were still worn in the 1940s for so-called Comic Strip Balls—see Wright).

In addition to that, the Yellow Kid "entered," or had an afterlife in, screen media such as television as a kind of in-joke visual device. Yellow Kid papier-mâché masks are used as a mise-en-scène prop in the television series *Dick Tracy* (1950–52). In the fourth chapter of the episode titled "The Mole" (which aired in 1950), an episode that content-wise deals with deceit, trickery, concealment, and deception, and in which the criminal named Mole (played by Raymond Hatton) attempts to kill Joker (played by William Tracy), the viewers will learn that wearing a Yellow Kid mask can either get you killed (a customer) or save your life (the Joker).[7] In one sequence, which takes place in a retail store, the Joker attempts to convince one of his customers to buy a Yellow Kid papier-mâché mask. The moment he puts on the mask in order to show to his customer how "scary" it looks, a woman (the Mole's accomplice, named Fluff) enters the store to spy on the Joker (who does not know Fluff) and to report to the Mole afterward what the Joker was doing. When the Mole comes in and sees a person wearing the mask, he shoots this person, assuming that it is the Joker. As it turns out, it was not the Joker but the customer who had put on the mask. At the end of the episode, the Joker is still alive (and Dick Tracy—played by Ralph Byrd—solves the case), and the papier-mâché mask is still available for sale.

---

6. Soper discusses the reenactments of the Yellow Kid in several of the Buster Brown comics (see Soper, "From Rowdy"). Reproductions of some of the pages can be found in Maresca; see also Blackbeard, plates 118–21.

7. See "The Mole." The episode and the respective chapters are viewable online on *YouTube*. My thanks to Ilka Brasch.

Knowledge about the Yellow Kid and the plurimedial proliferations is not necessary to understand the scenes and to enjoy the detective series. Pleasure can, however, in particular be derived from identifying the mask as a cultural artifact that was utilized both in the world of theater and advertising, and as a costume for parties at the turn of the century.

The creator of "The Mole" could have used a different mask to tell the story, that is for sure. But I think that this visual reference or mise-en-scène prop was planted strategically to cater to different generations—and communities—of consumers: Those who grew up with the Yellow Kid comics (or their reprints) and were familiar, those who encountered the many adaptations of the newspaper series for the theater stages (shows toured across the country up until at least 1908), and those who encountered Yellow Kid newspaper advertisements (as mentioned above), and who would be in their sixties when the popular detective series aired on television, may have enjoyed this mask as a nostalgic reminder of forms of entertainment of the past. In addition, I think that there is another implied addressee here, namely, Joseph "Yellow Kid" Weil, the most well-known Chicago-born con man of the early twentieth century (see O'Flaherty; "Card-swindling"; Weil)—he was ardent admirer of the comics series and was named after the Yellow Kid comic figure (see Weil, esp. 17–18). Weil outfoxed different people (on different continents) and swindled them out of millions of money for over thirty years, which he wrote down in his 1947 autobiography *"Yellow Kid" Weil*. His life and schemes were covered in the press up until his death in 1976, and he was admired for his skills. In "The Mole," it is the Yellow Kid—mask—that cons or dupes a villain (the Mole). For those familiar with Joseph "Yellow Kid" Weil, the Yellow Kid mask in "The Mole" triggers another form of amusement—based on a reading of the visual prop as a parody on Weil. The mask of a bald-headed, broad-grinning character is certainly an entertaining gimmick for everyone, but this prop elicits humor in particular for an in-group of viewers that share knowledge about the Yellow Kid (or "Yellow Kid" Weil).

An episode from the NBC television sitcom *Frasier* (1993–2004) is another interesting case in point in this regard. In "Daphne's Room," the director inserted a brief sequence in which the audience sees the reaction of the series' protagonist (Dr. Frasier Crane, played by Kelsey Grammer) to a particular item—a Yellow Kid watch or alarm clock; instead of words on his long yellow shirt, this Yellow Kid displays the time.[8] In "Daphne's Room," Frasier enters the bedroom of Daphne Moone (Jane Leeves), which he has

---

8. See "Daphne's Room." My thanks to Regina Schober.

never seen before. When he scans the room in search of a book Daphne had borrowed, Frasier discovers all kinds of curious items; among other things, he finds a photo pasted to the mirror (a photo of Prince Charles and Lady Diana, whose face has been glossed over by an image of Daphne). Whereas the Lady Di photo seems to amuse him—which allows Frasier to gain insight into the woman's longings (being married to Prince Charles)—there is another item in the bedroom, which seems to disturb him: On the vanity table he discovers something that does not really seem to fit with the other items placed on that table. The camera zooms in to the "thing" in yellow that has a bald head (except for one, antenna-like wisp of hair), large ears that stick out, and a grinning face (which we only see when the figure is turned around to face the audience; this is also the climatic moment when the laughter track sets off). Frasier's bodily and facial reactions to the Yellow Kid clock (which is not a merchandise item of the 1890s but a reproduction) convey that he regards this item as awkwardly tasteless. That this reference to the Yellow Kid in "Daphne's Room" coincides with the 1995 centennial celebrations of the "birth" of the Yellow Kid—celebrations that included, among other things, the publication of Bill Blackbeard's seminal study, art exhibitions, articles in the press, public lectures, and new merchandise products[9]—is, I think, far from accidental. These and presumably a host of other visual citations in screen media, which I am unable to map in this study, contribute to the reactualization and memorization of the Yellow Kid comic figure.

The Yellow Kid has been reappraised in different time intervals and for different purposes throughout the twentieth and twenty-first centuries.[10] The comic figure eventually also "reentered" the medium of comics, again as an in-joke device. Among other things, the Yellow Kid crossed into the superhero genre of DC (see Miller et al. 11) and Marvel. In *Captain America* (#401, titled "After the Storm"), Captain America, Hawkeye, and Iron Man visit a bar that is packed with cameo people and presences of the past. In one panel, the readers see Tony Stark asking two people at the bar whether he could join them; one of them is the Yellow Kid; the other, sitting right next to him, is Elvis Presley (Gruenwald et al. 16). The joke is obvious. In Marvel's *Runaways*—a series that is about, in simplistic terms, time trav-

---

9. In 1995, the US Postal Service, for instance, issued a thirty-two-cent Yellow Kid commemorative postage stamp (created by Carl Herrman).

10. In this context, see also the film reviews and newspaper articles about Disney's 1937 animation film *Snow White and the Seven Dwarfs*, many of which suggest that the character Dopey was modeled after the comic figure, aligned with new values (see Feinstein 6).

eling, shape-shifters, telepathic mutants, mad scientists, superpowers, and teamwork—the Yellow Kid has guest appearances as one of the members of the "Street Arab" gang that lives in a tenement district the gang calls Camelot in the year 1907; he appears as "notorious" Yellow Kid in *Runaways* (Whedon, *Runaways*, II#27, 15). In issue 30 of *Runaways*, the Yellow Kid has superpowers, which enable him to discharge yellow energy at his enemies (Whedon, *Runaways* II#30, 5, 10). The last time readers see him fighting is in issue 30, but this does not mean that he is killed. Though it is not mentioned explicitly in the narrative, the Yellow Kid lives on and continues to fight. In Marvel's *Blade*, readers would briefly encounter a vampire Yellow Kid thirsting for blood—in this series, he targets the homeless of New York City who live in an area called Skid Row (see Guggenheim, *Blade* III#5 12–16; see also Guggenheim, *Blade* III#12 14).[11]

As in all of these contemporary comics, I think it is safe to say that the yellow skin color and the bald round head of Frank Miller's Yellow Bastard character in the 1996 *Sin City* series is likewise a visual "anecdote" to emphasize the role the Yellow Kid played in the history of comics (see Voger 9), and I am certain there are more comics that play with references to the Yellow Kid—the Yellow Kid is reappropriated, reinscribed into new contexts (in distorted ways), while staying recognizable. The parts that are rewritten in *Runaways* and *Blade* are not only the iconic features of the Yellow Kid but also the setting he originally lived in—the backyards and alleys of the tenements in New York. Except for the bar he is sitting in in *Captain America*, the Yellow Kid continues to populate the street as a geographic space. These reiterations of the Yellow Kid are further manifestations of the comic figure's movements across time and media. Phrased differently: The artists who put into dialogue the past and the present are agents of continuation of the Yellow Kid's narrative of serial unfolding, if not in mainstream popular culture, at least in various academic disciplines and fan communities.

The serial Yellow Kid figure is a cultural artifact that had been perpetuated through diverse channels of dissemination in the nineteenth century and that has been activated by various social agents in the twentieth and twenty-first centuries. He remains available for appropriations in diverse contexts, and with the variety of items now accessible on the internet, new means of accumulation and circulation of the Yellow Kid are provided. I think it is worthwhile looking more closely at the ways in which the comic

---

11. For further information about Yellow Kid cameo appearances in superhero comic books, see Vandal.

figure is embedded in and thrives on today's digital world. This includes such file-hosting and file-sharing websites and blogging platforms as Pinterest, Imgur, Tumblr, and others; this includes also fan art productions posted online on the Comic Art Fans or Deviant Art websites, for example. These forms and practices of production, which rewrite the Yellow Kid in diverse ways, prompt a host of interesting research questions concerning their aesthetics and (trans)mediality, and concerning such issues as authorship and adaptation in contemporary culture. These are paths that the present study did not take, but I am hoping that future interdisciplinary research projects will address these issues.

Other paths I have not taken in this study include the transnational history of the Yellow Kid's comics series (and other newspaper and magazine cartooning art of that time period), and I am likewise hoping for scholars in such fields as comics, media studies, and art history to delve further into these subject matters. In his wonderful book on the *Origins of Comics*, Thierry Smolderen has argued: "To understand [the inception of the modern comic], we must consider the deep roots of graphic culture and comic tradition" (158), and this means looking at the transcultural "heritage" and developments, too. With regard to the Yellow Kid, I am not just thinking of the influence of European artists on American newspaper comics but also of, for instance, the inspiration provided by Japanese woodblocks and such artists as Utagawa Hiroshige III, Utagawa Sodahide, or Utagawa Kunitoshi.[12] That Japanese cartoonists such as Imaizumi Ippyō—who studied lithography in San Francisco in the 1880s before he returned to Japan in early 1890 to work for the *Jiji shinpō* (Current Events) newspaper that began publishing Sunday comic supplements *Jiji-Manga* in 1900 (see Bouissou 22)—or Yasushi (Rakuten) Kitazawa took inspiration from American newspaper comics of the late nineteenth and early twentieth centuries has been a subject matter in manga studies (see Ito; Johnson-Woods; Stewart, "An Australian" and "Manga").[13] Yet, the contacts between Japanese and American

---

12. My thanks to Birgit Michaelis. The cities of Boston and New York—as well as other cities—regularly held exhibitions on U-ikoyé art, which were covered in the press. The art critic, curator, and collector Ernest Francisco Fenollosa played a crucial role in circulating images and creating knowledge about Japanese art during the 1890s; in 1896 he published one of the first extensive catalogues on *The Masters of Ukioye*. For a critical discussion of the Japan craze in the 1890s and the conceptions of Japanese art today, see Nakashima.

13. Yasushi Kitazawa, known as Rakuten Kitazawa, first worked for the English-language weekly newspaper *Box of Curios*, published by Edgar Vooris Thorn in Yokoshama. Rakuten had access to American newspapers and humor magazines, among others, *Judge* and *Puck* (see Stewart, "An Australian" 89). In 1902, he began drawing

cartoon artists in the early to mid-1890s, and the "overlapping media environments of Japan and other parts of the World," still need to be closely examined, as Ron Stewart rightly points out ("An Australian" 91). Transcultural dialogues, the traveling of cultural artifacts, and the entanglements of national histories have been recurrent topics in transnational literary and cultural studies and in the scholarship on comics (see, for instance, Denson et al.). Yet, while the influence of Japanese art on practices and aesthetics in the fields of theater, advertising, and fine art has been discussed in studies of *Japonisme* (see Meech-Pekarik and Weisberg; Beckmann; Chiba), the impact of styles and design elements and printing techniques on American newspaper comics artists of 1890s has yet to be explored. What comes to mind in this context of transcultural constellations is the Australian-born cartoonist Frank Arthur Nankivell, who had lived and worked in Japan (he moved to Japan in early 1892, where he started as an illustrator for Edgar Thorn's English newspaper *The Box of Curios*) before he settled in the US in May 1894. Nankivell first sketched for Hearst's *San Francisco's Examiner*, as well as for the *Chronicle* and for the *San Francisco Call* (see Stewart, "An Australian" 91), and was then employed at *Puck* magazine in 1896 (see "Artist Nankivell Engaged by Puck"). Nankivell also contributed black-and-white illustrations to Pulitzer's *World* (see, for instance, Nankivell), and then, from October 1896 until August 1897, to Hearst's *Journal*. Nankivell drew comics for Hearst's American Humorist as well as a few cover illustrations for music portfolios (which were also printed in the American Humorist), and made a number of chromolithographic promotional posters for Hearst's newspaper. In 1897 Nankivell furthermore illustrated Edward Townsend's literary portrait of New York City, titled *Near a Whole City Full* (published by Dillingham, which at the same time also published the fictional autobiography of the Yellow Kid). These and other "networks," and probable mutual influences and cross-borrowings, and the role traveling newspaper and magazine artists—traveling in the sense of going abroad and visiting another country, and in the sense of moving between different print media (magazine, newspaper, book, poster)—and the circulation of printing techniques, drawing styles, and designs played in the evolution of the medium of comics at the turn of the century deserve to get more attention. Or, at

---

comics for the Sunday edition of *Jiji shinpō* (Ito 32). Later, Rakuten Kitazawa would also create the multicolor *Tokyo Puck* magazine (1905). For further information see, for example, Harder and Mittler; see also Scully.

least, I would like to see more scholars to engage with these issues and to put on historical lenses that will help us see the many intersections.[14]

There are many more reasons to revisit the decade in which comics became a mass medium and to explore the variety of visual and verbal forms of expression and experience, and I look forward to the future projects that will take us back in time and give us access to and help us read these incredibly fascinating "impressions for disposable consumption" (Greg M. Smith 230). With regard to the Yellow Kid newspaper comics, this study has focused on the serialized comic-tableaux of *Hogan's Alley, McFadden's Row,* and *Around the World* and has examined the aesthetic operations of varied repetition and branching in them. I just briefly discussed how the Yellow Kid also appeared in other comics formats such as captioned graphic narratives (e.g., *The Huckleberry Volunteers* or the serialized diary leaflets) and in comic strips, both in black and white and in color—the black-and-white strips were usually printed on Saturdays, sometimes on weekdays; the comic strips in color, some of which were produced collaboratively with other artists such as Joe Kerr or Richard Kendall Munkittrick, were published in the Sunday editions. All of these formats operate with different attention economies and generate different consumption practices of the visual and verbal signs.

The comic strips are forms of serial storytelling in which the Yellow Kid operates as a recurring figure, too. These comic strips of two or more framed or frameless panels are informed by two aesthetic principles of seriality[15]: (1) linear and chronological, as in "The Yellow Kid Indulges in a Cock Fight—A Waterloo" (November 29, 1896); that is, an action (a dura-

---

14. The question of how the newspaper comics of the 1890s borrow from media technologies from the same time period, such as chronophotography, and adapt them to the printed page are tackled in Schuldiner and Rosaler; Greg M. Smith. In this context, see also the serialized "Kinetoscope" comics that Carl Anderson produced for Hearst's *Journal*. Further inquiries into the remediations in the history of comics will follow soon, I hope.

15. By frameless, I mean that there are gaps between the panels but no framing lines that would enclose and demarcate the respective moments from the preceding or the following. The panel frames in the Yellow Kid comic strips differ greatly in terms of color and with regard to the line work and shape. We do not just find black boxes, so to speak, but quite a variety of enclosing modes, such as straight lines, wavy lines, intertwined threads, abstract floral patterns, and more, and sometimes a mise-en-scène element such as a perch functions to separate the images, and panel numbers indicate the reading direction. Moreover, the Yellow Kid comic strips operate with varying sizes (spacing) of the gaps (gutters) between the images. And often, the frames do not "hold" those that are supposed to be "inside"—parts of the animals or characters slop over the panel borders and intrude another image. For a broader perspective on the functions of frames and other artistic devices in comics, see Postema.

tion) is fragmented into sequentially organized parts (framed or frameless panels are placed next to each other), which in the reading process have to be put together again in order to become a meaningful coherent narrative,[16] and (2) episodic and nonprogressive. Sometimes these two aesthetic operations converge, as in "A Few Things the Versatile Yellow Kid Might Do for a Living" (November 22, 1896; see Figure 5.1).

In "A Few Things," ten frameless Yellow Kid images are juxtaposed in horizontal tiers, underneath each of which is a narrative caption written in first-person direct speech. Each image shows a Yellow Kid in a different pose and with different accessories such as laurels, a baseball cap, or a top hat and objects such as dice, musical instruments, a painting palette, and others. In the tried and tested way, the Yellow Kid's utterances are printed on the long yellow shirt, and in one of the images, we find words in the background, too (which tell the readers the story of the Yellow Kid's "origin" and how the comic figure first lived in Hogan's Alley and then moved to McFadden's Row). In terms of the visual elements, the comic strip provides a set of self-contained entities (or shots). Each image can mean by itself and is inclusive. It does not matter where you start; the images make sense without relation to the preceding or the following. It is a series of varied repetitions of the Yellow Kid that is not defined by temporal sequence. With regard to the narrative captions underneath the images, the contents of these text passages are either complementary or supplementary to what is depicted in the respective image (alluding to vaudeville shows and referring to extratextual events and real-life people, for example). The narrating agency in the passages is Mickey Dugan, who speaks in vernacular language. Whereas in the images, the Yellow Kid communicates with the reader through his message-bearing clothes, in the narrative captions, his words are presented in direct speech in quotation marks. If we connect the captions with the images and read them as a unit, as a panel, then each panel can still be meaningful without relation to the previous or next — with the exception of two. There are two narrative captions in the second row of panels that are composed to be read in connection with each other:

---

16. In a comic strip such as Outcault's "Cock Fight," narrative imagination — that is, creating temporal progression, linear evolvement, and coherency — is triggered by specific visual and verbal cues, such as the captions affixed below the images; the positions of the characters and animals in comparison to a preceding and a following panel; and through deictic expressions of time, such as "First" and "Second," and of space, such as "'Round the block" (Outcault, "The Yellow Kid Indulges"). But, as Charles Hatfield has pointed out, there is no "inherent connectedness" between the words and images in a comic strip or between the panels (135); reading a comic and making sense of a comic is a creative act that very much relies on "the invocation of learned competencies" (135).

FIGURE 5.1. Richard Felton Outcault, "A Few Things the Versatile Yellow Kid Might Do for a Living." *New York Journal*, 22 Nov. 1896, American Humorist, p. 8. San Francisco Academy of Comic Art Collection, The Ohio State University, Billy Ireland Cartoon Library & Museum.

"'It costs too much to be a real sport an' win prizes at the horse show'—," says the first-person narrator in one passage, the m-dash indicating that something will be added to his enunciation; the next caption concludes the idea by adding "'—but I tink I would be a good jockey an' a prize winner fer some one else" (Outcault, "A Few Things"). Thus, two panels in "A Few Things" operate with both the principle of continuous/linear and non-continuous/episodic seriality, which calls forth different forms of reader engagement and enables different forms of pleasure.

It is worth noting here that the attentive, regular reader of Hearst's American Humorist would notice that some of the comic strips that were printed between October and December 1896 refer to specific episodes in the *McFadden's Row* series, and a few of the Yellow Kid comic strips, such as "A Three Cornered Fight in McFadden's Flats" (December 6, 1896), explicitly relate to the geographic location of the *McFadden's* series—thus content flows between various formats. Those who would buy or borrow and read the illustrated autobiography of the Yellow Kid, which was published a few months later in 1897, would recognize that some of the visual as well as verbal elements in these comic strips were recycled in the book, too. This illuminates how the Yellow Kid is operative in a network of different modes of graphic storytelling, which invites readers to seek the connections.

The forms of serializations in the Yellow Kid's original newspaper carrier medium and their affordances certainly deserve more paragraphs than the lines I have just offered. The Yellow Kid grows and expands in and across different diegetic worlds—and in competing newspapers—and he disperses in and through differently organized serial formats (comic-tableaux, captioned narratives, and comic strips). The history of comics and the history of recurring comics characters do not begin with the Yellow Kid—for sure not—but I think the Yellow Kid newspaper comics are a good starting point to think further about practices and aesthetics of serial storytelling and how they evolved in new formats in the twentieth century and in comics today.

Hully Gee!

BIBLIOGRAPHY

Abel, Richard. *Americanizing the Movies and "Movie-Mad" Audiences, 1910–1914.* U of California P, 2006.

Adams, George Burton. "The United States and the Anglo-Saxon Future." *The Atlantic Monthly,* vol. 78, July 1896, pp. 35–44.

Adams, Katherine H., et al. *Seeing the American Woman, 1880–1920: The Social Impact of the Visual Media Explosion.* McFarland, 2012.

Adcock, John. "America's First Color Newspaper Supplement (1892)." *Yesterday's Papers,* 15 Nov. 2012, john-adcock.blogspot.de/2012/11/americas-first-color-newspaper.html.

Advertising. *Printers' Ink,* vol. 17, 16 Dec. 1896, p. 27.

"Advertising Novelties." *Printers' Ink,* vol. 19, no. 3, Apr. 1897, p. 30.

Ainsworth, William Francis. *All Around the World. An Illustrated Record of Voyages, Travels and Adventures in All Parts of the Globe. With Hundreds of Illustrations, after Drawings by Gustave Doré, Bérard, Lancelot, Jules Noël, and Other Eminent Artists.* Selmar Hess Publishers, 1894. 4 vols.

Allen, Irvin Lewis. *The City in Slang: New York Life and Popular Speech.* Oxford UP, 1993.

Allen, Jeanne Thomas. "Copyright and Early Theater, Vaudeville, and Film Competition." *Journal of the University Film Association,* vol. 31, no. 2, 1979, pp. 5–11.

Allen, Robert C. *Vaudeville and Film, 1895–1915: A Study in Media Interaction.* Arno P, 1980.

Allen, Rob, and Thijs van der Berg, editors. *Serialization in Popular Culture.* Routledge, 2014.

"American Affairs—Political and General: The Presidential Campaign." *Public Opinion: A Weekly Journal,* vol. 21, no. 3, 16 July 1896, pp. 69–80.

American Mask Manufacturing Company. *Illustrated Catalogue of Papier Maché, Linen, Wire, Gauze, Wax and Show Masks—Large Heads, Noses, Wigs, Beards, Dominos, Etc.* 1915.

"Amusements." *The Auburn Bulletin,* 28 Dec. 1896, p. 4.

"Amusements." *Lockport Daily Journal,* 20 Nov. 1897, p. 1.

Anderson, Benedict. *Imagined Communities: Reflections on the Origin and Spread of Nationalism.* 1983. Verso, 2006.

Appel, John J. "From Shanties to Lace Curtains: The Irish Image in *Puck*, 1876–1919." *Comparative Studies in Sociology and History*, vol. 13, no. 4, 1971, pp. 365–75.

"Arbitration and Manifest Destiny." *New York Journal and Advertiser*, 7 May 1897, p. 6.

Around the World with the Yellow Kid. Thomas & Wylie Lith. Co., 1897.

"Artist Nankivell Engaged by Puck." *The San Francisco Call*, 7 June 1896, p. 25.

"The Art of Advertising." *The Yellow Kid: A Fortnightly Magazine of Wit, Fiction and Illustration*, vol. 1, no. 3, 17 Apr. 1897, n. pag.

Assael, Brenda. "Art or Indecency? *Tableaux Vivants* on the London Stage and the Failure of Late Victorian Moral Reform." *Journal of British Studies*, vol. 45, no. 4, 2006, pp. 744–58.

"At the Lyceum Theater." *The Buffalo Courier*, 23 Mar. 1897, p. 6.

"At the Masque Balls." *The Milwaukee Sentinel*, 13 Feb. 1898, p. 2.

"At the Theatres." *The Syracuse Standard*, 27 Mar. 1898, p. 16.

Babbitt, E. H. "English of the Lower Classes in New York City and Vicinity." *Dialect Notes*, edited by the American Dialect Society, J. S. Cushing & Co., 1896, pp. 457–64.

Bailey, Peter. "Ally Sloper's Half-Holiday: Comic Art in the 1880s." *History Workshop Journal*, vol. 16, no. 1, 1983, pp. 4–32.

Baker, Charlie. "Yellow Kid Schottische." Union Mutual Music Co., 1897.

Baker, Nicholson, and Margaret Brentano. *The World on Sunday: Graphic Art in Joseph Pulitzer's Newspaper (1898–1911)*. Bulfinch Press, 2005.

"Baltimore." *The Clothier and Furnisher*, vol. 26, no. 5, Dec. 1896, p. 83.

"Baltimore." *The Clothier and Furnisher*, vol. 26, no. 6, Jan. 1897, p. 83.

Balzer, Jens. "Hemd voller Hieroglyphen. Zur Revision der Bild-Text-Beziehungen im frühen Comic." *Bildtext—Textbild. Probleme der Rede über Text-Bild-Hybride*, edited by Dirck Linck and Stefanie Rentsch, Rombach, 2007, pp. 117–54. Rombach Wissenschaften / Reihe Cultura 43.

———. "Hey, schau einmal her! Ein gelber Junge!" *Outcault: Die Erfindung des Comic*, written by Jens Balzer and Lambert Wiesing, Ch. A. Bachmann, 2010, pp. 13–34. Yellow: Schriften zur Comicforschung 3.

———. "'Hully Gee, I'm a Hieroglyphe'—Mobilizing the Gaze and the Invention of Comics in New York City, 1895." *Comics and the City*, edited by Jörn Ahrens and Arno Meteling, Continuum, 2010, pp. 19–31.

Banks, Elizabeth L. "American 'Yellow Journalism.'" *The Eclectic Magazine of Foreign Literature*, vol. 68, Sept. 1898, pp. 422–31.

Bannister, George J. "The Men Who Make Us Laugh." *Broadway Magazine*, vol. 11, no. 3, June 1903, p. 235.

Banville, Scott. "Ally Sloper's Half-Holiday: The Geography of Class in Late-Victorian Britain." *Victorian Periodicals Review*, vol. 41, no. 2, 2008, pp. 150–73.

Barber, X. Theodore. "The Roots of Travel Cinema: John L. Stoddard, E. Burton Holmes and the Nineteenth-Century Illustrated Travel Lecture." *Film History*, vol. 5, no. 1, 1993, pp. 68–84.

Barker, Kenneth. "The Comic Series of Joseph Pulitzer's New York Sunday World." *Inks: Cartoon and Comic Art Studies*, vol. 2, no. 1, 1995, pp. 26–32.

Barth, Gunther. *City People: The Rise of Modern City Culture in Nineteenth-Century America.* Oxford UP, 1980.

Bartholomew, Charles L. *Chalk Talk and Crayon Presentation: A Handbook of Practice and Performance in Pictorial Expression and Ideas.* Frederick J. Drake and Co., 1922.

Baxter, William. "How Pictures May Be Transmitted a Thousand Miles and Distant Friend Brought Face to Face." *The World*, 18 Oct. 1896, pp. 24–25.

B. C. T. "The Annual Dinner." *The American Stationer*, vol. 40, 31 Dec. 1896, p. 1106.

Becker, Stephen. *Comic Art in America: A Social History of the Funnies, the Political Cartoons, Magazine Humor, Sporting Cartoons and Animated Cartoons.* Simon & Schuster, 1959.

Beckert, Sven, and Julia B. Rosenbaum. Introduction. *The American Bourgeoisie: Distinction and Identity in the Nineteenth Century,* edited by Sven Beckert and Julia B. Rosenbaum, Palgrave Macmillan, 2010, pp. 1–8.

Beckmann, Thomas. "Japanese Influences on American Advertising Card Imagery and Design, 1875–1890." *The Journal of American Culture*, vol. 19, no. 1, 1996, pp. 7–20.

Beer, Thomas. *Stephen Crane: A Study in American Letters.* 1923. William Heinemann, Ltd., 1924.

Bengough, John Wilson. "An Irresponsible Infant." *The Globe*, 18 Aug. 1897, n. pag.

Benington, Arthur. "The Sunday Newspaper." *Journalism: Its Relation to and Influence upon the Political, Social, Professional, Financial, and Commercial Life of the United States of America,* edited by the New York Press Club, 1905, pp. 33–39.

Bentley, Nancy. *Frantic Panoramas: American Literature and Mass Culture, 1870–1920.* U of Pennsylvania P, 2009.

Bergengren, Ralph. "The Humor of the Colored Supplement." *The Atlantic Monthly*, vol. 98, Aug. 1906, pp. 269–73.

"The Best Song Yet! Given away Sunday with the Journal." *New York Journal*, 5 Nov. 1896, p. 3.

Betts Patent Headlight Company. "The 20th Century." *New York Journal*, 11 Apr. 1897, American Humorist, p. 8.

"Bicycles." *New York Daily Tribune*, 28 June 1896, p. 18.

"The Big Comedy Boom for 1899–1900." *The New York Dramatic Mirror*, 20 May 1899, p. 28.

Birmingham, Ernest F. "Note and Comment." *The Fourth Estate: A Newspaper for the Makers of Newspapers,* 16 July 1896, pp. 6–7.

———. "Note and Comment." *The Fourth Estate: A Newspaper for the Makers of Newspapers,* 1 Oct. 1896, pp. 6–7.

Birnkrant, Mel. "A Guided Tour of the Mel Birnkrant Collection: The Yellow Kid." *Melbirnkrant.com*, n.d., http://melbirnkrant.com/collection/page7.html.

Blackbeard, Bill. *R. F. Outcault's The Yellow Kid: A Centennial Celebration of the Kid Who Started the Comics.* Kitchen Sink P, 1995.

Blake, James W., and Michael Bernard. *The Belle of Hogan's Alley.* Howley Haviland Co., 1896.

Blakeney, Michael. "The Olney-Pauncefote Treaty of 1897—The Failure of Anglo-American General Arbitration." *Anglo-American Law Review*, vol. 8, no. 3, 1979, pp. 175–90.

Block, Adrienne Fried. "Matinee Mania, or the Regendering of Nineteenth-Century Audiences in New York City." *19th-Century Music*, vol. 31, no. 3, Spring 2008, pp. 193–216.

Block, Rudolph Edgar, and Richard Felton Outcault. "A Leaflet from the Yellow Kid's Diary." *New York Journal*, 13 Mar. 1897, p. 6.

———. "A Leaflet from the Yellow Kid's Diary—Monte Carlo." *New York Journal*, 6 Mar. 1897, p. 6.

"Bogus Yellow Kid Jailed." *New York Journal*, 11 Dec. 1896, p. 5.

Boime, Albert. "The Comic Stripped and Ash Canned." *Art Journal*, vol. 32, no. 1, 1972, pp. 21–30.

"The Bookman's Letter-Box." *The Bookman*, vol. 8, no. 2, 1898, pp. 160–61.

"The Bookman's Letter-Box." Letter to the editor by "A well-informed Baltimore lady," *The Bookman*, vol. 8, no. 5, 1899, pp. 482–84.

Boorstin, Daniel J. *The Image: A Guide to Pseudo-Events in America.* 1961. Athenaeum, 1987.

Boorum & Pease Company. A blank books and tablets advertisement with the Yellow Kid. *The American Stationer*, vol. 41, Feb. 1897, p. 227.

Böröcz, József. "Travel-Capitalism: The Structure of Europe and the Advent of the Tourist." *Comparative Studies in Society and History*, vol. 34, no. 4, Oct. 1992, pp. 708–41.

Bouissou, Jean-Marie. "Manga: A Historical Overview." *Manga: An Anthology of Global and Cultural Perspectives*, edited by Toni Johnson-Woods, Continuum, 2010, pp. 17–33.

Boutelle, C. A. "'Yellow Covered' Journalism." *Bangor Daily Whig & Courier*, 11 Oct. 1883, p. 2.

Brake, Laurel. "The Longevity of 'Ephemera': Library Editions of Nineteenth-Century Periodical and Newspapers." *Media History*, vol. 18, no. 1, 2012, pp. 7–20.

Branch, Edgar M. "'The Babes in the Wood': Artemus Ward's 'Double Health' to Mark Twain." *PMLA*, vol. 93, no. 5, 1978, pp. 955–72.

Brand, Dana. *The Spectator and the City in Nineteenth-Century American Literature.* Cambridge UP, 1991.

Braun, Alexander. *Jahrhundert der Comics. Die Zeitungs-Strip-Jahre.* Druckverlag Kettler, Huelsmann-Stiftung, 2008.

Brittain & Co. An advertisement with the Yellow Kid. *The San Francisco Examiner*, 26 June 1910, p. 34.

Brodhead, Richard. H. *Cultures of Letters: Scenes of Reading and Writing in Nineteenth-Century America.* U of Chicago P, 1993.

"Brotherhood of Commercial Travellers." *The Publishers' Weekly*, Jan. 1897, pp. 7–8.

Brown, Joshua. *Beyond the Lines: Pictorial Reporting, Everyday Life, and the Crisis of Gilded Age America.* U of California P, 2002.

Brown, Thomas Allston. *A History of the New York Stage from the First Performance in 1732 to 1901.* Dodd, Mead and Co., 1903.

Budra, Paul, and Betty A. Schellenberg. Introduction. *Part Two: Reflections on the Sequel*, edited by Paul Budra and Betty A. Schellenberg, U of Toronto P, 1998, pp. 3–18.

Buzard, James. *The Beaten Track: European Tourism, Literature, and the Ways to Culture, 1800–1918.* Oxford UP, 1993.

Byrne, James P. "The Genesis of Whiteface in Nineteenth-Century American Popular Culture." *MELUS*, vol. 29, no. 3/4, 2004, pp. 133–49.

Campbell, Joseph W. *Yellow Journalism: Puncturing the Myths, Defining the Legacies.* Praeger, 2001.

"Card-Swindling Charge 'Offends' Joseph Weil, Confidence 'Artist.'" *The Niagara Falls Gazette,* 9 Mar. 1931, p. 5.

Caron, James E. *Mark Twain, Unsanctified Newspaper Reporter.* U of Missouri P, 2008.

"Cartoonists on the Staff of the Colored Supplement of the Sunday World." *The World,* 19 July 1896, Colored Supplement, p. 4.

Castelberg's National Jewelry Co. Advertisement showing the Yellow Kid wearing jewelry. *The Evening Star* [Washington, DC], 1 Dec. 1896, p. 8.

Castelli, Alfredo, editor. *L'Altro Yellow Kid, 1896–1898: La Produzione dimenticata di George B. Luks.* Comicon, 2010.

Chanan, Michael. *Repeated Takes: A Short History of Recording and Its Effects on Music.* Verso, 1995.

Chapin, Robert Coit. *The Standard of Living among Workingmen's Families in New York City.* Charities Publication Committee, 1909.

Chapman, C. C. "Ammunition Guns and Sporting Goods." *Tucumcari News and Tucumcari Times,* 24 Dec. 1910, p. 10.

——. "Builders Hardware." *Tucumcari News and Tucumcari Times,* 15 Apr. 1910, p. 4.

——. "Heating Stoves That Heat." *Tucumcari News and Tucumcari Times,* 24 Sept. 1910, p. 3.

——. "Wire Fences That Last: They Are the Goods." *Tucumcari News and Tucumcari Times,* 5 Apr. 1910, p. 8.

Chapman, John, and Garrison P. Sherwood, editors. *The Best Plays of 1894–1899.* Dodd, Mead and Company, 1955.

Charosh, Paul. "Studying Nineteenth-Century Popular Song." *American Music,* vol. 15, no. 4, 1997, pp. 459–92.

Chiba, Yoko. "Japonisme: East-West Renaissance in the Late 19th Century." *Mosaic: An Interdisciplinary Critical Journal,* vol. 31, no. 2, June 1998, pp. 1–20.

"Children Sing 'The Yellow Kid.'" *The Washington Post,* 30 Dec. 1896, p. 4.

Clark, Francis, Rev., and Harriet E. Clark. *Our Journey Around the World. An Illustrated Record of a Year's Travel. With Glimpses of Life in Far Off Land. As Seen through a Woman's Eyes.* A. D. Worthington & Co., Publishers, 1894.

Cohen, Daniel. *Yellow Journalism: Scandal, Sensationalism, and Gossip in the Media.* Twenty-First Century Books, 2000.

Collier, Patrick. "Imperial/Modernist Forms in the *Illustrated London News.*" *Modernism/modernity,* vol. 19, no. 3, 2012, pp. 487–514.

Connerty, Michael. "Happy Ike, the Pink Kid, and the American Presence in Early British Comics." *International Journal of Comic Art,* vol. 19, no. 1, Spring/Summer 2017, pp. 538–46.

Connor, Steven. *Paraphernalia: The Curios Lives of Magical Things.* Profile Books, 2011.

Conolly-Smith, Peter. "Transforming an Ethnic Readership through 'Word and Image': William Randolph Hearst's *Deutsches Journal* and New York's German-Language Press, 1895–1918." *American Periodicals: A Journal of History, Criticism, and Bibliography,* vol. 19, no. 1, 2009, pp. 66–84.

Constable, Liz. "Fin-de-siècle Yellow Fevers: Women Writers, Decadence and Discourses of Degeneracy." *L'Esprit Créateur*, vol. 37, no. 3, 1997, pp. 25–37.

Cook, Charles Emerson. "Pictures by Telegraph." *Pearson's Magazine*, no. 3, Apr. 1900, pp. 345–48.

Coppersmith, Jonathan. *Faxed: The Rise and Fall of the Fax Machine*. Johns Hopkins UP, 2015.

"The Corps of Guides, Whose Services Were Donated to the Fair." *The Home Magazine*, vol. 8, no. 1, Jan. 1897, p. 6.

Cory, J. Campbell. "Four Days More and the Political Campaign of '96 Will Be Over." *New York Journal*, 30 Oct. 1896, p. 5.

———. Political cartoon with the Yellow Kid. *New York Journal*, 2 Nov. 1896, p. 3.

Cotkin, George. *Reluctant Modernism: American Thought and Culture, 1880–1900*. Twayne Publishers, 1992.

Couperie, Pierre, and Maurice C. Horn. *A History of the Comic Strip*. Crown Publisher, 1968.

"The Cretan Blockade." *New York Journal*, 23 Mar. 1897, p. 6.

Cross, Gary. *Kids' Stuff: Toys and the Changing World of American Childhood*. Harvard UP, 1997.

Cummins, Roger W. *Humorous but Wholesome: A History of Palmer Cox and the Brownies*. Century House Americana, 1973.

Dahl, Curtis. "Artemus Ward: Comic Panoramist." *The New England Quarterly*, vol. 32, no. 4, 1959, pp. 476–85.

Dale, Alan, and Archie Gunn. "The Mandarin." *New York Journal*, 5 Nov. 1896, p. 6.

"Daphne's Room." *Frasier*, directed by David Lee, performance by Kelsey Grammer, Jane Leeves, et al. Season 2, episode 17, Paramount Studios, 1995.

de Abruña, Laura Niesen. "Green Watermelons and Loaded Frogs: The Unexpected as Humor in Mark Twain's Lectures." *The Journal of the Midwest Modern Language Association*, vol. 20, no. 1, 1987, pp. 46–56.

DeGroot, William A. "Hogan's Alley Puzzle." N. pub., 1896.

De Haven, Tom. *Funny Papers*. Viking, 1985.

Denholm & McKay Co. "Boston Store." *Worcester Daily Spy*, 1 May 1897, p. 4.

Denning, Michael. "Cheap Stories: Notes on Popular Fiction and Working-Class Culture in Nineteenth-Century America." *History Workshop*, vol. 22, Special American Issue, 1986, pp. 1–17.

Denson, Shane. "'To be continued . . . ': Seriality and Serialization in Interdisciplinary Perspective." *Journal of Literary Theory Online*, 2011, www.jlt online.de/index.php/conferences/article/view/346/1004.

Denson, Shane, et al., editors. *Transnational Perspectives on Comics and Graphic Narratives: Comics at the Crossroads*. Bloomsbury, 2013.

Denson, Shane, and Ruth Mayer. "Grenzgänger: Serielle Figuren im Medienwechsel." *Populäre Serialität: Narration—Evolution—Distinktion. Zum seriellen Erzählen seit dem 19. Jahrhundert*, edited by Frank Kelleter, transcript, 2012, pp. 185–203.

"Denver." *The American Stationer*, vol. 41, Jan. 1897, 122.

De Sapio, Joseph. *Modernity and Meaning in Victorian London: Tourist Views of the Imperial Capital*. Palgrave Macmillan, 2014.

"The Descent of the Newspaper." Letter to the editor by "M.," *The New York Evening Post*, 20 Oct. 1896, p. 4.

"Descriptive Songs and Ballads." *The Phonoscope*, vol. 1, no. 1, Nov. 1896, p. 16.

DesRochers, Rick. *The New Humor in the Progressive Era: Americanization and the Vaudeville Comedian*. Palgrave Macmillan, 2014.

De Vinne, Theodore Low. *The Practice of Typography: Modern Methods of Book Composition, A Treatise on Type-Setting by Hand and by Machine and on the Proper Arrangement and Imposition of Pages*. The Century Co., 1904.

Dillon, Stanley. Letter to the editor. *Omaha World-Herald*, 22 Dec. 1898, p. 8.

Dirks, Rudolph. "First, the Anti-Cartoon Bill. Then, Perhaps This!" *New York Journal and Advertiser*, 20 Feb. 1898, American Humorist, p. 5.

Dormon, James H. "Ethnic Stereotyping in American Popular Culture: The Depiction of American Ethnics in the Cartoon Periodicals of the Gilded Age." *Amerikastudien/ American Studies*, vol. 30, no. 4, 1985, pp. 489–507.

Dreiser, Theodore. *Newspaper Days*. Edited by T. D. Nostwich, U of Pennsylvania P, 1991.

Dryer, Trevor D. "'All the News That's Fit to Print.' The New York Times, 'Yellow' Journalism, and the Criminal Trial 1898–1902." *Nevada Law Journal*, vol. 8, 2008, pp. 541–69.

Duer, Caroline. "The Yellow Age." *Current Literature*, vol. 20, no. 5, 1896, p. 391.

Dumont, Frank. *The Yellow Kid Who Lives in Hogan's Alley: A Burlesque*. De Witt Publishing House, 1897.

Duval, Romain. "Les centres marginaux: Outcault et les enfants pauvre d'Hogan's Alley." *Dessiner dans la marge*, edited by Boris Eizykman, L'Harmattan, 2004, pp. 95–127.

Eco, Umberto. "Innovation and Repetition: Between Modern and Post-Modern Aesthetics." *Daedalus*, vol. 134, no. 4, 2005, pp. 191–207.

EDGE. "The Great Sunday World." *The World*, 1 May 1897, p. 14.

———. "Thanksgiving Number." *The World*, 21 Nov. 1896, p. 14.

EDGE, and Robert H. Ingersoll & Bro. "The Ingersoll Yankee Dollar Watch." *The World*, 20 Dec. 1896, Comic Weekly, p. 4.

"Editorial Clippings." *Philadelphia Inquirer*, 15 Dec. 1896, p. 6.

Elliot, Judson W. "The Yellow Kid Waltz Song." Judson W. Elliot Publisher, 1897.

Elsing, William T. "Life in New York Tenement-Houses." *The Poor in Great Cities: Their Problems and What Is Being Done to Solve Them*, edited by Robert A. Woods et al., Kegan Paul, Trench, Trübner & Co., 1896, pp. 42–85.

Emery, Edwin, and Michael Emery. *The Press and America: An Interpretative History of Mass Media*. 1954. 4th ed., Prentice-Hall, 1978.

Endy, Christopher. "Travel and World Power: Americans in Europe, 1890–1917." *Diplomatic History*, vol. 22, no. 4, 1998, pp. 565–94.

"An Entertainment That Is Certain to Please All." *Middletown Daily Argus*, 4 Jan. 1897, p. 8.

Erdman, Andrew L. *Blue Vaudeville: Sex, Morals and the Mass Marketing of Amusement, 1895–1915*. McFarland, 2004.

"The Evolution of the Comic Picture and the Comic Artist." *The San Francisco Call*, 12 Nov. 1905, n. pag.

Ewen, Stuart, and Elizabeth Ewen. *Channels of Desire: Mass Images and the Shaping of American Consciousness*. 1982. U of Minnesota P, 1994.

Fahs, Alice. "Newspaper Women and the Making of the Modern, 1885–1910." *Prospects*, vol. 27, 2002, pp. 303–39.

"False Faces." *Los Angeles Times*, 21 Nov. 1897, p. 16.

"Father Puncherbocker, Greater New York's Quaint and Jovial Soul, Receives an Overwhelming Welcome." *The World*, 22 Dec. 1897, p. 14.

"Favus, a Clinical Study, with Special Reference to Treatment." *Pediatrics*, vol. 7, no. 1, 1 Jan. 1899, pp. 137–39.

FAX. "In Providence." *Printers' Ink*, vol. 21, 27 Oct. 1897, p. 27.

Feinstein, Robert. "The Phonograph in Hogan's Alley." *The Antique Phonograph Monthly*, vol. 33, no. 8, 1975, pp. 3–10.

Ferre, John P. "Sunday Newspapers and the Decline of Protestant Authority in the United States." *American Journalism*, vol. 10, no. 1–2, 1993, pp. 7–23.

The Filbert Grinding Co. Razor blades resharpened advertisement showing the Yellow Kid. *Evening Public Ledger* [Philadelphia], 6 July 1921, p. 15.

Fischer, Roger A. "Nast, Keppler, and the Mass Market." *Inks: Cartoon and Comic Art Studies*, vol. 4, no. 2, 1997, pp. 26–31.

———. *Them Damned Pictures: Explorations in American Political Cartoon Art*. Archon Books, 1996.

Floyd, J. F. *Our Tour Around the World. Containing Short Letters of Travel of A Tour Around the World, through America, Hawaiian Islands, New Zealand, Tasmania, Australia, Ceylon, Egypt, Palestine, Italy, France and England, Including Ten Years' Residence in New Zealand and Australia*. Charles H. Kerr & Company, 1896.

"Footlight Flashes." *The Philadelphia Inquirer*, 30 Aug. 1896, p. 16.

Frahm, Ole. "Every Window Tells a Story: Remarks on the Urbanity of Early Comic Strips." *Comics and the City*, edited by Jörn Ahrens and Arno Meteling, Continuum, 2010, pp. 31–44.

Freeman, Matthew. "Advertising the Yellow Brick Road: Historicizing the Industrial Emergence of Transmedia Storytelling." *International Journal of Communication*, vol. 8, no. 1, 2014, pp. 2362–81.

———. "Branding Consumerism: Cross-Media Characters and Story-Worlds at the Turn of the 20th Century." *International Journal of Cultural Studies*, vol. 18, no. 6, 2015, pp. 629–44.

French, George. "Along Newspaper Row." *The Printer and Bookmaker*, vol. 24, no. 2, Apr. 1897, pp. 50–53.

Friday, William H., Jr., and Homer Tourjée. "The Dugan Kid Who Lives in Hogan's Alley." The Homer Tourjée Music Pub. Co., 1896.

———. "The Yellow Kid." *New York Journal*, 8 Nov. 1896, American Humorist, pp. 7–8.

Frow, John A. "The Signature: Three Arguments about the Commodity of Form." *Aesthesia and the Economy of the Senses*, edited by Helen Grace, UWS Nepean, 1996, pp. 151–200.

Fuller, Wayne Edison. *RFD, The Changing Face of Rural America.* Indiana UP, 1964.

Furia, Philip. *The Poets of Tin Pan Alley: A History of America's Great Lyricists.* Oxford UP, 1990.

Gabriele, Sandra, and Paul S. Moore. "The *Globe* on Saturday, the *World* on Sunday: Toronto Weekend Editions and the Influence of the American Sunday Paper, 1886–1895." *Canadian Journal of Communication,* vol. 34, no. 3, 2009, pp. 337–58.

Gallienne, Le Richard. *Prose Fancies.* Second Series, John Lane, H. S. Stone & Co., 1896.

Galow, Timothy W. "Literary Modernism in the Age of Celebrity." *Modernism/ modernity,* vol. 17, no. 2, 2010, pp. 313–29.

Gambone, Robert L. *Life on the Press: The Popular Art and Illustrations of George Benjamin Luks.* UP of Mississippi, 2009.

Gandal, Keith. *The Virtues of the Vicious: Jacob Riis, Stephen Crane, and the Spectacle of the Slum.* Oxford UP, 1998.

Gardner, Ethellyn. *Letters of the Motor Girl.* The New England News Co.; Colonial Press, 1906.

Gardner, Jared. *Projections: Comics and the History of 21st-Century Storytelling.* Stanford UP, 2012.

Gerstle, Gary. *American Crucible: Race and Nation in the Twentieth Century.* Princeton UP, 2001.

Gilbert, David, and Claire Hancock. "New York City and the Transatlantic Imagination: French and English Tourism and the Spectacle of the Modern Metropolis, 1893–1939." *Journal of Urban History,* vol. 33, no. 1, 2006, pp. 77–107.

Gilfoyle, Timothy J. "Street-Rats and Gutter-Snipes: Child Pickpockets and Street Culture in New York City, 1850–1900." *Journal of Social History,* vol. 37, no. 4, 2004, pp. 853–82.

Gillies, Mary Ann. "The Literary Agent and the Sequel." *Part Two: Reflections on the Sequel,* edited by Paul Budra and Betty A. Schellenberg, U of Toronto P, 1998, pp. 131–43.

"Gilmore and Leonard." *The New York Dramatic Mirror,* 9 Apr. 1898, p. 28.

Gilmore & Leonard in Their Irish Nonsensicality Hogan's Alley. H. C. Miner Litho. Co., 1898.

Ginsburg, Jane C. "Licensing Commercial Value: From Copyright to Trademarks and Back." *The Law and Practice of Trademark Transactions: A Global and Local Outlook,* edited by Irene Calboli and Jacques de Werra, Edward Elgar, 2016, pp. 53–81.

"Giving Away Goods." *Printers' Ink,* vol. 25, 8 Apr. 1896, p. 34.

Glenn, Susan A. "'Give an Imitation of Me': Vaudeville Mimics and the Play of the Self." *American Quarterly,* vol. 50, no. 1, 1998, pp. 47–76.

"Glens Falls Opera House." *The Morning Star* [Glens Falls], 5 Dec. 1896, p. 5.

"A Glimpse in Holiday Windows." *The Clothier and Furnisher,* vol. 1, no. 5 [vol. 26 new series], Dec. 1896, p. 40.

Gordon, Ian. *Comic Strips and Consumer Culture, 1890–1945.* Smithsonian Institution P, 1998.

———. "Mass Market Modernism: Comic Strips and the Culture of Consumption." *Australasian Journal of American Studies,* vol. 14, no. 2, Dec. 1995, pp. 49–66.

Goris, An. "Happily Ever After . . . and After: Serialization and the Popular Romance Novel." *Americana: The Journal of American Popular Culture,* vol. 12, no. 1, 2013, n. pag., www.americanpopularculture.com/journal/articles/spring_2013/goris.htm.

Gossel, Daniel. *Medien und Politik in Deutschland und den USA. Kontrolle, Konflikt und Kooperation vom 18. bis zum frühen 20. Jahrhundert.* Franz Steiner Verlag, 2010.

"Gossip of the Town." *The New York Daily Mirror*, 25 Apr. 1896, p. 2.

"Gossip of the Town." *The New York Dramatic Mirror*, 21 Nov. 1896, p. 2.

Graham, Charles. "Tenement Life in New York—Sketches in the Fourth Ward." *Harper's Weekly*, 29 Mar. 1879, p. 245.

"The Graphic Christmas Number." *New York Daily Tribune*, 23 Dec. 1876, p. 10.

Green, Harvey. "Review." *The American Historical Review*, vol. 96, no. 2, 1991, pp. 615–16.

Gruenwald, Marc, et al. *Captain America* I#401. Marvel Entertainment, June 1992.

Grünewald, Dietrich. *Comics*. Niemeyer, 2000.

Guarneri, Julia. *Newsprint Metropolis: City Papers and the Making of Modern Americans*. U of Chicago P, 2017.

Guggenheim, Marc, et al. *Blade* III#5, Marvel Entertainment, Mar. 2007.

———, et al. *Blade* III#12, Marvel Entertainment, Oct. 2007.

Haenni, Sabine. *The Immigrant Scene: Ethnic Amusements in New York, 1880–1920*. U of Minnesota P, 2008.

Hagedorn, Roger. "Doubtless to Be Continued: A Brief History of Serial Narrative." *To Be Continued . . . : Soap Operas around the World*, edited by Robert C. Allen, Routledge, 1995, pp. 27–48.

———. "Technology and Economic Exploitation: The Serial as a Form of Narrative Presentation." *Wide Angle*, vol. 10, no. 4, 1988, pp. 4–12.

Hake, Ted. *Hake's Guide to Comic Character Collectibles: An Illustrated Price Guide to 100 Years of Comic Strip Characters*. Wallace-Homestead Book Company, 1993.

Hales, Peter Bacon. *Silver Cities. The Photography of American Urbanization, 1839–1915*. Temple UP, 1984.

Hallock, W. W. "Pernicious 'Yellow' Papers." Letter to the editor. *The New York Times*, 24 Mar. 1898, p. 5.

Hamilton, Grant. "Political 'Kids' out in the Cold." *Judge*, vol. 31, 12 Dec. 1896, n. pag.

———. "The Yellowest' Kid in Tammany Alley." *Judge*, vol. 31, 14 Nov. 1896, n. pag.

Hamilton, Grant, and Bernhard Gillam. "Judge's Brownies Spend Christmas in the National Store-Rooms." *Judge*, vol. 31, 26 Dec. 1896, n. pag.

Hamlin, Arthur S. *Copyright Cases, A Summary of Leading American Decisions on the Law of Copyright and on Literary Property, from 1891 to 1903*. G. P. Putnam's Sons, 1904.

Harder, Hans, and Barbara Mittler, editors. *Asian Punches: A Transcultural Affair*. Springer, 2013.

Harris, Neil. *Cultural Excursions: Marketing Appetites and Cultural Tastes in Modern America*. The U of Chicago P, 1990.

Harvey, Robert C. "How Comics Came to Be." *A Comics Studies Reader*, edited by Jeet Heer and Kent Worcester, UP of Mississippi, 2009, pp. 25–45.

Hatfield, Charles. "An Art of Tensions." *A Comics Studies Reader*, edited by Jeet Heer and Kent Worcester, UP of Mississippi, 2009, pp. 132–48.

Hayward, Jennifer Poole. *Consuming Pleasures: Active Audiences and Serial Fictions from Dickens to Soap Opera*. UP of Kentucky, 1997.

Henkin, David. M. *The Postal Age: The Emergence of Modern Communications in Nineteenth Century America.* U of Chicago P, 2006.

"Here Are the First Pictures Ever Telegraphed." *New York Journal*, 25 Oct. 1896, American Sunday Magazine, p. 31.

"Heroic Stand of Greece." *New York Journal*, 6 Mar. 1896, p. 6.

Herzberg, Oscar. "Advertising for Retailers." *Printers' Ink*, vol. 17, no. 8, 25 Nov. 1896, pp. 35–37.

Herzfeld, Elsa Goldina. *Family Monographs: The History of Twenty-Four Families Living in the Middle West Side of New York City.* The James Kempster Printing Company, 1905.

"High-Class Horses at Madison Square Garden This Week." *The World*, 8 Nov. 1896, Sunday Magazine, p. 31.

Hills, Matt. "Torchwood's Trans-Transmedia: Media Tie-Ins and Brand 'Fanagement.'" *Participations: Journal of Audience & Reception Studies*, vol. 9, no. 2, 2012, pp. 409–28.

Hodin, Mark. "Class, Consumption, and Ethnic Performance in Vaudeville." *Prospects*, vol. 22, 1997, pp. 193–210.

"Hogan's Alley." *The New York Daily Mirror*, 18 Apr. 1896, p. 17.

"'Hogan's Alley' A Big Hit." *The World*, 13 Oct. 1896, p. 9.

Holbo, John. "Redefining Comics." *The Art of Comics: A Philosophical Approach*, edited by Aaron Meskin and Roy T. Cook, Blackwell, 2012, pp. 3–30.

Holme, Pauline W. "Address to the National Purity Congress, Baltimore Yearly Meeting Committee." *The National Purity Congress, Its Papers, Addresses, Portraits*, edited by Aaron M. Powell, The American Purity Alliance, 1896, pp. 186–90.

Holt, Elvin. "'A Coon Alphabet' and the Comic Mask of Racial Prejudice." *Studies in American Humor*, vol. 5, no. 2, 1986–87, pp. 307–18.

Houston, Edwin J., and A. E. Kennelly. *Electric Telegraphy.* The W. J. Johnston Company, 1897.

Howell, William B. "'Yellow Kid' Copyright." *Synopsis of Decisions of the Treasury Department and Board of U. S. General Appraisers on the Construction of Tariff, Immigration, and Other Laws, for the Year Ending December 31, 1897*, edited by Lyman J. Gage, Government Printing Office, 1898, p. 363.

Howells, William Dean. "A Case in Point." *Literature—An International Gazette of Criticism* 2, 24 Mar. 1899, pp. 241–42.

H. P. Evan Co. *Instruction Book for the Standard Tailor System: A Self-Instructor with Object Lessons in the Art of Cutting All Styles of Garments, for Ladies, Gentlemen, Children and Infants.* H. P. Evan Co., 1896.

Hughes, Linda K., and Michael Lund. "Studying Victorian Serials." *Literary Research*, vol. 11, no. 4, 1986, pp. 235–52.

———. *The Victorian Serial.* UP of Virginia, 1991.

"Invention and Discovery." *The Great Round World*, vol. 1, no. 28, May 1897, p. 807.

Ito, Kinko. "Manga in Japanese History." *Japanese Visual Culture: Explorations in the World of Manga and Anime, 2008*, edited by Mark W. MacWilliams. Routledge, 2015, pp. 26–47.

James, Henry. "Chartres Portrayed." *The Tribune*, 29 Apr. 1876, p. 3.

———. "Paris as It Is." *The Tribune*, 25 Dec. 1875, p. 3.

———. "Parisian Life." *The Tribune*, 5 Feb. 1876, p. 3.

———. "Parisian Sketches." *The Tribune*, 22 Jan. 1876, p. 3.

"James M. Hamilton and Others in Costumes." [ca. 1910s]. *Montana State University Historical Photographs Collection—Montana State University*, http://arc.lib.montana.edu/msu-photos/item/56.

J. B. Lewis Co. "Wear-Resisters." *Boot and Shoe Recorder*, vol. 30, Jan. 1897, p. 135.

Jenkins, Henry. *What Made Pistachio Nuts? Early Sound Comedy and the Vaudeville Aesthetic.* Columbia UP, 1992.

Jenkins, Henry, et al. *Spreadable Media: Creating Value and Meaning in a Networked Culture.* New York UP, 2013.

Jess-Cooke, Carolyn, and Constantine Verevis. Introduction. *Second Takes: Critical Approaches to the Film Sequel,* edited by Carolyn Jess-Cooke and Constantine Verevis, State U of New York P, 2010, pp. 1–10.

"Jimmie's Paper." *The World,* 6 Dec. 1896, Comic Weekly, p. 2.

"Jimmie's Paper." *The World,* 13 Dec. 1896, Comic Weekly, p. 2.

Johanningsmeier, Charles. *Fiction and the American Literary Marketplace: The Role of Newspaper Syndicates, 1860–1900.* Cambridge UP, 1997.

———. "Newspaper Syndicates of the Late Nineteenth Century: Overlooked Forces in the American Literary Market-Place." *Publishing History,* vol. 37, 1995, pp. 61–82.

Johnson Bros. A holiday presents advertisement with the Yellow Kid. *The Kansas City Journal,* 9 Dec. 1896, p. 2.

Johnson-Woods, Toni. *Manga: An Anthology of Global and Cultural Perspectives.* Continuum, 2010.

Johnston, Patricia. Introduction. *Seeing High & Low: Representing Social Conflict in American Visual Culture,* edited by Patricia Johnston, U of California P, 2006, pp. 1–24.

Jones, Gavin. *Strange Talk: The Politics of Dialect in Literature in Gilded Age America.* U of California P, 1999.

Jones, Hayden. "Unique Scenes at the Commercial Travellers' Fair at Madison Square Garden." *New York Journal,* 18 Dec. 1896, p. 3.

Juergens, George. *Joseph Pulitzer and the New York World.* Princeton UP, 1966.

"Just in Time to Meet a Popular Demand." *New York Journal,* 7 Nov. 1896, p. 10.

Kaestle, Carl F. "Literacy and Diversity: Themes from a Social History of the American Reading Public." *History of Education Quarterly,* vol. 28, no. 4, 1988, pp. 523–49.

Kaindl, Klaus. "Visual Comics: Language, Pictures and Typography in the Translation of Comics." *META,* vol. 53, no. 1, 2008, pp. 120–38.

Kasanof, Lisa. *The Illustrations of Everett Shinn and George Luks.* PhD dissertation, University of Illinois at Urbana–Champaign, 1992.

Kasson, Joy S. *Buffalo Bill's Wild West: Celebrity, Memory, and Popular History.* Hill & Wang, 2000.

Keightley, Keir. "Hogan's Tin Pan Alley: R. F. Outcault and Popular Sheet Music." *The Musical Quarterly,* vol. 98, no. 1–2, 2015, pp. 29–56.

———. "Tin Pan Allegory." *Modernism/modernity,* vol. 19, no. 4, 2012, pp. 717–36.

Kelleter, Frank. "Five Ways of Looking at Popular Seriality." *Media of Serial Narrative*, edited by Frank Kelleter, Ohio State UP, 2017, pp. 7–34.

———. "From Recursive Progression to Systemic Self-Observation: Elements of a Theory of Seriality." *The Velvet Light Trap*, vol. 79, 2017, pp. 99–105.

———, editor. *Populäre Serialität: Narration—Evolution—Distinktion. Zum seriellen Erzählen seit dem 19. Jahrhundert*. transcript, 2012.

Kelleter, Frank, and Daniel Stein. "Great, Mad, New: Populärkultur, serielle Ästhetik und der frühe amerikanische Zeitungscomic." *Comics: Zur Geschichte und Theorie eines populärkulturellen Mediums*, edited by Stephan Ditschke et al., transcript, 2009, pp. 81–117.

Kemble, Edward Windsor. "Some X-Mas Gifts Which Would Fit—Perhaps Santa Claus Will Take This Advice." *New York Journal*, 20 Dec. 1896, American Humorist, n. pag.

Kensinger, Faye Riter. *Children of the Series & How They Grew, or A Century of Heroines & Heroes, Romantic, Comic, Moral*. Bowling Green State U Popular P, 1987.

Kersten, Holger. "The Creative Potential of Dialect Writing in Later-Nineteenth-Century America." *Nineteenth-Century Literature*, vol. 55, no. 1, June 2000, pp. 92–117.

———. "Using the Immigrant's Voice: Humor and Pathos in Nineteenth Century 'Dutch' Dialect Texts." *MELUS*, vol. 21, no. 4, 1996, pp. 3–17.

Kibler, M. Alison. "Pigs, Green Whiskers, and Drunken Widows: Irish Nationalists and the 'Practical Censorship' of McFadden's Row of Flats in 1902 and 1903." *Journal of American Studies*, vol. 42, no. 3, Dec. 2008, pp. 489–514.

Kielbowicz, Richard B. "Postal Subsidies for the Press and the Business of Mass Culture, 1880–1920." *Business History Review*, vol. 64, no. 3, 1990, pp. 451–88.

———. "Regulating Timeliness: Technologies, Laws, and the News, 1840–1970." *Journalism & Communication Monographs*, vol. 17, no. 1, 2015, pp. 5–83.

Kiler's Pharmacy Co. A Yellow Kid advertisement. *The Makio*, vol. 16, Apr. 1897, p. 343.

"Kill the Arbitration Treaty." *New York Journal and Advertiser*, 5 May 1897, p. 6.

Knobel, Dale T. "A Vocabulary of Ethnic Perception: Content Analysis of the American Stage Irishman, 1820–1860." *Journal of American Studies*, vol. 15, no. 1, 1981, pp. 45–71.

Kress, Gunther, und Theo van Leeuwen. *Reading Images: The Grammar of Visual Design*. 2nd ed., Routledge, 2006.

Krummel, Donald William. "Searching and Sorting on the Slippery Slope: Periodical Publication of Victorian Music." *Notes*, vol. 46, no. 3, 1990, pp. 593–608.

Kunzle, David. "The First Ally Sloper: The Earliest Popular Cartoon Character as a Satire on the Victorian Work Ethic." *Oxford Art Journal*, vol. 8, no. 1, Caricature, 1985, pp. 40–48.

———. "Precursors in American Weeklies to the American Newspaper Comic Strip: A Long Gestation and a Transoceanic Cross-Breeding." *Forging a New Medium: The Comic Strip in the Nineteenth Century*, edited by C. Dierick and P. Lefèvre, Vrije Universiteit Brussel P, 1998, pp. 157–85.

Laing, Dave. "A Voice without a Face: Popular Music and the Phonograph in the 1890s." *Popular Music*, vol. 10, no. 1, 1991, pp. 1–9.

Laird, Pamela Walker. *Advertising Progress: American Business and the Rise of Consumer Marketing*. Johns Hopkins UP, 1998.

Leach, William R. *Land of Desire: Merchants, Power, and the Rise of a New American Culture.* Vintage Books, 1993.

"Leander Sisters." Produced by James Henry White, camera by Frederick Blechynden. Thomas A. Edison Inc., 1897 [Library of Congress Online Catalog: https://www.loc.gov/item/00694233].

Lears, T. J. Jackson. *Fables of Abundance: A Cultural History of Advertising in America.* Basic Books, 1994.

Leary, John Patrick. "America's Other Half: Slum Journalism and the War of 1898." *Journal of Transnational American Studies,* vol. 1, no. 1, 2009, pp. 1–33, escholarship.org/uc/item/0v654385.

Lee, Alfred McClung. *The Daily Newspaper in America: The Evolution of a Social Instrument.* MacMillan Company, 1937.

Lee, James Melvin. *History of American Journalism.* Houghton Mifflin, 1917.

Lee, Judith Yaross. "Mark Twain as a Stand-up Comedian." *The Mark Twain Annual,* vol. 4, no. 1, 2006, pp. 3–23.

Lehuu, Isabelle. *Carnival on the Page: Popular Print Media in Antebellum America.* U of North Carolina P, 2000.

Lemke, Siglinde. *The Vernacular Matters of American Literature.* Palgrave, 2009.

Levine, Lawrence W. "William Shakespeare and the American People: A Study in Cultural Transformation." *The American Historical Review,* vol. 89, no. 1, 1984, pp. 34–66.

Levy, Lester S. *Picture the Songs: Lithographs from the Sheet Music of Nineteenth-Century America.* Johns Hopkins UP, 1976.

Lewis, Robert M. "Tableaux Vivants: Parlor Theatricals in Victorian America." *Revue française d'études américaines,* vol. 36, Apr. 1988, pp. 280–91.

——, editor. *From Traveling Show to Vaudeville: Theatrical Spectacle in America, 1830–1910.* Johns Hopkins UP, 2003.

Libbey, Laura Jean. "Kidnapped at the Altar, or The Romance of That Saucy Jessie Bain." *Fireside Companion—A Journal of Instructive and Entertaining Literature,* no. 1311, 10 Dec. 1892, n. pag.

Library of Congress Copyright Office. *Dramatic Compositions Copyrighted in the United States, 1870 to 1916.* Vol. 1, A To N. Government Printing Office, 1918.

——. *Dramatic Compositions Copyrighted in the United States, 1870 to 1916.* Vol. 2, O To Z. Government Printing Office, 1918.

"Local News and Notes." *Seneca County News,* 29 Dec. 1896, n. pag.

Lockwood, Allison. *Passionate Pilgrims: The American Traveler in Great Britain, 1800–1914.* Associated U Presses, 1981.

Lowitz, John Buckingham. "The Intercollegiate Boat Race in the Jungle." *The World,* 18 Oct. 1896, Comic Weekly, p. 8.

——. "Valentine's Day in Gay Gazoozaland." *The World,* 14 Feb. 1897, Comic Weekly, p. 8.

Luks, George Benjamin. "8 Funny Pages." *The World,* 9 Oct. 1897, p. 14.

——. "Bargain Day in Hogan's Alley." *The World,* 10 Jan. 1897, Comic Weekly, p. 4.

——. "A Cake Walk in Hogan's Alley." *The World,* 31 Jan. 1897, Comic Weekly, p. 4.

———. "A Genuine Horse Show in Hogan's Alley." *The World,* 8 Nov. 1896, Comic Weekly, p. 5.

———. "A Ghost Séance in Hogan's Alley." *The World,* 7 Mar. 1897, Comic Weekly, p. 4.

———. "The Great Baby Show in Hogan's Alley." *The World,* 25 Oct. 1896, Comic Weekly, n. pag.

———. "The Great Prize Fight in Hogan's Alley." *The World,* 6 Dec. 1896, Comic Weekly, p. 4.

———. "Hogan's Alley Attacked by the Hoboken Pretzel Club." *The World,* 31 May 1896, Colored Supplement, p. 8.

———. "The Hogan's Alley Inauguration." *The World,* 28 Feb. 1897, Comic Weekly, p. 4.

———. "Hogan's Alley Kids at the Continuous Performance." *The World,* 5 Dec. 1897, Comic Weekly, p. 5.

———. "A Hot Election Day in Hogan's Alley." *The World,* 1 Nov. 1896, Comic Weekly, n. pag.

———. "The Kalsomine Family's Glee Club in Full Action—The Trained Chicken Mose Conducts a Rehearsal." *The World,* 8 Aug. 1897, Comic Weekly, p. 8.

———. "The Masquerade Ball in Hogan's Alley." *The World,* 15 Nov. 1896, Comic Weekly, p. 4.

———. "Mose's Incubator—More Twins Born but There Are Others to Come." *The World,* 6 Mar. 1898, Comic Weekly, p. 8.

———. "Mose's Incubator—New Twins Hatched Each Week." *The World,* 30 Jan. 1898, Comic Weekly, p. 5.

———. "New Year's Celebration in Hogan's Alley." *The World,* 27 Dec. 1896, Comic Weekly, p. 4.

———. "The Open-Air School in Hogan's Alley." *The World,* 18 Oct. 1896, Comic Weekly, p. 3.

———. "Porkville's Four Hundred in the Merry Waltz." *The World,* 28 Nov. 1897, Comic Weekly, p. 5.

———. "President-Elect M'Kinley Visits Hogan's Alley." *The World,* 29 Nov. 1896, Comic Weekly, p. 5.

———. "Santa Claus Held Up in Hogan's Alley." *The World,* 13 Dec. 1896, Comic Weekly Christmas Number, p. 5.

———. "A Seeley Dinner in Hogan's Alley." *The World,* 24 Jan. 1897, Comic Weekly, p. 4.

———. "A Snowball Battle in Hogan's Alley." *The World,* 20 Dec. 1896, Comic Weekly, p. 4.

———. "A Sunday World Cartoonist's Impressions of Maggie Cline and 'Hogan's Alley.'" *The World,* 18 Oct. 1896, Sunday Magazine, p. 32.

———. "Thanksgiving Day in Hogan's Alley." *The World,* 22 Nov. 1896, Comic Weekly, p. 4.

———. "Training for the Football Championship Game in Hogan's Alley." *The World,* 11 Oct. 1896, Comic Weekly, p. 3.

———. "Valentine's Day in Hogan's Alley." *The World,* 14 Feb. 1897, Comic Weekly, p. 4.

———. "The Victoria Jubilee Celebration in Hogan's Alley—Queen Liz Reviews the Parade and the Kid Is Knighted." *The World,* 20 June 1897, Comic Weekly, p. 4.

Lynn & Co. "Yellow Kid Free." *The Black Cat: A Monthly Magazine of Original Short Stories*, vol. 19, Apr. 1897, p. 53.

Maguire & Baucus Ltd. *Fall Catalogue: Lumiere Films, Edison Films, International Films.* 1897.

Mancall, Peter C. "Introduction: Observing More Things and More Curiously." *Huntington Library Quarterly*, vol. 70, no. 1, Mar. 2007, pp. 1–10.

Manning, Ulysses G. Editorial comment on the Yellow Kid. *American Druggist and Pharmaceutical Record*, vol. 30, no. 2, 1897, p. 51.

———. "The Yellow Kid." *American Druggist and Pharmaceutical Record*, vol. 30, no. 4, 1897, p. 112.

Marks Arnheim Tailoring Est. "The Brilliant Results of Truth and Perseverance." *The World*, 13 Dec. 1896, Comic Weekly, p. 8.

Marschall, Rick, and Warren Bernard. *Drawing Power: A Compendium of Cartoon Advertising*. Fantagraphics, 2011.

Mason, Harry B., ed. *Window Displays for Druggists; Comprising for the Most Part Engravings and Descriptions of over a Hundred Attractive Displays which have been Designed and Used with Success by Druggists throughout the Country, Together with some Useful Suggestions on the Subject of Window Dressing in General.* E. G. Swift, 1908.

Mayer, Ruth. "Image Power: Seriality, Iconicity and *The Mask of Fu Manchu*." *Screen*, vol. 53, no. 4, 2012, pp. 398–417.

———. "Machinic Fu Manchu: Popular Seriality and the Logic of Spread." *Journal of Narrative Theory*, vol. 43, no. 2, 2013, pp. 186–217.

———. *Serial Fu Manchu: The Chinese Supervillain and the Spread of Yellow Peril Ideology*. Temple UP, 2014.

McCardell, Roy L. "Opper, Outcault and Company: The Comic Supplement and the Men Who Make It." *Everybody's Magazine*, vol. 12, 1905, pp. 763–72.

McCarthy, Dan. "The Great Sunday World." *The World*, 15 Oct. 1897, p. 12.

———. "The Horse Show—With No Show for the Horse." *The World*, 8 Nov. 1896, Comic Weekly, p. 8.

———. "The Popular Disease of the Day—Kleptomania." *The World*, 15 Nov. 1896, Comic Weekly, p. 5.

McDonald, Susan Waugh. "From Kipling to Kitsch Two Popular Editors of the Gilded Age: Mass Culture, Magazines and the Correspondence Universities." *The Journal of Popular Culture*, vol. 15, no. 2, 1981, pp. 50–61.

McDonnell, Pearl. "Library Meetings—Washington." *Public Libraries: A Monthly Review of Library Matters and Methods*, vol. 12, 1907, pp. 288–89.

McDougall, Walt. "New York's Great Reform Freak Show." *The World*, 17 Jan. 1897, Comic Weekly, n. pag.

———. "What Our Annual Horse Show Amounts To. Chiefly Display of the Gowns and Millinery of New York's Society Swells." *The World*, 10 Nov. 1895, Comic Weekly, n. pag.

McLean, Albert F. "US Vaudeville and the Urban Comics." *Theatre Quarterly*, vol. 1, no. 4, 1971, pp. 47–52.

McLoughlin Brothers. *McLoughlin Bros' Catalogue*. McLoughlin, 1895.

———. *McLoughlin Bros' Catalogue*. McLoughlin, 1897.

———. *Yellow Kid Puzzle*. McLoughlin, 1896.

McNair, J. R. "Chromolithography and Color Woodblock: Handmaidens to Nineteenth-Century Children's Literature." *Children's Literature Association Quarterly*, vol. 11, no. 4, 1986, pp. 193–97.

McReynolds, John O. "Othaematoma and Chronic Perichondritis of the Auricle." *Annals of Otology, Rhinology and Laryngology*, vol. 7, edited by T. Melville Hardie et al., Jones H. Parker, 1898, pp. 267–70.

McShane, Clay, and Joel A. Tarr. *The Horse in the City: Living Machines in the Nineteenth Century*. Johns Hopkins UP, 2007.

Meech-Pekarik, Julia, and Gabriel P. Weisberg. *Japonisme Comes to America: The Japanese Impact on the Graphic Arts, 1876–1925*. Abrams, 1990.

Mecklenburg, Virginia M. "Manufacturing Rebellion: The Ashcan Artists and the Press." *Metropolitan Lives. The Ashcan Artists and Their New York*, edited by Rebecca Zurier et al., National Museum of American Art in association with W. W. Norton, 1995, pp. 191–213.

Meinrenken, Jens. "Künstlermythen im Zeichen der Avantgarde: Zur Bedeutung der Malerei im amerikanischen Zeitungscomic." *Arbeit am Bild: Ein Album für Michael Diers*, edited by Steffen Haug et al. Walther König, 2010, pp. 122–26.

———. "Ver-rückte Bilder! Wenn Kunst- und Bildgeschichte sich im Comic begegnen." *kjl&m*, vol. 9, no. 3, 2009, pp. 46–52.

Meixner, Laura. "'Gambling with Bread': Monet, Speculation, and the Marketplace." *Modernism/modernity*, vol. 17, no. 1, 2010, pp. 171–99.

Melton, Jeffrey Alan. *Mark Twain, Travel Books, and Tourism: The Tide of a Great Popular Movement*. U of Alabama P, 2002.

Messent, Peter. "Tramps and Tourists: Europe in Mark Twain's *A Tramp Abroad*." *The Yearbook of English Studies*, vol. 34, 2004, pp. 138–54.

Metken, Günter. *Comics*. S. Fischer, 1970.

Meyer, August, and Herman F. Schlott. "The Yellow Kid." August Meyer Pub., 1897.

Meyer, Christina. "Medial Transgressions: Sheet Music—Theater—Advertising." *Mediality and Materiality of Contemporary Comics*, Spec. issue of *Journal of Graphic Novels and Comics*, guest editors Jan-Noël Thon and Lukas Wilde, vol. 7, no. 3, 2016, pp. 293–305.

———. "'Noch besser, bunter und mehr davon': Comicproduktion und Comicästhetik im 19. Jahrhundert." *Zur Ästhetik des Gemachten in Animation und Comic*, edited by Jan-Noël Thon and Véronique Sina, De Gruyter, 2018, pp. 151–75.

———. "Richard F. Outcault: Yellow Kid." *Handbook of Comics and Graphic Narratives*, edited by Sebastian Domsch et al., De Gruyter, forthcoming.

———. "Serial Entertainment / Serial Pleasure." *Media of Serial Narratives*, edited by Frank Kelleter, Ohio State UP, 2017, pp. 74–89.

———. "Topographien des urbanen Raums in Zeitungscomics der Jahrhundertwende." *Sehnsucht suchen? Amerikanische Topographien aus komparatistischer Perspektive*, edited by Christian Bachmann and Simone Sauer-Kretschmer, Christian A. Bachmann Verlag, 2014, pp. 169–91.

———. "Urban America in the Newspaper Comic Strips of the Nineteenth Century: Introducing the Yellow Kid." *ImageText*, vol. 6, no. 2, 2012, n. pag., www.english.ufl.edu/imagetext/archives/v6_2/meyer/.

Miller, Frank, et al. *All-Star Batman and Robin, The Boy Wonder*, #9. DC Comics, February 2008.

Mintz, Lawrence E. "Humor and Ethnic Stereotypes in Vaudeville and Burlesque." *MELUS*, vol. 21, no. 4, 1996, pp. 19–28.

"The Missouri Travelers' Mardi Gras Parade." *Meyer Brothers Druggist*, vol. 20, no. 9, Sept. 1899, p. 272.

"The Mole." *Dick Tracy*. Part IV, created by P. K. Palmer, directed by B. Reaves Eason, performance by Ralph Byrd, Raymond Hatton, William Tracy, et al., ABC, 22 Nov. 1950.

Montgomery, Maureen E. *"Gilded Prostitution": Status, Money and Transatlantic Marriages, 1870–1914*. 1983. Routledge, 2013.

———. "'Natural Distinction': The American Bourgeois Search for Distinctive Signs in Europe." *The American Bourgeoisie: Distinction and Identity in the Nineteenth Century*, edited by Sven Beckert and Julia B. Rosenbaum, Palgrave Macmillan, 2010, pp. 27–44.

Morgan, Wayne. "'If Your Grocer Does Not Keep the Ivory Soap': Palmer Cox, the Brownies, and 19th Century Marketing." *The Romance of Marketing History: Proceedings of the Eleventh Conference on Historical Analysis and Research Marketing*, 2003, edited by Eric H. Shaw, Association for Historical Research in Marketing, 2003, pp. 22–29.

Morgan, Wayne, and Sharilyn J. Ingram. "'If Palmer Cox wuz t' see yer, he'd git yer copyrighted in a minute': The Origins of Licensing." *Marketing History: Strengthening, Straightening and Extending: Proceedings of the 14th Biennial Conference on Historical Analysis and Research Marketing*, University of Leicester, June 2009, pp. 50–60.

Mott, Franklin Luther. *American Journalism: A History of Newspapers in the United States Through 250 Years*. The MacMillan Company, 1941. 2 vols.

Murphy, Maureen. "Bridget and Biddy: Images of the Irish Servant Girl in *Puck* Cartoons, 1889–1890." *New Perspectives on the Irish Diaspora*, edited by Charles Fanning, Southern Illinois UP, 2000, pp. 152–75.

Musser, Charles. "Passions and the Passion Play: Theatre, Film and Religion in America, 1880–1900." *Film History*, vol. 5, no. 4, Institutional Histories, 1993, pp. 419–56.

Myers, Gene. "Dance of the Hogan's Alley Hoboes." M. D. Swisher, 1896.

Myers, Robin, editor. *Serials and Their Readers, 1620–1914*. St. Paul's Bibliographies et al., 1993.

Nakashima, Tomoko. "Defining 'Japanese Art' in America." *The Japanese Journal of American Studies*, vol. 17, 2006, pp. 245–62.

Nalbach, Alex. "'Poisoned at the Source?' Telegraphic News Services and Big Business in the Nineteenth Century." *The Business History Review*, vol. 77, no. 4, 2003, pp. 577–610.

Nankivell, Frank Arthur. "Frank J. Cannon, of Utah: The Little Senator with the Big Negative Bang." *The World*, 17 Mar. 1896, p. 4.

Nasaw, David. *The Chief: The Life of William Randolph Hearst*. Houghton Mifflin, 2000.

National Cigarette & Tobacco Co. "The Cigarettes to Smoke." *Inaugural Ceremonies*. Program leaflet of the Inaugural Ceremonies. Gibson Bro., 1897, p. 28, *Hathitrust.com*.

———. "High Admiral." [circa 1896], n. pag.

———. "Outcaults Yellow Kid Cigarettes." [Cigarette hard pack]. New York [circa 1896], n. pag. *Morfauction.com*, 2018, http://morfauction.com/product/lot-107-yellow-kid-cigarettes-pack/.

Nelson, Cary, and Mike Chasar. "American Advertising—A Poem for Every Product." *US Popular Print Culture 1860–1920*, edited by Christine Bold, 2012, The Oxford His-

tory of Popular Print Culture, general editor Gary Kelly, vol. 6, Oxford UP, 2012, pp. 133–67.

"New England Notes." *The Electrical Engineer*, vol. 24, 11 Nov. 1897, p. 471.

"New McFadden's Row of Flats." *Niagara Falls Gazette*, 10 Feb. 1906, p. 5.

"New Records for Talking Machines." *The Phonoscope*, vol. 1, no. 2, 15 Dec. 1896, p. 18.

"Newspaper and Magazine Names Illustrated." *Printers' Ink*, vol. 18, no. 6, 10 Feb. 1897, p. 41.

A news snippet about a *Hogan's Alley* play. *Public Daily Ledger* [Maysville, KY], 27 Oct. 1897, p. 1.

Nicholson, Bob. "'You Kick the Bucket; We Do the Rest!': Jokes and the Culture of Reprinting in the Transatlantic Press." *Journal of Victorian Culture*, vol. 17, no. 3, 2012, pp. 273–86.

Niver, Kemp R. *Motion Picture from the Library of Congress Paper Print Collection, 1894–1912*, edited by Bebe Bergstein, U of California P, 1967.

Noel, Mary. *Villains Galore: The Heyday of the Popular Story Weekly*. Macmillan, 1954.

Norris, Frank. "The American Public and 'Popular Fiction.'" *The Responsibilities of the Novelist and Other Literary Essays*, Doubleday, 1903, pp. 103–8.

Norris, James D. *Advertising and the Transformation of American Society, 1865–1920*. Greenwood Press, 1990.

North, Michael. *The Dialect of Modernism: Race, Language, and Twentieth-Century Literature*. Oxford UP, 1994.

"Notes." *Printers' Ink*, vol. 17, 9 Dec. 1896, p. 38.

N. R. Jetic & Co. "Bidding Business." *The Clothier and Furnisher*, vol. 26, no. 5, Dec. 1896, pp. 53–55.

N. W. Ayer & Son. *N. W. Ayer & Son's American Newspaper Annual: Containing a Catalogue of American Newspapers, a List of All Newspapers of the United States and Canada, 1896*. UNT Digital Library, 2013, http://digital.library.unt.edu/ark:/67531/metadc9239/.

O'Flaherty, T. J. "Current Events." *The Daily Worker* [Chicago, IL], 21 Sept. 1923, n. pag.

Ogden, James R., et al. "Music Marketing: A History and Landscape." *Journal of Retailing and Consumer Services*, vol. 18, no. 2, 2011, pp. 120–25.

Ohmann, Richard Malin. *Selling Culture: Magazines, Markets, and Class at the Turn of the Century*. 1996. Verso, 1998.

"The Old Reliable McFadden's Flats—An Awful Bump." Russell and Morgan Print Co., 1902.

"The Old Reliable McFadden's Flats—Le'Ggo the Anchor." Russell and Morgan Print Co., 1902.

Olivier, Marc. "George Eastman's Modern Stone-Age Family." *Technology and Culture*, vol. 48, no. 1, 2007, pp. 1–19.

Olson, Richard D. "'Say! Dis Is Grate Stuff': The Yellow Kid and the Birth of the American Comics." *Syracuse University Library Associates Courier*, vol. 28, no. 1, 1993, pp. 19–34.

Orvell, Miles. *The Real Thing: Imitation and Authenticity in American Culture, 1880–1940*. U of North Carolina P, 1989.

"Our State Art Studio at Sing Sing." *New York Journal,* 7 Feb. 1897, American Sunday Magazine, p. 17.

"Outcault at Olympia." *The New York Dramatic Mirror,* 28 Nov. 1896, p. 19.

Outcault, Richard Felton. "At the Circus in Hogan's Alley." *The World,* 5 May 1895, untitled Sunday supplement, n. pag.

———. "The Bicycle Meet in Hogan's Alley." *The World,* 21 June 1896, Colored Supplement, p. 3.

———. "The Bud and Blossom of the Yellow Kid—His First and Latest Appearance." *The World,* 1 May 1898, Comic Weekly, p. 7.

———. "'Buster Brown and His Bubble'—8 'A Smooth Bit of Road.'" Souvenir Post Card Co., 1903.

———. "Buster Brown Meets the Yellow Kid." *New York American,* 7 July 1907, n. pag.

———. "The Crowd Gets up an Election Bonfire and the Yellow Kid Plays Nero." *New York Journal and Advertiser,* 7 Nov. 1897, American Humorist, p. 4.

———. "A Crying Need of the Day Is a Few More Popular Songs." *The World,* 5 Apr. 1896, Colored Supplement, p. 4.

———. "The Day after 'The Glorious Fourth' down in Hogan's Alley." *The World,* 7 July 1895, untitled Sunday supplement, n. pag.

———. "A Few Things the Versatile Yellow Kid Might Do for a Living." *New York Journal,* 22 Nov. 1896, American Humorist, p. 8.

———. "Hogan's Alley Children Spend a Day in the Country." *The World,* 19 July 1896, Colored Supplement, p. 3.

———. "Hogan's Alley Folk Have a Trolley Party in Brooklyn." *The World,* 9 Aug. 1896, Colored Supplement, p. 3.

———. "Hogan's Alley Folk Sailing Boats in Central Park." *The World,* 28 June 1896, Colored Supplement, p. 6.

———. "How the Yellow Kid Was Born: The Man Who Created It Tells for the First Time." *The World,* 1 May 1898, Comic Weekly, p. 7.

———. "An Illustrated Geography Lesson in Kelly's Kindergarten." *St. Louis Post Dispatch,* 27 Nov. 1898, Comic Weekly, n. pag.

———. "An Illustrated Geography Lesson in Kelly's Kindergarten." *The World,* 27 Nov. 1898, Comic Weekly, n. pag.

———. "A Leaflet from the Yellow Kid's Diary," *New York Journal,* 28 Feb. 1897, p. 6.

———. "Li Hung Chang Visits Hogan's Alley." *The World,* 6 Sept. 1896, Comic Weekly, p. 6.

———. "Merry Xmas Morning in Hogan's Alley." *The World,* 15 Dec. 1895, untitled Sunday supplement, n. pag.

———. "The Residents of Hogan's Alley Visit Coney Island." *The World,* 24 May 1896, Colored Supplement, p. 6.

———. "R. F. Outcault, of the New York Journal Finds Life 'One Grand Sweet Song,' with the 'Yellow Kid' Venues as an Inspiration." *The Fourth Estate: A Newspaper for the Makers of Newspapers,* 24 Dec. 1896, pp. 8–9.

———. "The Ryan's Arcade Gang Go Sleighing." *New York Journal and Advertiser,* 12 Dec. 1897, American Humorist, p. 4.

———. "The Sunday World's Hogan's Alley Folk on the Stage at Weber & Fields's Broadway Music Hall." *The World,* 6 Sept. 1896, Sunday Magazine, p. 27.

———. "Thanksgiving Day in Ryan's Alley." *New York Journal and Advertiser*, 21 Nov. 1897, American Humorist, p. 4.

———. "The War Scare in Hogan's Alley." *The World*, 15 Mar. 1896, Colored Supplement, p. 6.

———. "A Wild Political Fight in Hogan's Alley—Silver Against Gold." *The World*, 2 Aug. 1896, Colored Supplement, p. 6.

———. "The Yellow Dugan Kid." Letter sent to Librarian of Congress Ainsworth Rand Spofford, Copyright Office, Washington, DC, 7 Sept. 1896, www.loc.gov/pictures/item/acd1996005 836/PP/.

———. "The Yellow Kid at the Seat of War." *New York Journal and Advertiser*, 7 May 1897, p. 6.

———. "The Yellow Kid at the Seat of War: A Leaflet from the Yellow Kid's Diary." *New York Journal*, 23 Mar. 1897, p. 6.

———. "The Yellow Kid Indulges in a Cock Fight—A Waterloo." *New York Journal*, 29 Nov. 1896, p. 8.

———. "The Yellow Kid in Gay Paree." *New York Journal*, 20 Feb. 1897, p. 6.

———. "The Yellow Kid in Russia." *New York Journal and Advertiser*, 19 Apr. 1897, p. 6.

———. "The Yellow Kid Treats the Crowd to a Horseless Carriage Ride." *New York Journal and Advertiser*, 17 Oct. 1897, American Humorist, p. 8.

Outcault, Richard Felton, and Rudolph Edgar Block. "Around the World with the Yellow Kid." *New York Journal*, 24 Jan. 1897, American Humorist, p. 4.

———. "Around the World with the Yellow Kid." *New York Journal*, 14 Feb. 1897, American Humorist, p. 4.

———. "Around the World with the Yellow Kid. A Bull Fight in Honor of the Yellow Kid." *New York Journal*, 21 Mar. 1897, American Humorist, p. 4.

———. "Around the World with the Yellow Kid. An Eruption in Honor of the Yellow Kid." *New York Journal and Advertiser*, 16 May 1897, American Humorist, p. 4.

———. "Around the World with the Yellow Kid. At Balmoral Castle—A Lawn Party in the Yellow Kid's Honor." *New York Journal*, 7 Feb. 1897, American Humorist, p. 4.

———. "Around the World with the Yellow Kid. Fortune Smiles upon the Yellow Kid in Monte Carlo." *New York Journal*, 7 Mar. 1897, American Humorist, p. 4.

———. "Around the World with the Yellow Kid. High Life in Paris—The Yellow Kid (L'enfant Jaune) Takes an Airing." *New York Journal*, 21 Feb. 1897, American Humorist, p. 4.

———. "Around the World with the Yellow Kid. In the Louvre—The Yellow Kid Takes in the Masterpieces of Art." *New York Journal*, 28 Feb. 1897, American Humorist, p. 4.

———. "Around the World with the Yellow Kid. Mickey and His Friends Climb the Alps." *New York Journal*, 28 Mar. 1897, American Humorist, p. 4.

———. "Around the World with the Yellow Kid—Mickey and His Friends Hobnob with Royalty." *New York Journal*, 31 Jan. 1897, American Humorist, p. 4.

———. "Around the World with the Yellow Kid. Off for Europe—Where They Won't Do a Thing to the Effete Monarchies." *New York Journal*, 17 Jan. 1897, American Humorist, p. 4.

———. "Around the World with the Yellow Kid. The Yellow Kid Afloat on the Grand Canal." *New York Journal and Advertiser*, 18 Apr. 1897, American Humorist, p. 4.

———. "Around the World with the Yellow Kid. The Yellow Kid in Cairo." *New York Journal and Advertiser*, 9 May 1897, American Humorist, p. 4.

———. "Around the World with the Yellow Kid. The Yellow Kid Invades Germany." *New York Journal and Advertiser*, 4 Apr. 1897, American Humorist, p. 4.

———. "Around the World with the Yellow Kid. The Yellow Kid Returns." *New York Journal and Advertiser*, 30 May 1897, American Humorist, p. 4.

———. "Around the World with the Yellow Kid. The Yellow Kid Shakes His Trotters in Old Madrid." *New York Journal*, 14 Mar. 1897, American Humorist, p. 4.

Outcault, Richard Felton, and Archie Gunn. *Horse Show Number*. H. A. Thomas & Wylie Lith., Co., 1896.

Outcault, Richard Felton, and Edward Waterman Townsend. "McFadden's Row of Flats." *The Denver Evening Post*, 23 Oct. 1896, p. 9.

———. "McFadden's Row of Flats." *New York Journal*, 18 Oct. 1896, American Humorist, p. 5.

———. "McFadden's Row of Flats." *New York Journal*, 25 Oct. 1896, American Humorist, n. pag.

———. "McFadden's Row of Flats." *New York Journal*, 10 Jan. 1897, American Humorist, p. 4.

———. "McFadden's Row of Flats—A Merry Christmas in McFadden's Flats." *New York Journal*, 13 Dec. 1896, American Humorist, p. 4.

———. "McFadden's Row of Flats—A Turkey Raffle in Which the Yellow Kid Exhibits Skills with the Dice." *New York Journal*, 22 Nov. 1896, American Humorist, p. 4.

———. "McFadden's Row of Flats—Inauguration of the Football Season in McFadden's Row." *New York Journal*, 15 Nov. 1896, American Humorist, p. 5.

———. "McFadden's Row of Flats—McFadden's Flatters' Skating and Tobogganing Expedition." *New York Journal*, 6 Dec. 1896, American Humorist, p. 4.

———. "McFadden's Row of Flats—Receiving the Returns in McFadden's Row on Election Night." *New York Journal*, 1 Nov. 1896, American Humorist, p. 4.

———. "McFadden's Row of Flats—The New Year's Fancy Dress Ball in McFadden's Flats." *New York Journal*, 27 Dec. 1896, American Humorist, p. 4.

———. "McFadden's Row of Flats—The Opening Night in Kelly's Bowling Alley." *New York Journal*, 20 Dec. 1896, American Humorist, p. 4.

———. "McFadden's Row of Flats—The Season Opens with the Horse Show in McFadden's Row of Flats." *New York Journal*, 8 Nov. 1896, American Humorist, n. pag.

———. "McFadden's Row of Flats—The Studio Party in McFadden's Flats." *New York Journal*, 3 Jan. 1897, American Humorist, p. 4.

———. "McFadden's Row of Flats—The Yellow Kid Introduces A. Monk, Who Enlivens the Pool Tournament in McFadden's Flats." *New York Journal*, 29 Nov. 1896, American Humorist, p. 4.

Outcault, Richard Felton, and Paul West. "The Huckleberry Volunteers—An Old Acquaintance Meets Them in Cuba and Assumes Charge." *New York Evening Journal*, 16 Apr. 1898, p. 12.

———. "The Huckleberry Volunteers—They Make a Cavalry Charge on the Enemy." *New York Evening Journal*, 20 Apr. 1898, p. 12.

Paul, Albert. "The Yellow Kid Store." *Carlinville Democrat*, 3 Feb. 1898, n. pag.

Pearson, Susan J. "'Infantile Specimens': Showing Babies in the Nineteenth-Century America." *Journal of Social History*, vol. 42, no. 2, 2008, pp. 341–70.

Penn, William H., and Annie G. Callender. "The Little Yellow Kid." Mark Ament Music Co., 1896.

Petersen, Joyce Shaw. "Working Girls and Millionaires: The Melodramatic Romances of Laura Jean Libbey." *AMSJ*, vol. 24, no. 1, 1983, pp. 19–35.

Piacentino, Edward J. "The Poe–Longfellow Plagiarism Controversy: A New Critical Notice in The Southern Chronicle." *Mississippi Quarterly*, vol. 42, no. 2, 1989, pp. 173–82.

Pinkowski, Edward. *Forgotten Fathers.* Sunshine Press, 1953.

Pivar, David J. *Purity Crusade: Sexual Morality and Social Control, 1868–1900.* Greenwood P, 1973.

"Plays and Players." *Democrat and Chronicle*, 14 June 1896, p. 11.

"Plays Piano though Blind." *The San Francisco Call*, 4 Apr. 1904, p. 12.

Postema, Barbara. *Narrative Structure in Comics: Making Sense of Fragments.* RIT P, 2013.

"Programs of the Week." *Philadelphia Inquirer*, 7 Feb. 1897, p. 20.

Raphael's Inc. "Miscellaneous." *San Francisco Chronicler*, 17 Sept. 1897, p. 3.

Rawlings, Peter. "Grotesque Encounters in the Travel Writing of Henry James." *The Yearbook of English Studies* 34, 2004, pp. 171–85.

"Real Yellow Kid Fooled Cobblers." *New York Journal*, 14 Jan. 1897, p. 10.

"Reflections." *The New York Dramatic Mirror*, 13 June 1896, p. 2.

"Reflections." *The New York Dramatic Mirror*, 4 July 1896, p. 15.

Regent Manufacturing Co. "Whistle Knife." *The Iron Age*, vol. 59, Jan. 7, 1897, p. 86.

"Registered Trademarks." *Practical Druggist and Pharmaceutical Review of Reviews*, vol. 2, no. 4, Oct. 1897, p. 151.

Rehin, George F. "Harlequin Jim Crow: Continuity and Convergence in Blackface Clowning." *The Journal of Popular Culture*, vol. 9, no. 3, 1975, pp. 682–701.

Reusswig, H. W. "A 'Yellow Kid Window." Letter sent to Ulysses G. Manning. *American Druggist and Pharmaceutical Record*, vol. 30, no. 2, 1897, p. 51.

"R. F. Outcault, Father of Comic Strips, Dies." *Editor & Publisher and The Fourth Estate*, 29 Sept. 1928, p. 29.

Ridgway, Anthony James. "The Inner Voice." *IJES*, vol. 9, no. 2, 2009, pp. 45–58.

Riis, Jacob. "How the Other Half Lives: Studies among the Tenements." *Scribner's Magazine*, vol. 6, no. 6, Dec. 1889, pp. 634–62.

———. *How the Other Half Lives: Studies among the Tenements of New York.* Charles Scribner's Sons, 1890.

Robert Ingersoll & BRO. "Yellow Kid—Pins—Black Cat." *The Literary Digest*, vol. 14, no. 3, May 1897, p. 88.

Roby, L. S. "In Kansas." Letter to the editor. *Printers' Ink*, vol. 21, 6 Oct. 1897, p. 36.

Roeder, Katherine. *Wide Awake in Slumberland: Fantasy, Mass Culture, and Modernism in the Art of Winsor McCay.* UP of Mississippi, 2014.

Roggenkamp, Karen. *Narrating the News: New Journalism and Literary Genre in Late Nineteenth-Century American Newspapers and Fiction.* Kent State UP, 2005.

Rogin, Michael. "Making America Home: Racial Masquerade and Ethnic Assimilation in the Transition to Talking Pictures." *The Journal of American History,* vol. 79, no. 3, 1992, pp. 1050–77.

Rohrhand, Charles William. "The Journal's Exhibit at the Fair." *New York Journal,* 16 Dec. 1896, p. 10.

Rosenblatt, Louise M. "The Transactional Theory of Reading and Writing." *Theoretical Models and Processes of Reading.* 4th ed., edited by Robert B. Ruddell et al., International Reading Association, 1994, pp. 1057–92.

Rosenfeld, E. & Co. "For the Rest of the Country." *The Clothier and Furnisher,* vol. 26, no. 2, Sept. 1896, p. 32.

———. "For the Rest of the Country." *The Clothier and Furnisher,* vol. 26, no. 3, Oct. 1896, p. 40.

———. "Xmas Eve in Slum-Ber Alley." *The Clothier and Furnisher,* vol. 26, no. 5, Dec. 1896, p. 56.

———. "Xmas Eve in Slum-Ber Alley." *The Clothier and Furnisher,* vol. 26, no. 6, Jan. 1897, p. 44.

"Round the World with Nellie Bly." *The World,* 26 Jan. 1890, p. 21.

Rowe, John Carlos. "Mark Twain's Critique of Globalization (Old and New) in *Following the Equator, A Journey Around the World* (1897)." *Arizona Quarterly: A Journal of American Literature, Culture, and Theory,* vol. 61, no. 1, 2005, pp. 109–35.

Saalburg, Charles W. "The Colossus of Sunday Newspapers." *The World,* 29 Feb. 1896, p. 14.

———. "The Great Sunday World." *The World,* 21 Mar. 1896, p. 14.

———. "Inimitable 8 Funny Pages." *The World,* 22 Feb. 1896, p. 12.

———. "The Ting-Lings—The Brownies Welcome the Ting-Lings." *The Inter Ocean,* 29 Apr. 1894, untitled Sunday supplement, n. pag.

———. "Ting-Ling Types." *Inter Ocean,* 29 Apr. 1894, pp. 8–9.

Sabin, Roger. "Ally Sloper: The First Comics Superstar?" *A Comics Studies Reader,* edited by Jeet Heer and Kent Worcester, UP of Mississippi, 2009, pp. 177–89.

"The Salary of a Newspaper Illustrator." *The Inland Printer,* vol. 23, no. 6, 1899, p. 714.

Saltus, Edgar. "Mr. Saltus on the Great Event." *New York Journal,* 8 Nov. 1896, Sunday American Magazine, p. 1.

Santiago-Valles, Kelvin. "'Still Longing for de Old Plantation': The Visual Parodies and Racial National Imaginary of US Overseas Expansionism, 1898–1903." *American Studies International,* vol. 37, no. 3, Oct. 1999, pp. 18–43.

Sassatelli, Roberta. *Consumer Culture: History, Theory and Politics.* 2007. Sage, 2013.

Savory, Jerold, and Patricia Marks. *The Smiling Muse: Victoriana in the Comic Press.* Associated UPs, 1985.

Schuldiner, Michael, and Ruth Rosaler. "Film, Photographs and Saccades: Richard Outcault's Experiments with the Comic Strip Gutter in the Yellow Kid." *Studies in Comics,* vol. 9, no. 1, 2018, pp. 33–57.

Scully, Richard. "A Comic Empire: The Global Expansion of *Punch* as a Model Publication, 1841–1936." *International Journal of Comic Art*, 2013, pp. 6–35.

"Seen in Windows: Beautiful Displays Made by the Merchants." *The State* [Columbia, SC], 14 Nov. 1896, p. 8.

Seitz, Don Carlos. *Artemus Ward (Charles Farrar Browne): A Biography and Bibliography.* Harper & Brothers Publishers, 1919.

Severn, C. E. "In Chicago." *Printers' Ink*, vol. 21, 7 July 1897, p. 20.

Shardlow, F. C. "Dance of the Hogan's Alley Kid." W. J. Dyer & Bros, 1896.

Shaw, Milton M. *Nine Thousand Miles on a Pullman Train: An Account of a Tour of Railroad Conductors from Philadelphia to the Pacific Coast and Return.* Allen, Lane & Scott, 1898.

Sheldon, E. S. "What Is a Dialect?" *Dialect Notes*, edited by the American Dialect Society, J. S. Cushing, 1896, pp. 286–97.

Sheridan, Martin. *Comics and Their Creators: Life Stories of American Cartoonists.* Hale, Cushman, & Flint, 1942.

"The Shoe Men's Outing. A Grand Success From All Standpoints." *Boot and Shoe Recorder*, vol. 31, 15 Sept. 1897, pp. 79–81.

Shultz [Shults], Albert B. "The Advantage of Doing Things Yourself." *The World*, 17 Jan. 1897, Comic Weekly, p. 5.

Slocum, John P. "Is Richard Outcault an Artist?" *Broadway Magazine*, vol. 11, no. 6, Sept. 1903, p. 491.

Smith, Charlotte. "Charlotte Smith's Melancholy View." *New York Journal*, 8 Nov. 1896, Sunday American Magazine, p. 1.

Smith, Greg M. "Comics in the Intersecting Histories of the Window, the Frame, and the Panel." *From Comic Strips to Graphic Novels: Contributions to the Theory and History of Graphic Narrative*, edited by Daniel Stein and Jan-Noël Thon, De Gruyter, 2015, pp. 219–37.

Smolderen, Thierry. *The Origins of Comics: From William Hogarth to Winsor McCay.* UP of Mississippi, 2014.

Smythe, Ted Curtis. *The Gilded Age Press, 1865–1900.* Praeger, 2003.

Snyder, Robert W. "City in Transition." *Metropolitan Lives: The Ashcan Artists and Their New York*, edited by Rebecca Zurier et al., National Museum of American Art, in association with W. W. Norton, 1995, pp. 29–57.

———. *The Voice of the City—Vaudeville and Popular Culture in New York.* Ivan R Dee, 2000.

Snyder, Robert W., and Rebecca Zurier. "Picturing the City." *Metropolitan Lives: The Ashcan Artists and Their New York*, edited by Rebecca Zurier et al., National Museum of American Art, in association with W. W. Norton, 1995, pp. 85–189.

Soper, Kerry David. "From Rowdy, Urban Carnival to Middle-Class Pastime: Reading Richard Outcault's *The Yellow Kid* and *Buster Brown*." *The Columbia Journal of American Studies*, vol. 4, no. 1, 2000, pp. 143–67.

———. "From Swarthy Ape to Sympathetic Everyman and Subversive Trickster: The Development of Irish Caricature in American Comic Strips between 1890 and 1920." *Journal of American Studies*, vol. 39, no. 2, 2005, pp. 257–96.

Sorby, Angela. "A Visit from *St. Nicholas*: The Poetics of Peer Culture, 1872–1900." *American Studies*, vol. 39, no. 1, 1998, pp. 59–74.

"Sporting Goods." *The Evening Post* [New York, NY], 1 July 1896, p. 4.

"Star—McFadden's Row of Flats." *The New York Dramatic Mirror*, 14 Apr. 1900, p. 17.

Stewart, Ronald. "An Australian Cartoonist in 19th Century Japan: Frank A. Nankivell and the Beginnings of Modern Japanese Comic Art." *International Journal of Comic Art*, vol. 8, no. 2, 2006, pp. 77–97.

———. "Manga as Schism: Kitazawa Rakuten's Resistance to 'Old-Fashioned' Japan." *Manga's Cultural Crossroads*, edited by Jacqueline Berndt and Bettina Kümmerling-Meibauer, Routledge, 2013, pp. 27–49.

Stivers, Richard. *A Hair of the Dog: Irish Drinking and American Stereotypes*. Pennsylvania UP, 1976.

Stoeltje, Beverly J. "Rodeo: From Custom to Ritual." *Western Folklore*, vol. 48, no. 3, 1989, pp. 244–55.

Stowe, William W. *Going Abroad: European Travel in the Nineteenth-Century American Culture*. Princeton UP, 1994.

Strasser, Susan. *Satisfaction Guaranteed: The Making of the American Mass Market*. Smithsonian Books, 1989.

Strychacz, Thomas. *Modernism, Mass Culture, and Professionalism*. Cambridge UP, 1993.

Sullivan, C. J. "A Chapter from the Yellow Kid Diary." *The Makio*, vol. 16, Apr. 1897, pp. 303–5.

———. "Miscellaneous." *The Makio*, vol. 16, Apr. 1897, p. 228.

———. A Yellow Kid illustration. *The Makio*, vol. 16, Apr. 1897, p. 322.

"The Sunday World." *The World*, 25 Jan. 1897, p. 6.

Swift, Lindsay. "Atrocities of Color Supplements." *The Printing Art*, vol. 6, no. 6, Feb. 1906, pp. 343–45.

Swinnerton, Jimmy [James Guilford]. "Is It Possible That Messrs. George and Alexander—Put up a Job on the Journal Tigers?" *New York Journal and Advertiser*, 27 Feb. 1898, American Humorist, p. 5.

Tchen, John Kuo Wei. *New York before Chinatown: Orientalism and the Shaping of American Culture, 1776–1882*. Johns Hopkins UP, 1999.

Thon, Jan-Noël. *Transmedial Narratology and Contemporary Media Culture*. U of Nebraska P, 2016.

"Ting-Ling." *Inter Ocean*, 6 May 1894, p. 37.

"To-Morrow's Great Sunday World." *The World*, 20 June 1896, p. 14.

Townsend, Edward Waterman. *McFadden's Row of Flats*, directed by Gus Hill, music by Ivan L. Davis, produced at Graff and Jacob's Grand Opera House in Utica, performance by Rich K. Mullen, Charles A. Loder, George Leslie, Annie Dunn et al., 1897.

Townsend, Edward Waterman, and Richard Felton Outcault. *The Yellow Kid in McFadden's Flats*. G. W. Dillingham Co., 1897.

Trachtenberg, Alan. "Experiments in Another Country: Stephen Crane's City Sketches." *American Realism*, edited by Eric J. Sundquist, Johns Hopkins UP, 1982, pp. 138–54.

"Trade Items." *The American Stationer*, vol. 41, 18 Feb. 1897, pp. 255–61.

"Trade Items." *The American Stationer*, vol. 41, 20 May 1897, pp. 797–802.

Treasury Department. *Catalogue of Title Entries of Books and Other Articles.* No. 248, Mar. 30 to Apr. 4, 1896. Government Printing Office, 1896.

———. *Catalogue of Title Entries of Books and Other Articles.* No. 286, Dec. 21 to Dec. 26, 1896. Government Printing Office, 1897.

———. *Catalogue of Title Entries of Books and Other Articles.* No. 287, Dec. 28, 1896 to Jan. 2, 1897. Government Printing Office, 1897.

———. *Catalogue of Title Entries of Books and Other Articles.* No. 291, Jan. 25 to Jan. 30, 1897. Government Printing Office, 1897.

———. *Catalogue of Title Entries of Books and Other Articles.* No. 294, Feb. 15 to Feb. 20, 1897. Government Printing Office, 1897.

———. *Catalogue of Title Entries of Books and Other Articles.* No. 297, Mar. 8 to Mar. 13, 1897. Government Printing Office, 1897.

———. *Catalogue of Title Entries of Books and Other Articles.* No. 298, Mar. 5 to Mar. 20, 1987. Government Printing Office, 1897.

———. *Catalogue of Title Entries of Books and Other Articles.* No. 302, Apr. 1897. Government Printing Office, 1897.

———. *Catalogue of Title Entries of Books and Other Articles.* No. 314, July 5–July 10, 1897. Government Printing Office, 1897.

———. *Catalogue of Title Entries of Books and Other Articles.* No. 315, July 12 to July 17 1897. Government Printing Office, 1897.

———. *Catalogue of Title Entries of Books and Other Articles.* No. 336, Dec. 6–Dec. 11, 1897. Government Printing Office, 1897.

———. *Catalogue of Title Entries of Books and Other Articles.* No. 339, Dec. 27 to Dec. 31, 1897. Government Printing Office, 1897.

"Troublesome Yellow Kid." *The Fourth Estate: A Newspaper for the Makers of Newspapers,* 3 Dec. 1896, p. 3.

Turner, Frederick Jackson. "The Problem of the West." *The Atlantic Monthly,* vol. 78, Sept. 1896, pp. 289–97.

Turner, Mark W. "Periodical Time in the Nineteenth Century." *Media History,* vol. 8, no. 2, 2002, pp. 183–96.

———. "The Unruliness of Serials in the Nineteenth Century (and in the Digital Age)." *Serialization in Popular Culture,* edited by Rob Allen and Thijs van der Berg, Routledge, 2014, pp. 11–32.

"Types of the Tourists Who Constitute the Advance Guard for the Annual Exodus to Europe." *New York Journal and Advertiser,* 4 Apr. 1897, p. 60.

"An Unlamented Decease." *Munsey's Magazine,* vol. 18, no. 3, Dec. 1897, p. 473.

Urquhart, Colin K. "Roundabouts." *The American Stationer,* vol. 41, Apr. 1, 1897, pp. 524–25.

Vandal, Stuart [avatar name: Loki]. "Yellow Kid." *Marvunapp.com,* 2013, www.marvunapp.com/Appendix6/yellowkid.htm.

Veblen, Thorstein. *The Theory of the Leisure Class: An Economic Study of Institutions.* 1899. Oxford World's Classics, edited by Martha Banta, Oxford UP, 2007.

Voger, Mark. *The Dark Age: Grim, Great & Gimmicky Post-Modern Comics.* TwoMorrows Publishing, 2006.

von Lintel, Amy M. "Wood Engravings, the 'Marvellous Spread of Illustrated Publications,' and the History of Art." *Modernism/modernity*, vol. 19, no. 3, 2012, pp. 515–42.

Walker, Geneviève. "Two Scrapbooks/Manuscripts." Eden Hall School of the Sacred Heart, Torresdale, n. d.

"Wallingford." *New Haven Evening Register*, 22 Dec. 1896, p. 5.

Walls, Howard Lamarr. *Motion Pictures 1894–1912, Identified from the Records of the United States Copyright Office*. Library of Congress, Copyright Office, 1953.

Walsh, William Shepard. *Around the World in Eighty Minutes: Photographic Reproductions of the Most Magnificent Edifices, the Most Interesting Remains and the Most Beautiful Scenes on the Earth's Surface*. Henry Altemus, 1894.

The Waples-Platter Grocer Co. A Yellow Kid cigar advertisement. *Dallas Morning News*, 17 Feb. 1897, p. 2.

———. A Yellow Kid cigar advertisement. *Dallas Morning News*, 23 Feb. 1897, p. 12.

———. A Yellow Kid cigar advertisement. *Dallas Morning News*, 24 Feb. 1897, p. 3.

Warder, George Woodward. *The Cities of the Sun*. G. W. Dillingham Company, 1901.

Wardman, Ervin. "On the Tip of the Tongue: The Yellow Kids." *New York Press*, 26 Oct. 1896, p. 6.

———. "Yellow Is to Prevail." *The New York Press*, 27 Sept. 1896, p. 26.

Warner, Charles Dudley. "Editor's Study." *Harper's New Monthly Magazine*, vol. 90, Feb. 1895, pp. 481–84.

"The War Scare in America." *The Daily News* [London, UK], 17 Mar. 1898, p. 6.

Watson, Elmo Scott. *A History of Newspaper Syndicates in the United States, 1865–1935*. N. pub., 1936.

Weil, Joseph. *"Yellow Kid" Weil: The Autobiography of America's Master Swindler*, edited by W. T. Brannon, Ziff-Davis Publishing Company, 1948.

West, Richard Samuel. "Secret Origins of the Sunday Funnies: How the Comics Supplement Was Born." *Society Is Nix: Gleeful Anarchy of the Dawn of the American Comic Strip, 1895–1915*, edited by Peter Maresca, Sunday Press Books, 2012, p. 11.

Whedon, Joss, et al. *Runaways* II#27. Marvel Entertainment, Aug. 2007.

———. *Runaways* II#30. Marvel Entertainment, Aug. 2008.

Whitehill, Bruce. "American Games: A Historical Perspective." *Board Game Studies*, vol. 2, no. 1, 1999, pp. 116–41.

Wiener, Joel H. *The Americanization of the British Press, 1830s-1914: Speed in the Age of Transatlantic Journalism*. Palgrave Macmillan, 2011.

Wikoff, Brian W. "Lines That Move: Winsor McCay's Work in Performance and Comics, 1900–1920." Electronic thesis or dissertation, University of Cincinnati, 2009, *OhioLINK Electronic Theses and Dissertations Center*.

Williams, Allen S. "The First Commercial Travelers' Fair." *The Home Magazine*, vol. 8, no. 1, Jan. 1897, pp. 3–13.

Williams, J. R. Yellow Kid prize cartoon. *The World*, 28 June 1897, p. 10.

Wiltse, Ed. "'So Constant an Expectation': Sherlock Holmes and Seriality." *Narrative*, vol. 6, no. 2, May 1998, pp. 105–22.

Winchester, Mark David. *Cartoon Theatricals from 1896 to 1927: Gus Hill's Cartoon Shows for the American Road Theatre*. PhD dissertation, The Ohio State University, 1995.

———. "Hully Gee, It's a War!!! The Yellow Kid and the Coining of 'Yellow Journalism.'" *Inks: Cartoon and Comic Art Studies*, vol. 2, no. 3, 1995, pp. 22–37.

———. "Litigation and Early Comic Strips: The Lawsuits of Outcault, Dirks and Fisher." *Inks: Cartoon and Comic Art Studies*, vol. 2, no. 2, 1995, pp. 16–25.

Winterbottom, Percy [George A. Beckenbaugh]. "It Worked Both Ways." *The World*, 24 Jan. 1897, Comic Weekly, p. 3.

———. "Our Klondike Expedishun Obliged Too Return—(Continued from Last Weak.)." *The World*, 5 Sept. 1897, Comic Weekly, p. 4.

———. "A Romantick Ellopement." *The World*, 10 Jan. 1897, Comic Weekly, p. 3.

———. "Wee Are Off Four Klondike—By Percy Winterbottom, Inventor of the 'New Art.'" *The World*, 29 Aug. 1897, Comic Weekly, p. 4.

———. "Wie Trane Fore Our Fite with Fittssimmonz.—By Percy Winterbottom, Inventor of the New Art." *The World*, 5 Dec. 1897, p. 4.

Winwar, Frances [Francesca Vinciguerra]. *Oscar Wilde and the Yellow Nineties*. 1940. Harper & Brothers, 1958.

Withey, Lynne. *Grand Tours and Cook's Tours: A History of Leisure Travel, 1750 to 1915*. William Morrow, 1997.

"With the Retailers." *Boot and Shoe Recorder*, vol. 30, 3 Feb. 1897, p. 38.

"With the Retailers." *The Coal Trade Journal*, vol. 35, 9 Dec. 1896, p. 710.

Wood, Mary. "The Yellow Kid on the Paper Stage." *The Yellow Kid on the Paper Stage*, 2004, xroads.virginia.edu/~ma04/wood/ykid/yellowkid.htm.

Woods, Robert A., et al. *The Poor in Great Cities: Their Problems and What Is Being Done to Solve Them*. Kegan Paul, Trench, Trübner & Co., Ltd., 1896.

Woolf, Michael Angelo. *Sketches of Lowly Life in a Great City*. Edited by Joseph Henius, G. P. Putnam's Sons, 1899.

Wright, Charles A. "Thinking Out Loud: Move Over, M. Dier." *Our Town* [Narberth, PA], 29 Dec. 1948, n. pag.

W. W. Morgan Clothing Co. "The Yellow Kid." *Kansas City Star*, 10 Dec. 1896, p. 3.

Yaszek, Lisa. "'Them Damn Pictures': Americanization and the Comic Strip in the Progressive Era." *Journal of American Studies*, vol. 28, no. 1, Apr. 1994, pp. 23–38.

"'Yellow' Journalism." *Hampshire Telegraph and Sussex Chronicle Literary Supplement*, 24 Sept. 1898, n. pag.

"The Yellow Kid." *Morning Olympian*, 22 Dec. 1898, p. 3.

"The 'Yellow Kid.'" *Boot and Shoe Recorder*, vol. 31, 11 Aug. 1897, p. 32.

Yellow Kid advertisement. *The Yellow Kid: A Fortnightly Magazine of Wit, Fiction and Illustration*, vol. 1, no. 2, 3 Apr. 1897, p. 48.

The Yellow Kid: A Semi-Monthly Magazine of Wit, Fiction and Illustration. Howard Ainslee & Co., Publishers, 1897.

"The 'Yellow Kid' of the New York *World* and *Journal*." *Printers' Ink*, vol. 17, 25 Nov. 1896, p. 27.

"A 'Yellow Kid' Party." *The Capital*, vol. 5, no. 13, Mar. 1897, p. 14.

"Yellow Kid Schottische." *Arizona Weekly Journal-Miner*, 27 Jan. 1897, p. 1.

"The Yellow Kid Sees the German Kaiser." *New York Journal and Advertiser*, 12 Apr. 1897, p. 6.

"Yellow Kid Trouble." *The Fourth Estate: A Newspaper for the Makers of Newspapers*, 7 Jan. 1897, p. 4.

Young, John Philip. *Journalism in California: Pacific Coast and Exposition Biographies*. Chronicle Publishing Company, 1915.

Ziff, Larzer. *Return Passages: Great American Travel Writing, 1780–1910*. Yale UP, 2000.

Zumthor, Paul, and Catherine Peebles. "The Medieval Travel Narrative." *New Literary History*, vol. 25, no. 4, Autumn 1994, pp. 809–24.

Zurier, Rebecca, and Robert W. Snyder. Introduction. *Metropolitan Lives: The Ashcan Artists and Their New York*, edited by Rebecca Zurier et al., National Museum of American Art, in association with W. W. Norton, 1995, pp. 13–27.

INDEX

action-conducting: and competitions, 26–38; print forms, 38–47; technologies, 21–26, 38. See also seriality; social agents; spread, logic of; Yellow Kid

adapt/-ation, 13, 20, 32–34, 37–38, 41, 50–52, 70, 76, 83–85, 90n8, 121, 146n22, 157n8, 160, 160n13, 183, 190, 193, 195n14

addressees, 11, 99, 125, 139, 148, 171–72, 190

advertisements: and the comic supplements, 63, 64 fig. 1.8, 65 fig. 1.9, 66, 68–70, 121–23; in the form of a comic-tableau, 30–31, 31 fig. 1.2; promoting a newspaper, 27n8; 34, 44, 57 fig. 1.7, 61, 67; promoting a theater play (see theater shows); of tobacco wares, 44–47; by trading companies, 61; 61n23, 62. See also advertising; Printers' Ink; trade; Yellow Kid

advertising: and campaigns, 20–21, 29–30, 46, 48, 66, 187–88; field of, 14, 47, 61, 190, 194

aesthetic: and experience, 52, 81; operations/mechanisms, 11–12, 21, 47, 67, 71–72, 90, 101, 117–48, 153, 195–96; value, 127, 170, 174. See also comic-tableau/x; expansion; knowledge; repetition, logic of; seriality

afford/-ance, 2, 11, 47, 51–53, 92, 131, 131n8, 153, 164, 178–82, 198

agency. See social agents

Alex and George. See serial props

Alfy. See serial props

American Humorist (*New York Journal*), 6–8, 36, 38, 113, 120, 129, 145n21, 150, 156, 164, 183, 194, 198. See also comic strip; comic-tableau/x; Hearst, William Randolph

American Sunday Magazine, 21, 25 (*New York Journal*). See also supplements

Anderson, Benedict, 24n7

Anderson, Carl, 195n14

Around the World with the Yellow Kid (Outcault and Block), 8, 17, 42, 66, 71, 81, 83, 123, 148–67, 167 fig. 4.1, 168–78, 178 fig. 4.2–4.3, 179, 179 fig. 4.4–4.5, 180 fig. 4.6–4.8, 181–83. See also afford/-ance; repetition, logic of; sequel/-ization

artists appropriating the Yellow Kid comic figure for different purposes (not including George B. Luks/Richard F. Outcault), 2, 30, 31 fig. 1.2;

35–39, 40 fig. 1.3–1.4; 41–42, 56, 62, 129, 191–92. *See also* adapt/-ation; network; proliferation; social agents
Ashcan, 6, 73–74
audience: and diffuse/disparate, 2, 10, 13, 22, 29, 32, 42, 48n17, 50, 77–78, 113, 118–19, 141, 188; engagement, 11, 13, 29n10, 37, 41, 52–53, 104–5, 113–14; entertainment/theater show, 29n10, 30–33, 108n14, 114, 144–46, 160, 160n15, 161, 190–91; expanding, 12, 22, 61, 76–77; and middle-class, 9–10, 49, 76, 114, 136n15, 158, 158n11, 160, 160n15, 170n19; representations in the newspaper comics, 106–7, 169–71
authenticity, 37, 119–25, 125n5, 126–30. *See also* imitation; originality
authorship, 16, 21, 126, 188, 193. *See also* control; ownership

Balzer, Jens, 65, 77, 131
Barrison, Lona, 139; Sisters, 108n14, 136. *See also* Riccadonna Sisters
Beckenbaugh, George A., 100, 100n10, 101
Belle of Hogan's Alley, The (Blake and Bernard). *See* Blake, James
Bernhardt, Sarah, 81, 169
Blackbeard, Bill, 5, 7–9, 11, 27, 49, 75, 189n6, 191
Blade (comics series). *See* Guggenheim, Marc
Blake, James, 34–35, 69. *See also* competition; music; song sheet
Block, Rudolph Edgar, 8, 17, 81, 123, 150, 150n2, 151–66, 168, 173, 177n25, 178, 181–83. *See also* American Humorist; *Around the World with the Yellow Kid*; diary leaflets; narrative; Outcault, Richard Felton; travel
Bly, Nellie [Elizabeth Jane Cochran], 156–57, 157n9. *See also* Roggenkamp, Karen; stunt reporting; Verne, Jules
Boorstin, Daniel J., 154, 159
Brogan, Molly. *See* serial props
Brown, Buster. *See* Outcault, Richard Felton
Brown, Joshua, 10, 12, 23

Brownies characters (Cox), 41, 48–50, 159–60, 160n13
buttons: advertising/promotional, 46, 55; political campaign, 29, 69; souvenir, 29, 55; Yellow Kid pin-back, 29, 44, 46, 46n16, 54, 182

Campbell, Joseph W., 8, 19, 80
capitalism, 11, 15–16, 162, 188
Captain America (comics series). *See* Gruenwald, Marc
cartoons: as a basis for songs, 28–29; editorial, 2, 39; political, 38–39, 41, 83
chalk talks, 25
Chicago Sunday Tribune, 156
circulation: as availability, 3–4, 33n13, 34, 48, 72, 100, 107, 140n17, 152, 154, 157, 170, 183, 189, 192, 193n12, 194; figures (or numbers), 24n6, 48n17; as movement, 13, 15–16, 23–24, 29, 34, 61, 100–101, 192; of the reader's gaze, 130–31; wars, 19, 37
class: and differences, 113–15, 118, 131–32, 145, 148; discourses of class in the newspaper comics, 78–82, 104, 110–13, 118–20, 131–38, 142–47, 147n25, 148, 161–63, 165, 168–69, 176–77, 182; as economic status, 8, 154, 160, 165, 186; -inflected parodies, 82, 118, 129, 144; as social status, 32, 44, 49, 59, 74–75, 79, 165. *See also* audience
collaboration: and meaning-making, 10–11; as work between two or more artists, 7–8, 39, 149–50, 182–83, 195
columns. *See* narrative
comic strip, 1–2, 4, 74, 131, 131n9, 155, 183, 187, 194–95, 195n15, 196, 196n16, 197 fig. 5.1, 198; balls, 189
comic-tableau/x: definition of, 9–10; layout or composition of the, 9, 11, 30, 41, 51, 78, 102, 130–31, 131n8, 146, 152, 183; serial aesthetics of the, 16, 71–115, 188, 194–95, 198. *See also* afford/-ance; *Around the World with the Yellow Kid*; *Hogan's Alley* (comics series); expansion; humor; *McFadden's Row of Flats* (comics series); repetition, logic of; seriality; serial props

Comic Weekly (*The World*), 4–5, 9, 38, 63, 93–94, 99–101, 104, 120, 126–27, 129, 141–42, 156, 187. *See also* comic strip; comic-tableau/x; Pulitzer, Joseph

comics series: *Around the World in 30 Days* (Kemble), 156; *Blackberry Sisters* (Kemble), 145n21; *Captain Kidd Kids, The* (Lowitz), 156; *Coon Alphabet* (Kemble), 145n21; *Dinkies, The* (Saalburg), 156; *Gazoozaland* (*see* Lowitz, John Buckingham); *Great Trained Chicken, The* (Luks), 9; *Kalsomine Family* (Luks), 9, 90n7; *Katzenjammer Kids, The* (Dirks), 23n4, 39; *Kelly's Kindergarten* (Outcault), 23n3; *Kinder-Kids Abroad* (Feininger), 156; *Klondike* (Winterbottom), 101; *Little Nippers* (Luks), 87, 87n6, 90; *Merry-Go-Rounders, The* (Glackens), 156, 156n5; *Mose's Incubator* (Luks), 9, 90, 146n22; *Ryan's Alley* (Outcault), 9; *Ryan's Arcade* (Outcault), 9, 91; *Tigers* (*see* Swinnerton, Jimmy); *Ting-Lings* (*see* Saalburg, Charles); with the Yellow Kid in the weekly New York tenement settings (*see* American Humorist; Comic Weekly; competition; *Hogan's Alley* (comics series); *McFadden's Row of Flats* (comics series)). *See also* Luks, George Benjamin; Outcault, Richard Felton

competition: between *Around the World with the Yellow Kid* and other forms of travel writing, 154–64; between manufacturing companies, 20, 46, 46n16, 53; between music sheet composers and publishers, 20, 30–31, 34, 36–37; between newspapers and magazines, 72, 157n9; between the New York City newspapers (the *Journal* and the *World*) and their owners (Hearst and Pulitzer), 17, 37, 61, 91, 99, 127, 141, 155, 198; between retailers, 20; between theater show producers, 20, 30–34, 34, 37; between Yellow Kid comics series, 7, 9, 17, 20, 70, 72, 83, 86, 91, 99, 118; media, 31, 37, 189; over copyright (*see* copyright); as a topic in the comics, 106, 129–38, 143, 145–46. *See also* action-conducting

consumption activities/practices, 11–12, 16, 24–25, 28, 30, 43, 51–53, 62, 71–115, 142, 149, 160, 179, 195

control: and authorial, 18, 20–21, 23, 83, 153, 182, 187n4; discourse of, 185; legal, 20–21, 42, 83, 99, 123, 152, 182; loss of/without, 3, 13, 15, 20, 25, 123, 129, 187. *See also* copyright; ownership

copyright: and application, 27; catalogues, 27, 32–33, 53; competition over, 26; complete the, 27, 28n9; hold, 33, 33n13, 33n14, 37, 53; infringement, 121, 127; protection for, 27, 31, registration, 7n6, 27, 123–24; request for, 68, 99. *See also* authorship; False Notice of Copyright Act; Hamlin, Arthur; Howell, William B.; intellectual property; Library of Congress; ownership; Treasury Department

Cox, Palmer. *See* Brownies characters

Crane, Stephen, 74, 79–80

Cuba, 8, 8n7. *See also* Spanish-American War

cultural work of nineteenth-century newspaper comics, 2, 10–13, 16, 72–115, 117, 154

culture: and American, 79n1, 119, 137, 154; and contemporary, 53n21; 192–93; emergence of an audiovisual, 29n10; consumer, 12–13, 15, 20–21, 46, 48–49, 53–55, 62, 68, 73, 183, 189; of imitation (*see* imitation; Orvell, Miles); material, 119; print production, 12, 123, 145n21. *See also* capitalism

"Daphne's Room" (Lee), 190, 190n8, 191. *See also* in-joke; repetition, logic of; serialization

Darwinism, 105

Denson, Shane, 13, 117, 187n4, 194

dialect, 59, 80, 133; Bowery, 78–79, 82; in literature, 79n1, 80; as a representational technique, 78–79, 81; speech presentation, 30, 78–82; spelling, 103; as subject matter, 78–79, 81; writings, 79. *See also* language

232 • INDEX

diary leaflets, 7, 68n25, 163–64, 174–78, 195. *See also* addressees; afford/-ance; *Around the World with the Yellow Kid*; *McFadden's Row of Flats* (comics series); travel; travelogue
Dick Tracy (television serial). *See* "The Mole"
Dillingham Co., G. W., 14, 27, 42, 194. *See also* fictional autobiography
Dirks, Rudolph, 38–40, 40 fig. 1.3
dramatic/theatrical compositions, 15, 27, 29, 31, 37, 70. *See also* adapt/-ation; competition; copyright; Library of Congress; Winchester, Mark David; Yellow Kid
Dreiser, Theodore, 49n18
Dugan, Kitty. *See* serial props
Dumont, Frank, 32, 76
Dunnigan, Delia (Liz). *See* serial props
Duval, Romain, 9, 131

Eco, Umberto, 11
entertainment, 9–10, 29n10, 30, 63, 75–77, 79, 79n1, 80–81, 94n9, 118–19, 132, 144, 146, 168, 170, 184, 190. *See also* audience
ethnicity, 8, 10, 49, 75, 78, 83, 115; and difference, 118, 146–48; and humor, 77, 148, 167–68; and identity, 83–85; and prejudices, 147; and stereotyping (*see* stereotyping)
expansion: as structuring patterns in/of the comics, 12, 16–17, 87, 100–102, 153, 178–82; as social, political, economic initiative/process, 8, 16–17, 38, 53, 71, 91, 144, 153–54, 154n4, 176n24, 182, 188; of the Yellow Kid, 16, 38, 71, 91, 188, 198. *See also* proliferation; serial figure; seriality

False Notice of Copyright Act, 124n4
Feininger, Lyonel, 156
Feinstein, Robert, 5, 54n22
fictional autobiography, 14, 27, 42–44, 46, 52, 194, 198. *See also* Townsend, Edward Waterman
Fischer, Roger, 75
Flying Machine Boy. *See* serial props

focalization, 42–43, 71–72, 103–5, 171
Frahm, Ole, 11, 177n25
frame/-less, 9, 120–21, 130, 143, 195. *See also* comic strip
Frasier (television series). *See* "Daphne's Room"
Freeman, Matthew, 46, 52–53, 63

Gambone, Robert L., 6, 9, 68, 73, 87, 90, 90n7, 133n12, 146n22
Gardner, Jared, 10–11
gender, 8, 32, 115, 118, 167, 177n25
genre, 107, 144, 151, 155, 156n7, 157–59, 191. *See also* travel
Gilmore, Barney, 32–33, 35, 55, 69. *See also* competition; dramatic/theatrical compositions; *Hogan's Alley* (theater plays)
Glackens, William J., 73, 156, 156n5
Goat. *See* serial props
Gordon, Ian, 9–10, 24, 27, 63, 75, 84n5
Grand Tour, 151, 154–64, 176
Gruenwald, Marc, 191–92
Grünewald, Dietrich, 76–77
Guggenheim, Marc, 192
Guilbert, Yvette, 56, 107
Gunn, Archie, 61, 84. *See also* lithograph/-y; Outcault, Richard Felton

Hagedorn, Roger, 2n2, 150, 150n3
Hamlin, Arthur, 26, 124n4
Harvey, Robert C., 82
Hatfield, Charles, 11, 196n16
Hearst, William Randolph, 6–9, 19–22, 24–26, 36–37, 73–74, 145n21, 149–50; and Albert Pulitzer's *Morning Journal*, 6n5; and copyright (*see* copyright); and the editorial page/policies of his *Journal*, 7–8, 156n5, 163–64, 174–75; and nationalism, 176n24; outbidding Pulitzer (*see* competition); and political parties, 41; and promotional strategies, 44, 56–57, 57 fig. 1.7, 61, 66; and Richard F. Outcault's move from Pulitzer's newspaper to his *Journal* (*see* Pulitzer, Joseph); and the Sunday comic

supplement (*see* American Humorist); and the target audience of his newspaper, 137n15; and travel (see *Around the World with the Yellow Kid*; travel; travelogue); and the Travelers Fair of 1897, 55–56, 57 fig. 1.7; and the Yellow Kid comics (*see* comics series; comic strip; comic-tableau/x; cultural work of nineteenth-century newspaper comics); and *The Yellow Kid in McFadden's Flats* (*see* Dillingham Co., G. W.; fictional autobiography); and the *Yellow Kid Puzzle* (*see* McLoughlin Brothers). *See also* newspaper; supplements

Hill, Gus, 32–33, 33n14, 90n8

Hogan's Alley (comics series), 4–7, 9, 11–12, 23–24, 27, 30, 34, 35n15, 48, 52–53, 65–71, 74–75, 78–87, 88 fig. 2.1–2.2, 89 fig. 2.3–2.4, 90–96, 96 fig. 2.6–2.7, 97 fig. 2.8–2.10, 98 fig. 2.11–2.13, 99–104, 117–20, 123–25, 125n5, 126–27, 130–34, 135 fig. 3.3, 140–41, 141n18, 142–46, 146n22, 147–48, 153, 167, 177, 177n25, 188, 195. *See also* adapt/-ation; competition; copyright; readership; Yellow Kid

Hogan's Alley (plays), 27, 28n9, 28–34, 32n12, 32–35, 55–56. *See also* adapt/-ation; audience; dramatic/theatrical compositions; Gilmore, Barney; Leonard, John F.; Library of Congress; lithograph/-y; theater shows; Winchester, Mark David; Yellow Kid

Hogan's Alley (songs), 27, 28n9, 29–30, 34–36. *See also* musical compositions; song sheet; Yellow Kid

Hogan's Alley Puzzle, 27, 53. *See also* McLoughlin Brothers

Home Magazine, The, 57 fig. 1.7

Howell, William B., 27–28, 28 fig. 1.1. *See also* Treasury Department

Huckleberry Volunteers, The (Outcault and West), 8, 8n7, 195

humor, 39–44, 67, 99, 109–13, 118, 120–21, 129, 132–34, 136–48, 167–69, 190; ethnic (*see* ethnicity); magazines, 5, 9, 21, 41, 75, 85, 193n13, 194

iconic: and character, 181, 48n17; features/shapes, 13, 41, 58, 139, 192; Yellow Kid, 13–15, 38, 43, 62, 67, 87, 128. *See also* serial figure

ideology, 13, 85, 113, 143, 147, 176, 188

Illustrated Supplement (*The Inter Ocean*), 3–4

imitation: acts of, 57–58, 119; culture of, 119; in the comics, 107, 112–13, 118–19, 120–48; of pronunciation, 79–81, 133

immigrants, representations of, 8, 82–84, 110, 114–15

imperialism, 154, 176, 176n24

in-joke, 141, 189, 191

Ingersoll Co., 54, 63, 65 fig. 1.9

intellectual property, 26, 53, 126

Inter Ocean, The, 3–4, 48, 48n17

intermedial, 37, 47, 53n21, 69

interserial, 72, 86, 91–101, 119, 126, 141–42

intertextual, 42, 53n21, 178

intervention, 8, 176, 176n24. *See also* Cuba; diary leaflets; *Huckleberry Volunteers, The*; Spanish-American War

intraserial, 72, 95–101, 106–8, 119, 141–42

James, Henry, 159, 171n21

Jenkins, Henry, 53n21, 114

"Jimmie's Paper" (*The World*), 86–87, 95–96, 100, 100n10; 101. *See also* Beckenbaugh, George A.; Comic Weekly; Pulitzer, Joseph; supplements

Johanningsmeier, Charles, 10, 12, 23, 23n2, 24, 48n17

Jones, Gavin, 79, 79n1, 80

Journalist. *See* serial props

Judge, 9–10, 41, 193n13

Keightley, Keir, 30, 34, 37, 69

Kelleter, Frank, 2n2, 2–3, 9, 11, 16, 21

Kemble, Edward, 38, 145n21, 156

Kersten, Holger, 79, 79n1, 80–81

knowledge, 11, 78, 83, 99, 131, 160–61, 164, 168–70, 190, 193n12; areas of, 115, 117–18; hierarchies, 129, 138–39;

and memory cues, 62, 95, 104, 108, 141, 191; serial, 106–10, 138–41, 152–53. *See also* afford/-ance; audience; reading options/possibilities

Kunzle, David, 9, 48

Laird, Pamela Walker, 60–62, 161n16

language: and English, 78, 80, 133; and vernacular, 1, 36–37, 39, 41, 58, 61–62, 71–72, 74, 78–82, 161, 171, 186, 196

Lehuu, Isabelle, 10, 186n3

Lemke, Siglinde, 81

Leonard, John F., 33, 35, 55, 69. *See also* competition; dramatic/theatrical compositions; Gilmore, Barney; *Hogan's Alley* (theater plays)

Levine, Lawrence, 186n3

Libbey, Laura Jean, 169–70, 170n19

Library of Congress, 27n8, 35n15, 160n14; Copyright Office of the, 27, 99; and *Dramatic Compositions Copyrighted in the United States*, 27–28, 31–32, 33n14

liminal/-ity, 50, 85–86, 90, 117, 172

literacy, 8, 11, 82, 108, 131–33, 139

lithograph/-y, 12, 27, 51, 193: chromo-, 121, 194; companies, 14, 34; posters, 27n8, 34, 47, 157. *See also* advertising; Yellow Kid

Liz (Delia Dunnigan). *See* serial props

Lowitz, John Buckingham, 39–40, 40 fig. 1.4, 63, 156, 156n6

Luks, George Benjamin, 6–9, 12, 73–75, 84, 86–87, 88 fig. 2.1–2.2, 89 fig. 2.3–2.4, 90–95, 96 fig. 2.6–2.7, 97 fig. 2.8–2.10, 98 fig. 2.11–2.13, 99–101, 114–15, 126–32, 132n10, 133, 133n12, 135 fig. 3.3, 143–45, 145n21, 146–47; and blackface minstrelsy (*see* minstrelsy); and humor (*see* humor); and language in the comics (*see* dialect; language); parodying Richard Outcault, 68, 99, 140–41; and questions of originality (*see* authenticity; imitation; originality). *See also* comic-tableau/x; Comic Weekly; *Hogan's Alley* (comics series); Outcault, Richard Felton; Pulitzer, Joseph; serial props

Madison Square Garden, 102, 120, 129–32, 134, 137, 139, 140n17, 144n20, 146–47, 147n24

magazines: and artists, 2, 126n6, 194; for children, 2, 49–50, 160n13, 187; competition between (*see* competition); editors, printers, and publishers of, 5, 16, 23, 157n9; humor (*see* humor); travel writing in (*see* travel); in Europe, 2. *See also* periodicals; trade; *Yellow Kid: A Semi-Monthly Magazine, The* (Ainslee)

manufacturers, 50, 54, 54n22, 68

marketing: of comics, 48n17, 54, 57; of music, 29n10, 34; strategies, 48, 54, 57, 60–61, 68; value, 47, 61

Marschall, Rick, 46, 51n19, 188

Marvel, 191–92

mass culture, 2, 75, 91, 187

mass-produced/production, 3, 21, 29, 72, 77, 120

Mayer, Ruth, 2n2, 3, 13, 15–16, 38, 71, 101

McCarthy, Dan, 126, 134, 140, 147n24

McDougall, Walt, 41, 136

McFadden's Row of Flats (comics series), 7–9, 11, 23, 23n3, 25–27, 42–43, 51–53, 66, 68–72, 74–83, 83n4, 86, 101–8, 108n14, 109–15, 117–21, 122 fig. 3.1–3.2, 124, 124n4, 125–28, 130, 134, 135 fig. 3.4, 135–39, 143, 147–50, 152–53, 164–65, 167, 169, 171, 177–79, 181–83, 188, 195–96, 198

McFadden's Row (songs), 36–37. *See also* musical compositions; song sheet

McFadden's Row (plays), 30–32, 32n12, 33–35, 90, 90n8, 91. *See also* adapt/-ation; audience; Blake, James; dramatic/theatrical compositions; Hill, Gus; Library of Congress; lithograph/-y; theater shows; Winchester, Mark David; Yellow Kid

McLoughlin Brothers: and cross-promotion, 52–53; and *McLoughlin Bros' Catalogue*, 49, 51; and *Yellow Kid Puzzle*, 51–53

media: and competition (*see* competition); context/environment, 3, 12, 15–16, 20, 77, 99, 127, 153, 189, 194; options, 72–78, 117. *See also*

consumption activities/practices; serialization
medium: and carrier, 15, 20, 43, 187, 198; of origin, 38, 41, 50, 69
Meinrenken, Jens, 9, 105n11
Melton, Jeffrey Alan, 159–61
Miller, Frank, 191–92
minstrelsy, 114, 145–46, 146n22
modernity, 8, 11, 71–78, 108, 114
"Mole, The" (Palmer), 189, 189n7, 190. *See also* in-joke; masks; repetition, logic of; serialization
Mose's Incubator (Luks). *See* comics series
Munkittrick, Richard Kendall, 156n5, 156n6, 195. *See also* Glackens, William J.; Lowitz, John Buckingham
music: distribution of, 34–35; folios (*see* song sheet); halls, 15, 146n22; and marketing, 29, 34; songwriters and publishers, 20, 30–31, 34–37
musical compositions, 15, 27–28 28n9, 29–31, 35, 37, 70. *See also* competition; copyright; Yellow Kid

Nankivell, Frank Arthur, 194
narrative: and affordance (*see* affordance); columns by Edward W. Townsend, 8, 10, 52, 78, 83, 83n4, 102–15, 117, 123, 126, 134, 150–51, 155, 169, 171–72, 174, 177, 179, 181; graphic/illustrated, 8, 8n7, 17, 49, 130, 149n1, 155–56, 158–60, 160n13, 170, 195; levels (intra- or extradiegetic), 42, 85, 103, 105, 115, 132, 172–73, 177; liminality (*see* liminal/ity); passage, 107–8, 124, 150–51, 170–71; self-observational, 21, 66, 86; of serial unfolding, 15, 22, 37, 100, 192; travel, 148, 150–58, 158n10, 159–61, 168, 170n20, 179
narrator/narrating agency, 42–43, 50, 52, 68n25, 72, 83, 102–7, 111–12, 121, 124, 126, 131, 134, 149, 163–66, 168–77, 177n25, 181–83, 196, 198
National Cigarette & Tobacco Co., 46–47
network, 21, 46, 87, 194, 198. *See also* proliferation; serial figure; social agents; spread, logic of; Yellow Kid

New York Evening Journal, 8. *See also* Cuba; Hearst, William Randolph; *Huckleberry Volunteers, The*; Outcault, Richard Felton; West, Paul
New York Herald, 4n4, 22n1, 136n15, 160n15, 171n21
New York Journal. See Hearst, William Randolph
New York Journal and Advertiser, 6n5
New York Press, 173n22. *See also* Wardman, Ervin
New York Sun, 7, 150n2, 157n9
New York Tribune, 66, 159, 160n15, 171n21
newspaper: and color presses, 5, 12, 25; enticement strategies to create loyal customers and lure new consumers, 3n3, 36–37, 56, 61, 66–67, 124; fictive (*see* "Jimmie's Paper"); industry, 12, 20, 141n19; and printing plates, 3, 12, 23; readers (*see* audience); rivalries (*see* circulation; competition); and Sunday extras (*see* supplements); syndicate (*see* syndication)
Norris, Frank, 154
North, Michael, 79–80

Ohmann, Richard Malin, 55, 160
Olivier, Marc, 49–50
Opper, Fredrick Burr, 156
originality, 33, 37, 99, 119, 123n2, 125n5, 126–27, 130, 132, 152
Orvell, Miles, 119, 119n1
Outcault, Richard Felton, 4–9, 14–16, 21, 68–69, 75, 86–87, 120–21, 122 fig. 3.1–3.2, 123–27, 129–30, 132n10, 135 fig. 3.4, 136n15, 149, 149n1, 150–57, 163–64, 167 fig. 4.1, 178 fig. 4.2–4.3, 179 fig. 4.4–4.5, 180 fig. 4.6–4.8, 181–83, 186–87, 197 fig. 5.1, 198; and authorship (*see* authorship); and Buster Brown, 47, 188–89, 189n6; and the copyright application for the Yellow Kid (*see* copyright); giving drawing lectures, 25–26; and humor (*see* humor); as implied addressee, 99, 126–27, 140–41, 141n18, 141n19; and language in the comics (*see* dialect; language); and Mickey Dugan, 83–85; and the Outcault Advertising

Company, 188–89; and the teasing between him and George B. Luks, 91, 140; and *Trouble in Hogan's Alley*, 33n13; and Will S. Rising, 28–29. See also American Humorist, *Around the World with the Yellow Kid*; Block, Rudolph Edgar; chalk talks; collaboration; comic strip; comic-tableau/x; control; fictional autobiography; Hearst, William Randolph; *Hogan's Alley* (comics series); *McFadden's Row of Flats* (comics series); reading options/possibilities; readership; song sheet; Townsend, Edward Waterman; West, Paul

ownership, 20, 26, 42, 55, 99, 121, 124. See also intellectual property

panel, 4, 9, 100, 121, 131, 140n17, 149n1, 155; 183, 191, 195n15, 196, 196n16, 198. See also comic strip; frame/-less

masks: and face, 32, 35n15, 56, 140, 189; papier-mâché, 32, 48, 49n18, 54, 56, 189–90. See also theater shows

parody, 7, 41, 66, 68, 87, 90–91, 99, 118, 123, 127, 129, 134, 136–38, 140, 144, 147, 151, 156, 159–62, 177, 190. See also advertisements; serial props

periodicals, 2, 4n4, 22, 26, 34, , 75, 77, 80, 158–60. See also trade

photograph/y, 11, 56, 71, 74–75, 119, 189; chrono-, 195; engravings, 14, 44, 157

photogravure, 160, 160n14

pleasure, 2, 10, 17, 53, 63, 72, 77–78, 92, 95, 99, 108, 118–19, 133, 142, 153, 190, 198. See also afford/-ance; knowledge; reading options/possibilities

popular culture, 25, 154, 167, 170, 192

practices: and consumption (see consumption activities/practices); cultural, 2, 15–16, 20, 37, 48, 71–78, 117, 119n1, 137, 137n16, 153–54, 160, 193–94; of self-description, 21, 67–70; serial (see seriality; serialization; social agents; spread, logic of); writing, 156n7, 158, 158n10, 171, 171n21

Printers' Ink, 29, 46, 56–59. See also trade

proliferation: as logic of copying, 27, 29, 37, 66, 90–91, 151, 157n8, 181, 186–87; channels and circumstances of, 13, 16, 37, 20–21, 24–25; as plurimedial

sprawl; 15–16, 21, 68–69, 82, 86, 123, 128, 183, 190. See also sequel/-ization; seriality

Puck, 5, 9, 193n13, 194

Pulitzer, Joseph, 4–6, 9, 19–20, 72–73, 120–21, 129–30, 141–42, 147–48, 156–57, 183; and advertising in the Comic Weekly, 63–64, 64 fig. 1.8, 65, 65 fig. 1.9, 66; and the Associated Press, 6n4, 48n17; and comics spin-offs, 87n6, 90, 90n7; and the competition with William Randolph Hearst (see competition); as implied addressee, 104, 125; and "Jimmie's Paper" (see "Jimmie's Paper"); and the newspaper's political leaning, 41, 133n12; promoting *The World* (see advertisements); and Richard F. Outcault's move to Hearst's newspaper, 6–7, 27, 69, 103, 123–27, 140–41; and staff members of the *World*, 5–6, 72–73, 100, 126, 150n2, 156, 161n16; and the *St. Louis Post-Dispatch*, 23n3; and the target audience of *The World*, 136n15. See also newspaper; supplements

race, 8, 8n7, 90n7, 114–15, 118, 146, 146n22, 147, 167. See also class; ethnicity; gender; stereotyping

readership, 9, 23, 48, 73, 76, 99, 118, 158. See also newspaper

reading options/possibilities, 11, 17, 72, 76, 82, 86, 102–15, 109, 118, 120, 129, 133

recursivity, 17, 152, 182. See also afford/-ance; Gardner, Jared; Kelleter, Frank; seriality

Regent Manufacturing Co., 62

repetition, logic of, 12, 16–17, 38, 52, 54, 71, 90, 94, 101–2, 111, 117, 149–83, 188, 195–96

retail/-ing, 47, 51, 54, 56–60, 62. See also competition; Yellow Kid

rhetoric, 101, 176, 185. See also idiomatic expressions; language

Riccadonna Sisters. See serial props

Riis, Jacob, 74–75, 109n15

Robert Ingersoll & BRO., 54, 63, 65 fig. 1.9. See also advertisements; Yellow Kid

Roggenkamp, Karen, 156–57
Rosenfeld, E. & Co., 29–30, 69
Rowe, John Carlos, 161
Runaways (comics series). *See* Whedon, Joss

Saalburg, Charles W., 5, 48, 48n17, 67, 156
Sabin, Roger, 48–49
San Francisco Call, 4, 194
satire, 7, 41, 93n9, 102, 118, 132, 133n12, 137–38, 148, 161, 177, 183
self-description. *See* practices
self-referentiality, 14, 67–69, 82, 93, 127, 138
sequel/-ization, 150, 152–53, 155
sequence, 29n10, 131, 189, 196
sequentiality, 95, 153
serial figure, 13–16, 38, 113. *See also* action-conducting; expansion; proliferation; social agents; spread, logic of; serialization
serial props, 12, 72, 86–87, 92, 94–95, 117, 131, 153, 178–179, 181–82; Alex and George, 12, 87, 88 fig. 2.1–2.2, 89 fig. 2.3–2.4, 90–91, 92 fig. 2.5, 117, 141–42, 166; Alfy, 86, 92–95, 96 fig. 2.6–2.7; Flying Machine Boy, 86, 92, 94–95, 97 fig. 2.8–2.10, 142; Goat, 178 fig. 4.2–4.3, 179, 179 4.4–4.5, 182; Journalist, 86, 98 fig. 2.11–2.13, 95–101, 126–27, 140; Kitty Dugan, 83, 86, 91–92, 112–13, 138–40, 177n25; Liz (Delia Dunnigan), 86, 106–7, 111–12, 163, 166; Molly Brogan, 5, 86, 138, 162, 166, 179, 180 fig. 4.6–4.8, 182; Riccadonna Sisters, 108, 108n14, 112–13, 134
seriality: definition of, 2–3, 11, 16–17, 71, 188; principles of, 2, 2n2, 15, 17, 21, 70–115; 181, 195, 198; as a field of research, 2, 2n2, 3
serialization: as continuous game of outbidding (*see* competition); in and across different media, 2, 2n2, 3, 13–16, 20–21, 27, 37–38, 43, 46, 48, 48n17, 49–50, 53, 68–69, 82, 85–86, 90, 183, 185, 188, 192–94; of humor (*see* humor; knowledge); of stories, 7, 49, 81, 87, 95, 100n10, 111, 150, 150n2,

156n6, 157, 157n9, 159, 159n12, 160n13, 164, 170n19, 170n20, 188
Shelley, Mary, 187, 187n4
Sin City (comics series). *See* Miller, Frank
Sloper, Ally, 48–49, 49n18. *See also* marketing; masks; Sabin, Roger
Smolderen, Thierry, 130, 193
Smythe, Ted Curtis, 12, 19
Snyder, Robert W., 74, 76
social agents, 16, 47–61, 192–93
song sheet, 15, 29n10, 30, 34–37, 69, 194; as cutout/foldout feature, 4, 34; illustrated, 29n10, 36; represented in the comics, 30, 69, 130; production companies, 26, 31, 34–37
Soper, Kerry David, 10, 15, 83, 85, 133, 147, 156, 189n6
space: in/of comics, 7, 11, 30, 61, 65–66, 95, 102, 115, 120, 129, 142, 145–46, 151–52, 181, 195n15; geographic, 5, 17, 148, 151, 153, 166–67, 192; private, 15, 77, 80n2, 186; public, 13, 15, 29, 59, 77, 138–40, 147n25, 183, 186; urban, 8–10, 146. *See also* class
Spanish-American War, 2
spread, logic of, 13, 16, 20, 26, 47, 51, 71, 78, 80, 91, 100–101, 117, 121, 185–88. *See also* control; expansion; serial props
Stein, Daniel, 9, 11
stereographs, 160, 160n14
stereotyping, 8n7, 48–50, 77, 84–85, 114–15, 146n22, 148, 161, 166–68
Stewart, Ronald, 193–94, 193n13
stunt reporting, 156, 156n7, 157
Sunday: and the comic-tableaux (*see* comic-tableaux); editions, 3, 4, 9, 25, 61, 66–67, 72, 90, 129, 149, 157, 194n13, 195; leisure, 73, 76, 176, 186; extras/supplements (*see* supplements). *See also* American Humorist; Comic Weekly; readership; repetition, logic of; reading options/possibilities
Sunday Magazine (*The World*), 4, 93n9
supplements (not including the American Humorist/the Comic Weekly), 3–4, 4n4, 21, 25, 93n9; artists (not including George B. Luks/Richard

F. Outcault), 5, 38–39, 40 fig. 1.3, 40 fig. 1.4, 48, 48n17, 63, 67, 73, 91, 92 fig. 2.5, 101, 126n6, 136n15, 140n17, 147n24, 156, 156n5, 156n6, 193; competition between the (see competition); and criticism, 186; editors of the, 8, 72–73, 150, 150n2; the end of the Yellow Kid's life in the, 183, 188; interlinking parts in the, 99–101; in other newspapers, 3–4, 48, 48n17, 156, 159. See also advertisements; comics series; comic-tableau/x; Luks, George Benjamin; Outcault, Richard Felton; readership; syndication

Swinnerton, Jimmy, 38, 91, 92 fig. 2.5, 156

syndication, 1, 6n5, 12, 22–23, 23n2, 23n4, 24–25, 48, 48n17, 78

Tammany Hall, 4n4, 41

taste, 73, 111, 113, 118, 161–62, 185, 191

telegraph, 22n1, 140

tenement, 5, 8, 74–75, 78, 80, 82, 104, 109, 109n15, 111, 114, 132, 143, 150

theater shows: advertisements for, 32n12, 33–34, 56; producers, 30–32, 37, 55; illustrated in the comic-tableaux, 106–7. See also adapt/-ation; audience; dramatic/theatrical compositions; lithograph/-y; vaudeville; Winchester, Mark David

tobacco, companies, 29, 44–46, 46n16, 47, 54, 68

tourist, 154, 161, 165–66, 169. See also American Humorist; Around the World with the Yellow Kid; travel; travelogue

Townsend, Edward Waterman, 7, 33, 33n14, 42, 102–8, 108n14, 109–15, 120–21, 122 fig. 3.1–3.2, 124–30, 135 fig. 3.4, 147–49, 163–64, 194. See also American Humorist; collaboration; fictional autobiography; narrative; Outcault, Richard Felton; *Yellow Kid's Trip around the World*

toys, 15, 20, 32, 49, 50–51; books, 48n17; manufacturing, 47, 51, 53. See also McLoughlin Brothers; Yellow Kid

Trachtenberg, Alan, 74

trade, 129n7, 132, 154: cards, 44, 54–55; journals, 6, 19–20, 26, 29–30, 47, 54n22, 56–60, 70, 124n4; law, 121

trademark, 30, 54n22

transatlantic: and journalism, 153; journeys/voyages, 153–55, 160–62; marriage market, 163. See also space; travel; travelogue

transcultural, 193–94

transnational, history of comics, 193–94

transportation, 12, 24, 134

travel: and experience, 153–54, 158, 158n10; lectures, 160, 160n14, 160n15; as a popular genre, 150n2, 151, 153–64. See also narrative; transatlantic; travelogue

travelogue, 17, 151–53, 167. See also *Around the World with the Yellow Kid*; Block, Rudolph Edgar; Outcault, Richard Felton

Treasury Department, 27–28, 28n9, 35, 50. See also Hamlin, Arthur; intellectual property; Library of Congress; ownership

Turner, Frederick Jackson, 154n4

Turner, Mark W., 2n2

Twain, Mark, 159, 159n12, 161, 161n16

urban, 8, 72–76, 79, 113–14, 119–20, 142, 146; modernity (see modernity); space (see space)

vagabond, 42, 83. See also liminal/-ity; serial figure

vaudeville, 16, 69, 71, 76–77, 79–81, 83, 90n8, 106, 114, 118–19, 137n16, 138, 150

Veblen, Thorstein, 162

Verevis, Constantine, 2n2, 152. See also sequel/-ization

Verne, Jules, 156–57, 157n8

versatile, 13–14, 38, 43, 50, 172, 196, 197 fig. 5.1. See also liminal/-ity; serial figure; vagabond

Wardman, Ervin, 84, 186

Weil, Joseph, 24, 190

West, Paul, 8, 8n7
Whedon, Joss, 191–92
Winchester, Mark David, 20, 26–27, 28n9, 29–32, 33n13, 33n14, 62, 127
window displays, 47, 57–60, 68
Winterbottom, Percy. *See* Beckenbaugh, George A.
Wood, Mary, 76, 118, 133n12, 177
Woolf, Michael Angelo, 75
World, The. See Pulitzer, Joseph

Yaszek, Lisa, 11, 82, 113
yellow: and dress/shirt, 41, 43–44, 83–84, 87, 131, 136, 139; journalism, 15, 186, 186n2; peril, 85; press, 84; twins (*see* Alex and George; serial props)
Yellow Kid: and advertising, 15, 19, 21, 29–30, 41–42, 44, 45 fig. 1.5–1.6, 47, 50, 54, 56, 57 fig. 1.7, 59, 61–64, 64 fig. 1.8, 65 fig. 1.9, 66–70, 85, 187; appeal of the, 2–3, 15, 20, 43; backstory of the, 3, 83, 153; cardboard cutouts, 58, 187–88, 188n5; career/success of the, 3, 15–16, 19–21, 25, 31, 37, 42, 47–50, 58, 61, 70, 148, 153, 164, 185, 188; chewing gum, 54, 54n22; cigar/cigarette, 44, 45 fig. 1.5, 46, 68; copies and imitations of the, 22, 35, 58, 60, 62, 90, 120–29; and copyright questions (*see* copyright; intellectual property; ownership); costumes for theater plays and parties, 32, 48, 54, 56; dance, 35n15; drawing lectures, 25; games, 3, 3n3, 15, 27, 51–53, 157; and identifiable/memorable/recognizable, 1, 5, 13–14, 35, 39, 41, 59, 86–91, 149, 162, 192; items/objects, 15, 20–21, 29–30, 47–61, 50–51, 55, 58, 68; magazine (see *Yellow Kid: A Semi-Monthly Magazine, The* (Ainslee)); masks (*see* masks); modular quality of, 13, 182; posters, 19, 30, 44, 56, 58–59, 68, 125; records for talking machines, 35; recruiting cards, 19; and retail, 14, 47, 54–62; soap, 65n24; and songs (*see* music; musical compositions; song sheet); souvenirs, 29, 48, 54–55, 188; store receipts, 54. *See also* adapt/-ation; audience; buttons; comic strip; comic-tableau/x; competition; iconic; language; proliferation; serial figure; spread, logic of; theater shows; versatile; yellow
"'Yellow Kid' Copyright" (Howell). *See* Howell, William B.
Yellow Kid in McFadden's Flat, The (Townsend and Outcault). *See* fictional autobiography
Yellow Kid Puzzle. See McLoughlin Brothers
Yellow Kid: A Semi-Monthly Magazine, The (Ainslee), 14, 42–45, 45 fig. 1.5–1.6, 46, 50
Yellow Kid's Trip around the World (Townsend), 33n14

Zurier, Rebecca, 73–74

STUDIES IN COMICS AND CARTOONS
Jared Gardner and Charles Hatfield, Series Editors
Lucy Shelton Caswell, Founding Editor Emerita

Books published in Studies in Comics and Cartoons focus exclusively on comics and graphic literature, highlighting their relation to literary studies. The series includes monographs and edited collections that cover the history of comics and cartoons from the editorial cartoon and early sequential comics of the nineteenth century through webcomics of the twenty-first. Studies that focus on international comics are also considered.

Producing Mass Entertainment: The Serial Life of the Yellow Kid
    CHRISTINA MEYER

The Goat-Getters: Jack Johnson, the Fight of the Century, and How a Bunch of Raucous Cartoonists Reinvented Comics
    EDDIE CAMPBELL

Between Pen and Pixel: Comics, Materiality, and the Book of the Future
    AARON KASHTAN

Ethics in the Gutter: Empathy and Historical Fiction in Comics
    KATE POLAK

Drawing the Line: Comics Studies and INKS, 1994–1997
    EDITED BY LUCY SHELTON CASWELL AND JARED GARDNER

The Humours of Parliament: Harry Furniss's View of Late-Victorian Political Culture
    EDITED AND WITH AN INTRODUCTION BY GARETH CORDERY AND
    JOSEPH S. MEISEL

Redrawing French Empire in Comics
    MARK MCKINNEY